DATE DUE

Applications of the Sciences in Marketing Management

The Wiley Marketing Series

WILLIAM LAZER, Advisory Editor
Michigan State University

MARTIN ZOBER, *Marketing Management*

ROBERT J. HOLLOWAY AND ROBERT S. HANCOCK
*The Environment of Marketing Behavior—
Selections from the Literature*

GEORGE SCHWARTZ, Editor
Science in Marketing

EDGAR CRANE
*Marketing Communications—
A Behavioral Approach to Men, Messages, and Media*

JOSEPH W. NEWMAN, Editor
On Knowing the Consumer

STEUART HENDERSON BRITT, Editor
*Consumer Behavior and the Behavioral Sciences—
Theories and Applications*

DONALD F. MULVIHILL AND STEPHEN PARANKA
Price Policies and Practices

DAVID CARSON
International Marketing: A Comparative Systems Approach

BRUCE E. MALLEN
The Marketing Channel: A Conceptual Viewpoint

RONALD R. GIST
Management Perspectives in Retailing

JOHN K. RYANS AND JAMES C. BAKER
World Marketing: A Multinational Approach

JOHN M. BRION
Corporate Marketing Planning

NORTON E. MARKS AND ROBERT M. TAYLOR
Marketing Logistics: Perspectives and Viewpoints

JAMES BEARDEN
Personal Selling: Behavioral Science Readings and Cases

FRANK M. BASS, CHARLES W. KING, AND EDGAR A. PESSEMIER, Editors
Applications of the Sciences in Marketing Management

Applications of the Sciences
in Marketing Management

Edited by
FRANK M. BASS
CHARLES W. KING
EDGAR A. PESSEMIER

Krannert Graduate School of Industrial Administration
Purdue University

JOHN WILEY AND SONS, INC., New York · London · Sydney

Contributing Authors

ARNOLD E. AMSTUTZ, *Massachusetts Institute of Technology*

HENRY J. CLAYCAMP, *Stanford University*

JAMES F. ENGEL, *Ohio State University*

PETER T. FITZROY, *Marketing Science Institute*

RONALD E. FRANK, *University of Pennsylvania*

PAUL E. GREEN, *University of Pennsylvania*

ECKHARD H. HESS, *University of Chicago*

ROBERT J. HOLLOWAY, *University of Minnesota*

RONALD A. HOWARD, *Stanford University*

PHILIP KOTLER, *Northwestern University*

HERBERT KRUGMAN, *Marplan*

WILLIAM LAZER, *Michigan State University*

DAVID B. LEARNER, *Batton, Barton, Durstine, and Osborne*

LAWRENCE LIGHT, *Ohio State University*

WILLIAM F. MASSY, *Stanford University*

WILLIAM S. PETERS, *Arizona State University*

PATRICK J. ROBINSON, *Marketing Science Institute*

EVERETT M. ROGERS, *Michigan State University*

J. DAVID STANFIELD, *Michigan State University*

VOLNEY STEFFLRE, *University of California at Los Angeles*

F. J. VAN BORTEL, *Marplan*

Foreword

The chapters in this volume were presented originally at a symposium held at the Herman C. Krannert Graduate School of Industrial Administration, Purdue University, in July 1966. The purpose of the symposium was to survey and summarize recent research in marketing in order: (1) to develop an understanding of the state of knowledge in various areas, (2) to suggest possible avenues for future research, and (3) to determine the potential significance for management of these findings. Leading scholars were commissioned to write papers in the areas of their research specialization covering the diverse contributions of the behavioral and quantitative sciences to Marketing.

The quantity of significant research in marketing has increased greatly during recent years. Many research papers are necessarily narrow in scope. In many instances, little or no attempt has been made to relate the findings to other research or to interpret the results of the research generally. A basic premise underlying the organization of the conference, which led to this publication, was that papers that accomplished the three purposes outlined above would be valuable contributions toward the continued development of applications of science to marketing problems and toward the application of research findings to management decision making. We expect that a rapidly increasing body of scientific work relevant to marketing and a growing tendency on the part of marketing managers to rely on findings drawn from the basic disciplines will encourage a large increase in the number of papers that will meet the criteria for this symposium.

Although the subject matter of the material contained in this book is quite diverse, it, of course, was not possible to include all of the interesting new research topics in marketing. Nevertheless, we believe that the most significant basic research developments have been touched upon in the three parts: I. Consumer Behavior and Normative Models; II. Behavioral Theories of Consumer Behavior, and III. Experimental Methods and Simulation Models in Marketing Management. Some of the chapters reflect original theoretical or applied research contributions, since the need or the opportunity for this original work became apparent to authors while preparing papers on the state of the art in specific areas. We expect that the ideas and conclusions contained in the book will stimulate other contributions. In marketing, as elsewhere, research tends to create new questions more rapidly than it answers old ones.

We suspect that readers have some surprises in store for them in studying the conclusions reached in this book. This stems, we think, as much from the ideas and propositions that have been discredited or rendered doubtful as from the progress that has been made. We believe that this volume provides valuable information and insights for graduate students, decision makers, and scholars who are seriously concerned with research in marketing.

We thank the authors for their careful and conscientious efforts in preparing the material. Dean Emanuel T. Weiler and Dean John S. Day encouraged and supported the symposium that culminated in this book. We are especially grateful to Dr. Herman C. Krannert who generously supported this project, as he has supported so many others concerned with basic research in management.

THE EDITORS

Symposium Preface*

This symposium marks a significant milestone in the development of theory in marketing. Organized study in marketing on any significant scale did not appear until the 1920's, although sparse but significant contributions can be traced back to the turn of the century. The early writings were basically descriptive rather than analytical, and they continued to be descriptive until the 1950's. The qualitative descriptions of institutions and functions of the 1920's were augmented with quantitative detail in the 1930's—thanks to the first census of business in 1929 and similar counts in the early 1930's. But the exercise of counting and classifying businesses related to marketing and of adding up their respective shares of business did not lead to very profound new insights into an explanation of either the marketing structure or the decision-making processes within the firm.

Signs of a growing concern for theory in marketing became evident in the early 1950's when new or, at least, different and fresh approaches to a study of the discipline were emerging. Courses on marketing theory were introduced for the first time in a number of marketing curricula; the Cox and Alderson book on *Theory in Marketing* appeared, as did Joel Dean's classic on *Managerial Economics*; and the now well-known Marketing Theory Seminar was in its early beginnings as an institution in the quest for new insights into marketing phenomena. Later in the 1950's, the two famous reports (commonly referred to as the Ford and the Carnegie reports) gave additional impetus to change in all aspects of education and research in business, including marketing.

The outcome of the ferment and frustration of the 1950's has been an increased reliance upon classical disciplines—especially quantitative skills and behavioral sciences. Substantive concern has shifted from macro

* The chapters in this volume were prepared especially for presentation before a symposium on *Application of the Sciences in Marketing Management,* held at Purdue University under the leadership of the marketing faculty of the Herman C. Krannert Graduate School of Industrial Administration, July 11 to July 15, 1966.

descriptions and public policy matters to the managerial aspects of the business enterprise and the buying behavior of consumers. This new emphasis is evident both in the theme and in the specific coverage of the symposium.

Where research is concerned, the book demonstrates vividly the current state of the arts for that aspect of marketing which was set out for exploration, that is, *application of the sciences in marketing management*. The participants include and surely represent the scholars in the forefront who are currently blazing the new and significant trails. The papers reflect, through their careful and systematic selection, the main thrust of exciting research presently underway. They represent a good sampling both of the methodology and of the problem areas that are attracting the greatest attention of those currently working on the perimeters of knowledge about this aspect of marketing. Also, this collection of studies suggests that important areas of marketing are now being slighted or completely ignored. We might speculate that current patterns of emphasis are strongly influenced by availability of data and financial support. This suggests that a serious problem facing basic research in business administration (and marketing is no exception) lies in the lack of financial and other support for exploring the full spectrum of problems facing the very important institution of business in our society. The Federal Government provides a variety of support for the life sciences, the physical sciences, and the behavioral sciences, but practically no support for the study of business. The Ford Foundation is in the process of withdrawing its support from schools of business, and other foundations have been most frugal (to put it mildly) in their contributions in this direction. Trade groups and private firms make meager contributions, and financial support from these sources often is looked upon with suspicion. Conditions of this kind may have caused more than one good scholar to select problem areas on the basis of availability of data and the possibility of financial support rather than on the basis of critical importance. On the positive side, moving in directions of available money and data might serve to sharpen and experiment with research methodology. But, as a result, many critical research areas are slighted and some excellent methodology evolves, which is not readily transferable. Examples of this spotty attention paid to the full array of marketing problems include the considerable emphasis given to selected problems in the food industry and the lack of current inquiry by marketing scholars into many matters pertaining to market structure, market behavior, and public policy. Much of the mainstream of current research somewhat systematically avoids the growth segment of the market affiliated with affluence. Problems of brand loyalty and the like will continue to be important and worthy of intensive study, but they may not be as crucial as some other problems, as our marketing mechanism finds itself catering in greatly increased measure to more exotic tastes, backed by increased purchasing power. Emphasis then turns to individualization of offerings rather than to meeting mass market needs with quasi-standardized outputs. And conspicuous gaps appear in research effort relating to the full range of marketing problems associated with managing the enterprise. These deficiencies undoubtedly will persist until considerably more financial support is forthcoming.

This symposium was highly successful both from a professional point of view and in all other respects. Surely it served as an effective means of bringing the efforts of top talent to bear on some of the important issues of both substance and methodology in marketing management. Hopefully it will serve as a pattern for future seminars on other important marketing topics. Perhaps the excellent format of this symposium could serve as a basis for exploring sets of problems other than those concerned directly with marketing management. The recent contributions from economics, sociology (especially organization theory), and other social sciences might be explored as they relate to an understanding of macro marketing systems or arrangements, to marketing and economic development, and to relevant public policy issues. While our viewpoint is typically that of business management, possibly we should examine some problems from the vantage point of the consumer, or of society at large.

We speak for all of the participants of the symposium in conveying an expression of sincere thanks and appreciation to the faculty and administration of the Herman C. Krannert Graduate School of Industrial Administration for the excellent manner in which the symposium was organized and for the thought and care that went into the handling of each detail. We commend Dean Emanuel T. Weiler for the support that he has given to this effort. Special thanks are extended to Professors Frank M. Bass, Charles W. King, Edgar A. Pessemier, Dan Schendel, and Doyle Weiss both for their intellectual leadership in organizing the program and for their hospitality. An expression of appreciation is likewise extended to Stephen A. Baumgarten, Philip C. Burger, Leonard J. Parsons, John O. Summers, Richard D. Teach, and Douglas J. Tigert, all Ph.D. candidates at Purdue University, who helped in many ways to make the meeting a success.

SCHUYLER F. OTTESON
President, American
Marketing Association
1965-1966

Contents

Applications of the Sciences in Marketing Management

The Interdisciplinary Approach to Marketing—A Management Overview

The interdisciplinary approach to marketing has had significant impact on marketing thought in the past two decades. The objective of this chapter is to present an overview of the interdisciplinary approach and the specifics of the noneconomic and nonbusiness administration disciplines as they have contributed to marketing.

The chapter is divided into five major sections.

1. The interdisciplinary approach will be put into focus. It will be defined, the kinds of interdisciplinary relationships in marketing will be explored, and the current status of the approach will be assessed.

2. The interfaces among marketing and other disciplines will be investigated and the specific contributions, as well as an overall assessment of the value of other areas, will be noted.

3. The specific relationships with a number of other fields will be put into capsule form.

4. Several problems inherent in the approach will be discussed.

5. Some concluding observations will be presented.

THE INTERDISCIPLINARY APPROACH IN FOCUS

The Interdisciplinary Concept

To discuss the interdisciplinary approach with clarity, several related concepts should be examined, particularly transdisciplinary, multidisciplinary, and interdisciplinary. Transdisciplinary is the broadest concept.

It refers to the crossing of discipline boundaries. Both the multidisciplinary and interdisciplinary approaches, by definition, therefore, are transdisciplinary. There is, however, considerable difference between their respective approaches.

The multidisciplinary approach uses stores of knowledge and viewpoints from many disciplines. It borrows concepts and techniques. It expands a discipline and provides greater understanding and problem-solving capability. But it tends to leave the general discipline boundaries more or less intact.

The interdisciplinary approach integrates concepts and ideas, restructures fields, changes subject-matter boundaries, and bridges theoretical gaps. It tends to develop more coherent and logical structure, more adequate theories, and leads to new concepts, techniques, and even subjects. It synthesizes concepts, findings, and ideas. Sometimes it even results in new disciplines. Often the interdisciplinary approach follows the multidisciplinary.

From its inception, marketing has crossed disciplinary lines. It has built upon the ideas and concepts of other disciplines—particularly economics. The use of such concepts as demand, price determination, marginalism, elasticities, and market structure are examples.

Since marketing problems have been studied by subject-matter specialists external to marketing (for example, psychologists and sociologists), marketing has long felt the impact of a multidisciplinary approach. Specialists, however, investigate marketing problems from the perspectives of their own particular disciplines. A useful overflow from one area to another often occurs and disciplines are given new vitality, but they are not transmuted. Yet this very transfer of knowledge can challenge old categories and strain discipline boundaries.[1]

Marketing has borrowed from both the social and behavioral sciences. Initially, major contributions from the social sciences resulted in a heavy macro perspective. Later multidisciplinary contributions emphasized the behavioral sciences and a micro emphasis. This is to be expected since "the twentieth century marks the coming-of-age of the behavioral sciences."[2]

The interdisciplinary approach requires a true federation of disciplines.

[1] See William H. Ittelson, Martin Landow, and Harold Proshansky, "The Interdisciplinary Approach and the Concept of Behavioral Science," in Norman Washburne, editor, Decisions, Values, and Groups, Interdisciplinary Research Conference, University of New Mexico, Vol. II, 1950, pp. 7-24.

[2] Bernard Berelson and Gary A. Steiner, Human Behavior, an Inventory of Scientific Findings (New York: Harcourt, Brace, and World, 1964), p. 11.

It is not just a matter of borrowing among disciplines. It is concerned with the combination and integration of the endeavour of several specialized fields of study for the purpose of gaining marketing knowledge and solving marketing problems. The interdisciplinary approach offers tentative concepts, findings, postulates, working hypotheses, and methodology for the direction and organization of inquiry in marketing. It abandons reified categories of disciplines and tends to unify scientific inquiry.

The interdisciplinary approach, however, is not one unified approach—instead, it is many approaches. It is a loose coalition of perspectives, findings, and avenues. It can sometimes be a maze of conflicting hypotheses, findings, and ideas. This conflict, of course, can be challenging and desirable, and can lead to imaginative research.

Usually, the interdisciplinary approach to marketing is referred to in terms of an emphasis on behavioral, quantitative, or social sciences, or at best, nonbusiness administration areas. But it really covers the contributions of other functional fields of business administration, including management, organization theory, cost accounting, and financial administration.

By definition, the interdisciplinary approach to marketing refers to the use of all disciplines—social, behavioral, physical, quantitative, and business—to develop marketing insights, concepts, and theories and to illuminate, investigate, and solve marketing problems. It includes the application and integration of pertinent material to advance marketing. It refers to the blending and cross-fertilizations of various disciplines and their solidification in marketing thought. Through this integration, more widely applicable and useful marketing concepts and generalizations are evolving.

In relating to other disciplines, marketing has drawn from four discipline groups.

1. Those that are directly allied to marketing. This includes micro economics, management, organization theory, finance, and accounting. These disciplines investigate many marketing problems and subjects as part of their normal approach.

2. Those that study behavior, particularly human behavior such as psychology, sociology, and cultural anthropology.

3. Those that focus on broader societal issues and problems such as philosophy, political science, and macro economics.

4. The tool and technique disciplines, including mathematics, statistics, systems engineering, and computers.

Yet, marketers are placed in an uncomfortable position. They can study complex phenomena strictly within the limits of their specialized discipline while being cognizant that marketing phenomena cut across discipline boundaries and that problems are being viewed out of context. Or they can approach marketing problems from a broader base; they can seek interconnections, overlap, and unification with all other disciplines and become frustrated by the complexity of marketing situations and by the lack of simple principles and uniform and unifying theories. The first approach, while simple, lacks realism; the second approach can lead to confusing decision situations. In reality, a middle ground, termed the interdisciplinary approach, is usually selected.

It is significant that an intradisciplinary approach has also been felt in marketing. It leads to the integration and blending of concepts, ideas, and findings within the marketing discipline itself. It is being spurred by the acceptance of a systems approach to marketing. For example, physical distribution, the result of a systems approach, integrates transportation, storing, warehousing, distribution, handling, sorting, and moving. Marketing intelligence results from an amalgamation of various subjects dealing with gathering, analyzing, interpreting, and using data. Marketing promotion refers to the coordination of all promotional aspects—advertising, personal selling, and publicity.

Kinds of Interdisciplinary Contributions

The interdisciplinary approach to marketing results in three kinds of contributions: those that are direct and immediate, those that are direct but potential, and the indirect and potential contributions.

Direct and immediate contributions refer to these concepts, ideas, and findings that can be applied directly by marketing. Included are various techniques of measurement, concepts such as life cycle, social stratification, and data including income and demographic data. They result in an immediate infusion of knowledge. These contributions will be considered later.

Direct but potential contributions are those that appear to have direct carryover but require further research, development, or refinement. These constitute the bulk of the interdisciplinary contributions. For example, research on farm product innovations reveals that innovators and early adopters are more means oriented, tend to be more secure as individuals, and have greater ability to deal with abstractions. Is this true for other product categories?

Similarly, the following changes in values have been ascribed to our society.[3]

[3] Clyde Kluckhohn, "Have There Been Discernible Shifts in American Values during

1. Less emphasis on personal values and more on group standards and welfare.
2. Increased positive evaluation of psychological criteria.
3. Receding of value on future success in favor of respectable and stable security.
4. Rise in value of aesthetic considerations.
5. Greater value placed on explicit values.

A number of conclusions have been developed about conformity and resistance to change that have potential use in marketing management. For example:[4]

1. Individuals appear to be more susceptible to conformity pressures when expressing social opinions, idealogical attitudes, and abstractions that are not rooted in concrete experience than when they are well acquainted, or with personal preferences.
.2. Tendencies toward conformity and conversion are heightened when an individual is with at least three other persons, when others are in unanimous agreement, and when their reactions represent only small departures from the position.
3. A personality profile of the kind of individual who is least able to resist conformity pressures . . . would include such characteristics as submissiveness, lack of self-confidence, lack of originality, lack of achievement motivation, desire for social approval, and being uncritical, conventional, and authoritarian.

These conclusions seem to encompass implications for marketing but require further research.

Indirect potential contributions are those which are somewhat tangential but contain a glimmer of an idea, a concept, or suggest hypotheses that, with considerable work, may be useful. Resemblances, analogies, and identities often fall into this category. For instance, reasoning that marketing might be analyzed as a system, or seeking what correspondence the concepts of homeostasis, transaction, and transvection have in marketing, while indirect (at least initially) and requiring development, often proves useful.

Hart's two laws of social change: (1) the law of cultural acceleration, which states that the means for accomplishing purposes have increased at an accelerating rate, and (2) the law of logistic surges, which explains that the logistics curve describes specific instances of cultural accumulation, are examples of indirect potential contributions. They are suggestive

the Past Generation?" in Elting E. Morrison, editor, *The American Style* (New York: Harpers, 1958), p. 204.
[4] Albert D. Bederman and Herbert Zimmer, editors, *The Manipulation of Human Behavior* (New York: John Wiley, 1961), pp. 266-267.

in developing and understanding product innovation and acceptance.[5] Similarly, diagrammatic representation of ten theories of the direction of change have been offered. They seem to hold potential for developing marketing thought.[6]

Reasons for an Interdisciplinary Emphasis

The major reason for the use of the interdisciplinary approach is a pragmatic one. Interfaces exist among marketing and other disciplines. Marketing problems are not arranged to fit neatly the artificial isolation of specific subjects. The study of marketing is the study of behavior— behavior in a particular setting—the behavior of institutions and activities of the marketplace. Marketing factors are not readily compartmentalized or discipline bounded but are subject to common influences with other disciplines. Other subjects have demonstrated concretely that they have something to offer marketing. They offer a frame of reference, techniques, concepts, data, hypotheses, models, and theories. The result is that the interrelatedness of marketing and other disciplines is receiving greater attention than ever before.

Among the other reasons for the current interdisciplinary emphasis are the following.

1. Greater attention is being given to the societal aspects of marketing. This calls for an examination of marketing's broader dimensions and establishes the need for communication among a number of disciplines. Marketing is fundamental to the consideration of man in society and will, I feel, become one of the sciences of society.

2. Marketing, like all disciplines, is confronted with the challenge of dealing with an increasing rate of change and an explosion of knowledge. Change has been investigated by several disciplines. A variety of studies have been made of shifts of behavior, conformity, compliance, and other reactions. There are studies of repetitive cycles, changes in group structures, the dynamics of intergroup relations, and the consequences of inconsistent values and conduct. Indices of conformity and change exist. Change has been ordered. Social change, for example, has been ordered according to: changes in comprehensive social values; institutional change —changes in the forms of organization; changes in distribution of posses-

[5] Hornell Hart, "Social Theory and Social Change," in Llewellyn Gross, editor, *Symposium on Sociological Theory* (Evanston, Illinois: Row-Peterson, 1959), p. 202.
[6] Wilbert E. Moore, *Social Change* (Englewood Cliffs, New Jersey: Prentice-Hall), p. 38.

sions and rewards; changes in personnel; changes in abilities or attitudes of personnel.[7] They have meaning for marketing.

3. There exists a two-way pressure to link marketing with other disciplines. Our universities are now laboratories of society. They are problem oriented and a current interplay exists harnessing science and technology. The result is that many disciplines are progressing from their abstract theoretical orientations to problem solving. Marketing, on the other hand, is moving from its problem focus to theoretical bases. The result tends to be an amalgamation of disciplines and their concepts.

4. Systems-thinking is one of the current thrusts in marketing and other subjects. It is an approach borrowed from, and emphasizing, other disciplines, particularly biology, sociology, and systems-engineering. Systems-thinking stresses integrated wholes, feedback, and the interaction and adjustment of system elements. This integrated approach brings various discipline concepts together to solve problems. The analogies and tools of input-output systems, open and closed systems, and the concept of homeostasis, adaptation, adjustment, and survival are illustrative.

5. Various aspects of marketing are becoming rather technical. We are using increasingly complex tools of experimentation and measurement. Specialists from a variety of disciplines are attacking marketing problems. As specialties inevitably develop and grow, they foster research, discovery, theories, and inventions and become divided into finer and finer subsets for purposes of study and research. Specialization yields data and refined methodology. But marketing facts cannot stand by themselves. They need higher-order constructs to take on meaning. These constructs bring marketing into contact with other disciplines and in essence transmute both.[8] The interdisciplinary approach tends to bring coordination, synthesis, perspective, and the germination of ideas.

6. Related to the complexity of new techniques and the use of higher-order constructs is the use of models. The interdisciplinary approach has been particularly fruitful here. We are all familiar with the use in marketing of models such as the Markov process, linear programming, and queueing theory. A variety of qualitative models, including power-structure models, status models, and models of social stratification, have been valuable.[9] The interdisciplinary approach has, in fact, added dynamic

[7] Harry M. Johnson, *Sociology: A Systematic Introduction* (New York: Harcourt, Brace, and World, 1960), pp. 627-631.

[8] See William Lazer, "Philosophic Aspects of the Marketing Discipline," in William Lazer and Eugene Kelley, editors, *Managerial Marketing: Perspectives and Viewpoints* (revised edition) (Homewood, Illinois: Richard D. Irwin, 1962), pp. 606-612.

[9] See N. Rashevsky, "Two Models: Imitative Behavior and Distribution of Status,"

dimensions and new approaches to traditional marketing models which emphasized static marketing structures and marketing functions, but were not the best models for corporate decision making.

7. Our current approaches to the study of marketing are culture bound —they are American. But marketing is being interpreted in the light of other environments. The political-cultural-social contexts studied by other disciplines, therefore, become increasingly useful. Marketing is taking on international character and we are witnessing the process of acculturation—the transfer of culture and social elements from society to society.

Marketing is, in fact, a leading method of cultural contact across nations. Witness the transfer of marketing knowledge to other nations and the attempts to translate subsistence economies to better developed economies through the use of such ideas as the national market concept. For instance, consider the impact of advertising, supermarkets, and credit on other cultures.

8. The necessity of an interdisciplinary approach is inherent in our attempts to quantify marketing relationships. It has been suggested that perhaps the reason that we cannot quantify marketing activity very well is that the behavioral concepts basic to such measurement have not yet been developed. The challenge to the interdisciplinary approach is clear.

Current Status

What is the present status of the use of other disciplines in marketing? I feel that marketing's use of other disciplines to date may best be characterized as multidisciplinary rather than interdisciplinary. Yet, marketing, as an area of study, is moving from the multidisciplinary to the interdisciplinary stage. This current multidisciplinary emphasis is the prelude to the adoption of a more integrated interdisciplinary orientation. As a result of the current stage of progress, throughout the rest of the paper I shall not distinguish the multidisciplinary from the interdisciplinary.

Cronback's statement about the lack of integration of various psychological approaches is very appropriate for marketing. He states that if approaches are "kept independent, they can give only wrong answers or no answers at all regarding certain important problems."[10] For example, we cannot argue that marketing will deal with market forces and con-

---

in P. F. Lazarsfeld, editor, *Mathematical Thinking in the Social Science* (Glencoe, Illinois: Free Press, 1954), and K. Davis and W. E. Moore, "Some Principles of Stratification," *American Sociological Review,* 10, 242-249 (1945).

[10] Lee J. Cronback, "The Two Disciplines of Scientific Psychology," *The American Psychologist,* 12 (11), 673 (November 1957).

sumer behavior, while psychology will formulate the laws of motivation or change.

But the aim of the interdisciplinary approach should not be the cross-fertilization of ideas to unify the disciplines. Instead, it should be the use of various tools and concepts to come to grips with marketing problems. It should offer a joint attack on common problems in marketing, using the contributions of various disciplines, rather than promise unification of all disciplines.

The lines of the disciplines are blurring, and an integration and federation of some of them is occurring. It is becoming more difficult to differentiate parts of psychology and sociology from marketing, and vice versa. Will the disciplines be united into fewer and fewer subject-matter areas? Will the marketing boundaries vanish? The answer, I believe, is "No." Several forces will hold the marketing discipline intact. Its problems, theories, and methods; its instructional involvement; its identification with functions that are most significant to business; and its meaning for competition and international development, will insure that marketing will continue as a unit for teaching, research, and problem solving.

But the gaps among marketing and other areas will narrow. The tools will become similar. The concepts and ideas of many disciplines will continue to converge on marketing problems. More hybrid disciplines will emerge, and common concepts will evolve. Conceptual bridges between marketing and neighboring subject-matter areas will emerge.

Marketing's relationship with other disciplines will change. It will become more reciprocal in nature. Marketing is concerned with basic developments in our economy, culture, and society. It studies theoretical and significant problems that will advance thought in other areas. Such topics as consumer values, innovation, human behavior, market institutions, utilization of productive capacity, economic development, and life style are examples. "The field of marketing provides a testing ground on which to verify, modify, and extend the hypotheses which have been described by various behavioral sciences . . . marketing may become a basic source of concepts, hypotheses, and methodologies to be used by other disciplines."[11] These developments will legitimize the marketing discipline in the eyes of many.

In marketing, as in other areas, the transdisciplinary approach is evidenced in the development of hybrid disciplines. This refers mainly to the use of contiguous disciplines that merge to develop a different

[11] William Lazer and Eugene Kelley, "Interdisciplinary Contributions to Marketing Management," MTA Paper No. 5 (East Lansing: Michigan State University Bureau of Business and Economic Research, 1959), p. 7.

approach or new discipline. They focus on subject matter that "falls between the limits of discipline boundaries."[12] In the social and behavioral sciences, for example, this development would include social psychology, economic anthropology, and economic psychology. In marketing, we now see the development of marketing management, marketing communications, and marketing geography. As the interdisciplinary approach progresses, the tendency may become more pronounced.

The interdisciplinary approach to marketing recognizes the existence of two opposing situations: (1) that marketing is a discipline separate from the others and has unique problems and subject matter, and (2) that substantive marketing areas do exist where marketing can profit directly from joint study with other disciplines. The selection of distribution channels, the establishment of product-line or branding policy, and the evaluation of marketing effectiveness are examples of the first situation. The investigation of wants, needs, motives, status, and population changes reflects the second situation.

There are two stages to the integration of contributions from other disciplines. The first is the integration of relevant concepts, ideas, and findings by scientists, academics, and theoreticians, and their appearance in the literature. This is occurring on a wide front. The second refers to the implementation by practitioners. Currently, this is fairly limited. Yet, there have been a number of interesting applications as will be shown later in Table 1.2.

MARKETING AND OTHER DISCIPLINES

Marketing's Use of the Interdisciplinary Approach

In applying interdisciplinary contributions, there have been two tendencies. First, there is a tendency to use the extra-marketing specialist to solve marketing problems in terms of his major discipline. Here the psychologist, sociologist, or mathematician chooses his approach or perspective, often advocating its superiority. Sometimes it is better, but often it is not. At least it is different or novel, and that, too, can be helpful. The danger is that, instead of interpreting concepts and findings in terms of the marketing discipline, marketing may be refabricated in terms of the intellectual frameworks of other areas. In this sense, a discipline can become overly reliant on contiguous disciplines.

The second tendency is to develop a truly integrated and unified ap-

[12] Ibid., p. 2.

proach to marketing. This seeks to coordinate all the relevant results of contributing disciplines. The attempt is to achieve a total synthesis. There are evidences of some benefits of this attack, for instance, in Alderson's functionalism. Yet we are not at the point, and perhaps never will be, where this unification can be carried off totally. But, for marketing theory to progress, and for effective marketing management, unifying structures for marketing knowledge are required.

Interdisciplinary relationships have been brought in at various stages of marketing's evolution. They were helpful at the initial stage of natural observation of marketing activities, at the stage of discipline establishment, and at the current stages of quantification, experimentation, and concern with the development of formal theories.

The role of the interdisciplinary approach in marketing depends on and shapes the future direction of the discipline. For example, if marketing emphasizes the achievement of an understanding in terms of orderly, precise, logical elements, which omit reality and environments, then interdisciplinary concepts will be of limited use. If marketing accepts functionalism with its emphasis on environmental adaptation and probabilistic reasoning, the interdisciplinary approach will play a significant role. If marketing evolves into a number of specialties and develops micro theories and concepts, the interdisciplinary approach will be valuable in fostering synthesis, conceptual unity, and theories.

Currently, there are shifts in environmental factors encouraging the convergence of the research effort from many disciplines on marketing factors. Psychology, for example, is now feeling the impact of automation and abundance, and the "area of psychological research interest tends to shift from the producer to the consumer . . . what is needed is an understanding of consumer behavior."[13] These influences will buttress the interdisciplinary approach to marketing.

Interdisciplinary emphasis is affecting the development of marketing in yet another way. As both the marketing discipline, built on concepts from other disciplines, and the field of marketing became established, specialization spread. Marketing as a discipline turned inward and became fractionalized. With the interdisciplinary approach, marketing has turned outward, and the result is more meaningful perspectives, new concepts and theories, improved techniques, and a more useful body of knowledge. Wroe Alderson and Reavis Cox, almost twenty years ago, indicated the potential of this outward thrust for marketing when they

---

[13] Mason Haire, "Psychology and the Study of Business: Joint Behavioral Sciences," in Robert A. Dahl, Mason Haire, and Paul F. Lazarsfeld, *Social Science Research on Business Product and Potential* (New York: Columbia University Press, 1959), p. 54.

wrote "Here and there in the literature of several intellectual disciplines are appearing the elements from which an adequate theory of marketing will be constructed."[14]

An investigation of marketing management practice and marketing thought reveals that a more rigorous and penetrating analysis of marketing and business has resulted from multidimensional approaches to the study of marketing. Consider the use of economic theory. Demand, a core marketing concept, is now analyzed in terms of dimensions that extend well beyond those of the initial economic boundaries. It is viewed in terms of motivation, perception, status, imagery, symbolism, communications networks, conformity, resistance to change, levels of aspiration, life cycle, life style, mobility, search, and expectations. New questions are asked and new answers sought. Realistic involvement of many disciplines results. "A vast body of material which is potentially useful to marketing management exists in other disciplines."[15]

A variety of disciplines have given us a host of literature on values, opinions, interests, needs, motives, goals, and beliefs and are developing techniques to gauge them. The problems of images, perceptions, change, innovation, groups, power, status, and role are not indigenous to any one discipline. Yet they are the very stuff that marketing plans, product programs, and sales and advertising campaigns are built on.

Kapp has noted that "the essential characteristics of society are those of structural interdependence. Social structure is primary and from it all social inquiry must derive its basic scientific strategy."[16] In fact, some disciplines have been referred to as integrating disciplines. "For example, both anthropology and sociology are claimed to be 'integrating sciences,' the one taking 'culture' as the basic and integrating idea, and the other, 'social group or society.' "[17]

Viewed from this perspective, marketing is an integrating discipline. Markets are among the core institutions of our society. Marketing is characteristically American and exerts basic influences on our life style, culture, wealth, production, and values.

Marketing provides a common conceptual framework for studying many problems that cross disciplinary lines. The very scope and dimen-

[14] Wroe Alderson and Reavis Cox, "Toward a Theory of Marketing," *Journal of Marketing* (October 1948), p. 142.

[15] Lazer and Kelley, MTA Paper No. 5, op. cit., p. 1.

[16] K. W. Kapp, *Toward a Science of Man in Society* (Netherlands: Nijhoff, Heinman Imported Books, 1961), p. 203.

[17] Rollo Handy and Paul Kurtz, "A Current Appraisal of the Behavioral Sciences," Section 1 (Great Barrington, Massachusetts: Behavioral Research Council, 1963), p. 9.

sion of marketing problems carry theorists and practitioners over discipline boundaries. Although the "point of departure and the focus of study differ among the disciplines . . . there are frequently great similarities between marketing and other disciplines in both methodology and content."[18]

The interdisciplinary approach confronts the empirical findings of marketing with the conceptual and theoretical formulations of other disciplines, and vice versa. The result is that all confronted disciplines benefit. Marketing's direct and significant ties with economics and sociology are examples.

It seems that the most rapid period of progressive change in marketing is associated not with discoveries within the field but with the importation, borrowing, and diffusion of contributions outside marketing. In turn, however, these borrowed elements are changed in the assimilation process which results in new ideas and concepts.

In reality, marketing and its research are brought into existence to serve a purpose—a specific area of study. Yet as soon as marketing discovers ideas and information, it also serves other purposes and works with other subjects. As it does, it adds valuable dimensions and a wider purview to our understanding of both marketing and related areas. Marketing problems are seen in many dimensions.

Discipline Contributions Evaluated

It is often impossible to classify contributions by disciplines because of the cross-fertilization that has taken place. For example, people trained in one discipline work in another. There is a tendency to select concepts, tools, and techniques from any discipline and modify and adapt them as needed. This has often been done to solve marketing problems and the resultant blurring of discipline lines leads to arbitrary classifications.

Moreover, it is impossible to develop a rating scheme to evaluate objectively the overall contributions of various disciplines to marketing. Yet, I would feel remiss in carrying out this assignment if I did not present my feeling about the nature of discipline contributions. Other researchers will have different opinions, and an interchange of ideas should be useful.

I have rated the disciplines on the basis of whether they seem to have very limited application or perhaps undeveloped potential; whether they are useful in suggesting general approaches or as framework knowledge;

[18] Lazer and Kelley, MTA Paper No. 5, op. cit., p. 6.

whether they provide useful tools, theories, or concepts; or whether they are being actively applied and shape marketing. These categories are imprecise, and are not mutually exclusive nor collectively exhaustive, but I believe that the general meaning of the ratings will be clear.

Let me reemphasize that these ratings are subjective and represent one opinion at this point in time (see Table 1.1). I often encountered great difficulty in trying to pigeonhole discipline contributions. This is evidenced by the number of instances in which ratings embrace two categories.

Specific Use of Related Disciplines

Table 1.2 illustrates the direct and specific use of various concepts or tools from other disciplines in marketing. It lists various marketing sectors, the specific decision area in which interdisciplinary concepts are used, the related discipline and the concept or tool. Each of these contributions is keyed to a literature reference (listed at the end of this chapter). It is designed to be illustrative rather than comprehensive.

GENERAL RELATIONSHIPS WITH OTHER FIELDS

From our table of specific contributions to marketing problem solving, let us turn to a very brief consideration of some of the interfaces between marketing and various disciplines. The purpose here again is to be suggestive and not all-inclusive of either topics or disciplines.

Psychology

The fruitful and direct links between marketing and psychology are well known. Marketing's fundamental concern with consumer wants and needs has psychological underpinnings. Theories concerning motivation, learning, perception, symbolism, and association are useful. Psychoanalysis, with its emphasis on ego functioning and its role in human behavior, has lent useful projective techniques for marketing research. There has been a carryover in ways of measuring attitudes, beliefs, and opinions. Psychology's consideration of acceptance, adjustments, behavior, habit, instinct, cognition, responses, stimuli, desires, expectations, imagery, thresholds, perceptions, and testing is particularly apt for marketing.

TABLE 1.1   AN EVALUATION OF INTERDISCIPLINARY
ASSOCIATIONS AMONG NONBUSINESS
ADMINISTRATION DISCIPLINES
AND MARKETING[a]

Area or Discipline	Rating			
	Limited or Undeveloped Potential	Useful Perspectives and Approaches	Useful Techniques, Concepts, and Theories	Significant Applications
Anthropology— social and cultural		* * *	* * *	
Anthropology— physical	* * *			
Biology	* * *	* * *		
Computer Technology				* * *
Communications				* * *
Demography				* * *
Ecology			* * *	
Economics— international		* * *	* * *	
Economics— macro		* * *	* * *	
Economics— micro			* * *	* * *
Econometrics		* * *	* * *	
Engineering— electrical		* * *		
Engineering— human		* * *	* * *	
Engineering— systems			* * *	* * *
Esthetics		* * *		
Ethics		* * *	* * *	
Genetics	* * *	* * *		
Geography— economic		* * *	* * *	

TABLE 1.1 (Continued)

Area or Discipline	Rating			
	Limited or Undeveloped Potential	Useful Perspectives and Approaches	Useful Techniques, Concepts, and Theories	Significant Applications
History	***			
International Relations		***		
Law			***	
Land Economics		***		
Linguistics	***			
Mathematics			***	***
Natural Resources	***	***		
Operations Research			***	***
Philosophy of Science		***	***	
Political Science		***	***	
Psychiatry		***	***	
Psychology—behavioral				***
Psychology—clinical			***	***
Psychology—gestalt			***	***
Psychology—personality			***	
Social Psychology			***	***
Sociology				***
Sociology—rural			***	***
Statistics				***
Urban Planning	***			

[a] It is extremely difficult to rate the overall contributions of disciplines to marketing. Moreover, the categories used are not mutually exclusive, and different researchers will arrive at different assessments. Yet some trends are evident from such ratings.

TABLE 1.2 SPECIFIC USE OF RELATED DISCIPLINES IN MARKETING MANAGEMENT

Marketing Sector	Decision Area	Discipline	Concept or Tool	Literature Reference[a]
Market Communication	Personal influence, mass communication and adoption of innovation	Sociology	Two-step flow of communication, opinion leaders	1
	Communication and acceptance of innovation	Sociology	Trickle effect	2
	Communication of fashions	Sociology, Statistics	Innovators, adoption theory, communication behavior	3
Retailing	Choice of retail stores	Mathematics	Product-patronage matrix	4
	Store loyalty and promotional strategy	Psychology	Consumer panel	5
	Measurement of retail market position	Mathematics	Isolines	6
Pricing	Determining a pricing strategy	Statistics	Bayesian statistics	7
	Pricing	Psychology, Economics	Sensitivity analysis	8
Branding	Adjusting mature brands to changing markets	Sociology	Market segmentation and sequential purchasing behavior	9
	Brand and styles acceptance	Psychology	Tastes	10
Consumers and Consumer Behavior	Advertising strategy and consumer behavior	Psychology	Dissonance and consumers	11

17

TABLE 1.2 (Continued)

Marketing Sector	Decision Area	Discipline	Concept or Tool	Literature Reference[a]
Consumer and Consumer Behavior	Understanding consumer behavior	Psychology	Cognitive dissonance	12
	Consumer decisions	Psychology and Social Psychology	Risk taking and confidence	13
	Purchase influences	Sociology	Reference groups	14
	Determination of buying patterns	Sociology, Economics	Life cycle	15
	Understanding consumer behavior	Sociology, Economics	Life cycle, patterns, and elasticity of demand	16
	Status and consumer behavior	Psychology, Sociology	Status	17
Allocating Marketing Effort	Determination of marketing strategies		Marketing mix	18
	Proper allocation of marketing resources	Accounting, Management	Integrated information system	19
	Pretest and determination of market strategies	Mathematics, Electrical Engineering	Computer simulation	20
	Determination of value of alternative plans	Operations Research	Markov process	21
Market Segmentation	Expenditures by social class	Sociology	Social class position and mobility	22
	Tastes and purchase decisions	Sociology	High-, middle-, low-brow culture stratification of markets	23

TABLE 1.2 (Continued)

Marketing Sector	Decision Area	Discipline	Concept or Tool	Literature Reference[a]
Market Segmentation	Segmentation of markets	Sociology, Psychology	Segmentation analysis	24
	Consumption and social strata	Sociology	Social class stratification	25
	Market penetration and market segments	Sociology, Psychology	Consumption systems	26
Sales Effort	Selling effort and purchase behavior	Psychology	Communication systems	27
	Selection of salesmen	Psychology	Empathy and ego drive	28
	Measuring sales effectiveness	Accounting, Finance	Return on investment	29
Research and Forecasting	Predicting consumer attitudes	Economics	Habits, motives, expectations	30
	Determining expenditure for marketing research	Statistics	Bayesian statistics	31
	Allocations of research and development resources	Mathematics, Computers	Simulation	32
	Predicting sales for new products	Mathematics	Markov process	33
	Forecasting sales	Statistics	Time series analysis	34
New Product Acceptance	Market acceptance of new products	Sociology	Innovators, early and late adopters	35
	Determining acceptance of new products	Sociology	Mobility scales	36

19

TABLE 1.2 (Continued)

Marketing Sector	Decision Area	Discipline	Concept or Tool	Literature Reference[a]
New Product Acceptance	Encouraging product adoption	Law	Patents	37
Product Line	Adjusting product to consumer behavior	Anthropology	National character, subcultures, themes	38
	Elimination of weak products	Mathematics, Electrical Engineering	Product retention index, computer program	39
	Selection of new products	Accounting	Return on investment	40
	Use of information in product planning	Operations Research	Sales information	41
Advertising Strategy	Pretest of advertising strategies	Communication, Persuasion Research	Differential attitude technique	42
	Effects of advertising and selling	Psychology	Subliminal impact	43
	Measuring cumulative advertising effects	Economics, Statistics	Econometric model	44
	Selecting advertising strategies	Mathematics, Psychology	Computer simulation	45
	Measuring advertising effectiveness	Mathematics	Probability transition matrix	46
	Selection of media decisions	Computer Technology	Data breeder model	47
	Identifying advertising audiences	Sociology	Roster-reconstruction model	48

[a] References for this table are included at the end of this Chapter.

Sociology

Marketing is a social institution and has been explored as a social system. The fundamental relationships between marketing and sociology have been investigated. Jonassen enumerates:

. . . sociological concepts which appear later in marketing studies as important categories in terms of which data are gathered and analyzed.[19]

Sociologists investigate group action and dynamics, roles, expectations, conflicts, acculturation, mass, function, symbols, leisure, social class, households, consumption, life style, life cycle, mass communication, status, fashion, propaganda, and social values. Rural sociologists study innovation, product adoption, diffusion of information, change, models of power, urban and rural development. Direct contributions have also been made to surveys, interviews, sampling, scaling, and polls. Sociology has, in fact, been termed the discipline that has the greatest commonality of interest with marketing.

Political Science

Marketing thought and political science can interact fruitfully. Yet consideration to date has been confined mainly to regulatory activities of government. Other governmental influences, including purchasing activities, information, and research and development influences, are neglected.

Political science is concerned with man, society, political institutions, environments, influence, power, decision making, sanctions, and legitimacy. It studies these extrafirm forces so significant in marketing decisions.[20] It investigates bureaucracy, which leads to organizational considerations of marketing. The political scientist's interest in public opinion and propaganda are relevant for marketing, as are investigations of sovereignty and national policy.

Marketing and political science interact in the international sphere because marketing, more than any other part of a business, is directly exposed to the local operating environment.[21] Only recently has marketing started comparative analysis, but it is a mainstay of political science.

[19] Christen F. Jonassen, "Contributions of Sociology to Marketing," *Journal of Marketing* (October 1959), pp. 29-35.
[20] Hans Thorelli, "Political Science and Marketing," in Wroe Alderson, Reavis Cox, and Stanley Shapiro, editors, *Theory in Marketing* (revised edition) (Homewood, Illinois: Richard D. Irwin, 1964), pp. 125-136.
[21] Ibid., p. 129.

Political science can furnish us with models of western and nonwestern environments. Public administration and marketing can combine to promote economic development and the benefit of interdisciplinary contributions will be reciprocal.

Examples of possible contributions of marketing to political science stem from marketing operations in other countries. Consider the significance of the introduction of mass retail stores in Latin America, the establishment of supermarkets in Europe, or the role of advertising in Japan. The relationship between marketing, political science, and international development is direct and significant.

Quantitative Disciplines

Since a good part of this seminar is dedicated to a consideration of quantitative developments, I shall only make a few brief comments about them. Their impact on marketing as a discipline has been significant. Quantitative methods are helping marketing move from its prescientific or natural history base to a more scientific phase emphasizing more objective and precise methods of measurement, rigorous analysis, valid conclusions, and predictions. They are spurring marketing's development from impressionism to science.[22]

Marketing for the most part has concentrated on describing and classifying marketing phenomena. Quantitative disciplines stress measurement, both ordinal and cardinal, and this extends interdisciplinary horizons. The availability of new decision-making technology, including models and computers, affects our understanding of marketing, the decisions made, the quality of information, and methods of handling it. The result is greater attention to marketing planning, the creation of marketing information centers, and a reorganization of marketing tasks.

Anthropology

Marketing practice takes account of some anthropological findings. "A good case could be made for the thesis that marketing researchers do more anthropological research on modern cultures than do anthropologists."[23] Yet marketers and anthropologists have not found their common ground.

[22] Paul H. Dubois and David Goed, "Some Requirements and Suggestions for Quantitative Methods in Behavioral Science Research," in Norman F. Washburne, editor, *Decisions, Values, and Groups* (New York: Macmillan, 1962), pp. 42-65.
[23] Charles Winick, "Anthropology's Contributions to Marketing," *Journal of Marketing* (July 1961), p. 60.

Cultural anthropology seems to be the branch of anthropology that has the greatest relevance. It examines man and his works, including all the learned behavior of man. Anthropologists investigate differences that distinguish national groups. They explore the cultural and subcultural developments in terms of technology, language, symbols, rituals, and family behavior. Cultural anthropologists are educated to note cross-cultural differences and to understand other cultures. This is particularly relevant in dealing with global marketing. Anthropological investigations of cultural dynamics, cultural lag, assimilation, innovation, modes and standards of living, families, and status symbols have carryover for marketing.

Anthropomorphic measurements have been useful in designing products such as clothing and furniture. Anthropologists have helped marketers in developing advertising campaigns, introducing new products, styling clothing and packages, analyzing the meaning of symbols, rituals, taboos, and colors to various subcultures.[24] Their knowledge of patterns of living of various groups is particularly useful in our heterogeneous society. "There are at least three kinds of situations in which the knowledge of the anthropologist has been employed in marketing: specific knowledge, awareness of themes of a culture, sensitivity to taboos."[25]

Communications

That part of marketing concerned with advertising, sales promotion, personal selling, and public relations has a particularly close relationship with the communications discipline. Communications is, in fact, an excellent example of the direct benefit to marketing of contiguous disciplines. It has helped integrate the total promotional effort of the firm.

The following topics, investigated in communications, are suggestive of the interdisciplinary interfaces: the influence of mass media, message content and attitude change, the effects of propaganda, the impact of group pressures on communication, symbols and symbolism in communications, behavior and interaction in communication, the impact of environments on communication, subliminal and other psychoanalytical aspects, the diffusion of messages, communications models and theories, the perception of messages, learning and communication, motivation and communications, selective exposure and selective inattention, and information channels and networks. Also empirical investigations have offered some useful data, various theories, guides, and generalizations.[26]

[24] Ibid., pp. 56-59.
[25] Ibid., p. 56.
[26] See H. H. Hyman and P. B. Sheatsley, "Some Reasons Why Information Campaigns

Systems

Systems is more of an approach than a discipline. It has a heavy inter-disciplinary flavor and systems thinking in marketing is a carryover from such areas as systems engineering, operations research, sociology, and ecology.

The systems approach has been one of the major breakthroughs in marketing. It is resulting in a new level of sophistication in the understanding of marketing phenomena and processes. The marketing concept, the marketing mix, the communications, distribution, and product and service submixes, and physical distribution are systems concepts. When marketing is viewed as an integrated system of action, when the inter-relationships of elements are investigated, when the linkages among manufacturers, distributors, and consumers are studied for points of conflict and cooperation, when intersubsystem concessions are evaluated, better knowledge of marketing ensues.

The behavioral sciences offer conceptual frameworks for analyzing marketing systems in terms of three basic elements: (1) the conditions for marketing action including opportunity estimates, technology, territory, and size and time factors; (2) the master processes—communications, boundary maintenance, systemic linkages, structure, function and institutionalization, socialization, transmission of organizations, and social and marketing control; and (3) the specific system elements of objectives, facilities, norms, status-role, rank, power, authority-influence, sanctions, beliefs, and sentiments.

Systems engineering is providing new techniques for graphing and analyzing marketing systems in terms of quantifiable pressures and flows. Considerable progress has been made within the past five years, and the potential contributions seem to be significant.

Philosophy

Philosophy can provide a unifying force for marketing knowledge and can promote the development of marketing theory.[27] Logic and philosophy of science have immediate association with problem solving and marketing research. Social philosophers are concerned with the fundamental consequences of marketing for the United States and the international life style. Among the important philosophic questions for market-

---

Fail," in G. E. Swanson, T. M. Newcomb, and E. L. Hartley, editors, *Readings in Social Psychology* (New York: Holt, 1952), pp. 86-95.

[27] Lazer and Kelley, *Managerial Marketing: Perspectives and Viewpoints,* op. cit., pp. 606-612.

ing are: How does our concerted consumption orientation relate to basic social and individual influences and needs? Does marketing's emphasis on abundance, the purchase of more goods and services, and convenience and leisure, detract from the ideal or good life? Does marketing, per se, result in the generation of social animosity? Does marketing breed competition to the neglect of social welfare?[28]

Technology

Technological innovation and marketing are closely intertwined. While technology is science based, it is market dependent. The rate of technological change and the actual adoption of technology is market related.

Just as technology influences our life style, so marketing influences the enabling environment that stimulates, accepts, and infuses technology. Estimates made of research and development expenditures, which indicate that half of all these expenditures made in the United States have been made in the last ten years, point up the nature of future marketing implications. Increasingly, there will be a greater investigation of the intersection of marketing and technology.

Engineering

Various branches of engineering are becoming more relevant for the marketing discipline. Human engineering has a direct carryover. Systems engineering, with the development of new analytical techniques for depicting and analyzing marketing systems, has already been mentioned.

Ecology

There is a direct relationship between marketing and ecology in both approach and content. Ecology emphasizes the systems approach. It deals with population distribution, spatial and temporal relationships, metropolitan and rural communities, mass societies, intercity movement, and factors of diffusion.

History

Historians are not overly concerned with marketing and marketing issues. Neither are marketers adequately concerned with the contributions

[28] For a discussion of social philosophy and business, see Robert A. Dahl, "Business and Politics: A Critical Appraisal of Political Science," in Robert A. Dahl, Mason Haire, and Paul F. Lazarsfeld, *Social Science Research on Business Product and Potential* (New York: Columbia University Press, 1959), p. 43.

of history. Historical research, however, can become the source of valuable hypotheses. In turn, marketing can furnish valuable source materials about man in society to historians. To date, these contributions have been limited.

Biology

Biology has had an influence on marketing thought and action in two ways. First, there is a direct carryover from the concept of biological organisms and systems to marketing organisms and systems. Second, the biological ideas of evolution, growth, and change have their immediate counterpart in marketing.

PROBLEMS IN USING THE INTERDISCIPLINARY APPROACH

1. The interdisciplinary approach could result in the misguided direction of research and problem-solving activities in marketing. Attempts to manipulate the concepts, ideas, and findings of other disciplines to achieve unifying research results can lead to a neglect of marketing and its particular needs. Marketing activities may be shaped and structured to meet the dimensions, requirements, and constraints of other disciplines.

2. Although the problems, concepts, and findings of many disciplines have marketing relevance, the details, assumptions, and perspectives often vary. Researchers from other disciplines bring a different point of view, different training and experience to a problem. Researchers and discipline specialists often make marketing and marketing problems correspond to their own background and interests rather than the reverse. In reality, common concepts have different operational meanings to each specialist.

3. Controversies exist within and between the disciplines, and they are hard to resolve. Behavioral and social scientists are not unified in their approaches, concepts, and findings; bewilderment and confusion result. "For example, consider the important marketing subject area of motivation . . . rather than any one unified approach emerging, there are at least three major directions followed by psychologists pursuing motivation studies."[29] The integration of numerous conflicting explanations into practical solutions for marketing is a most perplexing task.

4. Marketers generally have tended to overstate the value of con-

[29] Herta Herzog, "Behavioral Science Concepts for Analyzing the Consumer," paper given at the Conference of Marketing Teachers from Pacific Coast States (Berkeley: University of California, September 9, 1958).

tributions of other areas. They have not evaluated situations realistically. The limitations of other areas are skirted or ignored. Consider, for example, the early reactions to motivation research or operations research. Marketing failed to examine and adjust the theories, concepts, and findings of other disciplines, and failed to modify them in light of its own knowledge and intellectual insights. Marketing has failed in its search to sort the contributions; it has failed to order the directly useful; it has failed to adjust and adapt the relevant, and to discard the irrelevant.

5. It is possible for the interdisciplinary approach to delay and even deter marketing developments. For instance, the uncritical application of stimulus-response theory, psychoanalytic tools, findings of "rat psychologists," or hypothetical economic models to marketing problems can lead to intellectual barrenness in various marketing areas. The concept of equilibrium, for instance, with its analog in the mechanical concept of forces and counterforces that reach a point of stability, has severe limitations when applied to energy and matter, or to the dynamic aspects of marketing.

6. The results of an interdisciplinary approach are often qualified and indecisive. Sometimes they are theoretical and cannot stand up to the pragmatic demands of problem solving. The assumptions made by other disciplines are often unreal or too limiting. Many times, the kinds of problems that can be handled best are often those that are not critical or which can be dealt with adequately at present.

7. Discipline specialists can only make a great contribution to marketing to the extent that we are able to communicate with and question them, and evaluate what they offer. Despite contiguous borders among disciplines, adequate communications are lacking. Jargon and terminology vary, and attempts to relate findings, theories, and constructs are usually very frustrating and ineffective. As specialization and compartmentalization increase and new hybrid disciplines evolve, communication tends to decrease.

8. There are also a number of problems associated with getting people from other disciplines to concentrate on marketing. Included are the problems of loss of identification and stature in one's discipline and the loss of security inherent in tackling new concepts and ideas.

CONCLUDING OBSERVATIONS

The interdisciplinary approach has shaped marketing developments significantly in the past two decades. New courses such as consumer behavior and marketing communications have emerged. Marketing books have been restructured. Basic ways of thinking about marketing have been altered, as is evidenced by functionalism, marketing management, and the systems approach. Marketing thought has been extended by borrowed theories and concepts. More precise experimentation and rigorous analysis have resulted from the application of computers, and mathematical and statistical techniques. The overall impact has been a more imaginative and fruitful attack on marketing problems and a better understanding of marketing systems than would otherwise be the case.

There is no doubt that marketing has borrowed more heavily from other disciplines than it has contributed. It has been applying, testing, refining, and modifying the methods and findings of many other areas. Although some reciprocal benefits have been realized, the significant reciprocal contributions will be realized in the future. Marketing will contribute in such areas as decision making, information, organization theory, motivation, imagery, persuasion, communications, scaling, competition, mergers, and innovation.

In concluding, I list, for consideration, several statements about the interdisciplinary approach to marketing.

1. The development of marketing science is closely tied to the amenity of marketing to the methods and findings of other disciplines, particularly mathematics, statistics, and the behavioral sciences.

2. Marketing is now, and will continue to be, one of the major environmental factors influencing man in society. Since the consideration of man in his environment is one of the tasks that pervades social and behavioral sciences, marketing is a natural area of interdisciplinary convergence for understanding human relationships, and its interdisciplinary role will become increasingly important. It will become one of the sciences of society.

3. The interdisciplinary approach has had a profound effect in shaping marketing thought, ideas, and research effort. As a result of the interdisciplinary approach, curricula have been restructured, courses revised, and new marketing subject-matter areas developed. It has had a more modest but still important impact on marketing action.

4. The greatest and most lasting contribution of the interdisciplinary approach may be its influence on ways of conceptualizing, formulating, and thinking about marketing problems instead of in providing marketing information and solutions for problems. The systems approach and functionalism are examples.

5. Most of the concepts, theories, hypotheses, and facts of other dis-

ciplines have only limited relevance for marketing. Marketing has failed to sift and sort, in a systematic fashion, the findings and concepts from other disciplines and to identify those that have direct importance for marketing. The result is that the interdisciplinary approach has not made the impact it could.

6. The successful injection of subject-matter specialists from other areas into marketing requires a rather unique individual. Competence in a behavioral, social, or quantitative discipline is not enough. People rooted in the marketing discipline, rather than behavioral or social scientists, or quantitative specialists, will contribute most to the future development of the marketing discipline.[30]

7. It is easier to use the concepts and approaches of other disciplines in a general way than it is to apply theories and findings to solve specific problems or to use specific data.

8. Much of the contribution of the interdisciplinary approach lies in data, concepts, and theories that have marketing overtones but which must be developed further. The direct transference of concepts or findings from other disciplines to marketing is often not practicable. Adaptation and adjustment is required to integrate them into marketing thought. To solve its problems, marketing faces the challenge of determining the necessary concepts, models, and theories, which are not available in other disciplines, and of developing them itself. These contributions, in turn, can shape the related disciplines.

9. Marketing is an integrative subject-matter area. Marketing problems may be viewed from social, behavioral, and measuremental perspectives. Marketing is a fundamental economic activity. The result is that marketing can contribute actively to the development of other disciplines.

10. Among the most direct and significant contributions to marketing thought are those from other business administration areas.

11. As an economy matures, the marketing problems come to the forefront and their sociological and psychological dimensions become more important. The tools of economics, then, must be bolstered by those of other behavioral and social disciplines. Theory, adequate to the demands of marketing tasks, must be concerned with the political, economic, sociological, cultural, and psychological dimensions. The multidisciplinary and interdisciplinary movement is a natural development.

12. As a direct result of transdisciplinary efforts, some of the findings and theories of a variety of disciplines will eventually be integrated into theories of market action that will parallel those of social action.

[30] Lazer and Kelley, MTA Paper No. 5, op. cit., p. 31.

REFERENCES

1. Elihu Katz, "The Two-Step Flow of Communication: An Up-to-Date Report on an Hypothesis," *Public Opinion Quarterly* (spring 1957), pp. 61-78.
2. Lloyd A. Fallers, "A Note on the Trickle Effect," *Public Opinion Quarterly* (fall 1954), pp. 314-321.
3. Charles W. King, *Communicating with the Innovator in the Fashion Adoption Process*, in "Marketing and Economic Development," Peter D. Bennett, editor, Proceedings of the fall conference of the American Marketing Association, Washington, D. C., pp. 425-439.
4. Louis P. Bucklin, "Retail Strategy and the Classification of Consumer Goods," *Journal of Marketing* (January 1963), p. 50.
5. Stanley J. Shapiro and Robert J. Colonna, "Store Loyalty as a Measure of Promotional Effectiveness of Supermarkets," *Business Horizons*, 7 (3), 67, 1964.
6. William Applebaum, "Measuring Retail Market Penetration for a Discount Food Supermarket—A Case Study," *Journal of Retailing* (summer 1965), p. 1.
7. Paul E. Green, "Bayesian Decision Theory in Pricing Strategy," *Journal of Marketing* (January 1963), p. 5.
8. Richard T. Sampson, "Sense and Sensitivity in Pricing," *Harvard Business Review* (November 1964), p. 99.
9. Robert Mainer and Charles C. Slater, "Markets in Motion," *Harvard Business Review* (March 1964), p. 64.
10. Herbert E. Krugman and Eugene L. Hartley, "The Learning of Tastes," *Public Opinion Quarterly* (winter 1960).
11. James F. Engle, "Are Automobile Purchasers Dissonant Consumers?" *Journal of Marketing* (April 1963), p. 55.
12. Harold H. Kassarjian and Joel B. Cohen, "Cognitive Dissonance and Consumer Behavior," *California Management Review* (fall 1965), p. 55.
13. Raymond A. Bauer, "Consumer Behavior on Risk Taking," Proceedings of the 43rd National Conference of the American Marketing Association, Robert S. Hanock, editor (June 15-17, 1960), pp. 389-398.
14. Francis S. Bourne, "Group Influences in Marketing and Public Relations," *Some Applications of Behavioral Science Research*, Resis Likert and Samuel P. Hayes, Jr., editors (Paris: UNESCO 1957), pp. 217-224.
15. S. G. Barton, "The Life Cycle and Buying Patterns," *Consumer Behavior*, Vol. II, New York University Press, edited by Lincoln H. Clark (1955), p. 28.
16. Janet A. Fisher, "Life Cycle Analysis in Research on Consumer Behavior," *Consumer Behavior*, Vol. II, New York University Press, edited by Lincoln H. Clark (1955), p. 28.
17. Burleigh B. Gardner, "Social Status and Consumer Behavior," *Consumer Behavior*, Vol. II, New York University Press, edited by Lincoln H. Clark (1955), p. 53.
18. Gordon E. Miracle, "Product Characteristics and Marketing Strategy," *Journal of Marketing* (January 1965), p. 18.
19. Richard A. Feder, "How to Measure Marketing Performance," *Harvard Business Review* (May 1965), p. 132.
20. William D. Wells, "Computer Simulation of Consumer Behavior," *Harvard Business Review* (May 1963), p. 93.

21. Jerome D. Herniter and John F. Magee, "Customer Behavior as a Markov Process," *Journal of Operations Research* (January-February 1961), p. 105.
22. Pierre Martineau, "Social Classes and Spending Behavior," *Journal of Marketing* (October 1958), p. 121.
23. R. Lynes, *The Tastemakers* (New York: Harper, 1957).
24. Daniel Yankelovich, "New Criteria for Market Segmentation," *Harvard Business Review* (March 1964), p. 83.
25. Richard P. Coleman, "The Significance of Social Stratification in Selling," Proceeds of the 43rd National Conference of the American Marketing Association, edited by Martin L. Bell (December 1960), pp. 171-184.
26. Harper W. Boyd, Jr. and Sidney J. Levy, "New Dimension in Consumer Analysis," *Harvard Business Review* (November 1963), p. 129.
27. Robert C. Brooks, Jr., "Relating the Selling Effort to Patterns of Purchase Behavior," *Business Topics* (winter 1963), p. 73.
28. David Mayer and Herbert M. Greensborg, "What Makes a Good Salesman," *Harvard Business Review* (July 1964), p. 119.
29. Michael Schiff, "The Use of ROI in Sales Management," *Journal of Marketing* (July 1963), p. 70.
30. George Katona, "The Predictive Value of Data on Consumer Attitudes," *Consumer Behavior,* Vol. II, New York University Press, edited by Lincoln H. Clark (1955), p. 66.
31. Frank M. Bass, "Marketing Research Expenditures—A Decision Model," *Journal of Business* (January 1963), p. 77.
32. William D. Barclay, "A Probability Model for Early Prediction of New Product Market Success," *Journal of Marketing* (January 1963), p. 63.
33. Edgar A. Pessemier, "Directing R & D for Profitable New-Product Development," *Communicating with the Innovator in the Fashion Adoption Process,* Charles W. King, "Marketing and Economic Development," edited by Peter D. Bennett, Proceedings of the fall conference of the American Marketing Association, Washington, D. C., pp. 425-439.
34. Robert L. McLoughlin, "The Breakthrough in Sales Forecasting," *Journal of Marketing* (April 1963), p. 46.
35. William Lazer and William E. Bell, "The Communications Process and Innovation," *Journal of Advertising Research,* forthcoming issue.
36. Steven J. Shaw, "Behavioral Science Offers Fresh Insights on New Product Acceptance," *Journal of Marketing* (January 1965), p. 9.
37. Carl E. Barnes, "Get Inventions Off the Shelf," *Harvard Business Review* (January 1966), p. 138.
38. Charles Winick, "Anthropology's Contributions to Marketing," *Journal of Marketing* (July 1961), p. 53.
39. Philip Kotler, "Phasing Out Weak Products," *Harvard Business Review* (1965), p. 107.
40. Philip A. Scheuble, Jr., "ROI for New-Product Policy," *Harvard Business Review* (November 1964), p. 110.
41. George H. Chacko, "An Operations Research Evaluation Technique of the Use of Sales-Research Information," *Journal of Operations Research* (May-June 1959), p. 313.
42. Harvey W. O'Neill, "Pretesting Advertising with the Differential Attitude Technique," *Journal of Marketing* (January 1963), p. 20.

43. Alvin W. Rose, "Motivation Research and Subliminal Advertising," *Social Research* (autumn 1958), pp. 271-284.
44. Kristian S. Palda, "The Measurement of Cumulative Advertising Effects," *Journal of Business* (April 1965), p. 162.
45. Raymond A. Bauer and Robert D. Buzzell, "Mating Behavioral Science and Simulation," *Harvard Business Review* (September 1964), p. 116.
46. Irvin M. Grossack and Robert F. Kelly, "Measuring Advertising Effectiveness: Use of PTM," *Business Horizons* 6(3), 83 (1963).
47. William T. Morgan, "Practical Media Decisions and the Computer," *Journal of Marketing* (July 1963), p. 26.
48. Laurence Roslow and Sidney Roslow, "A Low-Cost Method for Identifying TV Audiences," *Journal of Marketing* (April 1963), p. 13.

PART ONE

Consumer Behavior
and Normative Models

There are several possible ways to classify or categorize marketing models. Howard[1] distinguishes between normative and descriptive models. Normative models are prescriptive with respect to alternate courses of action, while descriptive models provide explanations of phenomena. Although this distinction is useful, it is significant that model-building activity in these two areas is not unrelated. There are descriptive elements in normative models and the sensitivity of the decision variables to the parameters of the descriptive models may be explored in order to determine the importance, or even the character, of the descriptive elements. While the focus of interest of descriptive models is upon understanding some phenomenon rather than on the development of a course of action, most descriptive models in marketing are suggestive of potential normative models. Therefore, even those descriptive models which have no immediate and obvious relation to decision problems may lead ultimately to results, ideas, or measurements which may be useful in connection with decision criteria. The distinction between descriptive and normative models is not unlike the distinction between pure and applied research.

If we associate science with that which is mathematically formal, with that which explores relationships, and with that in which formal measure-

[1] John A. Howard, *Marketing: Executive and Buyer Behavior* (New York: Columbia University Press, 1963).

ment is of primary importance, then it is clear that science in marketing is of recent origin. The era of the first generation of formal models of consumer behavior and marketing-decision processes has come to a close. The second generation builds upon and extends the first generation.

The descriptive and normative models included in Part One are concerned primarily with theoretical models of consumer purchasing behavior and the statistical methodology associated with the measurement of these phenomena. These chapters open up new avenues for exploration as well as indicate weaknesses and potentially rejectable hypotheses reflected in earlier models of consumer behavior. These chapters suggest more sophisticated models in the second generation of studies leading to the rejection of earlier, simpler and more naive assumptions. The results of numerous studies have been utilized to provide more coherent and more general conclusions than was heretofore possible.

The major thrust of descriptive model-building activity has been upon market segmentation and the dynamics of consumer behavior. The chapters in Part One deal with these areas as well as with normative marketing models.

MARKET SEGMENTATION

The concept of looking at the market for a product as being composed of segments which are homogeneous in some dimension has received widespread attention by those concerned with marketing strategy. Substantial research effort has been concerned with this concept since, if market segmentation as a strategy is to have real meaning, it is necessary to define precisely the relevant segments and to estimate the differences in response rates to marketing inputs between segments. For certain industrial products, the relevant segments of the market may be more or less obvious. Size and industry characteristics may be sufficient bases for segmenting the market. Similarly, for certain types of consumer products, some kind of segmentation may be possible without extensive research. For example, high-income families are more likely prospects for expensive cars and Carribean cruises than low-income families. Other demographic and socioeconomic variables such as age, size of family, and occupation may be related (but in a less obvious way) to buying propensities for these products.

The most challenging measurement problems associated with the market segmentation concept are in the area of consumer convenience goods. There are two possible approaches to the problem. First, we may start with observed differences in purchasing characteristics of different groups of consumers (that is, heavy versus light buyers) and attempt to discover those variables which are related to these characteristics. Second, we may start with those variables around which it might be feasible to build a strategy of segmentation and attempt to discover how purchasing characteristic differences are related to these variables.

In principle, it is possible to study the relationship between some measure of purchasing behavior and related variables by cross-classification procedures. However, as a practical matter, when the number of classifications is large, the sample size within cells tends to become so small as to render this technique useless even for fairly large samples. Multiple discriminant analysis has frequently been employed in order to obviate this difficulty. Thus, if there are two groups being studied, A and B, and two continuous functions $f_A(X/A)$ and $f_B(X/B)$ where X is a vector of measurements, the parameters of f_A and f_B may be estimated and, with the use of Bayes theorem, $h(A/X)$ and $h(B/X)$ may be calculated and used as a basis for classifying elements in the sample as a test of the predictive strength of the variables. In addition, significance tests may be employed to eliminate those variables not strongly related to group membership. In most studies, the distribution of X has been assumed to be joint normal, primarily because the existing computer programs make this assumption.

While it is clearly possible to raise questions concerning the statistical methodology employed in studies of group behavior, there have now been a sufficient number of studies (as revealed by Ronald E. Frank's rather exhaustive literature search) to warrant certain conclusions about the feasibility of applying a strategy of market segmentation to consumer convenience products. It has not been possible to discover strong association between demographic, socioeconomic, and such psychological variables as have been used and dependent variables (for instance, level of purchasing and brand loyalty). From the point of view of future research, it would appear that far more sophisticated measurements, probably psychological in nature, will have to be developed in order to understand more fully the variations in group behavior of consumers. Even if this is accomplished, it may not be possible to employ a strategy of segmentation or selective promotion since media audience composition patterns and media data may very well not permit selective utilization.

THE DYNAMICS OF CONSUMER BEHAVIOR

The earliest interest in the dynamics of market behavior was in the study of time-series sales behavior. Various sales-forecasting schemes have been developed which predict changes in sales fairly well. Few of these models, however, contribute anything at all to the understanding of consumer behavior since they do not include decision variables or explicit assumptions about the process of change in purchasing behavior.

The development of consumer panel data has permitted the study of dynamic purchasing behavior on an individual family basis. In recent years, there have been several studies of brand-switching behavior through time on an individual family basis. Many of these studies have postulated a first order Markov model of change. Thus, the time interval between purchase was assumed to be fixed, as was the transition matrix. It now appears that the Markov model, at least the first-order variety, may be safely rejected. It is worth noting that these models assume the market environment is stable, thus abstracting from changes in decision variables. Furthermore, even if the Markov model could be accepted, very little information would be gained about the motivating influences which yield this behavior pattern.

Ronald A. Howard, in the very illuminating discussion (Chapter Three) that appears in Part One, discusses the data difficulties associated with the study of dynamic behavior and develops a procedure that, among other things, relaxes the assumption about fixed time intervals between purchases, employs a Bayesian technique to incorporate information from the panel as a whole in estimating probabilistic behavior of individuals, and postulates changes in the market structure at discrete change points. In this way, the rigid assumptions of the earlier, more naive, models have been relaxed, and substantial flexibility has been added.

Two critical issues arise in connection with the study of the dynamics of consumer behavior. One of these issues is discussed by Howard. It is the issue of curve-fitting versus hypothesis testing. In adopting the Bayesian approach, we assume that the process is known and that the major problem concerns parameter estimation. This approach may be entirely satisfactory where the major interest is in decision making. However, when the primary concern is in the process itself, the Bayesian approach may contribute little to the reduction of uncertainty, even though it may force the model to fit the data well.

The second issue that arises in the study of the dynamics of consumer behavior deals with the question of the most appropriate level of aggregation with which to deal with the problem. The study of the influence of decision variables is greatly facilitated by models that deal with time-series aggregates. Many of the problems involved in micro models are simplified by aggregating the data. Furthermore, established econometric procedures may be more readily applied to test the models than is the case with most micro models. While macro models appear at present to offer greater promise for the study of the influence of decision variables, they also fail to reveal very much about the nature of consumer behavior beyond providing clues about the existence of gross relationships. In addition, when the decision variables of interest are those of brief duration, such as sales-promotional activities, the aggregation process frequently tends to conceal the short-term effect of these variables. The ultimate ideal, of course, is to develop macro models which are consistent with models of individual behavior. William F. Massy makes a contribution in this connection in developing a model which permits prediction of group behavior of nonhomogeneous consumers.

NORMATIVE MODELS

In the past, one of the major limitations of models-building activity has been the restriction of mathematical tractability. Thus, there has been a tendency to shape the model to fit mathematical convenience. Ideally, we should like to write down a detailed list of assumptions and then explore the implications of these assumptions with respect to goals. With the development of the high speed computer, it is now possible to extend the range of models to large, detailed, and complex systems.

Henry J. Claycamp and Arnold E. Amstutz describe a large micro-analytic simulation specifically designed for the prescription drug market. One of the important results of an activity of this kind is that it forces management to think through clearly and in some detail just what it does believe about market behavior. Moreover, the development of large-scale simulation models, of necessity, calls for joint effort of various people in an organization. Even if there are no other results than this, the effects of this collective effort may be beneficial.

Interesting points of comparison are possible between large simulation studies (for instance, that discussed by Claycamp and Amstutz) and complex systems models (for example, the one described by David B. Learner). Both models are structured around a chain of relationships. Thus, marketing decision variables affect sales through a series of intervening variables. Both models permit sensitivity analysis, although this is somewhat more difficult in the simulation study because of its complexity. Judgment plays an important role in measurement in both studies, but it appears that statistical estimation is of greater value in the model discussed by Learner than in the simulation model. The Learner model is considerably more general in application than the simulation model in that it is presumed to apply to a broad range of products. Neither model explicitly takes into account competitive interaction effects, and both models are essentially deterministic in character.

Market Segmentation Research:
Findings and Implications

The strategy of market segmentation is defined as the development and pursuit of different marketing programs by the same firm, for essentially the same product, but for different components (for example, heavy versus light buyers) of the overall market. The logic underlying this strategy is deceivingly simple and straightforward. Presumably the market for a product is made up of customers who differ either in their own characteristics or in the nature of their environment in such a way that some aspect of their demand for the product in question also differs. The strategy of market segmentation involves the tailoring of the firm's product and/or marketing program to these differences. By modifying either of these, the firm is attempting to increase profits by converting a market with heterogeneous demand characteristics into a set of markets that although they differ from one another, are internally more homogeneous than before.

For example, a cereal manufacturer may choose to develop products especially tailored to the younger set such as sugar-coated or alphabet-shaped cereals. Another example of segmentation is the attempt by many manufacturers to aim their promotion disproportionately at the heavy buyer of a product by choosing media that have a particularly strong appeal to this group.

The concept of segmentation was first articulated in a pioneering article by Wendell Smith in 1956 [31]. Since its publication, this concept has permeated the thinking of managers and researchers alike as much, if not more, than any other single marketing concept since the turn of the century. The importance of segmentation as a source of increased profits was highlighted in *Grey Matter:*

> Markets of the future will not only be segmented but each segment will be fragmented. Even fragments will offer great profit opportunities because of our

mushrooming population, expanding affluence, and spreading education. Advertisers who see the future clearly and develop the skill to cultivate *diverse segments and fragments* will sharpen their competitive edge [18, p. 4].

According to Smith:

The phenomenon of market segmentation suggests that, even in an economy characterized by imperfect competition, a drift toward equilibrium in market segments is discernible. It is worthy to note that the emergence of market segmentation as a strategy once again provides evidence of the consumer's pre-eminence in the contemporary American economy . . . [30, p. 3].

In other words, to the extent that firms take advantage of existing opportunities for market segmentation, their actions are apt to benefit not only themselves but also their ultimate consumers. On the other hand, the choice of segmentation as a strategy, when in fact it is unwarranted, can result in losses to both groups.

Marketing management is faced with two crucial decisions with respect to segmentation:

1. To what extent should the firm pursue a strategy of market segmentation?

2. If the market is to be segmented, upon what basis (or bases) should it be segmented?

It is normal to answer the first question in the affirmative if it can be shown that, on the average, certain segments (groups) of people buy more of the product under consideration than do other groups.

These customer segments are usually classified in terms of socioeconomic, life-cycle, or locational characteristics, although other dimensions such as personality variables may also be used. Groups for which the *average purchase rate* is high are identified as "target" market segments. Presumably, if average purchase rates were equal among all groups of a product's customers, segmentation would not be a profitable strategy.

How can we judge the validity of this conclusion? Are there criteria, other than the existence of differences in average purchase rate among various groups of customers, that are associated with opportunities for profitable market segmentation? The following section presents a conceptual framework for determining whether market segmentation will, in fact, result in higher profits. As we shall see, differences in average purchase rates are only one of several demand criteria for judging opportunities for profitable market segmentation.

This section is followed by a review of research on the usefulness of household socioeconomic, personality, and purchasing characteristics as bases for segmenting a wide range of grocery product markets. The majority of the work reported consists of investigations that I conducted with William Massy and Harper Boyd, Jr. This chapter concludes with a discussion of the implications of our work, to date, together with some suggestions for further research.

CRITERIA FOR SEGMENTATION

Management needs criteria for determining the extent to which segmenting a market would place it in a more beneficial position than would treating it as a homogeneous entity. What should these criteria be? Presumably a firm desires to achieve increased profits through segmentation. Under what conditions can these be obtained?

If the incremental costs of serving different customers in a market are the same, then there is only one condition under which a firm can achieve greater profitability through market segmentation: different groups of customers must have different responses to changes in the firm's marketing program. Consider, for example, a market in which some customers are very likely to switch brands in response to a cut in price while others are more sensitive to changes in national advertising. If we could identify these segments and find a way to reach them separately, greater profits could probably be achieved by charging somewhat different prices and aiming different levels of advertising at each group.

This idea can be restated as follows. "In the language of economics, segmentation is *disaggregative* in its effects and tends to bring about recognition of several demand schedules where only one was recognized before" [31, p. 5].[1] A demand schedule is simply an expression for the quantity of a product that is demanded at each of the number of different price or promotional levels.

Suppose, for example, that a firm is spending the same amount of promotional funds on all of its customers. Furthermore, suppose that it is trying to sell as much output as possible, in light of its promotional budget. An increase in promotional expenditures is contemplated. Should the firm extend the offer to all of its customers? If management knew that a particular identifiable group of customers (a market segment) would increase its expenditures on the product by $10 per unit sold, whereas other customers would tend to increase their total expenditures by only $5 per unit, it clearly would be better off if it cut its prices to the first group, thereby selling an increased proportion of its output to that

---

[1] For a more detailed statement of the logic underlying this point, see Ref. 29.

segment. This would continue until the incremental revenue associated with the sale of an additional unit was the same for the two groups. This is a well-recognized principle in the field of economics.

In other words, one crucial criterion for determining the desirability of segmenting a market along any particular dimension is whether the different submarkets have different elasticities with respect to the price and promotional policies of a firm. An elasticity is simply a summary measure that relates a percentage change in quantity demanded to the associated percentage change in some causal variable, such as price.

Where there are differences in the incremental costs involved in serving customers in the different submarkets, these cost differences should be matched against the effects of price and promotion upon demand in order to arrive at a criterion for judging the desirability of market segmentation. The treatment of costs in market segmentation is beyond the scope of this chapter; the important point for our purposes is that, whether costs are equal or not, the degree to which the demand elasticities in the various submarkets are different from one another remains a crucial criterion for market segmentation.[2]

In spite of the importance of response differences as a criterion for judging the appropriateness of market segmentation, only three studies have (1) reported results bearing upon this problem and (2) illustrated techniques for operationally defining the magnitude and nature of these differences [12, 14, 25]. All three of these studies have appeared in the literature since 1963. Variations in the response of customers to promotion, although not the only criterion for evaluating a given strategy of market segmentation, is the most neglected in the literature.

The most commonly discussed criterion is the extent of differences in the average purchase rate among various customer segments. It is frequently the practice in empirical research dealing with the demand for a given brand in a product class (for example, the Del Monte brand of canned corn) to base elasticity estimates on the response of the brand's market share to changes in pricing, retail advertising, and similar things. Although these response estimates are useful, they do not take into account differences in the average purchase rates for the various segments. Therefore, both elasticity and average purchase-rate criteria are required for an analysis of the usefulness of a given scheme of market segmentation.

In addition to these criteria, effective segmentation depends (in part) on the ability to communicate separately with whatever segments are of

[2] For a discussion of the relationship between costs and promotional sensitivities, see Ref. 1.

interest. To the extent that the segments are identical with respect to such characteristics as their socioeconomic status, personality, and media habits, the effectiveness of segmentation is severely constrained.

Summary of Criteria

We have found it useful to think of these criteria in terms of the following questions.

1. To what extent can members of each segment be identified in terms of characteristics such as socioeconomic status, personality, and media habits?
2. What is the degree of variation in the average level of customer demand for the product from one segment to another?
3. What is the degree of variation in customer sensitivity to changes in the firm's promotional policies as well as those of competitors? That is, do customers in one segment respond to a greater or lesser degree than those in another to changes in such promotional inputs as the rate of dealing and retail advertising as well as price level?

If customers belonging to different segments (for instance, high- and low-brand loyalty) have virtually identical incomes, personalities, and media exposures, then the effectiveness of segmentation based on this dimension is severely constrained because there is no way to tailor promotion to any one segment. Instead, segmentation must be directed at the entire population of customers.

In addition, if the average level of customer demand and customer sensitivity to changes in promotion is the same for all segments, there are no incremental profit opportunities to provide motivation for segmenting the market along the dimension being considered.

In contrast, where differences in average demand levels or sensitivities do exist, there is the possibility that segmentation will lead to increased profits. Whether increased profits are, in fact, associated with segmentation also depends on the magnitude of any incremental costs that are incurred in the tailoring of the marketing program to each segment.

SOME RESEARCH FINDINGS

The most frequently used bases for defining the market segments to be considered as targets for promotion are these household bases:

1. Demographic and socioeconomic characteristics, occasionally together with personality traits.

2. Purchasing characteristics, especially the total consumption of a product (that is, heavy versus light buyers) and brand loyalty.

In the following two sections of this chapter, each of these bases for segmentation is evaluated in terms of the three previously mentioned criteria. Although the findings presented do not completely resolve the issues that are discussed, they nevertheless provide a somewhat better basis for evaluation than has been previously available in the literature.

Demographic, Socioeconomic, and Personality Characteristics as Bases for Market Segmentation

The evaluation of demographic, socioeconomic, and personality characteristics as bases for market segmentation rests primarily on the answers to questions 2 and 3 in the preceding section; that is, the extent to which these characteristics are associated either with differences in *average purchase rates* or *responses* to the firm's promotional activities. The problem of identifiability is of somewhat less interest, since it is (in part) built into the definition of the segments. For example, obviously high- and low-income segments can be identified in terms of income.[3]

AVERAGE PURCHASE RATE DIFFERENCES. The most extensive investigation of the relationship between household purchase rate and demographic-socioeconomic characteristics was conducted by Frank, Massy, and Boyd [15]. Their study was based on *Chicago Tribune* panel data for 1961. These authors obtained a complete purchase history for 491 households for each of 57 product categories. The categories ranged from food products (such as regular coffee, carbonated beverages, margarine, and peanut butter) to household products (such as liquid detergents, scouring cleaners, toilet tissue, and food wrappers).

For a particular product category, we have a record of each individual purchase made by every household in the panel. The record of an individual purchase includes the brand purchased, the date of the transaction, the quantity, the package size, the total cost, the source from which the purchase was made, and whether a deal was associated with the transaction. A deal was defined as some special inducement to pur-

---

[3] The question of identification might be further pursued in this context by an analysis of the intercorrelations existing between demographic, socioeconomic, and personality characteristics. The intercorrelations between the demographic and socioeconomic variables used in the results to be reported are relatively small. An analysis of the relations between these variables and personality characteristics is in progress, although results are not as yet available [24].

chase (for instance, a 5¢-off label), a coupon allowing some reduction of price, or the inclusion of a premium with the purchase. (Many of the studies reported in this work were based on panel data. Although the panel involved differed from study to study, the type of data available did not. Thus, this description will not be repeated.)

Separate mutiple regression analyses were conducted for each of the product categories. The dependent variable was the quantity of the product purchased by the household during 1961, while the independent variables were fourteen socioeconomic characteristics (for example, size of family, income, occupation, education, and so on).

The multiple R^2's associated with each of the 57 regressions provided a measure of the proportion of variation in purchase rate from household to household that was accounted for by the net effect of the fourteen socioeconomic characteristics.

The highest proportion of variation in the quantity of product purchased from household to household was 0.29 for rice cereals. In 46 of 57 product categories, the proportion of variation explained was less than 0.20. In addition, less than 10 percent of household variation in consumption was explained in about one half (25) of the categories.

In 1961, Koponen published a study (based on J. Walter Thompson's panel data for 12 household products) that, although the products were not all identified, consisted of more than one grocery product [22]. The data base comprised purchase data for the 12 products (for an unspecified period of time), a record of household socioeconomic characteristics, and the results of the Edwards personal preference schedule for both the husband and wife in each household. The Edwards schedule generates measures of 15 personality traits for each individual (see Table 2.1 for a list of the measures). Most of Koponen's presentation was based primarily on two-way cross-classification analysis, which makes it virtually impossible to separate the effects of personality and socioeconomic characteristics on the expected household purchase rate for a product. Two products were singled out for regression analysis, neither of which were identified. In one analysis, only 100 households were included (out of 5000). There were 19 independent variables, 4 of which were socioeconomic, and 15 of which were personality (no indication was given of which 15 out of the 30 possible variables). In the case of the other product, the regression included all households in the panel. There were 20 independent variables (which were not defined). At any rate Koponen reports that, in the case of the first product only 13 percent of the variation in total household consumption was explained whereas, in the second regression, only 6 percent of the variation was explained. Neither house-

TABLE 2.1

---

1. Achievement: to do one's best, to accomplish tasks of great significance, or requiring skill and effort, and to do things better than others.
2. Deference: to get suggestions, follow instructions, do what is expected, accept leadership of others, and conform to custom.
3. Order: to have work neat and organized, make plans before starting, keep files, and to have things arranged to run smoothly.
4. Exhibition: to say witty things, tell amusing jokes and stories, talk about personal achievements, and have others notice and comment on one.
5. Autonomy: to be able to come and go as desired, say what one thinks, be independent in making decisions, and feel free to do what one wants.
6. Affiliation: to be loyal to friends, do things for friends, form new friendships, make many friends, and to form strong attachments.
7. Intraception: to analyze one's motives and feelings, observe and understand others, analyze the behavior of others, and predict their acts.
8. Succorance: to be helped by others, to seek encouragement, have others be kindly, to receive affection, and have others feel sorry when sick.
9. Dominance: to be a leader, to argue for one's point of view, make group decisions, settle arguments, and persuade and influence others.
10. Abasement: to feel guilty when wrong, accept blame, feel need for punishment, feel timid in the presence of superiors, and feel inferior.
11. Nurturance: to help friends in trouble, treat others with kindness, forgive others, do small favors, be generous, and show affection.
12. Change: to do new and different things, to travel, to meet new people, try new things, eat in new places, and live in different places.
13. Endurance: to keep at a job until finished, work hard at a task, keep at a problem until solved, and finish one job before starting others.
14. Heterosexuality: to go out with opposite sex, to be in love, to kiss, to discuss sex, and to become sexually excited.
15. Aggression: to tell others what one thinks of them, to criticize others publicly, to make fun of others, and to tell others off.

---

hold-demographic, socioeconomic, nor personality characteristics were highly associated with the amount of a product purchased by a household.

A subsequent study, using the same panel (JWT) that Koponen used, was conducted by the Advertising Research Foundation (ARF) [21]. The ARF study is based on toilet tissue purchasing behavior for 3206 members of the J. Walter Thompson panel in 1956. For each household, the ARF had a record of 15 socioeconomic characteristics and the results of the Edwards personal preference schedule for both husband and wife.[4]

[4] Twelve measures for both husband and wife were included. Three measures (achievement, dominance, and heterosexuality) were excluded because of the high level of multicollinearity associated with their presence in the equation.

The ARF conducted a multiple regression analysis aimed at determining the degree of association between household personality, socioeconomic characteristics, and total units purchased. Separate analyses were made for both one- and two-ply tissues.

The total predictive efficacy, as measured by the square of the multiple correlation coefficient, was 0.12 for one-ply tissue and 0.06 for two-ply tissue. The ARF results were quite consistent with those reported in the two preceding studies.

Massy, Frank, and Lodahl also conducted an analysis of the association between total household purchases and demographic-socioeconomic-personality attributes [26]. Their data base was the same as that used by the ARF (J. Walter Thompson panel data) except that they analyzed beer-, coffee-, and tea-purchasing behavior instead of toilet tissue-purchasing behavior. Table 2.2 presents separated analyses for each of the

TABLE 2.2   MASSY, FRANK, AND LODAHL STUDY RESULTS: TOTAL HOUSEHOLD PURCHASES

	R^2	F	F-ADD	Number of Households
Beer				486
Factor score	0.07	1.25	0.80	
‘ Number of units purchased	0.07	1.25	1.25	
Regular coffee				1283
Factor score	0.06	2.69[a]	1.61[a]	
Number of units purchased	0.07	3.04[a]	2.30[a]	
Tea				900
Factor score	0.07	2.18[a]	1.18	
Number of units purchased	0.07	2.31[a]	1.19	

[a] Significant at the 5% level.

three product categories and, within each category, for two different measures of total household purchases. The two measures are:

1. A total purchases factor score.
2. Total number of units purchased by a household.

The principal measure of total household purchases used by Massy, Frank, and Lodahl was the factor score. For each household in a given product category, a score was generated as a result of a factor analysis conducted on 29 measures of household-purchasing behavior. The 29 variables consist of measures of the rate of household consumption, the degree of brand loyalty, the degree of store loyalty, and the extent of dealing engaged in by the household. One of the factors that clearly stood out as a result of the analysis was total purchases. The total purchase factor scores, generated for each household, can be viewed as weighted averages of the 29 dimensions upon which the analysis was based, where by far the highest weights are given to measures such as the total number of units purchased, the number of shopping trips, and the like. The factors scores were used as dependent variables in place of these raw purchase variables.

The results are based on a multiple regression analysis that included 24 personality measures from the Edwards test and five household socioeconomic characteristics. For each combination of product and total purchases measure, three statistics are reported:

1. The square of the correlation coefficient (R^2) which measures the extent to which the 29 variables are associated with the particular measure of total purchases under study.

2. An F-ratio that provides information as to the extent which the observed degree of association is due to chance (F).

3. An F-ratio that measures the extent to which knowledge of husband and wife personality characteristics contribute to our ability to predict total household purchases once socioeconomic characteristics are known (F-ADD).

At best, only 7 percent of the variation in total household purchasing for a product is accounted for by the net effect of household demographic, socioeconomic, and personality characteristics. These results are not encouraging when considering these characteristics as bases for market segmentation. Based on this analysis, the heavy-buying houschold apparently has a profile of demographic, socioeconomic, and personality characteristics that is virtually identical to that of households exhibiting a lower rate of purchasing. Furthermore, the fact that only two of the F-ADD ratios are statistically significant means that the little degree of association that does exist is predominantly due to the demographic and socioeconomic (as opposed to personality) characteristics.

The last study to be described was conducted by Tucker and Painter [32]. They administered the Gordon personal profile test to 133 male marketing students at the University of Texas. The test was used as a basis for generating measures for four traits; that is, ascendancy, responsibility, emotional stability, and sociability. Separate analyses were conducted of the relationship between an individual's score for each trait and his consumption of headache remedies, vitamins, cigarettes, mouthwash, alcoholic drinks, deodorants, automobiles, and chewing gum, as well as his acceptance of new fashions. Tucker and Painter generated 36 two-way cross-classification tables (9 product categories × 4 personality traits). Of these, 13 were statistically significant at the 0.05 level or less. Although a high proportion of the observed relationships were statistically significant, the degree of association observed was nevertheless quite modest. In addition, the 36 sets of results were based on a set of independent variables, some of which (as the authors note) were intercorrelated. Nothing in the investigators' analytical procedures explicitly took into account these intercorrelations (for example, they might have used multiple regression or discriminate analysis). Thus, their procedures probably tend to overstate whatever effects are actually present.

Household demographic, socioeconomic, and personality characteristics appear to have, at best, a relatively low degree of association with total household purchases of any particular grocery product.

CUSTOMER SENSITIVITY TO PROMOTION.   The effect of demographic and socioeconomic characteristics on customer response to promotion was the subject of only one investigation, which was conducted by Frank and Massy [12, 25]. The investigation was based on household purchasing behavior for a single food product in one major metropolitan area over a 101-week period. The analysis was focused on the effect of demographic and socioeconomic characteristics on customer response to the pricing, dealing, and retail advertising activity of one particular brand (hereafter called brand M) as well as on that of competing brands.

The product in question is used by the vast majority of families in the United States. Purchases occur at the rate of several a month for many users. The product is sold through supermarkets and receives a significant amount of promotion at both the manufacturer and retailer levels.

Two sets of data are used in the analysis:

1. The purchase records of several hundred households who were members of the Market Research Corporation of America's Consumer Panel.

2. A sample of retail advertising lineage for the product covering every brand in the market. The sample included approximately 90 percent of the food lineage placed in the market during the 101-week period of the investigation.

Income, household size, wife's age, wife's employment status, and wife's education are used as a basis for defining market segments. Income and education are surrogates for social class, while wife's age and family size are related to the household's stage in the life cycle. Occupation, which is also related to social class, could not be included in the analysis because the distribution of households across the categories by which social class was defined did not permit breaking them down into meaningful groups.

Separate analyses were conducted for each of the five characteristics. In each case, the sample of households was divided into two groups on the basis of their relative standing on the socioeconomic dimension being investigated. The definitions of the groups are shown in Table 2.3. For

TABLE 2.3 BREAK POINTS, PERCENT OF HOUSEHOLDS, AND OUNCES IN LOW SEGMENT FOR EACH SOCIOECONOMIC CHARACTERISTIC

Socioeconomic Characteristics	Break Point	Low Percent[a]	Low Households Percent
Income	$6000	38.8	48.5
Household size	2 persons	61.5	58.5
Housewife			
Age	42 years	45.4	45.8
Employment	0[b]	69.7	69.0
Education	12 years	73.6	70.0

[a] Households belonging to the low segment have a value in terms of the relevant socioeconomic characteristic equal to or less than the one stated in this problem.
[b] "0" (zero) stands for a household with an unemployed wife while "1" is the code for a household where the wife is employed.

example, all families who earned more than $6000 a year were assigned to the "high-income group" and, conversely, families earning equal to or less than $6000 were assigned to the "low-income group." For each group, Frank and Massy next computed a weekly time series of M's market share, its price relative to the prices of competing brands, the magnitude of its dealing relative to competing brands, the extent of its dealing coverage, and the magnitude of its retail advertising as well as that of competitors. Using econometric techniques (based on multiple regression analysis), these two sets of time series were used as the basis for estimating the *current* and *long-run* effects on weekly market share for M of the changes in the pricing, dealing, and retail advertising activity of both M and its competitors.

The current effect of brand M's relative price was defined as the association between the relative price and M's current market share, while holding the effects of dealing and retail advertising constant. The long-run effect of price took into account not only its *current* effect but also the *carry-over* effects of past relative price levels (that is, the effects of M's relative price in the preceding two weeks on its current market share combined with the assumption that the effect of a given level of relative price declines exponentially over time). Analogous definitions pertain to both dealing and retail advertising. There were two sets of retail advertising variables. One set provided a measure of the current and carry-over effects of *nonfeature* (small-size) ads, while the other set of variables measured the effect on M's market share of varying the total amount of space in a given week devoted to feature (large-size) ads.

CORRELATIONS BETWEEN THE SEGMENTS. In analyzing the segmentation results, it is relevant to inquire whether the five pairs of equations tend to be orthogonal to one another. For example, the data might indicate that nearly the same set of families would be included in the "high-income" and "high-education" groups. If this were the case, we should expect that the regression results for these two groups would be nearly the same, just because of the overlap between the two data bases. Conversely, if the two groups are found to have fewer families in common, we are justified in making separate interpretations of the price, dealing, and advertising elasticities. Separate interpretations are valid only if the various pairs of groups are fairly orthogonal to (uncorrelated with) one another.

We might expect that some of the household traits included in this study would be correlated in the general population. In the data upon which the study was based, these traits were independent enough to justify separate analyses. The highest simple R between any pair of the five was 0.48, which was the degree of association between household size and age of housewife. The highest multiple R between any one of the five characteristics and the remaining four was 0.57 for age of housewife.

A factor analysis containing the five socioeconomic characteristics was performed to see if the nature of the intercorrelations of the characteristics led to any natural groupings with better orthogonality than the original five. The analysis generated four varimax factors. The only two variables that did not appear as separate factors were size of household and age of housewife. Therefore, Frank and Massy concluded that there was no need to revise their socioeconomic definitions.

The principal findings resulting from their analysis were the following.

1. *Housewife education.* For the most part, differences in the response pattern of low- versus high-education households were consistent with the notion that higher levels of education tend to be associated with both a faster rate and a greater degree of adaptive activity in the face of change. The long-run effects of changes in brand M's pricing, dealing, and feature retail advertising activity were greater for the highly educated market segment. In addition, the current response to market share in the highly educated market segment to changes in pricing, dealing, feature, and nonfeature retail advertising was consistently greater than that for the low-education segment.

The differences in the responses of these two groups to promotion, while not significant at the 0.95 level, were significant at the 0.90 level, so that we may be fairly confident that the two education groups respond differently (though the differences involved are slight).

2. *Housewife employment.* Households with unemployed housewives were more responsive to both current and long-run changes in price. Unemployed housewives may be more interested in the home, better informed, and in a more flexible position to spend the shopping time necessary to take advantage of price offers. There appears to be no clear-cut pattern to the current and carry-over effects of dealing. It seems as though the impact were some number close to zero with sampling variability accounting for the fluctuation in the observed direction of the effects.

Although the differences between the responses of the two groups are not significant at the 0.90 level, yet there is a fairly good chance that these differences, like those for education, are real but small in magnitude. This same argument pertains to the results for the income segments that are discussed in the next paragraph.

3. *Income.* We might expect that the lower a household's income the more sensitive it would be to changes in the offers made by manufacturers, especially changes in relative price. Although, at first, the results seemed to be inconsistent with this expectation in that the long-run elasticity with respect to price is greater for the low-income market segment as opposed to the high-income market segment (thus, confirming the hypothesis), the opposite was true of the current price elasticities. However, it may well be that high-income families do more stocking up in response to price changes than do their low-income counterparts, thus making the high-income families appear to have a greater price sensitivity in the short run. In other words, both inventory practices and sensitivity to price may vary by income.

The differences in response to dealing appear to have no consistent pattern, whereas the low-income elasticities for nonfeature advertising were consistently lower than those for the high-income segment. The responses of the two groups tend to converge when we look at feature advertising effects. It may be that low-income households have a higher threshold of response to retail advertising than do their high-income counterparts.

4. *Household size and age of housewife.* The observed differences with respect to segments formed on the basis of either household size or age of housewife were so slight that they did not justify detailed interpretation.

The two least-important socioeconomic characteristics, in terms of response differentiation, are household size and housewife age. Both of these characteristics are associated with the concept of life cycle. Education, income, and employment, relatively speaking, are more effective bases for segmentation. Education, income and, to a lesser extent, employment are associated with the definition of social class. In other words, in terms of response differentiation, social class seems to be a more important basis for market segmentation than does life cycle for the product under study.

> Based on the research reported in the preceding sections, for the most part socioeconomic characteristics are not particularly effective bases for segmentation either in terms of their association with household differences in average purchase rate or in response to promotion.

Household Purchasing Characteristics

The total amount purchased by a household and the degree of brand loyalty exhibited are used more often than any other household purchasing statistics as bases for market segmentation. Marketing literature abounds with references to contrasts involving each of the dimensions. It is often argued that two of the most valuable market segments to penetrate are the "heavy half" and those households that exhibit a high propensity to be brand-loyal. In the two sections that follow, each of these bases for segmentation is evaluated in terms of the three criteria previously mentioned.

Total Household Purchases

By definition, the segmenting of a market in terms of heavy and light customers results in between-segment differences in average household purchasing rates (the second of the three-evaluation criteria). Thus, the discussion that follows is focused exclusively on the extent to which customers in the different segments can be identified in terms of other characteristics (for example, socioeconomic and personality traits) as well as the extent to which the *responses* to promotion differ from one segment to another.

IDENTIFIABILITY. The issue of identifiability is of particular interest because different assumptions with respect to the nature and extent of differences between heavy and light customers can lead to quite different media-selection procedures.

Suppose that a manufacturer wants to concentrate his media budget on the "heavy half." For many promotional vehicles (newspapers, magazines, and TV shows), data are available concerning audience socioeconomic characteristics. It is often the practice to use this information as a basis for media selection. The implicit (at times explicit) assumption underlying this practice is that there is a correlation between various demographic and socioeconomic characteristics and total consumption for the product in question [34, 35].

Recently, this assumption has been questioned by Twedt [35] who also has suggested an alternative media-selection procedure. He asserts that household demographic and socioeconomic characteristics are not useful surrogates for total purchases for a broad range of grocery products. Assuming that this is true (he indicates, without presenting any data, that research confirms his assumption), Twedt then concludes that various media should collect audience purchase data for grocery products. He shows [35] how a media schedule for bacon (based on purchase data for a number of media) differs from those schedules that are based on demographic and socioeconomic profiles.

The same studies used to evaluate demographic and socioeconomic characteristics (in a preceding section of this chapter) as a basis for segmentation are relevant for evaluating average purchase rate as a basis for segmentation. To what extent can households with different average purchase rates be *identified* by using demographic and socioeconomic data?

Without repeating the review, let us repeat the conclusion: demographic and socioeconomic characteristics have only a relatively modest degree of association with household purchase rate for a wide range of grocery products.

This *conclusion* therefore supports Twedt's position.

CUSTOMER SENSITIVITY TO PROMOTION. A second assumption that under-lies the singling out of the "heavy half" as a special market target is that customers in this segment have different responses to promotion than do customers whose relative consumption is lighter. Only one investigation of response differences is reported in the literature. The results are from the same study (by Frank and Massy) discussed in the preceding section on demographic and socioeconomic characteristics as segmentation bases. The only difference is that, in this case, the customer segments were defined in terms of their purchase rates instead of in terms of their demographic and socioeconomic characteristics.

Light users of the product are defined as those households who pur-chased less than or equal to a certain specified annual rate during the period of the investigation. Heavy buyers are correspondingly those that purchased more than the rate specified. The rate is set so that approxi-mately one-half the number of ounces purchased in the market during the 101-week period are purchased by those households that are defined as light users.

What differences in response characteristics with respect to pricing, dealing, and advertising might we expect when contrasting light and heavy buyers?

On the average, light buyers buy less often than do heavy buyers. The per capita consumption rate for light-buying households is lower than that for the heavy-buying category. It is reasonable to assume that light-buying households tend to be less interested and less well informed with respect to current price, dealing, and advertising conditions in the market, let alone with respect to changes in these conditions over time. Probably a greater proportion of the purchases of light-buying house-holds are accounted for by special needs such as entertainment. In ful-filling these needs, more attention is probably paid to the nature and immediacy of the occasion than to the offers made by alternative brands.

These characteristics lead us to expect a lower proportion of the week-to-week variation in demand for brand M to be accounted for in the case of light buyers as opposed to heavy buyers. The results are consistent with this expectation. The proportion of variance in M's market share explained in the heavy-buyer segment is 0.59, while in the light-buyer segment it is 0.50.

In addition, light buyers are probably less sensitive to long-run changes in pricing policy. They are probably also less responsive to current price changes and tend to do less stocking up. Their results are consistent with this assertion. The current effect of a 1-percent cut in price on M's market share is greater for heavy buyers than for light buyers. However, the carry-over effects are also greater for heavy buyers. Heavy buyers apparently stock up more than light buyers. In spite of this difference in stocking up, the long-run sensitivity of heavy buyers to changes in relative price is still greater than that for light buyers.

The pattern of effects for dealing among heavy buyers is similar to that for pricing. The rationale is the same as that previously discussed.

The long-run effect of feature advertising is greater for light buyers than for heavy buyers, but the opposite is true for nonfeature advertising. Possibly a feature-sized ad is required to affect the awareness of a substantial proportion of light buyers. Small ads may tend to be selectively screened out by light buyers, leading to a considerably smaller net effect of market share. The change from a nonfeature ad to a feature ad accomplishes little by way of increased response among heavy buyers as opposed to light buyers, because of what is probably the already high level of their knowledge and awareness.

In spite of the fact that the observed differences in response between the heavy- and light-customer segments are consistent with expectations, these differences nevertheless are not significant at the 0.95 level. However, there is still a fair chance that there is a real (although modest) difference in response between the two groups.

SUMMARY. There is some support for total consumption as a basis for market segmentation, especially as a basis for media selection, if more media take on the responsibility of collecting purchase data from their respective audiences.

Brand Loyalty

The relevance of "brand loyalty" to the formulation of a profitable program of market segmentation has stirred the imaginations of practitioners and scholars alike ever since pioneering work by George Brown [4] and Ross Cunningham [5, 6] in the early 1950's. In contrast to the previously discussed bases for market segmentation, there has been considerable uncertainty expressed as to how brand loyalty should be defined as well as to the extent to which it actually exists. Before evaluating brand loyalty as a basis for market segmentation in terms of our three criteria (identifiability, average rate of purchase, and response to promotion), its definition and existence will first be discussed.

DEFINITION AND DEGREE. The discussion of the definition and degree of brand loyalty is based on the results of five investigations. Each investigator uses a slightly different definition of brand loyalty.

The first study, by George Brown [4], is based on the purchase histories of a sample of 100 households from the *Chicago Tribune* panel for 1961. The 9 product categories included are listed in Table 2.4. Although

TABLE 2.4   BROWN'S BRAND-LOYALTY ANALYSIS

Item	Undivided Loyalty	Divided Loyalty	Unstable Loyalty	No Loyalty
Margarine	21.1	13.8	27.5	37.5
Toothpaste	61.3	6.5	17.7	14.5
Coffee	47.2	18.1	29.5	5.2
All-purpose flour	73.2	7.1	14.1	5.6
Shampoo	44.0	10.4	12.3	33.3
Ready-to-eat cereal	12.5	22.7	18.2	46.6
Headache remedies	46.1	23.1	5.8	25.0
Soaps and sudsers	16.8	20.0	26.2	37.0
Concentrated orange juice	26.8	7.0	39.4	26.8

Brown experimented with a number of measures of brand loyalty, the one upon which he placed primary emphasis is as follows.

Any family making five or more purchases during the year was placed in one of four basic categories, depending upon the purchase pattern shown . . . :

1. Family showing undivided loyalty bought brand A in the following sequence: AAAAAA.
2. Family showing divided loyalty bought brands A and B in the following sequence: ABABAB.
3. Family showing unstable loyalty bought brands A and B in the following sequence: AAABBB.
4. Family showing no loyalty bought brands A, B, C, D, E, and F in the following sequence: ABCDEF [4, January 26, 1953, p. 75].

The results of applying this classification scheme are reported in Table 2.3. A majority of customers concentrate their purchases on relatively few brands and, consequently, by Brown's definition, exhibit brand loyalty. This is a particularly striking fact because customers are often exposed to as many as 10 or 15 brands in each of the categories included. In addition, week-to-week fluctuations in brand pricing and dealing are relatively substantial in most of the markets. There does appear to be some tendency for customers to stay with a particular set of brands even in the face of changing competitive conditions.

Ross Cunningham published an analysis of brand loyalty based on a 66-family sample from the *Chicago Tribune* panel covering their purchase histories for 7 product categories (toilet soap, scouring cleanser, regular coffee, canned peas, margarine, frozen orange juice, and headache tablets) from 1951 to 1953 [5, 6]. Cunningham defined brand loyalty in terms of the proportion of purchases that a household devoted to the brand it purchased most often. In the case of all 7 product categories, at least 50 percent of the households concentrated 43 percent or more of their purchases on the brand most often bought. For headache remedies, the percentage reaches a high of 72 percent, while the 43 percent figure pertains to toilet soap; scouring cleanser falls in the middle of the 7 categories with more than one half of the customers concentrating 53 percent of their purchases on the brand bought most often [5, p. 122].

Both Brown and Cunningham measured brand loyalty in terms of the extent to which customers tend to concentrate their purchases on a relatively few brands in a given product category. In contrast, studies by Guest [19, 20] as well as by Massy, Frank, and Lodahl [26] examine the stability of household-brand loyalty over time.

In 1941, Guest measured the brand preferences (the favorite brand) of 813 public school students for 16 product categories. Twelve years later (in 1953), he obtained preferences from 165 members of this group for the same products. Four of the 16 categories were food products, that is, coffee, cereal, bread, and gum. The percentage of respondents whose present and past preferences agreed are 35, 23, 31, and 29, respectively. In addition, a comparison was made between present use and past preference, which resulted in these percentages of agreement: 33, 25, 23, and 28. Considering that the results were based on the stability of individual behavior over a *12-year period*, they provide further evidence of the existence of "brand loyalty."

Massy, Frank, and Lodahl [26] based their analysis on the J. Walter Thompson panel data for regular coffee from July 1956 to June 1957. These authors split the purchase histories for each of the 670 households included into two 6-month time periods. Households making fewer than 6 purchases during the year were excluded from the analysis. They measured the share of purchases devoted to the brand bought most often in each of the two time periods (Cunningham's measure of brand loyalty).

They also measured the number of brands bought by each household in both time periods. Split-half correlation coefficients between the first and second time periods were then computed for each of these statistics. Thus, the coefficients measure the degree of association between a household's brand loyalty in one time period and that in the next time period. The coefficient for Cunningham's measure was 0.69, while that for the number of brands was 0.76.

Tucker [33] constructed an experiment as a vehicle for studying the formation of brand loyalty. Each of 43 housewives was presented 4 alternative brands of bread on each of 12 consecutive household deliveries. The loaves were virtually identical except that they had 4 different "brand names" (L, M, P, and H). Based on Tucker's definition, if no brand loyalty were present, we should expect 25 percent of each housewife's purchases to be made for each brand. More than one half of the respondents developed a higher degree of allegiance to 1 of the 4 brands than would be expected on the basis of this chance model. A number of customers became brand loyal even though there was no difference between the brands other than the "brand name" itself.

Whether we look at the concentration of household purchases among brands at a point in time or at its stability over time, there is marked evidence that brand loyalty is a "real" and reliable phenomenon—a phenomenon the understanding of which is a challenge to managers and researchers alike.

Identifiability

To what extent can brand-loyal customers be identified in terms of some subset of their personal attributes? Four investigations are either published or (in the case of one) are about to be published. All four analyze the relationship between the degree of brand loyalty exhibited by a household and its socioeconomic and personality attributes. The first two studies (by the ARF and Massy, Frank, and Lodahl) were described in a preceding section of this chapter, and therefore their full description will not be repeated.

The first of these is the ARF study based on household toilet tissue purchasing behavior. Separate analyses were conducted for both one-ply and two-ply tissue. In each case, a multiple regression analysis was conducted to measure the net degree of association between household brand loyalty and demographic, socioeconomic, and personality characteristics. Household brand loyalty was defined as the proportion of purchases devoted to the brand purchased most often.

The total predictive efficacy, as measured by the square of the multiple correlation coefficient, was 0.05 for one-ply tissue and 0.07 for two-ply tissue. In other words, they found virtually no association between personality, socioeconomic variables, and household brand loyalty.

Massy, Frank, and Lodahl [26] also conducted an analysis of the association between household brand loyalty and socioeconomic-personality attributes. This analysis was included in the previously mentioned study that used J. Walter Thompson panel data and was based on household purchases of beer, coffee, and tea.[5] Table 2.5 gives separate analyses for

TABLE 2.5   MASSY, FRANK, AND LODAHL STUDY RESULTS: BRAND LOYALTY

	R^2	F	F-ADD	Number of Households
Beer				486
Factor score	0.08	1.43	1.27	
Percent favorite brand	0.09	1.61[a]	1.41	
Number of brands	0.10	1.70[a]	1.40	
Regular coffee				1283
Factor score	0.05	2.42[a]	1.63[a]	
Percent favorite brand	0.05	2.05[a]	1.09	
Number of brands	0.07	3.13[a]	1.39	
Tea				900
Factor score	0.04	1.38	1.14	
Percent favorite brand	0.05	1.46	1.30	
Number of brands	0.05	1.70[a]	1.40	

[a] Significant at the 5% level.

each of the three product categories and, within each category, for three different measures of household brand loyalty. The results are directly comparable to those given in Table 2.2.

At best (for beer), only 10 percent of the variation in brand loyalty from one household to another is associated with personality and socioeconomic characteristics. Coffee and tea did only about one half as well. In any case, the results are not encouraging from the standpoint of de-

[5] Discussion of the split-half correlations in the preceding section was based only on coffee because the purchase rates for tea and beer are too low.

veloping a profile of the brand loyal customer. Based on this analysis, the "high brand–loyal" household apparently has a profile of personality and socioeconomic characteristics that is virtually identical to that of households exhibiting a lower degree of loyalty. Furthermore, the fact that only one of the F-ADD ratios are statistically significant means that the little degree of association that does exist results predominantly from the socioeconomic characteristics (as opposed to the personality characteristics).

A recent study published by Farley [8, 9] focused on the prediction of household brand loyalty separately for each of 17 grocery products. The data covered 197 households belonging to the Market Research Corporation of America's consumer panel in 1957; the households were residents of one market area. Attempts were made to predict two measures of brand loyalty (number of brands purchased and whether the household switched favorite brands from the first to the second 6-month period) based on knowledge of household income and size as well as the quantity of the product consumed by each household. The prediction of number of brands purchased was based on a multiple regression analysis. Of the 17 multiple R^2's that were generated, 11 were less than 0.04. The prediction as to whether a household switched favorite brands from one 6-month period to the next was based on a two-way multiple discriminant analysis. The results of both Farley's discriminant and regression analyses were quite consistent in that neither provides any managerially significant basis for identifying brand loyal customers.

In 1966, Frank and Boyd published an investigation of household brand loyalty to private brands [11]. The study is based on the purchasing behavior of 492 households who were members of the *Tribune's* panel throughout 1961. The investigators studied the association between the proportion of purchases a household devoted to private brands in a particular product category (for example, margarine, canned corn, potato chips, and regular coffee) and its socioeconomic characteristics, store shopping habits, and the total amount of the product purchased during the year. Separate analyses, based on multiple regression techniques, were conducted for each of 44 product categories.

Frank and Boyd found virtually no differentiation between private and manufacturer brand customers based on socioeconomic and total consumption characteristics. For 13 of the 44 products, the resulting squared correlation coefficients were 0.00, while for 32 of the products they were less than 0.23. Store shopping habits were correlated with private branding; however, this comes as no surprise. A customer who shops in the

A & P or Jewel stores is much more likely to buy private brands than a customer who shops in the smaller chains or in an independent food store.

> In spite of the reliability that households exhibit with regard to brand loyalty, research efforts aimed at identifying the brand-loyal customer have been notably unsuccessful.

AVERAGE LEVEL OF CUSTOMER DEMAND.   For each of the seven products included in Cunningham's analysis [5], he computed rank correlation coefficients between the quantity consumed by each of the 66 households and its level of brand loyalty. The coefficients are reported in Table 2.6.

TABLE 2.6   CUNNINGHAM'S AVERAGE LEVEL PURCHASED, AND BRAND LOYALTY RANK CORRELATION

Item	Correlation Coefficient
Toilet soap	0.109
Scouring cleanser	0.089
Regular coffee	0.003
Canned peas	0.195
Margarine	0.133
Frozen orange juice	0.028
Headache tablets	0.102

The highest, which is only 0.195, is for canned peas. There appears to be little relationship between purchasing activity and brand loyalty.

Massy, Frank, and Lodahl also examined this relationship. In addition to the brand loyalty factor generated by the factor analysis mentioned in the preceding section, a total activity factor was also identified. Scores for each household for both the brand loyalty and the activity factors were correlated. The resulting correlation for coffee was only 0.00, while those for tea and beer were 0.36 and 0.09.

Based on an analysis of frozen orange juice purchases from 1951 to 1953 for 650 households from the *Chicago Tribune* panel, Kuehn found that brand loyalty (as measured by the tendency for customers to repeat their purchase of the brand bought previously) was higher for heavy purchasers as opposed to light purchasers of the product [23]. These results are not consistent with those reported in either of the other studies. Kuehn's methodology is considerably more sensitive than Cunningham's; thus, we might place more weight on his results.

However, this does not explain the difference in conclusions reached by Kuehn and by Massy, Frank, and Lodahl. For two of the products studied, their results were consistent with Cunningham's conclusion, whereas for tea there did appear to be some association between activity and brand loyalty.

One possible explanation of the difference between these studies might be the products involved. For example, at the time of Kuehn's study, frozen orange juice concentrate was a relatively young product category. It may be that with respect to a new product, so closely tied to health, heavy users occur disproportionately in cases where a household feels that it has found a definitely superior brand. This effect might tend to disappear as the product becomes better established.

CUSTOMER SENSITIVITY TO PROMOTION.   The effect of brand loyalty on customer response to promotion is the subject of only two investigations. The first of these was the Frank and Massy study [12, 14, 25] of the response of brand M's market share in selected market segments to changes in its pricing, dealing, and retail advertising levels (described in a preceding section of this chapter).

The investigators computed the share of purchases that each household devoted to brand M as well as to competing brands. Those households that bought brand M more often than any other brand are called "loyal" and those that bought it less often "nonloyal." Frank and Massy then computed a weekly time series of brand M's market share, its price relative to the prices of competing brands, the magnitude of its dealing relative to competing brands, the extent of its dealing coverage and the magnitude of its retail advertising as well as that of competitors. Using econometric techniques (based on multiple regression analysis), these two sets of time series are used as the basis for estimating the current and carry-over effects on M's weekly market share of the changes in the pricing, dealing, and retail advertising activity of both M and its competitors.

These authors found no statistically significant difference between the price, dealing, and retail advertising elasticities for families who are loyal to brand M and those who are not. If loyalty were successful in building up the resistance of buyers to switch to other brands in the face of changes in market conditions, we might expect that the elasticities for loyal buyers would be less than those for the nonloyal group. However, this was not the case.[6]

The second investigation by Frank, Massy, and Morrison [25, 26] consisted of a study of the introduction of Folger's coffee into the Chicago regular coffee market. The data base consisted of *Chicago Tribune* panel data for 538 households from 1958 through 1960 for regular coffee as well as data covering 88 other food products for which *Tribune* records were kept for the same households from January to April, 1961.[7] The investigators estimated the extent to which household socioeconomic and purchasing characteristics (for both regular coffee and total household consumption of all food products reported by the panel members), during the 62-week period prior to Folger's introduction, predicted whether a household would either buy Folger's coffee more often than any other brand or not at all. Five socioeconomic and 15 purchasing characteristics are included in the two-way multiple discriminant analysis upon which their results are based. One of the purchasing characteristics is Cunningham's measure of brand loyalty (the proportion of purchases devoted to the brand purchased most often by a household during the period prior to Folger's introduction). Brand loyalty was associated with a resistance to adopting a new brand. The effect of loyalty, while it is probably "real," is nonetheless quite modest.

SUMMARY. The pattern of results for brand loyalty as a basis for market segmentation in food products is not encouraging. Brand-loyal customers almost completely lack identifiability in terms of either socioeconomic or personality characteristics. With the exception of one study by Kuehn, brand-loyal customers do not appear to have different average demand levels than nonloyal ones. Loyal customers do not appear to have economically important differences in their sensitivity to either the short-run effects of pricing, dealing, and retail advertising or to the introduction of new brands.

THE NEED FOR FURTHER RESEARCH

Neither the socioeconomic nor the purchasing characteristics that have been discussed appear to be particularly effective bases for market seg-

---

[6] For more detailed discussion of the rationales underlying this loyal-nonloyal analysis, see Refs. 12, 14, and 25.

[7] The four-month 1961 household purchase data had been previously obtained for use in another study. Ideally, we would have preferred to have this information as of 1958; however, it is unlikely that the Folger's introduction affected patterns of overall consumption in a way that would tend to confound the results.

mentation. Although most of the results consisted of only modest differences between segments, nevertheless these "negative findings" do have a positive value. For some of us, they add to the weight of evidence favoring what we already believed, while for others they may have had a somewhat greater surprise value.

Many practitioners have expressed doubt as to the usefulness of socioeconomic characteristics as bases for market segmentation [36]. In general, our findings are quite consistent with this conclusion. In contrast, the consistently negative character of our findings regarding brand loyalty comes as a surprise. In spite of the fact that brand loyalty appears to be a real, persistent phenomena, our research thus far has provided little insight into the process that generates loyalty proneness. Results, to date, contradict what we might expect.

The case for total consumption as a basis for market segmentation is somewhat stronger than that for brand loyalty as, by definition, different market segments contain customers with somewhat different demand characteristics. However, even in this case, the response to pricing, dealing, and retail-advertising differences between heavy and light market segments (although their directions were reasonably consistent with expectations) appear nonetheless to be of only a modest magnitude. This finding raises some doubt as to the usefulness of even this approach.

Although many of the results that have been discussed are quite provocative, they nevertheless are fragmentary in character. Clearly, there is a need for more research if we are to gain sufficient understanding of the determinants of customer purchasing behavior in order to be able to design more effective programs based on market segmentation.

At the very least, there are the following needs.

1. We should replicate the study of differential response of socioeconomic market segments to policy variables, over a wide range of product categories. (The results reported in this chapter are based on only one product category.)

2. We should extend the response models beyond pricing, dealing, and retail advertising to cover instore promotion as well as manufacturer spot television, radio, and newspaper coverage.

3. We should replicate the differential response analysis for both socioeconomic and purchase variables for the same product class in several different market areas. For example, we might work with market areas in which (1) there are different levels of total retail advertising, dealing, and pricing for the product in question (the response differences across customer segments may depend, in part, on the total level of industry

promotion for the product as well as on the brand's relative position), and (2) the brand under study has quite different market shares.

4. We should replicate studies of the correlates of brand loyalty across a broader range of product categories while at the same time experimenting with alternative definitions. For example, studying products with high prices as opposed to low prices per unit might reveal differences in the process by which brand loyalty is formed, as might a contrast of a product that usually has a low degree of personal risk associated with use versus a product with a high risk level.

5. We should conduct a more penetrating analysis of the association between psychological and sociological characteristics of buyers and the degree of brand loyalty they exhibit. It may be that the psychological dimensions that are idiosyncratic to the particular category being studied as opposed to, say, personal characteristics that are presumably enduring characteristics of the individual (that is, that are common to many, if not all, of the decision problems faced by the individual) are important determinants of brand loyalty.

6. We should extend the analysis of response differences to include the effects of variation in product characteristics. For example, we might study the extent to which different brands of cereals appeal to different customer segments. (In my opinion, this form of marketing effort can also be embraced by the concept of market segmentation. However, this view is not shared by some [28].)

In addition to these suggestions, there is a need to investigate systematically a much broader range of alternative bases for segmentation than have been considered thus far. One of the most promising attempts at achieving this objective has been launched by Pessemier, Teach, and Tigert [27]. These authors plan to investigate the relationship between household purchasing behavior in a number of grocery-product categories. They also plan to investigate household characteristics such as, for example, family and individual activities, brand preferences, and self-perception of risk involved in purchase, in addition to the more traditional socioeconomic characteristics. Their results are not yet available. Clearly, more work of this type is essential.

REFERENCES

1. William Baumol and Charles Sevin, "Marketing Costs and Mathematical Programming," *Harvard Business Review*, 35(5), 52-60 (September-October, 1957).
2. Kenneth Boulding, *Economic Analysis* (New York: Harper and Bros., 1955), pp. 608-615.
3. Brand Rating Index, *Report on the Marketing Value of Media Audiences*, March, 1965.
4. George Brown, "Brand Loyalty—Fact or Fiction?" *Advertising Age*, 23, 53-55 (June 19, 1952); 45-47 (June 30, 1952); 54-56 (July 14, 1952); 46-48 (July 28, 1952); 56-58 (August 11, 1952); 80-82 (September 1, 1952); 82-86 (October 6, 1952); 76-79 (December 1, 1952); and 24, 75-76 (January 26, 1953).
5. Ross Cunningham, "Brand Loyalty—What, Where, How Much," *Harvard Business Review*, 34(1), 116-128 (January-February, 1956).
6. ———, "Customer Loyalty to Store and Brand," *Harvard Business Review*, 39(6), 127-137 (November-December, 1961).
7. ———, "Measurement of Brand Loyalty," *The Marketing Revolution*, New York: American Marketing Association (December 27-29, 1955).
8. John Farley, "Brand Loyalty and the Economics of Information," *Journal of Business*, 37(4), 370-381 (October, 1964).
9. ———, "Testing a Theory of Brand Loyalty," *Proceedings of the American Marketing Association Winter Conference*, pp. 308-315 (December, 1963).
10. Ronald E. Frank, "Is Brand Loyalty a Useful Basis for Grocery Product Market Segmentation?" mimeographed (December, 1965).
11. ——— and Harper Boyd, Jr., "Are Private-Brand-Prone Food Customers Really Different?" *Journal of Advertising Research*, 5(4), 27-35 (December, 1965).
12. ——— and William Massy, "Estimating the Effects of Short Term Promotional Strategy in Selected Market Segments," *Market Response to Sales Promotion*, a volume to appear in the Marketing Science Institute Series (New York: McGraw-Hill) (forthcoming).
13. ———, "Innovation and Brand Choice: The Folger's Invasion," *Proceedings of the American Marketing Association Winter Conference*, pp. 96-107 (December, 1963).
14. ———, "Market Segmentation and the Effectiveness of a Brand's Price and Dealing Policies," *Journal of Business*, 38(2), 186-200 (April, 1965).
15. ———, William Massy, and Harper Boyd, Jr., "Correlates of Grocery Product Consumption Rates," mimeographed (April, 1966).
16. ——— and Donald Morrison, "The Determinants of Innovative Behavior with Respect to a Branded, Frequently Purchased Food Product," *Proceedings of the Winter Conference of the American Marketing Association*, pp. 312-323 (December, 1964).
17. Norton Garfinkle, "A Marketing Approach to Media Selection," *Journal of Advertising Research*, 3(4), 7-15 (December, 1963).
18. Grey Advertising Agency, "Herd Hysteria: a Mounting Marketing Hazard," 36(5) (May, 1965).
19. Lester Guest, "A Study of Brand Loyalty," *Journal of Applied Psychology*, 28, 16-27 (1944).

20. ———, "Brand Loyalty—Twelve Years Later," *Journal of Applied Psychology*, **39**, 405-408 (1955).
21. Ingrid Hildegaard and Lester Krueger, "Are There Customer Types?" *Advertising Research Foundation*, New York (1964).
22. Arthur Koponen, "Personality Characteristics of Purchasers," *Journal of Advertising Research*, **1**(1), 6-12 (September, 1960).
23. Alfred Kuehn, "An Analysis of the Dynamics of Consumer Behavior and Its Implications for Marketing Management," unpublished Ph.D. Dissertation, Carnegie Institute of Technology (May, 1958).
24. Thomas Lodahl, William Massy, and Ronald Frank, "The Intercorrelation Between Demographic, Socioeconomic, and Personality Characteristics," forthcoming, 1966.
25. William Massy and Ronald Frank, "Short Term Price and Dealing Effects in Selected Market Segments," *Journal of Marketing Research*, **2**(2), 171-185 (May, 1965).
26. ——— and Thomas Lodahl, "Buying Behavior and Personality," Graduate School of Business, Stanford University, working paper (forthcoming, June, 1966).
27. Edgar Pessemier, Richard Teach, and Douglas Tigert, *Consumer Behavior Research Projects*, Purdue University, Krannert Graduate School of Industrial Administration (August, 1965).
28. William H. Reynolds, "More Sense About Market Segmentation," *Harvard Business Review*, **43**(5), 107-114 (September-October, 1965).
29. Joan Robinson, *The Economics of Imperfect Competition* (London: Macmillan, 1955), pp. 179-188.
30. Wendell Smith, "Imperfect Competition and Marketing Strategy," *Cost and Profit Outlook*, **8**(10) (October, 1955).
31. ———, "Product Differentiation and Market Segmentation as Alternative Marketing Strategies," *Journal of Marketing*, **21**(1), 3-8 (July, 1956).
32. W. T. Tucker and John J. Painter, "Personality and Product Use," *Journal of Applied Psychology*, **45**, 325-329 (1961).
33. ———, "The Development of Brand Loyalty," *Journal of Marketing Research*, **1**(3), 32-35 (August, 1964).
34. Dik Warren Twedt, "How Important to Marketing Strategy is the 'Heavy User'?" *Journal of Marketing*, **28**(1), 71-72 (January, 1961).
35. ———, "Some Practical Application of 'Heavy Half' Theory," *Proceedings of the 10th Annual Conference of the Advertising Research Foundation* (October, 1964).
36. Daniel Yankelovich, "New Criteria for Market Segmentation," *Harvard Business Review*, **42**(2), 83-90 (March-April, 1964).

Stochastic Models
of Consumer Behavior

Ever since the existence of consumer panels first provided the opportunity to observe the repetitive purchases of frequently purchased items by individual consumers, management scientists have been developing and refining stochastic models to attempt to explain the observed behavior. Some of the attempts were crude, some were ingenious; as we might expect, their results ranged from total failure to qualified success. I shall not attempt here to review the progress of stochastic models because adequate documentation already exists.[1]

However, there have traditionally been a number of issues in such models that deserve more extensive treatment. They are all concerned with this question: If we knew the real probabilistic mechanism governing the consumer, how would we use the data of the consumer panel to calibrate the model and make predictions? The major difficulties that arise in answering this question are (1) that the data from the panel are somewhat limited, (2) that aggregation of data over customers requires special care that is not always taken, (3) that changes in a customer's characteristics over time inherently limit time-averaged procedures for establishing parameters, and (4) that independent factors (for example, stockouts and family visitors) may cause an apparent change in buying habits even though the customer's underlying probabilistic model remains the same. In fact, all of these problems occur at the same time, thus complicating their analytic treatment. However, by considering them one (or perhaps two) at a time, we can gain considerable insight into the process we are discussing. For the sake of clarity and convenience, we

---

[1] Jerome D. Herniter and Ronald A. Howard: "Stochastic Marketing Models," *Progress in Operations Research*, Hertz, ed. (New York: John Wiley & Sons, 1964), pp. 33-96, and bibliography.

shall confine our remarks to the case where the underlying customer model is Markovian, or semi-Markovian, although this restriction is not necessary in much of the following.

MARKOVIAN MODELS

To fix ideas, let us begin with a description of the underlying customer model we shall consider. Each customer produces a purchase pattern in time for a particular product class. Each purchase might be described by its brand, size, number, price, color, type, and so on. We divide the purchase descriptors into a finite number of mutually exclusive and collectively exhaustive sets that we call states. For simplicity, we can consider the state to be simply the brand purchased.

The time scale can be divided into fixed intervals or left as a continuous variable. In most early work, the fixed time scale was used. Within each time interval, the brand that the customer purchased was recorded; the phenomenon of interest was the change of brand from one interval to the next. Of course, that model could be readily applied only when exactly one purchase was made within each time interval. If no purchase was made, or if more than one purchase that included different brands was made, then an operational problem arose. Practical men resolved this difficulty by treating "no purchase" as a brand, and by devising arbitrary rules for the multipurchase case. Other investigators ignored the actual timing of purchases and focused only on the brand of successive purchases. Thus, in any case, the investigator was left with a brand sequence or state sequence showing the successive brands purchased by the customer. Since there was often marked changing of brands over a year's time, probabilistic models were quickly employed. No doubt the earliest was a multinomial model, which we can think of as having the customer select the brands to be purchased from a run with replacement. However, the run lengths of purchases of the same brand were too great to be accounted for by a multinomial model. For this reason and for the more compelling reason that brand selection should intuitively be an inertial process, the multinomial model was not seriously considered for long.

The next logical step was to allow the probability of purchasing a brand to depend on the previous history of brand purchases. The simplest model of this type is the Markovian process, where the probability of purchasing each brand depends on the brand bought on the last purchasing occasion. Thus, we assume that if a person bought brand i last

time, he will buy brand j next time, with some transition probability
The probabilities p_{ij} determine the transition matrix P that specifies t
process. If we desire to extend the amount of relevant purchase histo₁,
or two, three, or any other finite number of purchases into the past, we
can do so by extending the state description to include such information.
However, this type of extension exacts a large computational penalty.

The Markov model produced some very interesting results. It seemed
to do markedly better than the multinomial model in providing plausible dynamic patterns; but on a number of other points, such as the consistency of the transition probability matrices over time, the Markov
model either produced results that challenged the Markovian assumption
or else it could not be checked because of limited data. At this point, a
number of different paths were followed. Some investigators postulated
models that apparently made the probability of purchasing each brand
dependent upon the entire purchase history. However, close examination
often revealed many similarities between these models and Markovian
models, and in many cases their validity was no more convincing than
that of the Markovian models.

Another path of investigation involved the treatment of the time scale.
Since the interpurchase interval was a random variable, models were developed that allowed this phenomenon implicitly.[2] In particular, the
semi-Markov process considered the succession of brands purchased to
be governed by a transition probability matrix P of the kind we have described but, in addition, permitted the time between the purchase of
brand i and the purchase of brand j to be a random variable τ_{ij} with a
density function $h_{ij}(\cdot)$ specific to the transition. We call these density
functions the holding-time density functions for the process; the matrix
$H(\cdot)$ of holding-time density functions and the transition probability
matrix P constitute a complete description of the process.

The more versatile semi-Markov model enriched the concept of Markovian modeling. Since all semi-Markov processes do not have Markov
processes that are equivalent in their behavior over time, the evidence
that had developed that customer behavior was not Markovian could not
be so easily interpreted—the problem could have arisen in the treatment
of timing. But, of course, the more complicated semi-Markov model also
had higher data requirements and was open to charges that it had so
many parameters that it could fit anything.

And so the researchers' problems grow. Is the semi-Markov model (or

[2] Ronald A. Howard: "On Methods: Stochastic Process Models of Consumer Behavior," *Journal of Advertising Research*, 3(3), 35-52 (September, 1963).

some other model) an adequate representation of repetitive purchasing behavior? Who can say? In view of the problems of limited data in an uncertain environment, it is very difficult to answer this question. It is as if an early twentieth-century physicist were presented with a modern model of the nucleus and asked whether it was an appropriate model. All he could say was that it passed the tests of his present apparatus.

Let us now examine the various modeling difficulties. The first is the question of limited data.

LIMITED DATA

Since we have a suspicion that the market environment is changing continually, we are reluctant to use purchase histories spanning several years for the calibration of a customer model. Yet the result is that, for even frequently-purchased items, we must deal with observations that number in tens rather than in hundreds. If we have, for instance, twenty purchases by a customer and we enumerate the transitions he made and the holding times for those transitions, we see that our data are puny with respect to the task of assigning a matrix of transition probabilities and a matrix of holding time density functions. (In a three-brand market, these would both be 3 x 3 matrices.) It is clear that short of extending the time of observation to obtain more data, and thus running the risk of an important change in the environment, the only alternative we have is to develop a method for using the available data in such a way as to supplement rather than substitute for other information on the customer. The formal technique that can be used here is Bayesian updating, where initial probability assignments for transition probabilities and holding time density functions are modified as each new purchase is made by the customer. This model has the advantage that it allows us to make probability assignments on the future behavior of customers even in unusual situations, such as when the customers do not purchase at all within the period of observation.

To apply the Bayesian inference approach to the semi-Markov model, we could, for example, postulate a multidimensional beta distribution over each row of the transition probability matrix.[3] Furthermore, we could use the family of Gamma distributions to describe each holding-

[3] E. A. Silver: "Markovian Decision Processes with Uncertain Transition Probabilities or Rewards," *Operations Research Center Technical Report No. 1*, Massachusetts Institute of Technology, Cambridge (August, 1963).

time density function and let the two parameters of each Gamma be themselves given by a joint probability distribution. We shall call the the multidimensional Beta and the probability distributions on the Gamma parameters the prior-prior distributions. The prior-prior distributions would be assigned on the basis of our knowledge of variability in transitions and holding times for the panel as a whole. These are likely to be quite broad distributions. Then, as each purchase of a panel member is examined, we update these prior-prior distributions in the way indicated by Bayes' theorem. After processing all the data on a customer, we then have a new probability assignment consisting of a new multidimensional beta and a new joint distribution on the parameters of each gamma holding time. This result is quite different from obtaining specific transition probability and holding-time density function matrices for the customer. In particular, the variance in the number of purchases of each brand will be different for the two situations.

Few Bayesian models of this type have been implemented, but their results are promising. They provide an answer to the question of limited data and, also, a firm logical foundation that may be used in approaching our other difficulties.

AGGREGATION

The problem of aggregation arose when investigators attempted to find a single transition probability matrix with great accuracy for all customers by considering all purchase sequences of all panel members as parts of one long sequence. Although the resulting matrix has well-determined elements, it ends up describing no one, rather than everyone. The desire to model the panel as a whole is quite commendable because most promotional decisions will be based on overall purchasing. However, aggregation is helpful only when it is done according to a clearly defined procedure. The simplest procedure is to consider the panel as a vector semi-Markov process.[2] Such a process is the summation of independent semi-Markov processes; in this case, one process for each member of the panel. Since the summation of Markov or semi-Markov processes is not necessarily a process of the same kind, we see that searching for "aggregate Markovian" behavior is a doomed way of locating individual Markovian behavior.

The concept of the vector Markov process is primarily important because it keeps us thinking clearly about the aggregation problem. The assumptions that are inherent when transition probabilities are assigned by taking ratios of successive state occupancies are illuminated by the vector Markov modeling concept.

DYNAMIC CUSTOMER CHARACTERISTICS

We would be very much surprised if the same customer model described a customer over a long period of time. There appear to be so many perturbations in the market that any such constancy would be the exception rather than the rule. When I think of my own attitudes in purchasing the same type of item over and over again, I have the feeling that I get into a rut and buy the same brand repeatedly, apparently without conscious thought. Then something may persuade me to try a new brand, and if I like it I shall likely get into another rut of buying the new brand; otherwise, I shall return to my old rut. Such a process is not necessarily well-modeled by a Markov or semi-Markov process. The appropriate model would be more like one that had internal states that might or might not change from time to time as the result of external influences.

One model that has been developed to treat processes of this type is the dynamic inference model.[4] In this model, we assume that the customer has internal states that are not observable by us. At change points generated by a renewal process, the internal state of the customer may change. The parameters of the change point generation process would depend on the perturbations in the market (for instance, advertising campaigns, price reductions, and the like). The change in the internal state can be governed by a variety of stochastic processes. For example, the new state may be independent of the previous state and simply selected from a probability distribution. A more complicated situation arises when the new state depends on the previous state in a Markovian sense so that it is selected from a probability distribution conditional on the previous state. We could even have the new state depend probabilistically on both the previous state and some characteristic of the change point. However, regardless of the specific mechanism used, both the generation of change points and the change process itself cannot be observed.

What can be observed are the purchases of the customer—we call these purchases the observable variables. The observable variables are generated by a stochastic process that has the internal states as param-

4 Ronald A. Howard: "Dynamic Inference," *Operations Research,* **13**(**5**) (September-October, 1965).

eters. Since we cannot observe either the internal states or their times of change, we must use the observable variables to make inferences about the internal states and, thus, probability assignments on future purchases. Crudely, we could say that we are going to make inferences on customer preferences by observing customer purchases.

The mathematical formulation of this model is beyond our present scope, but it is contained in footnote 4. Let us, therefore, concentrate on clarifying the model by interpreting one of the examples from footnote 4 in a marketing context. Suppose that we observe, on each purchase occasion, whether a customer bought our brand or some other brand. We designate his buying our brand by setting a variable x equal to 1 and his buying some other brand by setting it to zero. The chronological sequence of buying our brand twice in succession, then some other brand twice in succession, would imply the purchase pattern 1100.

We characterize the customer's preference for our brand by assuming that on each purchase occasion he decides whether to buy our brand by making a Bernoulli trial with the probability of buying our brand equal to p. The number p is therefore his internal state and, consequently, is not observable. As long as no changes occur, the value of p remains the same. However, when a perturbation or change point occurs, the value of p will change. For simplicity, we assume that the new value of p is independent of the value before the change and is selected from a uniform probability density on the interval $(0,1)$. The choice of the distribution would depend on our relative competitive position in terms of price and quality and on the degree of logic exercised by the customers. This distribution could even change in calendar time, if required. The new value of p will govern the customer's behavior until the next change point occurs.

We assume that the change points themselves are generated by a renewal process and, in our example, by a very simple one. We assume that a change occurs with probability γ just before each purchase occasion. This change mechanism implies that the number of purchases between changes is geometrically distributed with a mean of $1/\gamma$. In practice, the value of γ would be selected to correspond to the amount of activity in the market in terms of price, quality, or promotional change.

A very interesting question to ask of this model is: Given a purchase pattern, what is the probability that the customer will purchase our brand next time? If we restrict attention to purchase patterns of length four, then there will be sixteen different possible patterns. Table 3.1 shows the probability of purchasing our brand next time for each of these patterns as a function of γ, the change probability. A more complete dis-

TABLE 3.1 DYNAMIC INFERENCE BASED ON THE UNIFORM DISTRIBUTION (0,1)

Reverse binary	Purchase Pattern				Change Probability: γ										
	x(4)	x(3)	x(2)	x(1)	0	0.05	0.10	0.15	0.20	0.25	0.30	0.35	0.40	0.45	0.50
0	0	0	0	0	.167	.192	.216	.239	.262	.284	.304	.324	.344	.362	.379
1	1	0	0	0	.333	.324	.322	.323	.328	.336	.345	.355	.367	.378	.391
2	0	1	0	0	.333	.340	.346	.353	.359	.366	.373	.381	.389	.397	.406
3	1	1	0	0	.500	.453	.424	.406	.396	.391	.390	.392	.396	.402	.409
4	0	0	1	0	.333	.352	.369	.383	.395	.406	.414	.422	.428	.434	.439
5	1	0	1	0	.500	.485	.473	.464	.456	.451	.448	.446	.445	.445	.445
6	0	1	1	0	.500	.495	.489	.483	.476	.470	.465	.461	.457	.455	.455
7	1	1	1	0	.667	.613	.571	.540	.515	.497	.482	.472	.465	.460	.457
8	0	0	0	1	.333	.388	.429	.460	.485	.504	.518	.528	.535	.540	.543
9	1	0	0	1	.500	.505	.511	.517	.524	.530	.535	.539	.543	.545	.546
10	0	1	0	1	.500	.515	.527	.536	.544	.549	.552	.554	.555	.555	.553
11	1	1	0	1	.667	.648	.631	.617	.605	.594	.586	.578	.572	.566	.561
12	0	0	1	1	.500	.547	.576	.594	.604	.609	.610	.608	.604	.598	.591
13	1	0	1	1	.667	.660	.654	.647	.641	.634	.627	.619	.611	.603	.594
14	0	1	1	1	.667	.676	.679	.677	.672	.665	.655	.645	.634	.622	.609
15	1	1	1	1	.833	.808	.784	.761	.738	.717	.696	.676	.657	.638	.621

Past ← → Future

Entries are probabilities of purchasing the brand on the next occasion

TABLE 3.1 (continued)

Reverse binary	Purchase Pattern				Change Probability: γ									
	x(4)	x(3)	x(2)	x(1)	0.55	0.60	0.65	0.70	0.75	0.80	0.85	0.90	0.95	1.00
0	0	0	0	0	.395	.410	.424	.438	.450	.462	.472	.482	.491	.500
1	1	0	0	0	.403	.415	.428	.440	.451	.462	.472	.482	.491	.500
2	0	1	0	0	.415	.425	.434	.444	.454	.463	.473	.482	.491	.500
3	1	1	0	0	.417	.426	.435	.444	.454	.463	.473	.482	.491	.500
4	0	0	1	0	.444	.449	.454	.460	.465	.471	.478	.484	.492	.500
5	1	0	1	0	.449	.452	.456	.460	.465	.471	.478	.485	.492	.500
6	0	1	1	0	.455	.456	.459	.462	.466	.472	.478	.485	.492	.500
7	1	1	1	0	.456	.457	.459	.462	.467	.472	.478	.485	.492	.500
8	0	0	0	1	.544	.543	.541	.538	.534	.528	.522	.516	.508	.500
9	1	0	0	1	.545	.544	.541	.538	.534	.528	.522	.516	.508	.500
10	0	1	0	1	.551	.548	.544	.540	.535	.529	.523	.516	.508	.500
11	1	1	0	1	.556	.551	.546	.541	.535	.529	.523	.516	.508	.500
12	0	0	1	1	.583	.575	.565	.556	.546	.537	.527	.518	.509	.500
13	1	0	1	1	.585	.575	.566	.556	.546	.537	.527	.518	.509	.500
14	0	1	1	1	.597	.585	.572	.569	.549	.538	.528	.518	.509	.500
15	1	1	1	1	.605	.590	.576	.562	.550	.539	.528	.518	.509	.500

Past ←   → Future

Entries are probabilities of purchasing the brand on the next occasion cussion of Table 3.1 appears in reference cited in footnote 4, but we shall point out one unusual feature. Consider the purchase pattern 1100. If $\gamma = 1$, a change occurs before every purchase, the purchase pattern is irrelevant, and probability 0.5 must be assigned to a purchase of our brand next time. If $\gamma = 0$, then there are no changes and we know that all the purchases in the purchase pattern are relevant to the inference on p. Since the pattern 1100 consists of equal numbers of purchases of our brand and other brands, it again results in an assignment of 0.5 probability to a purchase of our brand next time. The entries in Table 3.1 for the purchase pattern 1100 and the values $\gamma = 0$ and $\gamma = 1$ confirm these observations. But what happens to the probability of purchasing our brand next time as the change probability is increased from 0 to 1? Table 3.1 shows that, at first, the probability decreases down to a minimum of 0.390 when $\gamma = 0.30$ and then gradually increases again up to the value 0.5.

We can provide a rough explanation of this phenomenon by saying that, when $\gamma = 0.30$, it becomes likely that the first purchase in the pattern was made during another change cycle, and so this purchase is not very relevant to our probability assignment. This reasoning would lead to placing more weight on the purchases of other brands and, thus, result in a value of p below 0.5. We observe that the same phenomenon of a row minimum occurs elsewhere in Table 3.1, and that the same kind of reasoning is helpful in explaining it. The provocative phenomena observed in this simple example indicate the value of distinguishing between the internal state of a customer and his actual purchasing behavior.

To illustrate an actual marketing use of the dynamic inference model, we consider consumer panel data published by Herniter.[5] In the first table of his study, Herniter lists the fraction of panel members who actually purchase product A as a function of their previous purchase pattern for that product. The previous purchase patterns range from length zero to length four. Table 3.2 of our chapter reproduces this data in column 1; the purchase pattern notation is the one we have been using.

These data were fitted using the dynamic-inference model. The criterion for fitting was minimum squared error over the entire set of data; however, the results are not particularly sensitive to the choice of criterion. We assume that the distribution of p is the beta distribution,

$$f_\beta(p|r',n') = \frac{\Gamma(n')}{\Gamma(r')\Gamma(n'-r')} p^{r'-1}(1-p)^{n'-r'-1}, \qquad 0 \leqslant p \leqslant 1,$$

[5] Jerome D. Herniter: "Stochastic Market Models and the Analysis of Consumer Panel Data," presented at the Twenty-Seventh National Meeting of the Operations Research Society of America, Boston, Massachusetts (May 6-7, 1965).

TABLE 3.2   AN APPLICATION OF THE DYNAMIC
                INFERENCE MODEL

Purchase Pattern	Probability of Purchase on Next Occasion	
← Past Future →	Determined Empirically from Consumer Panel Data (1)	Computed from a Fitted Dynamic Inference Model (2)
—	.26	.25
0	.14	.14
1	.57	.57
00	.11	.11
10	.31	.37
01	.38	.42
11	.72	.69
000	.09	.09
100	.25	.27
010	.23	.30
110	.44	.47
001	.31	.35
101	.53	.53
011	.50	.55
111	.80	.75
0000	.08	.07
1000	.19	.21
0100	.22	.23
1100	.32	.33
0010	.19	.26
1010	.34	.40
0110	.37	.41
1110	.52	.52
0001	.28	.32
1001	.38	.43
0101	.43	.45
1101	.62	.60
0011	.41	.50
1011	.61	.61
0111	.62	.63
1111	.84	.79

which is described by the two parameters r' and n'. For example, the uniform distribution used in developing Table 3.1 is a beta distribution with $r' = 1$, $n' = 2$. The fit of the consumer panel data in Table 3.2 required a beta distribution with parameters $r' = 0.3$, $n' = 1.2$. This distribution has a mean 0.25 and is U-shaped with an unbounded height at the ends of the $(0,1)$ interval. We notice that its shape implies that panel members are likely to select with a very small or a very large value of p when a change point occurs.

The remaining feature of the model that must be specified is the change probability γ. The fitting process produced a value $\gamma = 0.06$, which would correspond to an average of about sixteen purchase occasions between changes.

Determining the three parameters r', n', and γ completely specifies the dynamic-inference model. Column 2 in Table 3.2 shows the predictions of purchase probability on the next occasion based on this model. We see that the fit is quite good over the entire set of data. Indeed, the situations where the larger discrepancies between the model and the panel data arise cast more doubt on the data than they do on the model. For example, the pattern 010 shows an actual fraction purchasing of 0.23 and a model prediction of 0.30. Yet we observe that the pattern 100, which implies a previous purchase occasion more remote into the past, has an actual fraction 0.25, which is, of course, greater than 0.23. This suggests that the value of 0.23 is suspiciously low and that the discrepancy between empirical results and the model may, in fact, be less than appears at first glance. Incidentally, the same argument applies when these patterns are preceded by a zero to form the patterns 0010 and 0100, as we may verify in Table 3.2.

When we consider that the dynamic-inference model we have used has but three parameters, the results of the fitting process are especially satisfying. The dynamic-inference process offers an attractive possibility for formulating useful models of repetitive purchasing.

THE FILTERING PROBLEM

We know that distribution flaws and changes of purchasers in the family could result in purchases of brands that are not the preferred brand. Although the dynamic-inference model we have discussed could be interpreted in this light, we shall find it helpful to discuss a version of this model that we shall call <u>Markovian dynamic inference</u>. Suppose that a customer's internal state of brand preference can change from purchase to purchase according to a Markov process with transition matrix P. However, the fact that the customer has an internal preference for a certain brand does not necessarily mean that he will buy that brand—because of flaws in distribution and other extraneous events. Instead, we assign a probability q_{ik} that the customer will purchase brand k when his internal preference is for brand i. Thus, we have defined an observation probability matrix Q that relates purchases to internal states. In this marketing example of Markovian dynamic inference, we find it convenient to think of Q as a square matrix by having the same set of possible purchased brands as we have internal states. We would expect the diagonal elements of Q to be larger than the off-diagonal elements because we expect a customer to be able to realize his preference in the majority of cases.

Once this structure is established, we can use the theory of probability to assign probabilities to the purchasing of each brand on the next purchase occasion, given the purchase sequence that has been observed. Since the Markov process provides us with a prior distribution on the sequence of internal states of the customer, and since the observation probability matrix allows us to assign a probability to any purchase pattern given the sequence of internal states, we can use Bayes' theorem to write immediately the probability to be assigned to each sequence of internal states given an observed purchase pattern. When these probabilities are summed over all states but the last state occupied, we obtain the marginal probability distribution on the internal state in view of the observed purchase pattern. We can then use this marginal distribution to find the probability that each brand will be purchased on the next purchase occasion. The computations are theoretically straightforward, but tedious, and therefore very suitable for digital computation.

The main advantage of the Markovian dynamic model is that it allows us once more to distinguish between the internal state of the customer and his observable purchase. Thus, purchase patterns that would not in themselves appear Markovian may be quite consistent with a Markovian internal model and a separate process for the generation of purchases given internal state.

Of course, there is no reason why changes in the internal state are restricted to a simple Markov process. The semi-Markov model we discussed earlier is equally feasible and considerably more general in application. The computational requirements of the semi-Markovian dynamic-inference process are only slightly above those of the Markovian version.

GENERAL COMMENTS ON MODELING

We have discussed various difficulties in the modeling of repetitive purchasing patterns using, as an underlying model, an essentially Markovian structure. However, other models like the learning models have been proposed, and most of what we have discussed would apply to them with minor modifications. The Markovian models are in many ways easier to analyze and compute than their competitors, but since the trend seems to be going in the direction of simulation, this observation may not be very significant.

One problem that every modeler must face is that of model fitting. We note that if we take a Bayesian point of view, then we build all our information into the model and accept its probability assignments for the future as being logical and consistent with our state of information. The question of evaluation per se never arises. In fact, it is very similar to the question of how to evaluate a weather forecaster who uses subjective probability in making his forecasts.

A more traditional point of view on model fitting and evaluation would be to use part of the data for the fitting of the model parameters by employing some system like least-squares or minimum chi-square, and then to compare the predictions of this model against what took place in the remainder of the data, probably using a subjective evaluation criterion.

Much has been written on the question of model fitting and evaluation, but the problem is far from resolved. To a scientist, the test of a model may be how much insight it gives him into the process and how many of the observed phenomena it explains. To the marketing executive, the test is whether he can make more profitable marketing decisions using the model than he can without it. It is quite possible that we need a double standard in modeling—the Bayesian view for the manager concerned with profit and the traditional view for the scientist concerned with reproducibility. Any discussion of model evaluation will have to recognize the possibly differing goals of the management scientist and the manager.

However, there is one test of any proposed model and its associated computational scheme that both manager and scientist would find interesting. Assume that the proposed model is, in fact, the actual model for the customer. Choose reasonable parameters and simulate the amount and kind of data on the process that will be available from the consumer panel. Then apply the proposed computational scheme to the simulated data. Observe the values of the parameters that the scheme assigns and the implied probabilistic predictions of future behavior. Finally, compare these predictions with the predictions of the actual parameters. A surprising number of analytic procedures cannot pass this test. However, only a test like this that includes both the computational scheme and the available data can build confidence in a proposed analytic modeling procedure.

CONCLUSION

The problem of modeling repetitive consumer purchases is extremely complicated—it may, in fact, be too complicated to be analyzed by using consumer panel data. Studying consumer behavior through consumer panels may be like studying atomic structure through the physical properties of matter. We appear to need much more imagination in marketing experimentation so that we can isolate a portion of customer behavior that can be meaningfully studied. Perhaps individuals with training in the physical sciences would be most capable of providing the kind of help necessary. Indeed, we can even postulate an experimental management scientist who brings to this area the experimental skills so valuable in physical science.

The development of causal models for repetitive purchasing has only begun. A major investment of technical and financial resources must be made if some of the glimmerings of hope we now see are to flourish into real achievement.

FOUR | *WILLIAM F. MASSY**

Stochastic Models for
Monitoring New-Product Introductions

The number of new products introduced to the market each year is large
and growing. Thousands of items have been added to the class of frequently purchased products alone during the past few years. Although
many of these newcomers represent modifications of products or brands
already on the market, many of the products are true innovations. Our
notions about the definitions of certain product classes have had to be
revised because of the large number of new-product offerings that cannot
be forced into one of the established molds.

Managers of new-product introduction campaigns need information
about how their product is doing in test markets and how it is doing
during the critical months after the beginning of national or regional
distribution. Their needs are often greater than those of managers responsible for marketing established products because of the dynamic nature
of the new-product adoption process, the difficulty of obtaining reliable
information from nonmarket sources, and the tremendous risks that are
often connected with bringing out a new product.

The factors that increase the information needs of new-product managers also make it difficult to provide this information. Workers in the
field are familiar with the "humped" nature of the sales curves for many
new products, for example. Sales rise as more and more consumers try
the product (perhaps in response to an introductory offer) but then often
taper off as repeat purchases become more and more scattered in time.
This phenomenon is accentuated if factory rather than retail sales are
monitored, because of the effects of pipeline filling. In view of the fact

* The author wishes to acknowledge the assistance of Dr. I. J. Abrams, Vice President
of Technology of the Market Research Corporation of America (MRCA); and Dr.
Donald Morrison, Assistant Professor at the Graduate School of Business, Columbia
University.

that early sales trends are usually poor indicators of eventual product performance, it has been necessary to develop methods for "looking behind the sales curve."

The purpose of this chapter is to present a mathematical model that can be used to describe the adoption process for new frequently purchased products and to make forecasts of long-run sales volumes. The model is "objective" in the sense that it depends only on sales statistics for the new product. The sales statistics to be utilized must be obtained from consumer panels, as these panels provide the only source of continuing information on the purchases of a cross section of consuming families. Although other kinds of data (for example, results from consumer preference or image studies on test panel households) might be incorporated into such a model, this topic will not be considered here. We discuss the theoretical and intuitive considerations that lead to specification of the new model, outline some of its properties, and suggest some ways in which the model might be put to use. A more extensive and technical treatment can be found in Massy [1966a], upon which the present work is based.

Models of Consumer Purchasing Behavior

The construction of stochastic models for describing and forecasting consumer purchasing behavior with respect to frequently purchased products has been proceeding for some ten years now, and some impressive results have been attained. Unfortunately, few models seem to meet the information needs of managers of *new*-product marketing efforts. We shall review some of these models and comment on their relevance to the problem of new-product adoption.

MODELS FOR BRAND CHOICE. The major developments in the field of stochastic representations of purchasing behavior have involved models for choice of brand within a particular product class. These models attempt to specify the probability law for selection of one brand or another, assuming that a purchase of the product class does in fact occur. These models are best couched in terms of the selection process that operates at the level of the individual family. These processes are then aggregated according to rules contained in the model so that the probability law governing brand shares at the total market level are obtained.

The simplest model for brand choice is the stationary, homogeneous multinomial law. Consumers are assumed to make selections according to fixed probabilities, which are the same for all families and do not change over time. Then the share of each brand in the market can be described in terms of a multinomial distribution with parameters p_1, p_2, . . . , and N, where N stands for the total number of families in the market. The shortcomings of this model are obvious: different families are known to have different brand-choice probabilities and the probabilities are sure to change in response to market forces and continuing experience with the product.

The stationarity assumption was attacked first. Although all formal models of behavior must ultimately be stationary in some sense, the objective is to push the stationarity assumption as far upstream as possible. In the purchasing behavior context, we shall call a model "stationary" if the probability elements determining the frequency of purchase events or choices of particular brands remain the same through time. The model is said to be "nonstationary" if these elements tend to change. Nonstationary models should include specifications for the laws that determine the change process of the probability elements defined above. Whether deterministic or stochastic, these laws must ultimately rest on some stable elements of the behavior complex under study. By pushing the stationarity property "upstream," we mean that the law of the change process is made to include more and more of what we believe is important about the time variation in behavior.

The first attempts to relax the stationarity assumption of purchasing behavior models were made by users of homogeneous first-order Markov process [see Lipstein, 1959, and Styan and Smith, 1964]. The brand-choice probabilities are assumed to depend on the brand last purchased so the stationarity assumption is shifted from the brand-choice probability vector to the matrix of transition probabilities. Lipstein [1965] considers the characteristics of linear operators that carry a transition matrix that is observed in one time period into a different transition matrix that is observed later. This amounts to specifying a law of change that works on the transition matrix of the Markov process, thus pushing the ultimate stationarity of the model a step further upstream. In another development, Howard [1963] has discussed the aggregation of family-specific Markov models with homogeneous transition matrices to obtain results for the over-all market.

Stationarity can be relaxed in other ways. Kuehn [1962] has argued that, although the brand purchased last changes the probability vector, the resulting probability level depends also on the initial conditions. Kuehn's linear learning model amounts to a first-order Markov process operating on the state space of the probability vector rather than on the state space of the brand-choice alternatives themselves. Kuehn also points out that the probability of purchasing a particular brand tends toward the share of the market for that brand as the time since the last purchase of the product class increases. This finding has considerable intuitive appeal, since "front-of-mind awareness" with respect to particular brands will tend to fade over time in the absence of reinforcement or further learning. Herniter [1965] has reported the same phenomenon, except that he pegs the asymptotic probability level at the brand's advertising share rather than at its market share.

Coleman [1964] and Montgomery [1966] report work on a zero-order evolutionary probability model. Here the probability vectors are assumed to change through time according to a probability law that does not depend on the incidence of purchases or particular choices of brand. The required probability law can be derived from a model that is closely akin to the nonstationary stimulus sampling models of mathematical psychologists [see Montgomery, 1966]. The probability law implies that individual purchase probabilities should trend, on the average, to a brand's share of the market and, thus, provides theoretical support for the empirical phenomenon discussed above. It also appears that the model can be generalized to include the effects of learning: the author has done some exploratory work on his subject, although results will probably not be forthcoming for some time.

Howard [1965] has developed yet another type of nonstationary model that can be applied to the problem of brand choice. His "dynamic inference" procedure assumes that the elements of the probability vector change from time to time in accordance with some probability law that is independent of actual purchase outcomes. The probabilities are drawn from a (stationary) prior distribution each time a change occurs. The objective of the analysis is to find the probability that a particular brand will be purchased on the next occasion, in view of a short history of past purchases.

Morrison [1965a and b] was one of the first to deal explicitly with the problem of heterogeneity among the probability vectors of different consumers. He introduces the idea of a prior distribution of purchase probabilities for the case of stationary multinomial models and extends his approach to cover first-order Markov processes with certain specified structures. The essence of the idea is that, if different consumers have different probabilities, we must take this fact into account when using aggregate market data to test hypotheses about the structure of the brand-selection process. Although the purchase probabilities of individual facilities usually cannot be observed directly, we can estimate the parameters of the frequency function describing the incidence of different values over members of the population (the "prior" distribution) and use these results in our calculations. Morrison's work was motivated by that of Frank [1962], who pointed out the dangers of the homogeneous-population assumption. Massy [1966b] has demonstrated the kinds of interpretation errors that are likely to arise when applying this assumption to the simple Markov model. Population heterogeneity has also been assumed by Coleman, Montgomery, and Massy [1965] in connection with their treatments of the zero-order evolutionary and learning models. It is likely that Kuehn has also used the assumption in his later work.

All of the models considered above share the characteristic pointed out at the beginning of this section: they concentrate on the problem of brand choice, given that a purchase does occur. The problem of predicting when a purchase will occur is not considered as part of these models, though machinery for treating it might be added in some cases. The lone exception to this rule is provided by Howard [1963], who introduced the idea of a semi-Markov process to the marketing literature. Such a process includes the probability law for time between purchases as well as for brand choice.

It is also worth noting that the models discussed above have solid bases in probability theory. I believe that this is essential if serious mistakes of interpretation are to be avoided and forecasting procedures placed on a firm footing. This is particularly true with respect to the question of aggregation. We take issue with a recent article by Ehrenberg [1965] on this point, and also in connection with his treatment of the "problem" of process reversibility.

MODELS FOR PURCHASE INCIDENCE.   Work on models for describing the incidence of purchases of a certain product class is much less extensive than that dealing with the problem of brand choice. Three types of models have been used to date. One type deals with the distribution of total quantity of product purchased by members of a consuming population, the second type of model focuses on the question of purchase timing, and the third type concentrates upon the speed of penetration of newly introduced products.

One of the only models for predicting the quantity of purchases for a frequently purchased consumer product was presented by Ehrenberg in a now classic paper [1959]. He showed that if the occurrence of purchases by individual families can be described by Poisson probability process with parameter M, and if M varies over the population of consumers in accordance with a gamma (chi square or Pearson Type III) distribution, then the total number of purchases made by all members of the population in a given interval of time is distributed as a negative binomial random variable. In the terminology used earlier, the Poisson distribution represents the basic or primary probability law for the purchasing process, while the chi-square assumes the role of a prior distribution. This model is obviously nonhomogeneous, although it is stationary in the sense that the parameter for a particular family is assumed to remain constant through time. The model to be presented in this chapter is a generalization of the basic approach introduced by Ehrenberg.

A model for predicting the timing of purchases for an established product has been suggested by Massy and Frank [1964]. The model focuses upon the consumer's pantry shelf inventory and assumes that a purchase will occur whenever the inventory becomes depleted. Although inventory levels cannot be observed directly in most studies, inferences about these levels that are sufficient for estimating the model's parameters can be obtained from consumed panel data with suitable assumptions.

Models of the incidence of purchases for new products are illustrated in papers by Woodlock [1963] and Fourt and Woodlock [1960]. They use penetration models of the general type that has long been familiar in economic research. The percentages of families in the population who have tried the product once, twice, three times, and so on, are used as dependent variables. The model specifies the form of the growth curve for these percentages and the model's parameters are estimated from panel data. Under certain conditions, the levels of penetration in future periods can be obtained by extrapolating the growth curves, but this method of forecasting must be used with caution. The growth laws can be fairly complicated, and the assumption of nonhomogeneous consumer populations can be introduced without difficulty. The models have a stochastic interpretation, although they are often viewed deterministically. Anscombe [1961] has shown how maximum likelihood estimates can be obtained for the parameters of the mixed (that is, nonhomogeneous) exponential (Poisson) penetration model. Anscombe's methods are used in connection with the model to be presented in this chapter.

Considerable experience with the use of penetration models for handling the practical problems of monitoring new product introductions has been acquired by practitioners in the field. By examining the penetration curves obtained for different depth of repeat classes, it is often possible to identify marketing problems before they become serious. Rough forecasts can also be obtained even where the growth curve itself cannot be extrapolated accurately beyond the range of the available data. These forecasts take the form of statements like "the new product will probably be successful" or "it will probably fail." The forecasts are obtained by comparing the product's pattern of penetration in successive depth of repeat classes with norms previously established through experience with similar products.

A "Good" Model of New Product Adoption

What characteristics should we seek when building a model of the new-product adoption process? What kind of model is likely to be "good" in the sense of being intuitively plausible, technically rigorous, operationally viable, and—most important—useful for management?

We believe that a number of such characteristics can be listed.

1. The model should have a firm intuitive and theoretical basis; that is, its parts should have intrinsic meaning in terms of the structure of the process being modeled. Results should be derived from these structural postulates by using probability theory or other logically consistent means. Some reasons for this view were given above. Models that rely on mechanical extrapolation may be useful in the short run but will not be able to keep up with the ever-growing information needs of managers or to take full advantage of the expanding capabilities of data processing devices.

2. The model must allow for heterogeneity among purchasing rates or probabilities of different members of the population. This should be a cardinal rule for every type of stochastic model of the consumer purchasing process.

3. The model should not assume that purchase probabilities are stationary. The characteristics of the new-product adoption process deny the stationarity assumptions, since the very essence of innovation involves change. Both learning and time-evolution are likely to be important. (Time-evolution can be regarded as a surrogate for the effects of the marketing activities of various firms and the "bandwagon" effect due to word-of-mouth advertising as the product begins to catch on.)

4. The model should not place great reliance on the researcher's ability to define the product class in question. This implies that models that deal with changes in the probability vectors for brand choice (if a purchase of some member of the product class is about to occur) are likely to be of limited usefulness in the new-product adoption context.

The last criterion seems to be the only one that is likely to generate much controversy. While the author would not claim that brand-choice models are *never* useful in the new-product context [see, for example, the work of Montgomery, 1966, and Carman, 1965, on the adoption of fluoridated toothpaste], there is one strong factor which works against them. Consider the process by which a manager chooses from among alternative new-product ideas. According to the textbooks, he should generally seek to find a product that fills some combination of consumer needs that is not already being strongly exploited by competitors. While comparative advantages in production or marketing may sometimes lead a firm to enter a market in which substantial competition already exists, there can be no doubt that the lucrative but sparsely populated cells of the "market grid" usually offer the best opportunities for new-product success.

One of the attributes of the sparsely populated market-grid cell is that there are no close substitutes for the new product. This means that it will be difficult or impossible to define a neat "product class" into which the product falls—in the sense that all members of the class can be freely substituted for one another. For example, are pop tarts in the bread class, the jam class, the breakfast food class, or still another product class? How can we use a probability vector that is defined over all of these possibilities? Many similar examples could be given, and I am impressed by the proportion of cases in which the new-product problem is defined in these terms by experienced market researchers. Finally, we should note that it is precisely in the cases where the product "fits between" product classes that management's information needs are greatest, as these products represent the greatest innovative effort and involve the most uncertainty. Therefore, we would do well to design our new-product demand models with these situations in mind.

A STOCHASTIC EVOLUTIONARY ADOPTION MODEL
FOR NEW PRODUCTS

The model to be described in this section is designed to meet the criteria given above. It represents certain important characteristics of the adoption pattern for new frequently purchased products by means of mathematical statements about the relations between purchase events, and the probabilities of purchase events, as they occur at different times for different families. Purchasing data obtained from consumer panels can be summarized in a concise and meaningful form by estimating the parameters of the model. If certain assumptions about future values of these parameters are made, forecasts of purchase rates can be deduced from the model. We call the model STEAM, which stands for *ST*ochastic *E*volutionary *A*doption *M*odel.

The model is a diagnostic and forecasting device. It is not "causal" in the sense of offering hypotheses about why consumers behave as they do. Instead, it is designed to exploit consumer-panel data to help meet information needs described by executives responsible for new-product introductions.

Specification of the Model

Specification of a stochastic model takes the form of making explicit statements about a probability law that is believed to describe the behavioral process under study. A number of different laws, some stochastic and some not, will have to be specified in order to provide a reasonable model for the process of new-product adoption. First, we introduce a *primary model*, representing the purchasing decisions of individual families in particular time intervals. Second, there is a series of *secondary models* which describe the ways in which the parameters of the primary model vary from individual to individual, over time, and in response to certain classes of events. In combination, the primary and secondary models define a *composite probability law* for the new-product adoption process, as seen in the aggregate. The composite probability law is the most relevant for the business firm, at least from the forecasting point of view, since the firm is concerned with the total number of purchases made by all consumers.

INCIDENCE OF PURCHASE EVENTS. Purchases are discrete events that occur in time. As such, they may be described in terms of a stochastic counting process of the type discussed by Parzen [1962, p. 117]. The purpose of the model is to predict the number of events that will occur in a fixed time interval. More precisely, the stochastic process model defines the probability that the number of events that have been counted will be, for example, X_1 at time t_1, given that it was X_0 at time t_0. Our primary model for the occurrence of events will take the form of a stochastic counting process, where an "event" is defined as the occurrence of a purchase regardless of the size of the purchase.[1]

The simplest and best known representation of a counting process is provided by the Poisson distribution:

$$P\{N(t) = x | \mu\} = e^{-\mu} \frac{\mu^x}{x!}, \qquad x \geq 0. \tag{4.1}$$

[1] That is, a "purchase" may involve one small package of the product or several large ones. See Section 3.3 of Massy [1966a] for an approach to a composite model of purchase incident and size of purchase.

The random variable $N(t)$ is defined as the number of counts and the parameter μ is the mean rate of occurrence of the counts in the interval $[0, t]$. Ehrenberg [1959] uses the Poisson distribution in his model of the consumer purchasing processes. A more extensive justification for its use is provided by Massy [1966a, pp. 17-19].

The Poisson process can be generalized slightly to provide a more specific link to the new-product adoption problem. Suppose that the housewife's preferences for different types of packaged dinners can be represented by a vector of probabilities. If the purchase of these dinners is a Poisson process and if the probability that she will choose a particular new variety (assuming that she has decided to buy TV dinners, in general) remains constant over the interval from t_0 to t, then the occurrence of purchases of the new variety can also be described by a Poisson process. It can be shown that:

$$P\{N(t) = x | v, \eta\} = e^{-v\eta t}[(v\eta t)^x]/x!, \qquad (4.2)$$

where $N(t)$ = number of purchases of variety A in $(0,t)$

η = mean purchase rate for packaged dinners

v = probability of purchase variety A, given that some type of packaged dinner is going to be bought

The composite parameter $(v\eta)$ thus represents the mean purchase rate for variety A and is equivalent to the "μ" of Eq. 4. It should be noticed that an assumption of stability for the probability element v denies the existence of either learning or evolutionary effects. That is, relative preferences for variety A are not affected by product usage or exposure to promotion. The same assumptions apply to the process that generates use opportunities for packaged dinners in general, as summed up by the mean use rate η. (The introduction of secondary models will relax these restrictions.)

The user of panel data will not be able to observe the incidence of use opportunities directly. However, if the product class in question is well defined, we may count all purchases of any brand or variety of product and, thus, produce estimates of the mean usage rate parameter η. The share of these purchases devoted to variety A then provides an estimate of the choice probability v. Share figures often suffice for the purpose of analyzing consumer preferences, in which case there is no need to consider the counting process at all. The methods discussed in this chapter are designed to be applied to situations where the class of use opportunities is not well enough defined to permit observation of total usage through panel data. One advantage of our approach is that even where the boundaries of the product class are not clear, it is still possible to deal with models couched in terms of the composite parameter μ. As this represents the use rate for the new product or variety directly, it is possible to proceed without depending upon any notion of product class.

DISTRIBUTION OF INTERPURCHASE TIMES. The primary model given above represents the probability law for the number of purchases made by a given family in a particular interval of time. It will be more convenient, however, to consider the distribution of the length of time between one purchase and the next rather than the distribution of the number of purchases occurring during a fixed interval of time.

The intervals between successive events in a counting process are called the waiting or interarrival times of the process. It is well known that the waiting times of a homogeneous Poisson process are exponentially distributed. In our case, however, the parameters of the primary purchasing model will be assumed to vary with time. Such a model is called "nonhomogeneous." (In the present context, nonhomogeneous refers to time. Our model is also nonhomogeneous over families because of the mixed population assumption introduced below.) The distribution of waiting times for the nonhomogeneous Poisson process can be written as follows [see, for example, Parzen, 1962, p. 125]:

$$f[t|\mu(t)] = e^{-m(t)}\mu(t), \qquad (4.3)$$

where t is the waiting time to the next purchase and $\mu(t)$ is a generalization of the purchase rate parameter (given in Eq. 4.1), which allows for the effects of time. The term $m(t)$ is called the "mean value function" of the counting process: it is defined as

$$m(t) = \int_0^t \mu(x)\, dx.$$

The distribution of waiting times will be considered further in a later section.

PRIOR DISTRIBUTION OF PURCHASE RATES. Purchase events have been assumed to occur according to a Poisson counting process, but nothing has been specified about the manner in which the parameter of the process varies over different families. From the arguments given above, we can see that it would be extremely unlikely for all families to generate use opportunities for the product at the same rate and have the same relative preference for the new product as a means of fulfilling their requirements. That is, aggregate purchasing behavior must be represented by a mixture of Poisson processes with different parameters. This idea was first applied to a consumer behavior model by Ehrenberg [1959]. The problem

is formally similar to the one encountered in analyses of accident proneness, on which a considerable literature has accumulated [see Bates and
Neyman, 1952].

It is convenient to use the Pearson Type III function as the prior distribution for the parameters of a Poisson process. We shall consider a
particular parameterization of this function, which has been termed
the "gamma-1" distribution by Raiffa and Schlaifer [1961, p. 225]. It
is represented by:

$$f(\mu|\alpha, \beta) = \frac{\beta e^{-\beta\mu}(\beta\mu)^{a-1}}{\Gamma(\alpha)}, \qquad \mu \geq 0, \qquad (4.4)$$

where the random variable μ is the parameter of our primary purchasing
model and $\Gamma(\alpha)$ is the gamma function of α. The parameters of this
function can be interpreted by considering the mean and variance of μ:

$$E[\mu] = \frac{\alpha}{\beta}, \qquad \text{var } [\mu] = \frac{\alpha}{\beta^2}.$$

Both the mean and variance of μ are proportional to α, which is called
the number of degrees of freedom of the distribution. The parameter β
acts as a scaling factor. The random variable μ can be standardized so
that its mean and variance are equal through multiplication by β. Since
the gamma distribution can assume a wide variety of shapes, we may
expect a reasonably good fit to many of the unimodal distributions of
Poisson parameters which might be encountered in real situations.

LEARNING. The act of purchasing and using any item in the product
class is likely to affect the family's assessment of relative preference for
the various brands (leading to a change in v), the mean rate at which
the product class is consumed (leading to a change in η), or both.
Kuehn has argued that a learning process exists at the level of v, and
he indicates that it can be described by a modification of the linear
learning model. We believe that learning is likely to be a very important
component in the process of new-product adoption, but we doubt that
the linear model is applicable to new-product adoption processes.

A major simplification is available when we consider learning in the
context of new-product adoption. It seems plausible to assume that the
largest learning effect occurs in connection with the purchase and use of
the *new* member of the product class. Although the use of older alternatives must continue to affect subsequent purchasing behavior, it seems
likely that the impact of new experience with respect to the innovation
will swamp the learning effects due to using the older products, at least

for awhile. Thus, we are justified in neglecting learning effects due to purchase of older members of the product class. Indeed, this course of action is required when we deal with product classes that are not well defined since, in that case, it is often impossible to monitor purchases other than those of the particular new product under study.

It is difficult to formulate a reasonable model for representing the effect of purchases of the new product on the parameter of the primary counting model. It seems likely that trial will tend to increase usage rates if consumers like the product. On the other hand, the possibility of trial followed by rejection is much more likely in the new-product context than in the case of many of the established products studied by Kuehn; this would imply that μ could decline with use. Finally, the effects of increased experience are not necessarily monotonic. Cases where several trials are required before the consumer accepts or rejects a new product or variety are quite common. It is not unusual to find that μ will increase after the first four or five purchases and then decrease. In fact, this is the rule rather than the exception with "fad" products. Unfortunately, it is often very difficult to determine the extent to which early acceptance of new products is "faddish": this often represents one of the primary purposes of consumer research in the new-product context. The considerations given above imply that the effect of learning on μ will not always be linear or exponential. A quadratic form is the minimum for describing faddishness, and even that would seem to be somewhat restrictive.

We shall handle the problem of learning by assuming that a different prior distribution of μ's exists for families who have made different numbers of purchases of the new product. The panel data can be stratified by depth of repeat class, and the values of α and β in Eq. 4.4 estimated separately for each stratum. Thus, the form of the learning effect can be inferred after the fact from the series of $E(\mu)$ and $\text{var}(\mu)$ for the various depth of repeat groups. The fact that stratification by depth of repeat class is a familiar device to workers in the new-product research field makes the above procedure attractive.

TIME OF CONVERSION. In view of the fact that the prior distribution of μ is assumed to vary with the number of previous purchases of the new product, it seems reasonable to inquire as to whether the timing of the previous purchases would also be likely to have an effect. The answer is "yes," as can be seen by examining the following example.

Suppose that we have only two groups of families in the population: one group with high initial purchase rates for the new product and one group with low initial rates. We begin observing the population at the time the new product is introduced and we find that some families make their first purchase early, others make their first purchase late, and still others never purchase the new product at all. With the Poisson model, it can easily be shown that, while it is possible for a family with a small value of μ to be among the early adopters, most members of this group will have the higher initial purchase rates. The converse is true for members of the late adopter and diehard (disinterested) groups. We now inquire about the probable distribution of μ's after one trial of the product. If a family's assessment of the product's attributes after use is positively correlated with its prior assessment (as seems likely for many products), we should expect to find that the mean of the distribution describing post-trial preferences would be larger for people who converted from the "0" to the "1" depth of repeat class soon after the product was introduced than for those people who waited for a considerable period of time. This would be true because members of the first group would tend to have had larger initial μ's than members of the second group. The process just described is related to that discussed by Frank [1962], who demonstrated the results of self-selection on the interpretation of aggregate brand-switching statistics. However, we must not forget that, in the present case, the effects of self-selection are moderated by the existence of the learning phenomenon.

We shall handle time-of-conversion effects by incorporating them into our mathematical structure through another secondary model. Suppose that the ith family in our sample makes its kth purchase at time t. Let us represent this family's "time of conversion" to the kth depth of repeat class by τ_{ki}, which will be defined as

$$\tau_{ki} = t - \tau_{k*} + 1,$$

where τ_{k*} is defined as the average time at which the first few families entered the kth depth of repeat class.[2] Remember that we are concerned with the prior distribution of purchase probabilities for each depth of repeat class. (These probabilities are labeled for the kth class, although they actually refer to the upcoming $(k+1)$st purchase.) We shall assume

[2] The time at which the first family entered the kth depth of repeat class was used as an estimate for τ_{k0} in an early version of the model. A reader pointed out that since this time is a random variable, the fit of the model could easily be affected by one "improbable" event. This difficulty is overcome by smoothing: that is, by averaging the conversion times of the first five families or so. Of course, it will be necessary to modify the definition of τ_{ki} for the earliest of these families, so that τ_{ki} is always greater than or equal to one as required by the model.

that the α parameter of the gamma-1 prior distribution depends on τ_{ki} in the following manner:

$$\alpha = \alpha^* \, \tau_{ki}{}^\gamma, \qquad\qquad (4.5)$$

where α^* and γ are new parameters. To simplify notation in the sequel, the original parameter will be written in functional notation as $\alpha(\tau_{ki})$ and α^* will be shortened to α. The restriction on τ_{ki} is implied by the definition given above.

Equation 4.5 provides a flexible monotonic representation of the effect of τ_k on the prior distribution. The α parameter of the prior distribution for the first few families to enter the kth depth of repeat class is given by $\alpha(1) = \alpha^*$. Then it changes with τ_k in one of the number of different ways shown in Fig. 4.1, depending upon the value of γ. The arguments given earlier suggest that $\gamma < 0$ if the correlation between preference assessments before and after a trial is positive; while this is the expected situation, we should not be too surprised if the contrary should occur. However, we should expect that $-1 < \gamma < +1$ to avoid the possibility of explosive behavior. Finally, we should note that, although there was no strong theoretical reason for selecting α as the parameter of the prior distribution to be made dependent on τ_k, the fact that β is interpreted as a scale parameter while α is linearly related to both the mean and variance of the distribution made this course of action intuitively attractive. The present formulation also leads to mathematically tractable results.

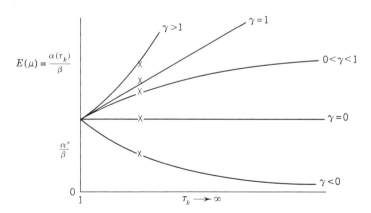

Figure 4.1.   Relation between mean of prior distribution and time of conversion for different values of γ.

TIME SINCE CONVERSION. The probability of repurchasing a given brand has been shown to change systematically as the time since the last purchase of the product class increases. The idea that consumers tend to "forget" the influence of the brand last purchased and eventually respond in proportion to the aggregate of market forces is relevant for our model of the adoption of new products. We have argued that consumers have relative preference for different ways of satisfying their needs, and that the new product represents one way of responding to these needs when they arise. The needs are considered to be use opportunities, which may arise more or less at random with rate η, while the families' relative preferences are summed up by the probability element v. It is reasonable to assume that the latter variable will change as the period since the last time a similar use opportunity was satisfied increased. As we cannot observe the timing of use opportunities that do not elicit purchases of the new product, however, we shall have to assume that the relevant time interval is the time since the last purchase of the new product itself. This assumption states that the probability of choosing the new product when a use opportunity arises declines as the length of time since the last trial of the new product increases. Since the probability element v is not observable in the absence of methods for defining use opportunities, we shall frame our model in terms of the composite measure μ. This will also allow for interactions between the time since the trial of the new product and the process that generates use opportunities, if any should exist.

Our specific assumption is that μ varies exponentially with the time since the last purchase:

$$\mu(t_{ki}) = \mu^* t_{ki}^{\lambda}, \tag{4.6}$$

where

$$t_{ki} = t - \tau_{ki} + 1 \geqslant 1.$$

The variable t_{ki} represents the time since the ith family entered the kth depth of repeat class—that is, since the family made its last purchase. The measure is incremented by one in order to insure that it will never be less than unity. In view of this restriction, Eq. 4.6 takes on values similar to those graphed in Fig. 4.1 for the previous secondary model, depending on the sign and magnitude of λ. We shall again simplify notation by writing the original parameter as $\mu(t_{ki})$ and shortening μ^* to μ.

The above model provides for exponential changes in purchase rates for individual families as the length of the period since their last trial of the new product increases. While the lower asymptote is fixed at zero and the function is unbounded above, it may be expected to provide a good fit to the results reported by Kuehn and Herniter for short ranges of time. We should expect that $\lambda < 0$, so that the purchase rate declines with time; thus, the behavior of the function in the positive range is not particularly important. The assumption of a zero lower asymptote is not consistent with the results reported for established products, but it may be reasonably appropriate in the present context where cases of total rejection of the new product are not unknown.

Properties of the Model

The specifications of the model are reviewed in Eq. 4.7, using a consistent notation.

Primary model for interpurchase times.

$$f\{t_{ki}|\mu_{ki}(t_{ki})\} = e^{-m_{ki}(t_{ki})} \mu_{ki}(t_{ki}), \tag{4.7a}$$

where

$$m_{ki}(t_{ki}) = \int_1^{t_{ik}} \mu_{ki}(t) \, dt.$$

Secondary model for effect of time since conversion.

$$\mu_{ki}(t) = \mu \, t_{ki}^{\lambda}, \tag{4.7b}$$

where

$$t_{ki} = T - \tau_{ki} - \tau_{k*} + 2 \geqslant 1.$$

Secondary model for mixed populations.

$$f\{\mu|\alpha(\tau_{ki}), \beta\} = \frac{\beta e^{-\beta\mu}(\beta\mu)^{\alpha(\tau_{ki})-1}}{\Gamma(\alpha(\tau_{ki}))}. \tag{4.7c}$$

Secondary model for effect of conversion time.

$$\alpha(\tau_{ki}) = \alpha \, \tau_{ki}^{\gamma}, \tag{4.7d}$$

where

$$\tau_{ki} = T - \tau_{k*} + 1 \geqslant 1.$$

The variables used in the models are defined as follows:

i An index used to designate families. Each family in the panel is assigned a unique value of i.

k An index used to designate depth of repeat classes.

T An index used to designate time. It may be defined as the total number of weeks (months, and so on) since the product was introduced.

t_{ki} The length of time since the ith family made its kth purchase (entered the kth depth of repeat class), incremented by one.

τ_{ki} The time period at which the ith family made its kth purchase, taken relative to the time origin of kth depth of repeat class, incremented by one.

τ_{k*} The "time origin" of the kth depth of repeat class.

The lower limit of integration in Eq. 4.7a is "1" because t_{ki} has its origin at one rather than at zero, as was implicitly assumed in Eq. 4.3.

The nature of the various time indices used in the model can be clarified by reference to Fig. 4.2. The purchase histories of two hypothetical families are presented, each family having made its first purchase at point P_1 and its second at P_2. The time origins of the 0th, 1st, and 2nd depth of repeat classes are also given. The conversion times (τ_{ki}) and waiting times (t_{ki}) are defined in terms of the data described above, as shown in the figure. (The unit increment that applies to each time index is not shown.)

The model contains four free parameters, which may be interpreted as follows:

λ The intensity with which a family's expected purchase rate changes with respect to time since the last purchase. The model requires $-1 < \lambda$. For $\lambda < 0$ the expected purchase rate declines with time, as would normally be expected. We require $\lambda < 1$ to avoid explosive behavior.

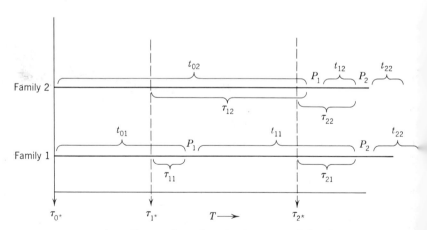

Figure 4.2.   Time indices for two hypothetical families.

β   The scale factor in the distribution of initial expected purchase rates. The model requires $\beta > 0$.

α   The number of degrees of freedom in the distribution of expected purchase rates for the first few families to enter a given depth of repeat class. The parameter is proportional to the mean of the prior distribution. The model requires $\alpha > 0$.

γ   The intensity with which the mean of the prior distribution of expected rates changes with respect to the period of time since the first family entered the given depth of repeat class. We should expect that $-1 < \gamma < +1$ in order to avoid explosive behavior.

If λ and γ are equal to zero, our model reduces to that of Ehrenberg [1959]. Examples of how the values of these parameters might be used as diagnostic tools for managers of new-product introduction campaigns will be presented later.

CONDITIONAL DISTRIBUTION OF $t|\mu$.   The conditional distribution of interpurchase times is obtained by operating on Eq. 4.7b as indicated in Eq. 4.7a. Performing the indicated operations gives us the following expressions for the density and distribution functions:

$$f(t|\lambda, \mu) = \mu t^{\lambda} e^{-[\mu/(\lambda+1)](t^{\lambda+1}-1)}, \qquad t \geqslant 1, \qquad (4.8)$$

and

$$F(t|\lambda, \mu) = \frac{\mu e^{\mu/(\lambda+1)}}{(\lambda+1)} \int_{1}^{t^{\lambda+1}} e^{-[\mu/(\lambda+1)]x} \, dx = 1 - e^{-[\mu/(\lambda+1)](t^{\lambda+1}-1)}. \qquad (4.9)$$

It is apparent from Eqs. 4.8 and 4.9 that the parameter λ must be constrained to the range of values greater than -1 in order for the conditional density and distribution functions to be properly defined. If $\lambda = -1$ the ratio $\mu/(\lambda+1)$ is infinite, while if $\lambda < -1$ the ratio is negative and the probability mass does not converge to one as t becomes large. Equation 4.8 is a form of the Weibull distribution, which is used extensively in reliability engineering.[3] The Weibull is itself a member of the broader class of Polya frequency densities of order 2 [see Barlow, Marshall, and Proschan, 1963].

---

[3] Our distribution differs from the Weibull in that its time origin is one rather than zero. Therefore, standard expression for the moments of the Weibull do not apply. The results given above are valid because they depend only on the kernel of the density.

UNCONDITIONAL DISTRIBUTION OF t.   The unconditional density of the interpurchase times is obtained by integrating μ from the conditional density function. Equation 4.7c defined the prior distribution of μ as gamma-1 with parameters $\alpha(\tau)$ and β, while the definition of $\alpha(\tau)$ was given in Eq. 4.7d. In Massy [1966a, p. 42], we prove the following results:

$$f(t|\alpha,\beta,\gamma,\lambda; \tau) = \alpha\tau^\gamma \beta^{\alpha\tau^\gamma} (\lambda+1)^{\alpha\tau^\gamma} \frac{t^\lambda}{[t^{\lambda+1} + \beta(\lambda+1) - 1]^{\alpha\tau^\gamma+1}}. \tag{4.10}$$

$$F(t|\alpha,\beta,\gamma,\lambda; \tau) = 1 - \left[\frac{\beta(\lambda+1)}{t^{\lambda+1} + \beta(\lambda+1) - 1} \right]^{\alpha\tau^\gamma}, t \geqslant 1. \tag{4.11}$$

Expressions by which the mean and variance of the unconditional distribution of interpurchase times can be evaluated from tables of the incomplete beta-function are also derived in the above reference.

The unconditional distribution of interpurchase times gives our best assessment of the probabilities that a certain consumer will make his next purchase in a particular time interval, provided that (1) we do not know that consumer's value of μ and (2) we do know the time τ of his last purchase and we know or have estimates of the remaining parameters of the model. Put another way, the unconditional distribution applies to cases where we sample at random from a group of families with known values of α, β, γ, λ, and τ: families picked from this population will all have the distribution of interpurchase times given by Eq. 4.11. On the other hand, if we could somehow know the value of μ for a particular family, we could make more accurate probability assessments by using the conditional distribution of interpurchase times, as given in Eq. 4.9. Since μ cannot be empirically estimated unless families with different values can be segregated *a priori*, however, we must base our analyses on the unconditional distribution.

POSTERIOR DISTRIBUTION OF μ GIVEN NO PURCHASES IN $(1,t)$.   Consider a situation where (1) a family has been randomly sampled from a population with known (or estimated) parameter values and (2) the family does not purchase the new product during the period of observation, for instance, $(1,t)$. Although it is true that at the beginning of the observation period we could not make any statement about this family's purchasing intensity (μ) that was not already implied by the prior distribution $f(\mu|\alpha,\beta,\gamma,\tau)$, the fact that no purchases are recorded in the subsequent period does allow us to make such statements after the fact. The sample information suggests that this family's μ-value probably was not as high as those of some of the families that were drawn from the same population and did purchase in the interval $(1,t)$. Quantification of this relation is important in making forecasts of purchase rates.

We shall denote prior distributions and parameters with single primes $(')$ and posterior quantities with double primes $('')$. The event that no purchase is recorded in the interval $(1,t)$ for a particular family is given by $N(1,t)$. Then we can show that the posterior distribution of purchase intensities for that family is gamma-1, the same as the prior, with parameters:

$$\beta'' = \frac{t^{\lambda+1} - 1}{\lambda + 1} + \beta', \tag{4.12}$$

and

$$\alpha'' = \alpha'.$$

The mean and variance of a gamma-1 distribution are proportional to $1/\beta$ and $1/\beta^2$, respectively. Therefore, we can see that the posterior density of μ shifts to the left and becomes more concentrated as the length of the period without a purchase increases. In the limit, the probability mass would all be concentrated at the origin. This would imply that a family which "never" purchased the product had an initial purchasing intensity of zero. Furthermore, the rate at which the density shifts toward the origin increases with the value of λ. This means that the initial value of purchasing intensity would have to be smaller in cases where the intensity tends to rise with time $(\lambda > 0)$ than in cases where the intensity declines from its initial value $(\lambda < 0)$, assuming that a family is observed not to have purchased in some interval $(1,t)$. This is in line with common sense.

Estimation of Parameters

Space does not allow the development of parameter estimation procedures for STEAM to be included in this chapter. Viable methods have been derived in our previous work. Computer programs for performing the necessary calculations have been written and are now being tested.

Several different methods for estimating the four parameters of the model have been explored. They include two variants of maximum likelihood as well as the minimum chi-square and minimum modified chi-square procedures. All of the proposed methods are consistent and enjoy the best asymptotically normal property commonly associated with "good" estimators, and all are based on the likelihood principle. While the maximum likelihood estimators have somewhat smaller variances than the chi-square estimators for all finite sample sizes, the choice between the alternative methods will hinge on questions of computational convenience.

None of the estimating methods result in closed-form expressions for the parameters. Rather, it is necessary to use numerical procedures for maximizing or minimizing the appropriate criterion function. However, we have been able to prove that at least one form of the likelihood function is concave with respect to three of the parameters and almost concave with respect to the fourth, so numerical maximization is not difficult. A nonlinear programming algorithm developed by Wilson [1964] has been adapted for the purpose. Since optimization of a well-behaved objective function with only four variables is a relatively easy nonlinear programming problem, the lack of closed-form estimating equations is not a serious drawback as far as the application of STEAM is concerned.

Some Possible Applications

One of the advantages of a model is that it permits the researcher to focus upon those aspects of the behavior under study which appear to be particularly sensitive or important. The model is an abstraction of the real behavior. As such, it can hopefully lay bare the interactions among factors which govern the process under study. By doing this, the model can suggest what kind of information should be collected in order to monitor the behavior process and indicate how the information should be processed, presented, and interpreted.

In the case of STEAM, the four parameters of the model provide the sense of direction indicated above. Where estimated from empirical data, the specifications of the model provide the intuitive backdrop against which interpretations can be made. To review briefly, the four parameters of the model provide information on two different aspects of the purchasing process. The first three of them (α, β, and γ) deal with the distribution of purchasing propensities among different members of the consumer population. The last one (λ) is related to the effect of "forgetting"—that is, a tendency for strong positive (or negative) dispositions toward the product to decay with the passage of time in the absence of reinforcement.

We shall illustrate the use of model-based statistics by considering the following situation. Suppose that a new product has been undergoing test-marketing activities for a period of several months, and that con-sumer responses have been monitored by means of a test panel throughout this period. At the end of the observation period, we might have the situation shown in Table 4.1 with respect to the number of families in various depth of repeat classes.

TABLE 4.1

Depth of Repeat Class	Number of Families	Cumulative Sample Size
0	300	600
1	200	300
2	75	100
3	25	25
	600	

That is, some 300 families did not purchase at all during the observation period, 200 families purchased once, and so on. The model's parameters are estimated separately for each depth of repeat class, with sample sizes indicated in the last column of the table. The sample sizes are cumulative because the parameters for the first depth of repeat class are estimated from data for all the families in the panel, the parameters for the second depth are based on all families who have purchased once or more, and so on.

How might the model's parameters provide information that might be useful for marketing management? Remember that the mean of the prior distribution of purchase rates is given by α/β, and the variance by α/β^2. Neglecting the effects of time since conversion for a moment, these two parameters determine the form of the prior distribution for all families in the depth of repeat cell under study. Suppose that the data produce estimates which imply the prior distributions given in Fig. 4.3. How might these be interpreted? First, we might not be surprised to see that the prior distribution for the 0th class is fairly flat, although without extreme positive values. Before having purchased the new product, the population might be fairly homogeneous with respect to evaluations of its utility, although no one may be very excited about it. The hypothetical distributions for the first and second depth of repeat classes are successively more peaked than the original one, and the means are somewhat further to the right. Two processes are involved here. First, the self-selection process discussed earlier might easily lead to a reduction in the variance of the distribution and to an increase in its mean. Second, the learning phenomenon can also lead to shifts in the mean. Finally,

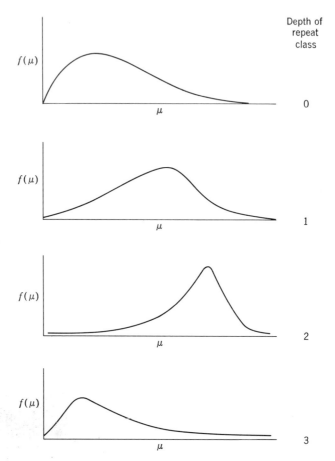

Figure 4.3. Hypothetical prior distributions for three depth of repeat classes.

we notice that the distribution for the third depth of repeat class has a much lower mean than the others, although it has a long positive tail. If this were observed in practice, we might conclude that experience with the product leads to disenchantment on the part of most consumers (the mean is reduced), even though some consumers respond very favorably (there is a large positive tail). We should be anxious to observe the parameters for the fourth depth of repeat class when new data become available, in order to determine whether this trend continues for groups having even more experience with the product.

In addition to the four basic parameters of the model, it might be interesting to consider the mean and variance of the distribution of waiting times to the next conversion for each depth of repeat class. These statistics, and particularly the mean, sum up the effects of all four parameters on the mean purchase rate for the aggregative process.

An additional summary statistic should be added to our inventory. Consider the families who entered the kth depth of repeat class at time t_j and are still there at the end of the observation period. The group of 300 families who have not purchased during the period of observation provide a good example of this: all of them "entered" the 0th class at time t_0 and are still there at the end of the observation period. Remember that the posterior distribution of purchase rates can be calculated for the families in any such group by means of Eq. 4.12, given estimates of the parameters for the group and the amount of time during which the families were in the class prior to the end of the observation period. Thus, we can form a statistic for the mean posterior purchase rate (which we shall denote by μ'') by taking a weighted average of the posterior means for all the t_j's in the kth depth of repeat class. That is:

$$\mu''_k = \frac{\Sigma\, n_{jo}\, \alpha \tau_j{}^\gamma / \beta''_j}{\underset{j}{\Sigma}\, n_{jo}},$$

where

$$\beta''_j = \frac{T_j{}^{\lambda+1} - 1}{\lambda + 1} + \beta$$

according to Eq. 4.12. The summary μ's provide information about the future purchasing behavior of families currently in the various depth of repeat classes. (It is possible that under some circumstances families with very small posterior values for $\alpha \tau_j{}^\gamma / \beta''_j$ could profitably be dropped from the panel, or at least be asked to report less frequently than other panel members.)

Finally, we shall often wish to consider a measure of the model's "goodness of fit." To this end, we can calculate the value of chi-square for the given depth of repeat class according to standard procedures. The resulting value of the statistic is distributed as χ^2 with $\Sigma_j T_j$ degrees of freedom under the null hypothesis that the data were generated by the model.

The reader will recognize that many of the interpretations suggested above are highly subjective in nature. The parameter estimates and summary statistics are subject to many errors of sampling and misspecification of the model. (Lower bounds on the former could be obtained by applying the Cramer-Rao conditions for BAN estimates.) Even if the estimates were exact, there would be additional problems of interpretation because of the complexity of the underlying processes being studied. These difficulties are common to all classes of models, however, so they should not discourage us.

The STEAM model is flexible enough to accommodate a wide range of behavior, yet its applications to consumer-panel data appears to be practical. The parameters are intrinsically interesting; by considering them and the related summary statistics, it is possible to gain fresh insights about the purchasing process. In view of certain assumptions about how the model's parameters are likely to evolve in the future, STEAM can be used to forecast future purchase rates. Expressions for the mean and variance of forecast statistics are developed in Massy [1966a, Section 3]; an approach for generalizing the forecasting procedure to include the amount as well as the rate of purchase is also provided.

STEAM is now being empirically tested in a variety of real problem situations. We believe that it will prove to be a useful marketing tool. We also hope that some of the ideas contained in the model will lead to further developments in the area of stochastic models of consumer behavior.

REFERENCES

F. J. Anscombe, "Estimating a Mixed-Exponential Response Law," *Journal of the American Statistical Association*, **56**, 493-502 (September, 1961).

R. E. Barlow, A. W. Marshall, and F. Proschan, "Properties of Probability Distributions with Monotone Hazard Rates," *Annals of Mathematical Statistics*, **34**, 375-389 (1963).

G. E. Bates, and J. Neyman, "Contributions to the Theory of Accident Proneness. I. An Optimistic Model of the Correlation Between Light and Severe Accidents. II. True or False Contagion," *University of California Publications in Statistics*, 215-76 (1952).

J. Carman, (Working paper on the Application of the Linear Learning Model to the Introduction of Crest Toothpaste.) University of California, Berkeley (spring 1965).

J. M. Coleman, *Models of Change and Response Uncertainty* (Englewood Cliffs, N.J.: Prentice-Hall, 1964).

A. S. C. Ehrenberg, "An Appraisal of Markov Brand-Switching Models," *Journal of Marketing Research*, **2**, 347-363 (November, 1965).

A. S. C. Ehrenberg, "The Pattern of Consumer Purchases." *Applied Statistics*, **8**, 26-41 (March, 1959).

L. A. Fourt, and J. W. Woodlock, "Early Prediction of Market Success for New Grocery Products," *Journal of Marketing*, **25**, 31-38 (October, 1960).

R. E. Frank, "Brand Choice as a Probability Process," *Journal of Business*, **35**, 43-56 (January, 1962).

J. D. Herniter, "Stochastic Market Models and the Analysis of Consumer Panel Data."

Presented at the Twenty-Seventh National Meeting of the Operations Research Society of America, Boston, Massachusetts (May 6-7, 1965).

R. A. Howard, "Stochastic Process Models of Consumer Behavior," *Journal of Advertising Research*, 3, 35-42 (September, 1963).

R. A. Howard, "Dynamic Inference," *Journal of the Operations Research Society of America* (fall 1965).

A. A. Kuehn, "Consumer Brand Choice—A Learning Process?" *Journal of Advertising Research*, 2, 10-17 (December, 1962).

B. Lipstein, "The Dynamics of Brand Loyalty and Brand Switching," *Better Measurements of Advertising Effectiveness: The Challenge of the 1960's*. Fifth Annual Conference of the Advertising Research Foundation, New York (1959).

B. Lipstein, "A Mathematical Model of Consumer Behavior," *Journal of Marketing Research*, 2, 259-265 (August, 1965).

W. F. Massy, "A Dynamic Model for Monitoring New Product Adoption." Working Paper No. 95, Graduate School of Business, Stanford University (March, 1966)(a).

W. F. Massy, "Order and Homogeneity of Family-Specific Brand Switching Processes," *Journal of Marketing Research*, 3, (February, 1966)(b).

W. F. Massy, "Estimation of Parameters for Linear Learning Models." Working Paper No. 78, Graduate School of Business, Stanford University (October, 1965).

W. F. Massy, and R. E. Frank, "A Theoretical Model for Purchase Timing." Working Paper No. 17, Graduate School of Business, Stanford University (April, 1964).

D. B. Montgomery, (Ph.D. Dissertation), Graduate School of Business, Stanford University (1966).

D. G. Morrison, "Stochastic Models for Time Series with Applications in Marketing." Technical Report No. 8, Joint Program in Operations Research, Stanford University (1965)(a).

D. G. Morrison, "New Models of Consumer Behavior: Aids in Setting and Evaluating Marketing Plans." Proceedings: Fall Conference of the American Marketing Association, Washington, D.C. (September 1-3, 1965)(b).

E. Parzen, *Stochastic Processes* (San Francisco: Holden-Day, 1962).

H. Raiffa, and R. Schlaifer, *Applied Statistical Decision Theory*. Boston: Division of Research, Graduate School of Business Administration, Harvard University (1961).

G. P. H. Styan, and H. Smith, Jr., "Markov Chains Applied to Marketing," *Journal of Marketing Research*, 1, 50-55 (February, 1964).

R. Wilson, "Subroutine SOLVER." Working Paper of the Western Management Science Institute, University of California, Los Angeles (June, 1964).

J. W. Woodlock, "A Model for New Product Decision." Presented to the Chicago Chapter of the American Marketing Association (November 22, 1963).

FIVE | *HENRY J. CLAYCAMP AND*
ARNOLD E. AMSTUTZ

Simulation Techniques in the
Analysis of Marketing Strategy

The complexity of the marketing process and the losses which frequently result from making poor decisions have caused marketing scholars and practitioners to constantly search for better ways to predict the outcomes of alternative strategies. The typical marketing manager has little direct contact and virtually no control over those whose actions ultimately determine the success or failure of his strategies. Changing competitive conditions and consumer circumstances; interactive effects of advertising, product quality, price and distribution; and time delays in response make it difficult to evaluate, much less predict, the effects of a specific program.

In spite of these difficulties, significant progress has been made recently in developing new methods of analyzing complex interactive systems and decision processes such as those found in marketing. In particular, the development of simulation techniques that utilize the amazing computational power and data handling capacity of large-scale computers has greatly increased researchers' ability to handle complex problems through the use of formal, symbolic models.

The purpose of this chapter is to assess the current use and future potential of computer simulation in marketing. In the first part of the chapter, we shall discuss the nature of the technique, some of the advantages and limitations associated with its use, and review selected studies which indicate how it has been applied to marketing problems. In the second part, we shall discuss the steps involved in developing and testing a complex simulation and describe the structure of a microanalytic model of buyer behavior that was designed to aid management in the generation and evaluation of alternative strategies.

CHARACTERISTICS AND APPLICATIONS
OF COMPUTER SIMULATION

Although the term "simulation" has been used to describe many kinds of applications of abstract models to real situations, most operations researchers limit the meaning to:

1. The use of models which represent the essential elements of a real system or operation.

2. The use of observations of the model's output or behavior under different experimental conditions to test hypotheses or make predictions about the real phenomenon.[1] In computer simulation, the model consists of mathematical and logical statements and the computer is used to calculate specific outcomes when different data inputs, parameter values, or structural relations are specified.

Advantages

The approach given above stands in sharp contrast to the classical use of symbolic models where general analytical solutions are used to deduce a model's properties. Since analytical solutions are not required in performing simulations, simple models are not essential for reasons of tractability. If necessary, hundreds of mathematical and logical statements and thousands of variables can be used to build a realistic model of a complex system. Freedom from the "solution constraint" allows the researcher to let his judgment about the importance of a variable be the primary determinant of whether it should be included in the model. It has also stimulated the development of new kinds of models that can be used in a wide variety of problem situations. Some of these models will be described later in this chapter.

Morgenthaler [10] points out that simulation can be used to overcome other difficulties encountered in applying the scientific method of investigation. Once a simulation model has been found to be a reasonable representation of the phenomenon under study, observations of the behavior of the model can be used to derive and test new theories and hypotheses. This use of a model is particularly important when it is difficult or impossible to induce experimental changes and observe responses in the real environment. The idea of "artificial experimentation" with a model to deduce the effects of possible changes in real-world structure

[1] For example, see [5] and [10].

is not unique to simulation. Indeed, these deductions are the ultimate goals of most model-building efforts. The advantage of simulation is that it allows these experiments to be conducted in a more complex, and usually more realistic, "artificial environment" than would be possible using purely analytical methods.

However, it should be pointed out that the ability to handle large-scale models through simulation does not imply that complexity is desirable for its own sake. The principle of parsimony has not been repealed by the advent of the computer. In many cases, the power of the simulation method can best be exploited by creating complex systems made up of relatively simple components. Where this is possible, we can combine the advantages of parsimonious representation of microstructures with the ability to handle highly complex macrostructures. The term "microanalytic simulation" is used to describe this approach to model building.[2]

The characteristics pointed out above make simulation a valuable marketing tool. There is little difference between using a simulation as an experimental device for evaluating theoretical models and using it to derive the implications of alternative marketing strategies. Thus, artificial experimentation through simulation can be used to produce direct inputs to management decision making.

More specifically, the major advantages of using simulation in marketing can be summed up as follows.

1. The simulation process can be used to explore the implications of management's perceptions about the external environment. Executives, salesmen, agency personnel, researchers, and other members of the firm's marketing team can pool their intuitive resources and readily available market data in order to come up with a series of statements about the behavior of consumers, middlemen, and competitors, and the effect of specific marketing actions. Researchers can translate these statements into mathematical and logical analogues, and put them together in the form of a simulation. If the process is done well, the output of the simulation has some claim representing the implications of the perceptual inputs that went into the model. Aberrant results may be traced to errors in the interpretation of manager's statements or, more significantly, to errors or inconsistencies in the original formulations themselves.

2. Simulations can be used to integrate and systematize large quantities of information obtained from past marketing research studies and

---

[2] For an excellent example of this approach, see [11].

secondary sources. A model helps to place formerly isolated pieces of data in perspective and often increases the net amount of information that can be obtained from them.

3. A simulation model which has been accepted as a reasonable representation of the real world can be used to guide future research activities. With confidence in the overall structure of the simulation, the researcher can perform sensitivity analyses with respect to specific parameters or component characteristics. In addition to gaining general knowledge about the system's performance characteristics, these tests help to indicate what kinds of additional empirical or theoretical research will have the greatest impact upon the overall accuracy of the model. Research can then be concentrated in areas where potential results are known to be important.

4. Once a market simulation model has been validated to the satisfaction of both research and management personnel, the method of artificial experimentation can be used to derive forecasts of sales levels, market penetration rates, profits, or other criterion variables conditional upon alternative specifications of the elements of the firm's marketing mix. The model can act as a kind of synthetic test market and can be used to screen alternative strategies without incurring the risk or expense of experimentation in the real world. While some experimentation in the real world may always be desirable to settle crucial policy questions and maintain a continuous check on the validity of the simulation, the ability to screen a larger number of test candidates through artificial experimentation is likely to produce both substantial savings and better candidates for experimentation in the real environment.

The payoffs outlined in paragraph one through four above can be viewed as forming a kind of pyramid. We may start with a purely intuitive model, supplement it with data from existing sources, and use the model to generate additional research leads that can, in turn, be fed back to improve the accuracy of the simulation. The apex of the pyramid is attained when both intuitive confidence in the model and formal validity checks on its performance are sufficiently positive to warrant its use as a tool for helping to solve "on-line" marketing decision problems.

Another possible application of the simulation model is in the area of managerial education. Military officers have participated in war games for many years. Modern war games simulate the outcomes of strategic and tactical decisions by means of highly complex computer models. In the business game, executives or students who are responsible for managing companies in a simulated environment have the opportunity to obtain highly realistic experience in decision making and analysis. If the simulation model represents the marketing environment of a particular company or industry with reasonable accuracy—that is, if it meets the validation criteria implied in connection with three and four above— the training experience can be specialized to the point where executives from the firm or industry can take away specific knowledge about market characteristics that will be immediately useful in solving day-to-day problems.

Finally, the effort required to build and test a simulation model usually yields an important by-product in the form of the learning experience it affords managers and researchers involved in the study. A great deal of interaction is required between managers who have the intuitive grasp of the marketing process and researchers who have the technical skill to create the simulation. This is particularly true if the model is designed to be used as a direct aid to decision making. The manager is forced to be specific about his assumptions as to how the market operates—more specific than he is used to being in his normal day-to-day activities. Moreover, he is asked to contribute to the resolution of "ify" questions about how various outputs of the model will be used in decision making.

On the other side, the researcher must always be alert to questions of managerial relevance and is often required to compromise in matters of technical formulation and elegance. Although the task of assimilating unfamiliar concepts and communicating in an unfamiliar vernacular can lead to friction between manager and researcher, experience has shown that open-minded and intelligent attempts to resolve these problems will pay off. The effort devoted to specifying assumptions in precise terms (the computer is totally unforgiving of ambiguity), to carefully considering and integrating all available data, and to identifying important variables and interactions to be included in the model, invariably leads to new insights about the firm's marketing environment and policies even before simulation runs are performed.

Problems

Although there are many advantages and payoffs associated with the use of a complex simulation, there are also important problems and limitations.

First of all, computer simulation is inherently expensive. Skilled model builders, computer specialist, and substantial amounts of computer time are required to develop, test, and maintain a large-scale system. Even relatively simple models can involve major expenditures if special studies are required to generate data for parameter estimation and model validation. While the cost of a project is obviously related to its scope, some idea of the level of expenditure often involved is indicated by a recent survey of simulations of social, political and economic systems. Of 41 projects for which financial information was available, 20 were reported to have cost between $10,000 and $100,000, and 17 over $100,000. Some projects involved expenditures of as much as $2,500,000 [1].

The creation and use of complex simulation systems also involves significant technical problems. Foremost among these is the question of system design for efficient computation. Although almost anyone with elementary knowledge of computer programming can translate individual elements of a model into computer language, considerable skill is required to design a large-scale simulation. The basic problems involve program overlay and file manipulation. Simulation programs of the kind emphasized in this chapter are frequently too large to fit into the core memory of a computer. Under these conditions, it is necessary to divide the program into segments and bring each segment into core as needed to process information. Similarly, most simulations must bring large quantities of data into core, process it, and return it to external files. While many computers can perform calculations at the rate of a million or more per second, the operations required to transfer programs and data between internal and external memory take place at a much slower rate. Hence, it is essential to minimize such activity. Seemingly trivial differences in the organization of data files and the order in which computations are performed can make the difference between an efficient simulation system and one that is economically impractical to operate.

Care must also be taken in the design of systems that will permit experimentation with different data inputs and parameter values. In some cases, special input editor routines that identify different classes of control information and check for syntactical and logical inconsistencies may be required to reduce the effort involved in introducing these changes and lessen the chances of executing a costly simulation run containing input errors.

Output systems must also be designed carefully. The following general considerations are relevant. First, output from sectors of the model, and sometimes even individual functions, must be available for performance testing. Secondly, procedures must be developed for translating results obtained from simulation runs into measures that can be validated against real-world data and used by management in decision making. Finally, efficient assimilation of information requires adequately labeled and conveniently formatted output—the latter often involves consideration of graphical as well as numerical modes of display. The development of effective output procedures is usually a nontrivial part of the design of the total simulation system.

Formidable problems are also present in the testing phase. Most simulation models, even those of moderate size, contain so many parameters that it is impossible to do sensitivity analyses on all possible combinations of values. Thus, the researcher must use judgment or a formal technique (for instance, random sampling) to select specific values to be included in sensitivity tests—and hope that feasible, but untested, values will not cause the model to behave in an erratic fashion.

Ascertaining the validity of a simulation model is also a complicated task. The researcher must decide which aspects of the real system are to be used as evaluative criteria and how close the model output must be before it can be said to be valid. Although the purpose the model was designed to serve provides guidelines for selecting variables to be compared, there is no simple way to determine when correspondence between model output and real-world data warrants the conclusion that the model is a valid representation of the underlying process.

Finally, it is important to reemphasize the limitations inherent in the use of any model. Regardless of complexity and amount of detail, a model is by definition an abstract of reality. If important variables are omitted, and inaccurate assumptions and data are used, a model cannot be expected to produce highly accurate output. This fact seems to be easily forgotten, especially when the output is nicely formatted and consists of precise numbers calculated by a computer.

Marketing Applications

The diagram of a marketing system shown in Fig. 5.1 provides us with a convenient way to categorize applications of computer simulation in marketing. Each block in the diagram represents a population of individual behavioral units whose decisions control the flow of product, information, and money throughout the system. Although it is possible to simulate marketing systems using detailed models of the decision processes of individual consumers, middlemen, and manufacturers, few attempts to do so have been made. Most marketing simulations have focused on specific kinds of decisions or variables and have treated other aspects of the total system at a high level of aggregation or have ignored them entirely.

For example, simulation has been applied to the study of physical distribution systems by Shycon and Maffie [12] and Kuehn and Hamburger

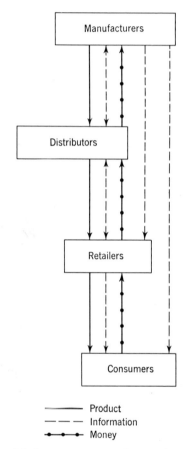

Figure 5.1.   A simplified representation of a consumer marketing system.

[9]. In the Shycon and Maffie study, a model describing the location of factories and customers and the transportation costs from feasible warehouse locations was created. Since the model also included functions describing inventory carrying costs and warehouse operation costs at various volume levels, it could be used to calculate the total distribution cost of servicing the firm's customers with a specific warehouse configuration. By specifying different warehouse locations, the costs of alternative distribution strategies could be evaluated.

The Kuehn and Hamburger study was also designed to evaluate the economic implications of alternative warehouse locations. However, this simulation does more than evaluate the cost of a given system. It also selects the locations to be tried in the model from a feasible set which has been specified by the user. Although the heuristics employed to select locations do not guarantee that the optimal set will be found, they do insure that each location added and retained in the solution results in lowered costs for the total system. Both of these simulations ignore marketing factors other than physical distribution and treat the patterns of demand by consumers as given.

One important aspect of information flow—exposure of consumers to formal advertising media—has been simulated by the Simulmatics Corporation [13]. The Media-Mix model was developed to estimate the reach and pattern of exposures of alternative media schedules. Census statistics for specific market areas were used to create artificial populations of consumers with representative distributions of important demographic variables. Data from audience and readership studies were used to develop equations that would yield the probability of a particular type of consumer being exposed to a given media vehicle at a particular point in time. The model gives each of the 2944 simulated consumers an opportunity to be exposed to each insertion in a media schedule that has been specified by the user. The stochastic outcomes are recorded and tabulated in reports that show, by consumer type, the reach and frequency of exposure resulting from the insertion schedule. As the content and format of advertisements are not considered, the model does not provide information about the impact of the messages on consumer orientations.

Simulation has also been used to study decision processes of marketing executives and consumers. For example, Howard and Morgenroth simulated the way in which one executive in a large manufacturing firm set prices on the firm's products [7]. After extensive interviewing of the executive, a model was created that described the way in which information from several sources was used to determine a specific price. Validation tests were conducted by selecting, at random, 31 pricing decisions made by the original executive and 130 decisions made by executives who were not studied. In each of the 161 cases, the model predicted the price accurately.

Similar studies have been made of retail ordering and pricing decisions. March, Cyert, and Moore created models of the decision processes employed by executives in one department of a large department store [6]. The performance of the model in predicting markups, markdowns, and sale prices was particularly impressive—188 of 197 markups, 140 of 159 markdowns, and 56 of 58 sales prices were predicted to the penny.

Simulations like the above are of immense value in understanding and improving the way in which specific decisions are made. Moreover, these simulations have indicated that it may be possible to let the computer make many of the repetitive decisions that take large amounts of executive time.

Although it is known that at least one company had a detailed simulation model of consumer decision processes and buyer behavior, there are few published studies in this area. As far as we know, the model of doctor-prescribing behavior (discussed later in this chapter) is the most detailed simulation of this nature to be constructed to date.

A recent article by Kotler demonstrates the use of simulation in the study of interactions between major elements of the marketing system [8]. Models describing market and competitive responses were created and used to analyze the results of new-product introduction strategies for two hypothetical companies. Thirteen different strategies were postulated for each of the duopolists. Tests were run on each of the 78 strategy combinations and comparisons were made of profits and market share over a five year period. Kotler used these results to draw generalizations about the market position, rate of return, and amount of risk associated with different classes of strategies. While the model is generalized (that is, it does not represent identifiable companies and products), it is easy to see how similar models of a specific nature can be developed.

The Balderston and Hoggatt simulation of the lumber industry is one of the few attempts to use microanalytic simulation to study interactions between manufacturers, wholesalers, and retailers [4]. While the primary purpose of the project was to study market structure and the way it is affected by different message costs and various methods of determining the parties to a transaction, the authors indicate that, with relatively minor modifications, the model could be adapted to permit evaluation of alternative marketing strategies. Experiments performed on the model made it possible to draw generalizations about the dynamics of market segmentation and the effect of the experimental variables on profitability and concentration at each of the levels of distribution. In addition to being an excellent example of microanalytic simulation, the documentation provided in *Simulation of Market Processes* makes this book a must for anyone interested in the technique.

The Total Market Environment Simulation (TOMES) is, we believe, one of the most detailed simulations of a total marketing system now in operation.[3] This simulation (currently being used as a marketing game) contains artificial populations of consumers, retailers, distributors, and salesmen. In the consumer model, one thousand individual decision-

---

[3] The Total Market Environment Simulation was developed by A. E. Amstutz, H. J. Claycamp, C. R. Sprague, and J. D. C. Little. It is currently being used in marketing courses at M.I.T. and Stanford University. For a more detailed discussion of the use of the model, see [3].

making units are simulated in each of nine census regions of the United States. Each consumer is described by socioeconomic characteristics, by probabilities of being exposed to specific media, by awarenesses of brand names, and by attitudes toward retailers, product characteristics, appeals, and specific brands of product. Awarenesses and attitudes about brands of products are formed by selectively perceiving the communication content of advertisements in print media, television, point of sale displays, and word-of-mouth messages generated by other simulated consumers. Individual consumers make explicit decisions to shop, purchase, and generate word-of-mouth messages as a result of interactions between socioeconomic variables and perceived brand images of specific products.

Individual retailers and wholesalers form profit expectations on the basis of communications received from manufacturers and observed consumer demand. If they decide to stock a specific brand they forecast their own sales, determine order quantities, and set their own prices.

Participants managing competing companies in this simulated environment can employ amazingly realistic marketing strategies. It is possible to vary product characteristics of a specific brand, place individual advertisements in specific regional or national media, employ individual salesmen and allocate their efforts to specific kinds of retailers, use direct or indirect distribution, and so on.

Realistic research can also be done to provide information for decision making and evaluation of strategies. For example, simulated commercial services provide audits of retail sales and inventories and readership studies of specific advertisements. In addition, consumer research can be done by purchasing surveys of random samples of individual consumers in any of the nine regions.

While this simulation system was designed to teach marketing planning and decision making, it can be used as a research environment for evaluating alternative strategies and developing new analytical techniques. The system also serves to illustrate the kind of richness that can be embodied in a microanalytic simulation and the variety of uses that this type of model can serve.

DEVELOPING AND TESTING COMPLEX SIMULATION SYSTEMS: AN EXAMPLE

The remainder of this chapter is devoted to a discussion of the process of developing and testing complex simulation systems.[4] The procedure

---

[4] The work described in this chapter was done in part at the Computation Center of the Massachusetts Institute of Technology and Project MAC.

outlined here has been followed in developing models of markets for food products, appliances, services, securities, and electronic subsystems, in addition to the prescription-drug market example discussed in this chapter.[5]

General Steps in the Process

Microanalytic simulations designed for marketing management use focus on the processes through which management attempts to influence behavior in the external environment. The steps followed in creating, testing, and implementing a market-oriented behavioral simulation may be summarized as follows.

1. A conceptual framework encompassing relevant attributes of the problem environment is delineated.
2. Elements of the environment considered important by management are established as the focus of a systematic study of market activity.
3. A theoretical structure encompassing relevant elements and processes is defined.
4. Relationships between elements and processes are expressed in quantitative and measurable terms.
5. Observed or assumed relationships are summarized in systems of equations compatible with a computer simulation structure.
6. Individual functions, system subsegments, and the total simulation are related to data obtained from the "real-world" environment.
7. Criteria of validation and performance measurement are established and model precision and accuracy are determined.

Step 1 in this process is to develop a broad description of important factors in the marketing environment. This qualitative description serves as the basis for a nonmathematical but orderly structure that can be used to define key elements and processes.

Step 2 involves the design of gross macro flow models encompassing previously defined elements and processes. These preliminary descriptions of market activity define major interaction patterns and, thus, serve as cornerstones of models providing more complete and detailed descriptions of actions within relevant subsectors of the marketing system.

Steps 3 to 5 encompass quantification of relevant behavior and development of detailed sector models. The models produced at this stage

---

[5] A discussion of system elements common to these various applications is also given in [2].

must provide sufficient scope and refinement so that a representation of the total relevant environment may be synthesized in a single computerized simulation.

Steps 6 and 7 in this process involve practical implementation. The performance of the simulation must be validated against data obtained from the actual environment in which management is operating.

In the final analysis, the objective of simulation development is to produce a usable model—a model on which operations can be performed in lieu of operation in the actual physical environment.

The Problem Environment

The system discussed in this chapter was designed to provide the management of an international drug company with a new aid in the analysis, evaluation, and planning of marketing activities.[6] The specific objective of the project was the design of a complete simulation of the prescription-drug market that would enable management to investigate in a synthetic environment the implications of alternative strategies and policies without making the commitment of resources required for comparable investigation in the real world.

In developing specifications for the system, management directed that it should facilitate: (1) evaluation of promotional (media) effectiveness; (2) evaluation of salesmen (detail men) effectiveness; (3) testing of alternative policies and strategies for marketing particular products to a given market segment; (4) evaluation of the probable success of new products at an early stage of market development; (5) assessment of the validity of management's understanding of the dynamics of the prescription-drug marketing system.

While the constraints of this chapter do not permit a complete exposition of the methodology or results of this activity, highlights of the development procedure and system performance are discussed in the following pages.

System Development in Detail

In developing a simulation of competitive market behavior, the firm and its competitors are viewed as input generators. The external-market simulation is then designed to duplicate the response characteristics of

6 Work on this simulation was started by us in 1963. Some aspects of the total system are still in development.

comparable real-world markets to the inputs generated by the competing firms.

BOUNDARY DEFINITIONS. System development activity normally begins with a definition of the boundary conditions that limit the scope of the system to be developed. In most instances, this preliminary specification is relatively crude. Management generally attempts to describe a limited number of sectors. The description may be of the form illustrated in Fig. 5.2. This figure shows management's preliminary conception of the prescription-drug market environment. Lines connecting various sectors of the illustration indicate management interest in interactions between these market elements.

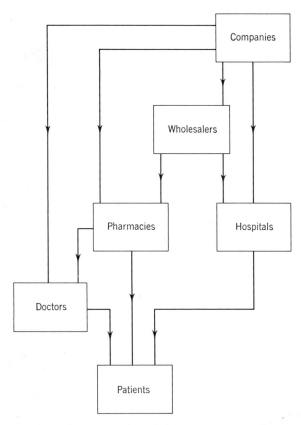

Figure 5.2. Boundary definitions—an example.

At the outset, management must also specify the objectives that they hope to achieve through use of the system once it has been developed, validated, and implemented. Objectives of the type defined above frequently determine whether a particular aspect of the environment will be included or excluded. Proposed applications also determine the level of detail and accuracy that management requires of the operating system.

Once the desired scope and objectives have been specified, macro descriptions of behavior within the environment to be simulated can be undertaken.

MACRO SPECIFICATION DEVELOPMENT. Macro specification is designed to achieve two interrelated objectives. First, it initiates the process of quantitative model formulation. Second, it provides an opportunity for managers and researchers to establish the conceptual framework and preliminary definitions of key variables.

During the macro specification phase, major emphasis is placed on stating that which management knows, assumes, and hopes. Underlying assumptions about the nature of the environment are given close scrutiny. Boundary conditions established in preliminary discussions are refined to the point where the scope and detail of future analysis and evaluation may be established. Thus, macro specifications formalize the preliminary model structure and establish the frame of reference for all subsequent model development.

Figure 5.3 illustrates this step in the process of system specification. Concepts illustrated in Fig. 5.2 have been expanded through recognition of additional sectors and more complete definition of interactions between sectors. Flows of information, orders, prescriptions, and product have been identified.

Beginning with the company in the upper left-hand corner of the flow chart, product flow is followed through wholesalers, chain outlets, pharmacies, and hospitals. Parallel order flows are noted from wholesaler, hospital, and pharmacy levels. Distribution-facilitating information generated by the company is indicated as an important input to salesmen, wholesalers, pharmacies, and doctors. Information inputs to the company include observer reports, salesman reports, panel research, and direct mail research.

Salesmen are represented as receiving information from the company and transmitting it to wholesalers, pharmacies, hospitals, and doctors.

Wholesalers are perceived as receiving information directly from the company and through its salesmen, transmitting orders to the company, and receiving products from it. The small oval to the left of the whole-

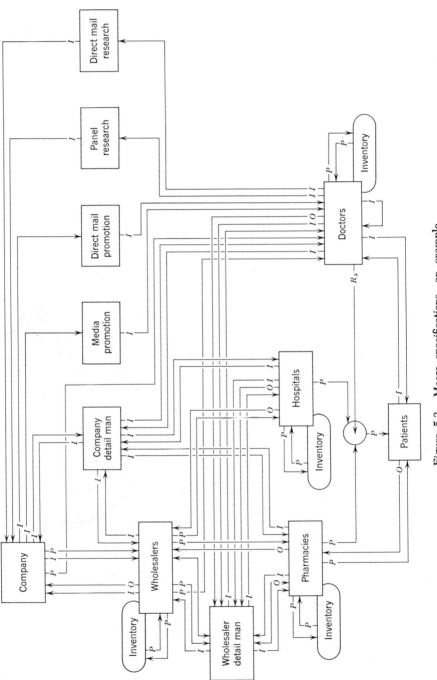

Figure 5.3. Macro specifications—an example.

saler sector indicates product inventory at the wholesaler level. Inputs to the wholesaler are indicated as originating in the hospital, pharmacy, and salesman sectors. Wholesaler salesmen are represented as order takers.

Pharmacies receive information from the company through its salesmen and some wholesaler salesmen. The possibility of both direct and through-salesman order procedures is noted. Inventory maintenance is indicated by the oval to the left of the pharmacy sector.

At the level of detail represented in the Fig. 5.3 flow chart, the hospital is analogous to a pharmacy.

The doctor is described as receiving information from the company salesmen, media, and direct mail promotion. An additional source of information is represented by the information line leaving the lower right-hand corner of the doctor rectangle and returning to that same sector. This line represents doctor interaction and the generation of "word-of-mouth" communication. The company receives information inputs about the doctor sector through observer reports, panel, and direct-mail research.

The patient is shown as interacting with the doctor, receiving prescriptions under control of the doctor, and, under certain circumstances, initiating refill procedures.

Although competitors are not illustrated in this flow chart, the actions of relevant companies are considered in detail in the actual simulation.

The process of macro specification is frequently iterative. Initial specifications provide the basis for preliminary definitions which are then modified in the light of additional conceptual development, market studies, and data constraints. For example, once preliminary formulations for the drug market simulation had been developed, substantial time was spent in discussing these formulations with members of management as well as practicing physicians. These interactions, additional analysis, and empirical research led to refinement of the initial structures.

DATA REQUIREMENTS. Macro specifications refine boundary conditions to the point where specific data requirements may be established. Figure 5.4 summarizes representative data requirements associated with the drug-market simulation. The two sections of this figure distinguish between data required for model structuring and initialization and that used as input during operating runs.

Data sources included monthly audits of drugstore invoices, weekly audits of prescriptions written, audits of the distribution and content of journal advertising, quarterly reports from panels of doctors who recorded

Figure 5.4
EXAMPLES OF DATA REQUIREMENTS FOR INITIALIZATION AND
INPUT—DRUG SIMULATION

I.   Specification and Initialization
   A.   Identification of indications
      1.   Name
      2.   Code number associated with name
      3.   Prevalence of indication
      4.   Prioritization of indications
      5.   Duration of indications
   B.   Identification of drugs
      1.   Name
      2.   Code number associated with name
      3.   Classification code
      4.   Manufacturer code
   C.   Initialization information for drugs
      1.   Drug code number
      2.   Uses of specific drugs for specific indications
      3.   Existing promoted brand image
   D.   Identification of distribution channels
      1.   Major wholesales
      2.   Major drug outlets
      3.   Major hospitals
   E.   Identification of company salesman
      1.   Territory code
      2.   Average number of calls per day to doctors, hospitals, and
           pharmacies
   F.   Identification of competitive companies
      1.   Company name
      2.   Manufacture code
      3.   Number of salesmen
      4.   Average number of calls per day to doctors, hospitals, and
           pharmacies
   G.   Indication—action—appeals matrix
      1.   By indication
      2.   By specialty
   H.   Number of doctors by type
      1.   Drug usage record
      2.   Media availabilities
      3.   Proportion of indications treated
II. Input
   A.   Variance in incidence of indication
      1.   By indication
      2.   By time period

B. Media advertising—specified for each advertisement
1. Date of release
2. Media code
3. Drug promoted
4. Ad format
5. Ad content

C. Direct mail specification
1. Date of mailing
2. Region mailed
3. Proportion of each specialty mailed
4. Content

D. Company salesman detail
1. Date of release
2. Drug promoted
3. Priority
4. Content of detail

E. Company sample handling
1. Drug code
2. Sample size
3. Number of samples
4. Proportion of specialty covered
5. Territories sampled
6. Date of sampling

F. Convention presentations
1. Date
2. Physician attendance
3. Product presented
4. Content of presentations

G. Symposia
1. Handled as conventions

H. Public relations releases
1. Handled as advertising

---

individual patient treatment, direct-mail promotions, and salesman details (sales messages for specific drugs). Specialized research studies were also employed to determine doctor knowledge, experience, attitudes, and treatment procedures.[7]

[7] Generation of the data required for a simulation of this magnitude is in many cases a monumental task. However, the pharmaceutical industry is unusually rich in commercial data services, and the company sponsoring this simulation has an especially effective market research department. Thus, much of the data required for this simulation was already in existence and only needed to be integrated into the model.

MICRO SPECIFICATION DEVELOPMENT. Once key decision and response elements have been identified, the focus of model development shifts to micro specification. The first activity in this phase is the creation of detailed models based on management hypotheses regarding the problem environment and verified, where possible, by reference to behavioral theory and existing data. Working within the structure supplied by the macro specifications, each decision point is described in terms of inputs to and outputs from that decision. Hypothesized relationships between inputs and observable behavior are formulated in terms of measurements that permit validation of the model against data from the real world. Each functional relationship is explicitly described in mathematical or logical expressions, and instructions for computer system design and programming are established.

Simulations of the type being considered here involve unusually complex computer programs. As a result, a major portion of micro specification normally focuses on the creation and testing of computer programs required for data packing, multilevel system control, and overlapped processing.

DESCRIPTION OF A DECISION PROCESS. The conceptual framework summarized in the macro specification hypothesizes a doctor's decision to prescribe particular drugs for a patient exhibiting specified indications (illnesses). Treatment may take place in the doctor's office, a hospital, or the patient's home. In any case, the fundamental problem facing the physician is selection of the appropriate therapy on the basis of his present knowledge, attitudes, and experience.

Basic characteristics of the simulated drug-selection procedure are summarized in Fig. 5.5. This flow chart begins with the initialization of a doctor decision matrix, DRDECM. All elements of this matrix are initialized at zero. Thus, in the beginning of the process, the doctor is assumed to have no predisposition other than that reflected in his memory of associations and experience.

The indication(s) exhibited by the patient are noted by the doctor who recalls one or more drugs which might be used in treatment. This process is simulated by placing a 1 in the drug-decision matrix position representing each drug that has been associated with treatment of the exhibited indication(s). If, upon completion of this process, the matrix is zero, the association process has failed and the doctor adopts a more complex procedure.

The second procedure involves a systematic evaluation of the doctor's past experience with relevant drugs. In the simulation, this process is initiated by setting appropriate drug matrix positions to 1, indicating that

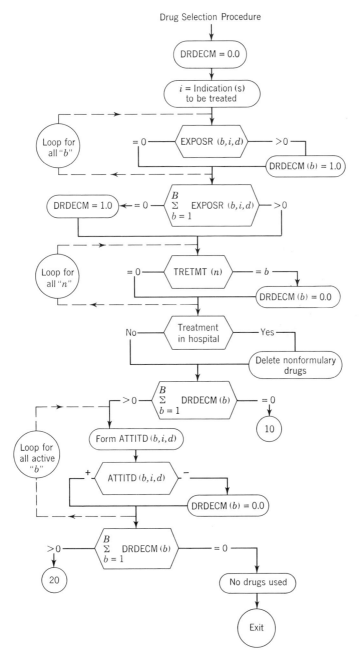

Figure 5.5.   Drug selection procedure.

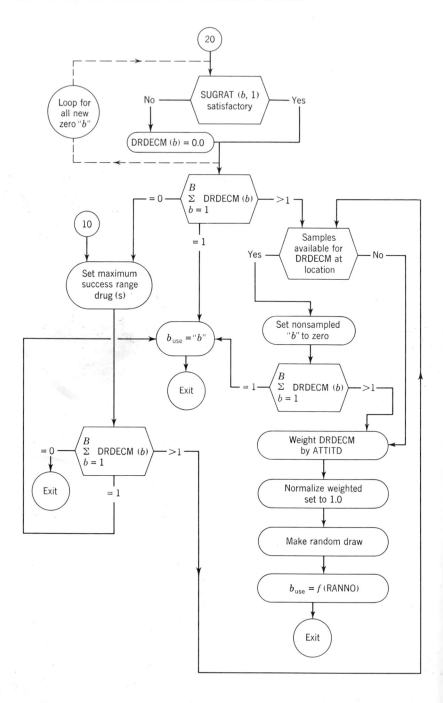

all drugs in the set are equally appropriate for consideration. The doctor deletes from consideration those drugs toward which he has a negative attitude as a result of previous experience. (Drugs previously used in treating each patient are recorded in the patient's treatment record to facilitate identification.) At this point in the decision process, if the doctor is in a hospital, all drugs not included in the hospital formulary are deleted from consideration.

If the matrix is zero following this process, reconsideration is effected using modified standards (as specified at location 10 in Fig. 5.5). If the matrix contains one or more nonzero entries, the doctor's attitude toward each remaining drug is established. All drugs for which the resulting attitude is negative are then removed from consideration. If there are no drugs toward which the doctor has a positive orientation, no drug is used. On the other hand, if one or more positive-attitude drugs remain, the process continues to the entry (specified as position 20) in Fig. 5.5.

At position 20, the doctor considers each remaining drug in terms of his past success in achieving desired therapy in similar circumstances. Historically unsatisfactory drugs are rejected with the corresponding entries in the drug matrix set to zero. If, following this procedure, all drugs are eliminated, drugs deleted because of unsatisfactory historical performance may be reconsidered with a less stringent performance requirement.

If several drugs remain to be considered after either the initial or revised test, the doctor makes a choice based on his attitude toward each drug remaining under consideration. If his attitude toward all drugs is equivalent, he will have an equal probability of choosing any one of the drugs. If, on the other hand, his attitude toward one drug is more favorable, his choice is biased in favor of that drug.

ADDITIONAL FUNCTION FORMULATION. In a similar manner, each decision and response function encompassed by macro specifications is investigated. In some instances, initial theoretical constructs are validated. In others, empirical evidence suggesting alternative constructs is obtained and the process of formulation is repeated for revised structures.

The final structure established by micro specifications includes processes through which the doctor is exposed and responds to media, conventions, salesmen, and word-of-mouth communication; evaluates indications exhibited by a patient; establishes desired actions, efficacy, and safety; and schedules the patient for a return visit.

EXPLICIT DECISION REPRESENTATION. Decision and response functions are formulated and tested as probabilities since data from the real-world environment are in the form of frequency distributions. Generation of explicit decision outputs for each cell within a simulated population requires conversion of the probabilistic statement into explicit yes/no decisions. A number drawn randomly from a rectangular distribution of range 0 to 1.0 is compared with the stated probability to determine each probabilistic event.

An Example of the Simulation Process

Behavior within each sector of the simulated environment must be described in terms of interrelated decision and response functions of the type illustrated above. In addition to describing functional relationships, the system designer must develop a representation of the dynamic processes that produce behavior observed within and between sectors of the market.

The operation of a microanalytic simulation can be most easily described by discussing the basic flow of information through the system and examining characteristics of the processes through which behavior is created. The basic structure of the prescription-drug market simulation is illustrated in Fig. 5.6.

SYSTEM INITIALIZATION. On entry, the system prints certain title and control information on output tapes (A-3) and the on-line printer. Tables developed by a preprocessor program are then read into core storage to establish information to be referenced during the simulation cycle and initialize operating parameters.

DOCTOR FILE INPUT. Each stimulated doctor is described by the content of a doctor file record. Doctor files are recorded on tape sequentially by geographic region. A single doctor file is held in core at a given point in time. After simulating the doctor's activity for a specified number of weeks, the file is updated to reflect his experiences, and written on tape. A new doctor is then read into core, and the procedure is repeated.

THE TIME LOOP. As indicated above, the system is structured so that time is moved past each doctor in turn. This organization of the system is necessitated by the large size of the doctor-file record which makes it impractical to move doctors in and out of core or to maintain more than one doctor in core at a given point in time.

During most simulation runs, the time period considered is one simulated year. The time step is one week and the time index (IT) proceeds sequentially from 1 through 52. Events occurring during a particular week are identified by a monotonic date code which, during processing of the simulation, is referenced to the time index (IT).

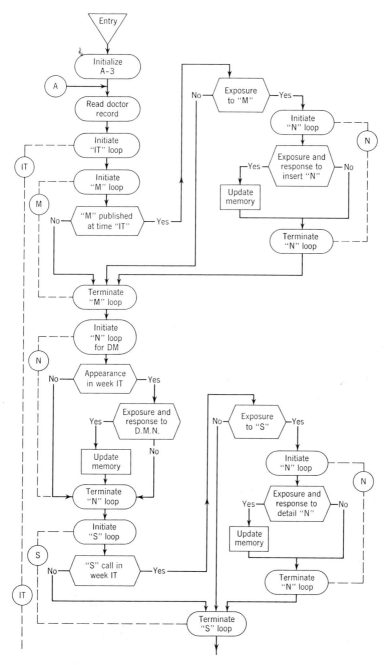

Figure 5.6. Macro flow chart of system operation.

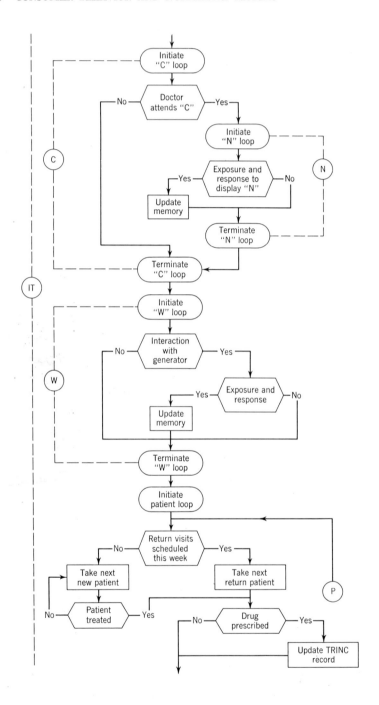

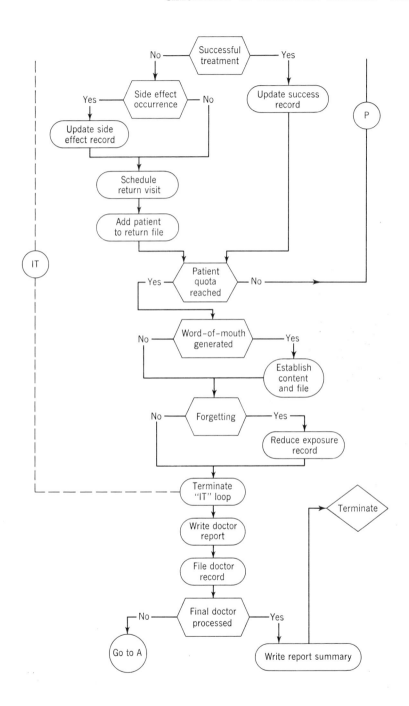

DOCTOR RESPONSE TO MEDIA PROMOTION. During each week in simulated time, the publication frequency of each relevant journal is tested to determine whether it is published during the week under consideration. If a particular journal appears, the probability of the doctor then under consideration being exposed to that journal is developed. If, on the basis of this probability, it is determined that the doctor will be exposed to the journal, each advertisement appearing in an advertisement schedule table for that journal is examined to determine whether or not the doctor will be exposed to and assimilate any new information. When an advertisement is assimilated, the doctor's response to the message is established and his memory updated to take account of information content. This process is continued for all media messages and doctors at each point in time.

DIRECT-MAIL RESPONSE. The handling of direct-mail response is structured in a manner analogous to media promotion. During each simulated week, a comparison is made to determine whether any direct-mail pieces appear. If a direct-mail piece is being sent during the week in question, exposure probabilities are developed to determine whether the particular doctor then being considered will be exposed to the specified mailing. If exposure occurs, assimilation probabilities are generated and if, on the basis of these probabilities, it is determined that the doctor will assimilate portions of the communication, his response is determined and his memory updated.

RESPONSE TO SALESMAN DETAIL. In developing a representation of the doctor's response to salesman communication, the probability of exposure is first determined on the basis of parameter values in the doctor-file record that establish the probability that the doctor will receive a call from a salesman representing any one of the relevant companies. If the doctor is exposed to a salesman from a particular company, the schedule of details (sales messages for a specific drug) presented by that salesman is examined to determine which details are being presented to doctors of the indicated specialty during the week under consideration. If a particular detail is presented and assimilation occurs, the doctor's memory is updated. As in the case of all other communication response loops, this procedure continues until all sales messages have been considered.

RESPONSE TO CONVENTION ACTIVITY. Exposure to presentations at a convention is based on a convention schedule that specifies the probability of a doctor of a particular specialty and residence attending a convention held at a particular time. In keeping with the previously established procedure, the convention schedule is examined once each simulated week to determine whether a convention is being held. If a convention is being held, the probability of the doctor then in core attending that convention is determined and, if the doctor is found to attend the convention, procedures similar to those outlined above are used to determine exposure to and assimilation of relevant information.

RESPONSE TO WORD-OF-MOUTH COMMUNICATION. Within the structure of the simulation, messages generated by doctors in a particular region are accumulated along with descriptors of the generating doctor in a table of word-of-mouth messages. Thus, when a particular doctor is in core, messages generated at various points in time by doctors preceding him are available in the world-of-mouth table. This table is referenced in a manner analogous to the schedule and content table discussed for other media. The probability of interaction between the doctor in core and the message-generating doctor who preceded him is established. If the doctor is exposed to the word-of-mouth communication, the probability of assimilation is developed in a manner analogous to other communication functions and the doctor's memory is updated to reflect the word-of-mouth interaction.

TREATMENT OF PATIENTS. The stimulated doctor is exposed to patients from an artificial patient population that is supplied as an input to the simulation. An average patient load parameter in each doctor-file record determines how many patients will be treated in a given week. In treating a patient, the simulated doctor determines what drug or drugs, if any, will be prescribed for the exhibited indication(s) of the patient.

Once treatment has been decided upon, the probability that it will achieve desired results is established on the basis of clinical data. If it is determined that the treatment undertaken will not prove effective within a specified period of time, the patient is maintained in a backlog of patients who will return to the doctor at some time in the future. If the outcome of treatment is successful, the patient is, for all practical purposes, dropped from the model. In either instance, the trial and outcome (including possible side effects) of a particular treatment is noted.

After the first simulated week, the doctor has two sources of patients: (1) patients in the population from which his original patient group was drawn; and (2) patients who require continuing treatment. During subsequent time periods, the doctor's first source of patients is the returning-patient file. After all patients previously treated and scheduled to return have been treated, the doctor considers new patients from the outside population.

GENERATION OF WORD-OF-MOUTH COMMUNICATION.   As the doctor considers various drugs in context of the treatment during the simulated week, a record of his attitude toward his experiences is maintained. Following completion of the treatment cycle for a particular simulated week, this record is examined to determine whether the doctor will generate word-of-mouth communication regarding some aspect of his recent treatment experience. If such word-of-mouth communication is generated, communication content is established, dated, and stored in the word-of-mouth communication file for later referencing by other doctors.

FORGETTING.   At certain prescribed time intervals, the doctor's memory is examined to determine whether forgetting would have occurred during the lapsed time period. The memory record for each drug is examined and if forgetting has occurred, the record is reduced.

TIME CYCLE COMBINATION.   The basic process described above is repeated for each week in the simulated year for each doctor in the artificial population. Once the final week ($IT = 52$) for a particular doctor is completed, an activity report is generated and the doctor-file record is updated to reflect his experiences during the simulated year. This record is then written on tape to serve as an input for simulation of future time periods.

Following completion of a given doctor record, the simulation returns to the point in the Fig. 5.6 flow chart labeled "A," reads another doctor record from the tape file, and repeats the process as described. After all doctors have been considered for the specified period of simulated time, a final summary report is written and the simulation terminates.

Testing

Once a simulation has been developed to the point where it can be used to produce artificial behavior, the emphasis shifts to testing. Although the ultimate test of any model is its usefulness, the stability, reliability, and validity of a simulation should be ascertained before it is used as an operational tool.

STABILITY TESTING.   Stability tests are concerned with the reasonableness of the model's performance when it is subjected to different, but feasible, parameter values and input data, and run for substantial periods of time. The major problems encountered in stability testing are selection of specific parameter values, definition of "reasonable" performance, and determination of an appropriate time period for the test.

RELIABILITY TESTING. Tests of reliability focus primarily on the question of reproducibility of results. The basic problem is one of determining stochastic variations of important outputs when different series of random numbers are used to determine specific outcomes within the system. Confidence intervals for important outputs can be established using various statistical techniques.

VALIDITY TESTING. Tests of validity are concerned with "truth." Although reliability may be assessed using standard statistical techniques, there are no objective measures of truth. Consequently, the researcher must turn to a subjective evaluation of the accuracy of the assumptions used to create the model and of the consistency of its performance with theory and empirical data. In the final analysis, a model is realistic if it duplicates the relevant characteristics of the real phenomenon. For example, Turing has suggested that a model may be called "realistic" if a person knowledgeable in the subject being modeled—that is, a person having experience with the relevant reality—cannot distinguish model output from output generated by the real system. Thus, once the validity of assumptions has been established, tests must be made of model output.

The procedure normally followed in testing the validity of a microanalytic simulation is to proceed sequentially through analyses of individual functions, individual cell behavior and total population behavior.

FUNCTION VALIDATION. Since the number of functions involved in a large-scale simulation usually precludes exhaustive testing, this activity is limited to investigation of the performance of functions which are known to be essential to system operation.

CELL LEVEL VALIDATION. The objective of validation at the cell level is to establish that the behavior of an individual within the simulated population cannot be differentiated from that of a similar member of the real world population. Figures 5.7 and 5.8 illustrate the kind of output which can be obtained from the drug simulation for purposes of cell validation. Figure 5.7 summarizes the characteristics of a single fictitious doctor at the time when he began a particular week of simulated activity. The doctor in question is a general practitioner between 45 and 60 years of age in private practice in the Midwest. He employs a nurse-receptionist and treats an average of 136 patients per week. Data following these

```
                       TURING TEST RE MULTIPLE DRUG USE --- MARCH 26, 1966
DOCTOR      1, OF SPECIALTY  1, S.M.A. 1 IN      REGION 2, PRACTICE TYPE 1, AGE CAT. 3 IS NOW BEGINNING

AVERAGE PATIENTS TREATED PER WEEK 136 SCREENING EMPLOYEE INDICATOR 1

CIRCULATION PROBABILITIES
 1.0000  0.5750  0.3050  0.9480  1.0000  0.9220  1.0000  0.5030  0.0440  0.9410  0.9510  0.9080  1.0000

MEDIA EXPOSURE PROBABILITES
  0.2280  0.1640  0.1280  0.2670  0.3620  0.2560  0.1510  0.1410  0.1220  0.2520  0.3080  0.1130  0.1850

COMPANY EXPOSURE PROBABILITIES
 0.2700 0.2000 0.1400 0.1000 0.       0.2000 0.1400 0.1600 0.0200 0.4800 0.5300 0.1500 0.1300 0.1800 0.450
 0.3900 0.3700 0.3100 0.1900 0.1600 0.1300 0.      0.1800 0.3300 0.3300 0.0800 0.4700 0.      0.1400 0.170
 OR WEIGHTING     1
```

Figure 5.7.

descriptors indicate the doctor's media habits expressed in terms of circulation and exposure probabilities for major journals encompassed by the simulation. Company exposure probabilities indicate this doctor's historical frequency of interaction with salesmen from companies included in the simulated environment.

```
 PATIENT      1 IS A GERIATRIC, SEEN  1 TIMES PREVIOUSLY AND GIVEN APPOINTMENT IN WEEK  5
 PATIENT EXHIBITS INDICATIONS URI      WITH  0 ACTIONS DESIRED ,       ,
                      CONDITION IMPROVING.
                 ANXREA WITH  2 ACTIONS DESIRED , ADEPRE, TNCGEN,
                      CONDITION UNCHANGED.
 PRESENT TREATMENT DRUGS NONSIM, TOFRAN,        . NO PRIOR TREATMENT.
 DRUG     1 EQUANL NOTED AS ASSOCIATED WITH INDICATION  47 ANXREA
 DRUG     2 LIBRUM NOTED AS ASSOCIATED WITH INDICATION  47 ANXREA
 DRUG     3 MILTWN NOTED AS ASSOCIATED WITH INDICATION  47 ANXREA
 DRUG     6 MARPLN NOTED AS ASSOCIATED WITH INDICATION  47 ANXREA
 DRUG     8 RITALN NOTED AS ASSOCIATED WITH INDICATION  47 ANXREA
 DRUG     9 TOFRAN NOTED AS ASSOCIATED WITH INDICATION  47 ANXREA
 DRUG     9 TOFRAN DELETED DUE TO PRIOR TREATMENT
 DRUG   1 EQUANL ATTITUDE FORMED =        3 FOR IND. 80 URI    AND   47 ANXREA
 DRUG   2 LIBRUM ATTITUDE FORMED =        2 FOR IND. 80 URI    AND   47 ANXREA
 DRUG   3 MILTWN ATTITUDE FORMED =        0 FOR IND. 80 URI    AND   47 ANXREA
 DRUG   6 MARPLN ATTITUDE FORMED =        2 FOR IND. 80 URI    AND   47 ANXREA
 DRUG   8 RITALN ATTITUDE FORMED =        0 FOR IND. 80 URI    AND   47 ANXREA
 DRUG   3 MILTWN DELETED DUE TO NEG. OR ZERO ATD.
 DRUG   8 RITALN DELETED DUE TO NEG. OR ZERO ATD.
```

```
 DETERMINING HIGHEST CRITERIA DRUG, IPATH = 1, ICASE = 1
 DRUG   1 EQUANL, CRITERIA VALUE =  3.000
 DRUG   2 LIBRUM, CRITERIA VALUE =  2.000
 DRUG   6 MARPLN, CRITERIA VALUE =  2.000
    1 UNSATISFIED ACTIONS  TNCGEN
 DRUG   2 LIBRUM ATTITUDE FORMED =        0 FOR UNSATISFIED ACTIONS
 DRUG   3 MILTWN ATTITUDE FORMED =        0 FOR UNSATISFIED ACTIONS
 DRUG   4 STELAZ ATTITUDE FORMED =        0 FOR UNSATISFIED ACTIONS
 DRUG   5 THORAZ ATTITUDE FORMED =        0 FOR UNSATISFIED ACTIONS
 DRUG   6 MARPLN ATTITUDE FORMED =        0 FOR UNSATISFIED ACTIONS
 DRUG   7 PARNAT ATTITUDE FORMED =        0 FOR UNSATISFIED ACTIONS
 DRUG   8 RITALN ATTITUDE FORMED =        0 FOR UNSATISFIED ACTIONS
 DRUG  10 NOLDAR ATTITUDE FORMED =        0 FOR UNSATISFIED ACTIONS
 DRUG  11 PLACOL ATTITUDE FORMED =        0 FOR UNSATISFIED ACTIONS
 NO DRUG FOR UNSATISFIED ACTIONS
 EVALUATION COMPLETED, TEMP SET    0  0     1  0     0  0 ID1      ID2 EQUANL ID3
 FATE, RETURN  0, SUCCESS 1  1  0,  S.E. 0 0 0
```

Figure 5.8.   Patient treatment.

Figure 5.8 illustrates a simulated doctor's treatment of a geriatric patient suffering from an upper respiratory infection. The output indicates that, on a prior contact with this patient, the doctor prescribed two drugs. On this visit the patient's condition is improving; however, the doctor is now concerned with an anxiety reaction and undue fatigue exhibited by the patient. Noting this condition, the doctor is seeking anti-depressant and general tonic actions. The Fig. 5.8 output provides a detailed account of the process through which the doctor elects to prescribe a new drug.

The Turing test of cell behavior was conducted by developing exhibits (for instance, those shown in Figs. 5.7 and 5.8) that describe patient treatment by actual and simulated doctors. These profiles were then examined by practicing physicians who assessed the "reasonableness" of the exhibited behavior. The results of tests involving many different kinds of therapy indicated the simulation produced highly realistic behavior at the cell level.

It is important to note that the physicians were not asked to evaluate the quality of the treatment given patients by the artificial doctors. They were to evaluate whether or not the simulated behavior was equivalent to behavior generated by similar doctors in comparable real-world circumstances. Since the simulation is designed to be an accurate description of the real-world environment, normative questions are irrelevant.

Once the legitimacy of simulated behavior of the type outlined in Figs. 5.7 and 5.8 has been established through Turing tests, the system may be used to produce behavior over time.

Figure 5.9 illustrates the cumulative prescription market shares generated by two general practitioners operating in the simulated environment during one year. These two doctors prescribed only one relevant drug during the first two weeks of simulated activity. However, as the year progressed, they tried six other drugs. The doctors' cumulative brand shares for the ten brands are shown at week 52. Output of the type illustrated in Fig. 5.9 is used primarily to test system stability.

POPULATION LEVEL VALIDATION. Meaningful tests of population behavior require aggregation of simulated cell behavior. In the doctor case, population behavior is validated by analyzing the proportion of prescriptions allocated to each brand (brand shares), and changes in knowledge, attitudes, and perceived brand images of important segments of the population.

For example, Fig. 5.10 illustrates the brand shares of ten frequently used drugs resulting from 100 simulated-doctors' treatment of several thousand patients. In conducting such tests, the population is initialized to duplicate the distribution of relevant parameters as they existed at a specified point in time in the real-world environment. In the case of the Fig. 5.10 run, the artificial population was initialized to correspond to conditions existing at the beginning of 1961.

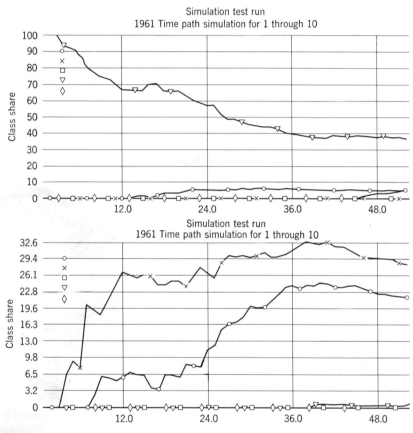

Figure 5.9.   Sample output—two doctors.

Inputs to the simulation during performance tests describe conditions existing in the real world during the relevant time period. In this case, inputs specified the content and media allocation for all journal, direct mail, salesman detail, and convention promotion generated by competitors operating in the relevant market area during 1961. Tests performed following this simulation run established that the rank order of brand shares at the end of 1961 in the real and simulated worlds were equivalent (Fig. 5.11) and the maximum error for any one brand was less than six percentage points.

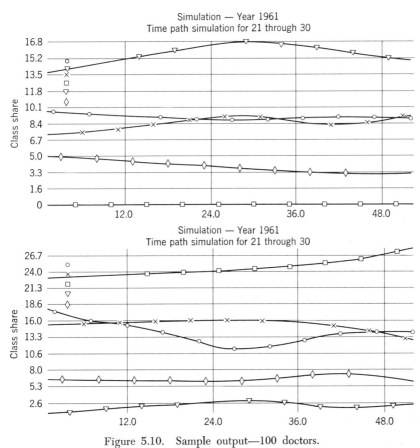

Figure 5.10.   Sample output—100 doctors.

It should be pointed out that this test is a duplication of history—not a prediction of the future. A great deal of real-world data was used in providing inputs for this test and in estimating important parameters. When the model is used for prediction of the future, subjective judgment

Figure 5.11

RANK ORDER BRAND SHARE COMPARISONS

Identification	Rank as Initialized	Year End Rank	
		Simulated	Actual
1–Y	4	2	2
1–0	5	6	6
1–X	6	5	5
1–+	8	8	8
1–□	10	10	10
2–□	1	1	1
2–0	2	3	3
2–X	3	4	4
2–+	7	7	7
2–Y	9	9	9

must be used to develop inputs, and assumptions must be made about the stability of important parameters.

MANAGEMENT USES OF MICROANALYTIC SIMULATION

With a system of the type described in this paper, management must assess system performance in terms of intended applications. If, in management's opinion, performance is sufficient to warrant use of the simulation as a representation of the real-world environment, applications of the type outlined below may be appropriate. However, if, in their opinion, the simulation fails to duplicate salient attributes of the real-world environment, further development leading to a more refined system must be undertaken or the use of the technique rejected.

TESTING IMPLICIT MODELS.   One of the first benefits to accrue from the development of a simulation system is the systematic testing of management conceptions of the environment in which they operate. In reviewing alternative formulations and evaluating functions, cell-model behavior, and total population performance, management must make explicit the implicit models that they use in decision making.

THE "WHAT IF?" QUESTION.   If management accepts simulation performance as indicative of real-world response under comparable conditions, the simulation becomes a test market without a memory in which management may examine with impunity the implications of alternative policies and strategies. Whether introducing new products or considering modification of a marketing program, management may apply alternative strategies in the simulated environment and evaluate the implications of these strategies under various assumed competitive conditions.

The effectiveness of such pretesting is dependent on management's ability to predict probable competitive responses to proposed actions, as well as the accuracy of the simulation system. Management may find it profitable to examine the impact of best- and worst-case competitive response patterns. In most instances, the best case assumes that competition will continue with programs developed prior to initiation of company actions, while the worst case assumes full competitor knowledge of the proposed company program and actions designed to thwart company efforts.

PERFORMANCE REFERENCES. The simulated environment also provides the reference points against which the progress of operations in the real world may be measured. Given a simulation pretest, management can determine, by monitoring appropriate variables, whether or not a program is progressing as planned. If conditions producing satisfactory performance in the simulated environment are encountered in the real world, it is assumed that final results will be comparable.

SUMMARY

In this chapter, we have attempted to discuss the general characteristics of computer simulation, and the process of creating, testing, and using a complex simulation system. In discussing marketing applications, we have emphasized complex models and microanalytic simulations since we believe that they best illustrate the differential advantages of the simulation technique.

Finally, the future of simulation in marketing appears to be particularly promising for at least two reasons. First, although systems such as the drug-market simulation tax the capacity of the largest commercially available computers, new computers with larger memories and even greater computational speed are being developed. And second, in spite of the expensive nature of computer simulation, increasing numbers of marketing scholars and executives are coming to agree with the philosophy voiced by a top executive of the firm sponsoring the drug simulation —"Even if there are significant errors in prediction, it is worth the expense because of the way it makes people think."

REFERENCES

1. Clark C. Abt et al., *Survey of the State of the Art: Social, Political, and Economic Models and Simulations* (Cambridge, Mass.: Abt Associates, November 1965), pp. 64-65.
2. Arnold E. Amstutz, "A Marketing Oriented Behavioral Theory of Interactions within Consumer Product Markets," unpublished Ph.D. Dissertation, MIT, June 1965.
3. Arnold E. Amstutz and Henry J. Claycamp, "The Total Market Environment Simulation: An Approach to Management Education," *Industrial Management Review*, 5, 47-60 (spring 1964).
4. Frederick E. Balderston and Austin C. Hoggatt, *Simulation of Market Processes*, Berkeley, Institute of Business and Economic Research, University of California, 1962.
5. C. West Churchman, "An Analysis of the Concept of Simulation," in Austin Curwood Hoggatt and Frederick E. Balderston, editors, *Symposium on Simulation Models: Methods and Applications to the Behavioral Sciences* (Cincinnati: Southwestern Publishing Co., 1963), p. 12.
6. R. M. Cyert, J. G. March, C. G. Moore, "A Specific Price and Output Model," *A Behavior Theory of the Firm* (Englewood Cliffs, New Jersey: Prentice-Hall, 1963), pp. 128-48.
7. John A. Howard and William M. Morganroth, "A Positive Model of Executive Decision," *Management Science* (forthcoming).
8. Philip Kotler, "Competitive Strategies for New Product Marketing Over the Life Cycle," *Management Science*, 12, 104-119 (December 1965).
9. Alfred A. Kuehn and Michael J. Hamburger, "A Heuristic Program for Locating Warehouses," *Management Science*, 9, 643-66 (July 1963).
10. George W. Morgenthaler, "The Theory and Application of Simulation in Operations Research," in Russell L. Ackoff, editor, *Progress in Operations Research* (New York: John Wiley), p. 367.
11. Guy H. Orcutt et al., *Micro-Analysis of Socio Economic Systems: A Simulation Study* (New York: Harper, 1961).
12. Harvey M. Shycon and Richard B. Maffie, "Simulation—Tool For Better Distribution," *Harvard Business Review* (November-December 1960).
13. *Simulmatics Media Mix: Technical Description* (New York: Simulmatics Corporation, October 1962).
14. A. M. Turing, "Computing Machinery and Intelligence," *MIND*, pp. 433-60 (October 1950).

Profit Maximization through New-Product Marketing Planning and Control

Over the years, the statistics of new-product introduction and innovation have been reviewed at great length. The success ratio that is most representative depends, to a great extent, upon who your favorite expert is. New products are a clear marginal concern with the highest priority, because new products are the main competitive vehicle in consumer packaged-goods product categories. The high rate of failure, whatever it may be, has cast an aura of mystery and black magic around the business of introducing new products. If there were no mystery, success might occur more frequently than it does.

The key perspective for dealing effectively with this problem requires that we view new-product marketing as a managerial process and, like any managerial process, it must be effectively planned and controlled in a systematic manner. DEMON is such a management planning and control system. In the context of DEMON, planning means examining a wide range of alternative marketing plans and selecting, from among them, the most profitable plan for implementation. This step involves developing the marketing details and the marketing actions that must be taken to accomplish the desired objective.

DEMON also refers to control, and the essence of useful management control is performance feedback. The feedback of information about the way the world responds to each marketing effort makes the DEMON system flexible and adaptable during its application.

The feedback control of marketing implies continuously changing input to the marketing system; this may occur for a variety of reasons. The general economic environment and competitive activities can change the inputs to marketing effort; similarly, corporate policy can change. These corporate policies are the ground rules chosen for operating the company. Finally, the marketing plan itself changes the environment. This last is, of course, to be expected—because the very purpose of marketing is to make the world change in the manner in which you want it to change. Awareness of these changes and the ability to capitalize upon or compensate for them, depending upon which side of the goal they fall, are key management functions.

THE MARKETING SYSTEM

A marketing plan represents both the criteria for evaluating how well the plan is implemented and for supplying the means for controlling the marketing variables that are the means for achieving the objectives. We might consider, for example, that a marketing plan is composed of a variety of elements, each of which must realize some goal in order to achieve the overall objective. These elements might be the advertising appropriation, the media plan, the product, the sales force, consumer promotion appropriation, and the price. Each of these marketing elements is a control variable since marketing management controls advertising and promotion expenditures, the size of the sales force, the formulation of the product, and the content and execution of the advertising. In turn, these elements control, to a greater or lesser extent, the consumer's reactions.

Management plans the media purchases to achieve media objectives, defined in such operational terms as reach and frequency. They also plan a product to achieve a specific level of conversion of first-time buyers (triers) to repeat purchasers (users). They plan a sales force to achieve distribution.

Most marketing professionals have an intuitive notion of the relationship between different factors; for instance, the amount spent on advertising and the sales response. These relationships have been examined and a substantial correlation has been found. Other investigators, looking into different product categories and following the same procedure, find similar results. Actually, both sides are probably right. Each is examining a limited view of the total range of the performance of the marketing variables involved. Where one investigator finds a relationship, another might find none, since each is looking at different segments of the total relationship between advertising expenditures and sales response. The true relationship might be highly complex (see

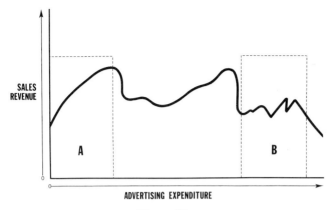

SALES
REVENUE

A

B

ADVERTISING EXPENDITURE

Figure 6.1.

Fig. 6.1). The first has analyzed sector *A* (a linear relationship); the second, dealing with sector *B*, finds no relationship at all.

Although this problem of interpretation faces all investigators, the fact remains that knowledgeable marketing people maintain that there are useful relationships between the budget and sales in a marketing plan. This conflict between theory and experience directed attention away from gross input-output studies and toward a closer examination of the relationships among *elements* in the marketing plan. Using this direction as a point of departure, empirical data describing each element in the marketing plan was correlated with data describing other elements in the marketing plan (see Fig. 6.2). The arrows in this diagram signify the relationship of one marketing element to another. The examination on this relatively microscopic level not only uncovered useful mathematical

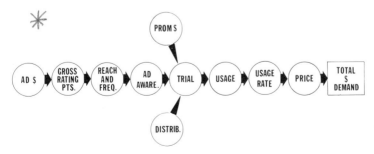

Figure 6.2.

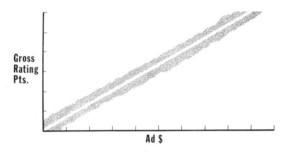

Figure 6.3.

relationships, but found that they were quite constant across a wide range of product categories. For example, data relating cumulative advertising expenditures with audience size provides a useful mathematical relationship between advertising expenditures and gross rating points (a measure of audience size). This relationship is quite linear (see Fig. 6.3). As expenditures accumulate over time, so also do gross rating points accumulate. Thus, time is an underlying variable. The rate at which gross rating points are accumulated can change depending, in part, upon the media discounts available to a given manufacturer. Thus, instead of a linear relationship, an exponential curve (Fig. 6.4) reflects these discounts.

DON'T NEED —UNDER STAND THOUGH

The relationship between advertising expenditures and gross rating points is not perfect, if only because the measurements of audience size are fallible. There is an uncertainty, a variance, surrounding such a relationship, as is true of any statistical estimate. That variance is represented by the dispersion of points around the trend line.

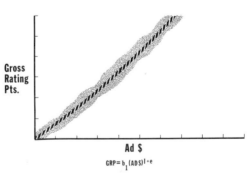

$$GRP = b_1 (ADS)^{1+e}$$

Figure 6.4.

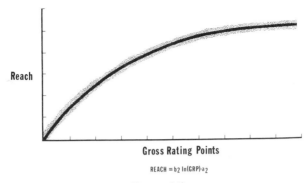

Gross Rating Points

REACH = b_2 ln(GRP)-a_2

Figure 6.5.

Similarly, gross rating points can be usefully related to the undupli-
cated audience to whom the message is transmitted once, twice, three
times, and so forth. Thus, gross rating points provide an estimate of the
net audience and figures of the media schedule. This relationship is best
expressed by a logarithmic function (see Fig. 6.5). Gross rating points
serve not only as a dependent variable relative to advertising expenditures, but also as an independent variable relative to net audience.
Similarly, net audience serves not only as the dependent variable related
to the number of gross rating points, but as the predictor of advertising
awareness. Advertising awareness is defined as the number of people in
the target audience who can recall having seen or heard the advertising
message (people who not only recall the brand, but also are aware of
the advertising message).

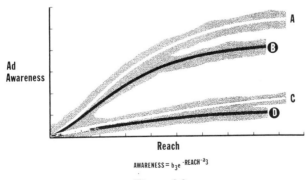

Reach

AWARENESS = $b_3 e^{-\text{REACH}^{-a_3}}$

Figure 6.6.

The relationship between reach and advertising awareness is highly nonlinear. The empirical measurements relating reach and advertising awareness may be described by many different curves, as in Fig. 6.6. These different curves are members of a family of curves arising from the same basic mathematical function $\beta e^{-R-\alpha}$. Beta is the ratio of brand-advertising expenditures to the average advertising expenditure in the product category.

Thus, a ratio of 1.0 means that the introductory brand will spend at the same rate as the average of the product category; if beta is 1.5, spending is 50% more than the average for the product category; similarly, if beta is 0.5, spending is one half the rate for the product category.

In operational terms, minus alpha is, as yet, undetermined. No variable that can be experimentally manipulated has been related to the values of the minus alpha parameter. Alpha appears to be related to the creative execution of the advertising. In practice, it is quite possible to determine alpha through survey measurements. The range of minus alphas that determines which member of the family curves is pertinent is known from past field studies, while measurements can be made to determine the current parameter value in a specific new-product introduction.

Advertising awareness, in part, leads to trial of a new product. Trial is defined as the proportion of people in the target market who purchase the product for the first time. It is the response to the question in a survey that asks: "What brands of floor wax have you ever tried?" If twenty out of one hundred replied "Brand X," Brand X trial rate is 20%, at that time. This relationship between advertising awareness and trial is linear, as seen in Fig. 6.7. Although it is linear across product categories, parameter values (trial rates) for different product categories may discriminate one category from another.

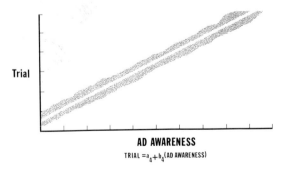

AD AWARENESS

$\text{TRIAL} = a_4 + b_4 (\text{AD AWARENESS})$

Figure 6.7.

In a similar manner, product trial leads to repeat purchase. If a consumer purchases the product a second time, he is a user; that is, someone who responds positively to the question "What brand of floor wax do you have on hand now?" If one hundred people were interviewed, and ten replied "Brand X," that is 10% usage. The conversion rate of triers to users is linear, as shown in Fig. 6.8. It might appear that a high correlation is forced because the data are constrained, since consumers cannot be second purchasers if they have not purchased the product once. Examining this relationship by constraining the second value to be less than the first value, when chosen randomly, showed that the random correlation coefficient is about 0.33. The actual trial-usage correlation coefficient is 0.94, which is significantly greater than 0.33.

With this estimate of the number of users and the distribution of the rate at which the product is used (how many times it is used once in a year, twice in a year, three times in a year, and so on), unit prices can be factored in to arrive at an estimate of sales or total revenue.

As it stands, this model is an incomplete statement of consumer response, since trial is also dependent upon how and whether the brand is promoted to the consumer. In this context, promotion means any vehicle used to place the product in the consumer's hands, either by giving it to him (in the form of a sample, sent through the mail or hung on a door knob), by mailing a coupon that allows purchase at a reduced price, or by printing a price-off coupon in an advertisement or using any other of a variety of direct inducements to the consumer.

Field data shows the conversion between expenditures on differing promotions and the number of people that try the brand. For example, one and a half percent may become triers from a coupon mailing, and ten percent from a sample mailing. This fairly well-documented informa-

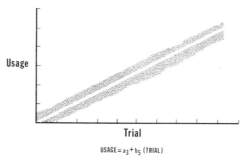

Usage

Trial

$$USAGE = a_3 + b_5 (TRIAL)$$

Figure 6.8.

tion has a degree of accuracy that allows reasonable estimates of the number of people likely to try the brand on the basis of any of a variety of consumer promotions.

The other modifier of trial is distribution coverage. The extent to which retail distribution is achieved makes the pool of people available to try the product larger or smaller. If fifty percent distribution is reached, the entire United States is not the market because the brand can only be bought in fifty percent of the country's outlets. The size and efficiency of the sales force and the trade promotion in great part controls the extent of distribution achieved for a particular brand. Many manufacturers are quite well supplied with data on the number of sales calls, the number of salesmen, and other salesforce performance measurements. These data can be related to the retail distribution achieved at any point in time to determine a useful relationship.

Each of the variables in these relationships exists both as an independent variable and as a dependent variable. In this sense, the relationships can be linked one to another to provide a system of equations that may be solved recursively (like a series of falling dominoes) to provide an estimate of consumer sales for any level of advertising and promotion expense. The result is clearly a statistical estimate, since each relationship is imperfect and has a great deal of uncertainty associated with it. One factor with which DEMON is concerned centers upon the size of the uncertainty of the sales estimate. The issue is not, as product managers usually phrase it, "How good are the data?" since what the manager really wants to know is how bad the data are—that is, how bad relative to a specific objective. If the data are sufficiently bad to reduce the odds of achieving a million-dollar profit target from four out of five to three out of five, the question of data quality is put into a decision context. On the other hand, if all that can be said is "Here is a standard deviation of twelve percent," that is not managerially useful information. Each of the relationships in this market-planning model has a variance about it. All of the variances in the system can be accumulated (as a root mean square) to derive an overall measure of the uncertainty of the estimate of sales volume.

BUDGET INPUT-PROFIT OUTPUT

These relationships can be linked to develop a marketing plan that specifies how much to spend on advertising, how much to spend on promotion, what media to use, the target level of advertising awareness, the product performance, distribution levels, usage rate, and price. If these targets are developed on a quarterly basis, a quarterly marketing plan results; if the targets are set on an annual basis, an annual marketing plan is developed. These annual plans can be cumulated for five years, for example, to cover a planning period of that length. In this fashion, marketing plans would be developed in a coherent time-phased program. By developing such a conditional estimate of the sales volume in each year, through the transfer function between expenditures (input) and profits (output), each marketing parameter can be adjusted to make the profit as large as possible over the planning period.

The inputs to this system are advertising and promotion expenditures. It is quite possible to have a product, advertising, and a salesforce—but without the stimulus of funds, these elements will not function. Thus, for a specific set of parameter values (each of which represents the performance of a marketing element), the level of advertising and promotion funds required to maximize profits over the planning period may be determined (Fig. 6.9). A set of these parameters is an index of the likely market accomplishment of each element in the marketing plan. Thus, if 20% of the consumers try Brand X, and 10% repeat their purchase, the conversion ratio (that is, the parameter between trial and usage) would be 50%. That 50% index represents the consumer response to a specific chemical formulation of Brand X. If the chemical formulation is altered in some fashion, resulting in a different product, a different conversion ratio would also result from changed consumer response. Perhaps 60, of 100 consumers in a test, repurchase the product. The reformulated product now has a 60% conversion ratio. Thus, each of the two conversion parameters represents a different product formulation.

A marketing plan represented by a specific set of parameters (one for

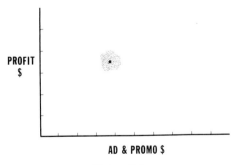

AD & PROMO $

Figure 6.9.

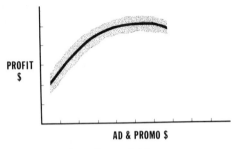

AD & PROMO $

Figure 6.10.

each element in the marketing model) can result in different profit results, depending upon how much is spent on advertising and promotion. If these expenses are systematically examined over a wide range of values (Fig. 6.10), various estimates of profitability for the same set of parameter values (marketing plan) but different levels of input will result. This overall relationship between expenditures input and profit output is compounded from the functional relationships among the elements of the marketing plan used in arriving at the profit estimate. Because of the statistical nature of the relationships, each estimate is an expected profit. The greatest value in the curve (see Fig. 6.10) is the maximum expected profit produced by that set of parameter values over a range of expenditures.

If the parameter value in any functional relationship changed, a different overall relationship between expenditure input and profit output would be expected. This altered input-output relationship might produce a curve like that in Fig. 6.11. A third set of parameter values might pro-

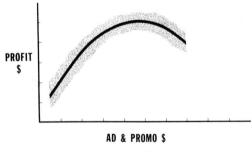

AD & PROMO $

Figure 6.11.

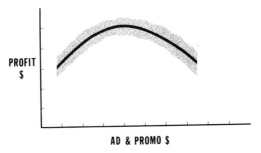

PROFIT
$

AD & PROMO $

Figure 6.12.

vide a profit curve like that in Fig. 6.12. Each input-output relationship is thus composed of many expected profits; the greatest value in each curve is the maximum expected profit.

Each profit curve represents a different marketing plan. They are different because each has different parameters representing, for example, consumer response to alternate product formulations as represented by the conversion ratio of triers to users. Other marketing plans might have different media mixes, represented by the ratio of gross rating points to reach. Another plan might have different advertising execution, represented by the relationship of frequency to advertising awareness. Thus, each profit curve represents a different marketing plan. Each plan has a maximum expected profit over a range of expenditure inputs. If, in Fig. 6.13, the different marketing plans (on the Z-axis) are related to the range of inputs (on the X-axis), a three dimensional surface will result

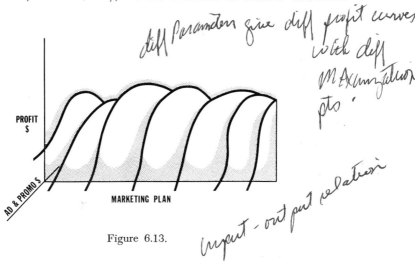

diff Parameters give diff profit curves
with diff
MAximization
pts.

input - output relation

PROFIT
$

AD & PROMO $

MARKETING PLAN

Figure 6.13.

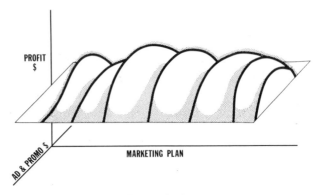

Figure 6.14.

when the profit output (on the Y-axis) of each plan is determined. Recollecting that each plan is a different combination of parameters, the output of these plans is a profit-response surface of all marketing plans across all input values. Each marketing plan has a maximum profit, and the greatest profit on the entire response surface is the maximum expected *maximum* profit (see Fig. 6.14). In this double maximization, the first maximum tells the value that is the maximum expected profit; the second maximum tells which of all of the maximum is the largest.

GO-ON—NO-GO

It is quite possible that this results in a maximum profit so low that it is not considered worthwhile pursuing. Although it may indeed be maximum profit, management policy would not accept such a meager maximum as adequate, considering the risks involved in introducing the new product. These policies would filter out those marketing plans that provide maximum profit below a minimum level, as in Fig. 6.15. In essence then, there are maximum-profit marketing plans where the profits are just not maximum enough to be considered within the framework of the policies by which management runs the company.

It is also likely that some range of profit, although worth examining, is not sufficiently great to warrant prompt implementation of the marketing program. Perhaps further development of the plan, based on additional information, could uncover greater potential profits that are not now readily observable. Alternatively, the uncertainty associated with

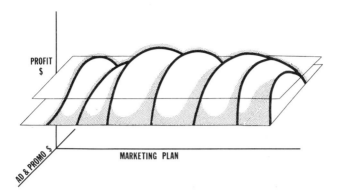

PROFIT $

AD & PROMO $

MARKETING PLAN

Figure 6.15.

the current marketing plan may be of a magnitude to imply financial risk greater than is judged acceptable. These two development possibilities suggest that devoting further effort to the search for better parameter values (representing better product, better advertising, and so on) would result in a profitable marketing effort. DEMON considers each of these conditional decisions to postpone a GO-national decision based on the likelihood that better parameter can be uncovered from additional market development effort, thus providing greater profit.

In this fashion then, profit expectations that fall below the minimum level justify the "NO-GO" decision. Profit expectations greater than minimum, but not achieving the target, fall within the "ON" decision. The third alternative, profit expectations that exceed the target level, represents the "GO" decision. Because the double maximization seeks the maximum expected maximum profit, the greatest of the "GO" marketing plans is the desired objective. There are indeed many marketing plans that might lead to a "GO" decision. The objective of DEMON though, is to identify the maximum profit "GO" plan.

Each of these decision alternatives will be correct, with more or less assurance of the results. The extent of such assurance is determined by accumulating the uncertainties and subtracting these from certainty. Four major sources of uncertainty reduce the assurance of achieving maximum profit. The first arises from the statistical inaccuracies of the marketing relationships in the planning system. The second source is the uncertainties in the market place. The third source comes from the forecast product-category sales volume during the planning period. The fourth source of uncertainty is the market research survey data. The total of these four sources of uncertainty can affect the extent to which profits satisfy managerial targets. If profit falls between the two cut-off levels, an ON-decision directs the selection of the marketing element most likely to increase profitability, while reducing the uncertainty associated with achieving such profit. The selection of the marketing element to be revised is accomplished by finding the parameter with the greatest leverage on profit. Consider, for example, the awareness to trial ratio. Changing the related marketing element requires developing new advertising content. This creative revision is then tested in the market place by appropriately conceived market research; the uncertainties and inaccuracies of this research are reflected in the total uncertainty measure. The newly developed advertising test results provide a new parameter for advertising performance that replaces, in the input-output relation, the parameter describing the previous advertising. Thus, the new advertising and the new parameter reflecting its performance have led to a new marketing plan. Once again, the advertising and promotion expenditure required to maximize profit would be determined through the input-output relationship. In this manner, the detailed operational elements of the marketing plan are developed. Further managerial information of the marketing plan would show the odds of achieving any target level of profit and the best decision alternative based on the information at hand.

This planning component of DEMON is basically a behavioral model. The sequential relationships among the marketing-plan elements convert expenditures into observable behavorial responses that are then converted back to revenue dollars. In the process of these conversions, specific behavioral objectives are set, providing a basis for evaluating new measurements derived from market research. These measurements of consumer behavior are primarily evaluative measures and are of only limited value as diagnostic measures that tell, for example, how the product performance may be enhanced. DEMON uses these evaluative measurements as a management control device, measuring system performance and providing feedback control over the total marketing plan, managerial policies, and decisions at hand.

PAY-OUT POLICIES

The impact of managerial policies on the marketing plan is best illustrated by the notion of pay-back. The payback concept (payout, break-even) was introduced into marketing as a management control on financial investment. Over the years, its function has become distorted and it now serves not merely as an investment-risk constraint but also as an objective of marketing. Thus, a product manager, when asked "What are your objectives for this new brand?" replies that he wants a ten share of market *and* payout in three years. He thus indicates that payout is one facet of the objective for marketing the product. Payout then, has historically been dealt with either as an objective or as a constraint. In the context of DEMON, payout can be handled with equal facility in both roles. The managerial and the marketing implications of alternative payout policies can be examined to uncover their constraining effect on the profit performance of the marketing effort. As a practical matter, many payout policies constrain not only the size of the investment, but they also serve to limit the attainable profit. Marketing plans requiring investments greater than can be recouped using conventional straight-line payback concepts are not considered, even though their profit contribution may be far superior as a result of fully exploited marketing opportunities.

Other financial criteria (for instance, cash flows, discounted cash flows, the rate of return on capital employed) may be used since they are simply transforms of the maximum expected maximum profit.

SYSTEM VALIDITY

What has been learned by using the DEMON system? The issue of the validity of the system can be considered on three different levels. The first is face validity. Does it look right? Thus far, our experience has been that results make sense to marketing people. The face validity is enhanced because the marketing goals in the system are highly specific. Previously, brand managers rarely defined their target level of advertising awareness, or what the product performance *ought* to be, or how big the salesforce *ought* to be.

Another level, component validity, explores whether the functional relationships in the planning system are valid. These relationships have been cross-validated on new samples. The existing relationships accounted for 80% to 90% of the uncertainty when predicting results for the new samples. These cross-validity indices are quite high, at least in the context of economic and behavioral data.

In foreign markets (in England and West Germany), purchased data have been analyzed. These data, gathered independently of DEMON specifications, show virtually the same index of correlation between each of the pairs of relationships. Obviously, there are different parameter values in these relationships, because of differences in the scale of the economies involved. These results add more evidence to the component validity of each of the relationships.

Overall system response has been verified by an eighteen-month test of alternative marketing plans in parallel test markets. The performance of marketing plans developed in the conventional manner was compared with the performance results of a DEMON-developed marketing plan. Although all elements of the two plans were similar, the advertising expenditure in the DEMON plan required to achieve maximum profits was exactly one half the budget required for the market share objective in the conventional plan. Over eighteen months, a comparison of the two plans in two pairs of matched test markets was carried out. One pair of test markets was selected for each plan on the basis of appropriate controls for size, consumption, and other marketing factors. The comparison started in January, 1965 and concluded in July, 1966. The basis for accepting DEMON planning rested on DEMON results exceeding 50% of the profits achieved by the conventional plan. Conversely, if the DEMON plan provided profit less than 50% of the conventional plan, then it would be rejected as a planning and control system. At the end of the test, the DEMON marketing plan provided 134% of the profit of the conventional marketing plan. This maximum profit premium by itself is quite satisfactory. When the use of the available 50% of the advertising budget is added, these results become formidable.

These component and systems validations have accumulated during eighteen months of DEMON use. There are other managerial conclusions that have resulted from these limited DEMON applications. For example, DEMON points out how critical it is to collate retail distribution with advertising expenditures so that advertising does not occur in areas where the product is unavailable and so that the product is not on the shelf without advertising pressure to move it. This conclusion may appear obvious; however, many sophisticated marketing organizations regularly spend advertising funds in areas where the product is not distributed, because their planning approach has neglected to integrate the two functions.

In organizational terms, DEMON has added great flexibility to the role of the product manager. Because the DEMON system directs the manager's attention to those marketing elements with the greatest priority, the manager spends much less time searching out the problem, and can direct his energy to fixing it. These efficiencies allow him to take on additional managerial assignments, thus multiplying his role.

These and other managerial and organizational implications of

DEMON are not fully exploited at this time. As system experience is accumulated, it is quite likely that entirely new marketing opportunities and organizational structures will result. Such an occurrence should not be minimized, since business history shows clearly that new ideas are slow to gain acceptance, but competitive pressures propel their adoption when results are demonstrated.

REFERENCES

1. A. Charnes and W. W. Cooper, "Chance-Constrained Programming," *Management Science* (October, 1959).
2. ——— and ———, "Deterministic Equivalents for Optimizing and Satisficing under Chance Constraints," *Operations Research,* **11** (1) 18-39 (January-February, 1963).
3. A. Charnes, W. W. Cooper, J. K. DeVoe, and D. B. Learner, "DEMON: Decision Mapping Via Optimum GO-NO Networks—A Model for Marketing New Products," *Management Science,* **12** (**11**), (July, 1966).
4. ———, ———, ———, and ———, "DEMON Mark II: An Extremal Equation Approach to New Product Marketing" (submitted to *Management Science* for publication).
5. ———, ———, ———, and ———, "DEMON Mark II: An Extremal Equation Solution and Approximations."
6. D. B. Learner, "Marketing Innovation and Management Science," paper delivered at the *American International Meeting of the Institute of Management Sciences,* New York (September, 1963).
7. ———, "DEMON: A Management Planning and Control System for Successfully Marketing New Products," *Proceedings of the 47th National Conference of the American Marketing Association,* R. M. Kaplan, editor (June, 1964).
8. ———, "DEMON New Product Planning: A Case History," *Proceedings of the 48th National Conference of the American Marketing Association,* Frederick E. Webster, Jr., editor (June, 1965).

PART TWO

Behavioral Theories of Consumer Behavior

During the past thirty years, significant progress has been made in developing the field of marketing as a legitimate discipline. That progress has been based, in large part, on the recognition by marketers of the interrelationships between marketing and the other disciplines of the social sciences, particularly mathematics and the behavioral sciences. The objective of Part Two is to discuss the application of the behavioral sciences to marketing management and to present four chapters that discuss major areas of the behavioral sciences in terms of marketing implications.

THE BEHAVIORAL SCIENCES

Despite the interest in the behavioral sciences among marketers, few precise definitions of the broad field exist. At the outset, the behavioral sciences should be distinguished from the social sciences. Broadly defined, the social sciences include anthropology, economics, education, history, law, political science, psychology, and sociology. The behavioral sciences are a subset of the social sciences and include those disciplines that focus primarily upon explaining and predicting human behavior using the scientific method of inquiry. Traditionally, anthropology, psychology, and sociology have comprised the basic behavioral disciplines. More recently, subsections of other social-science disciplines have emerged to focus on broad "behavioral" issues (for example, social geography and demography, behavioral economics and consumer behavior, psychiatry and political science) and deserve affiliation with the behavioral sciences.

In developing expectations regarding the contributions of the behavioral sciences to marketing, it must be recognized that the behavioral sciences do not represent mature disciplines compared with mathematics and the physical sciences. Although a long history of social commentary and conceptual discussion about the behavior of man back to Aristotle can be found in the older social sciences of philosophy, literature, history, and political history, systematic empirical study of human behavior through the scientific method originated as late as the nineteenth century. The behavioral sciences are actually still in the "growth stage" of their development.

Anthropology, psychology, and sociology have only recently achieved status as legitimate disciplines.[1] Anthropology traces its origin to British researchers in the late nineteenth century. The first academic department of anthropology was not established in the United States until 1890. The first experimental laboratories in psychology were established by Wilhelm Wundt in Leipzig, Germany, and William James in the United States during the 1870's. The early sociological investigations of social-reform movements were also products of this period. While the behavioral sciences grew during the 1920 to 1930 era, the great launch for the disciplines came with World War II. Social psychology as a legitimate area is largely of post-World War II origin. Since that time, the number of professionally trained behavioral scientists and the volume of empirical research has burgeoned.

In essence, the behavioral sciences represent a field less than a century old in its modern form with its most significant growth in the past thirty years. The field is introspective, critical of its fragmentation and internal provincialism, yet in a period of continuing transition. Berelson and Steiner have commented, ". . . as the seventeenth and eighteenth centuries saw the maturing of the physical sciences, and the nineteenth that of the biological sciences, so the twentieth century marks the coming-of-age of the behavioral sciences."[2]

Although the overall growth of the behavioral sciences is impressive,

[1] For an interesting review of the development of the behavioral sciences and current trends, see Bernard Berelson (ed.), *The Behavioral Sciences Today* (New York: Basic Books, 1963).

[2] Bernard Berelson and Gary A. Steiner, *Human Behavior: An Inventory of Findings* (New York: Harcourt, Brace, and World, 1964), p. 11.

not all of this growth has even indirect relevance to marketers. Within anthropology, for example, archaeology and physical anthropology contribute little to understanding the marketing process, while cultural anthropology has greater significance. Likewise, *within cultural anthropology*, studies of primitive tribes may have less relevance than studies of contemporary societies, communities, and groups. In the broad field of psychology, physiological psychology, animal psychology, abnormal psychology, and educational psychology have little to offer the marketer, while the literature generated by psychologists on learning theory, perception, cognitive style, language and semantics, motivation and personality, and the development of attitudes, values, and opinions may have great significance. Areas of sociology such as social class, social mobility, interpersonal communication, leadership, and reference-group theory may make significant contributions to understanding marketing phenomena, while the sociological research on crime, racial prejudice, and race differences, for instance, may contribute little.

MARKETING AND THE BEHAVIORAL SCIENCES

Although the behavioral sciences offer potential for providing greater insights into marketing problems, too little behavioral research is *directly* transferable from its context of origin to the marketing arena. The charge facing the marketer in applying behavioral science concepts in marketing involves searching, selecting, translating, and applying from the burgeoning volume of behavioral research to the marketing context. The marketer must *search* the relevant areas of behavioral research for concepts and methodologies of relevance to particular marketing issues. The marketer must *select* those findings that appear most relevant. The marketer must *translate* these findings from the laboratory experimental setting (that uses college sophomores as subjects) into the context of the contemporary consumer market for convenience goods, for example. Lastly, the marketer must *apply* the concepts in actual marketing strategy or in research ultimately directed at developing marketing strategies.

APPLYING THE BEHAVIORAL SCIENCES IN MARKETING: HISTORICAL PERSPECTIVE

Although application of the behavioral sciences in marketing has received impetus in the last decade, astute marketers have been aware of the potential of the behavioral disciplines for decades. The recognition of the importance of behavioral concepts to marketing is reflected in the earliest marketing literature. A leading textbook used in the first marketing courses, developed in the 1900 to 1910 era, was *Psychology of Advertising* by Walter Dill Scott, published in 1908.[3] In later volumes, behavioral concepts were presented, although supported with only meager anecdotal evidence. DeBower,[4] for example, in his volume, *Fundamentals of Advertising* (published in 1917), discussed, with insight born of experience, issues that behavioral scientists today would identify as motivation, selective perception, and communication, semantics and psycholinguistics, visual impact, and persuasability and message content. Butler,[5] for example, highlighted the implications of class for consumer behavior long before the Lynds and Middletown or Warner and Lunt and the Yankee City Series dealing with social stratification.[6]

In addition, Butler discussed "word-of-mouth advertising" in advance of the classic Katz and Lazarsfeld research on personal influence.[7] Likewise, during the 1930's, marketers were reportedly using organized rumor campaigns and word-of-mouth communication to promote products or sabotage competitor's campaigns.[8]

In the early marketing research literature of the 1930's, an awareness of the role of the behavioral sciences was also apparent. In the first volume of the *Journal of Marketing*, for example, empirical research was reported dealing with consumer attitudes, values, and brand preferences,[9] social mobility and retailing strategy,[10] and psychological research on

---

[3] Walter Dill Scott, *Psychology of Advertising* (New York: McGraw-Hill, 1908).

[4] Herbert F. DeBower, *Advertising Principles* (New York: Alexander Hamilton Institute, 1917).

[5] Ralph Starr Butler, *Marketing and Merchandising* (New York: Alexander Hamilton Institute, 1923).

[6] R. S. Lynd and H. M. Lynd, *Middletown* (New York: Harcourt, 1929) and R. S. Lynd, and H. M. Lynd, *Middletown in Transition* (New York: Harcourt, 1937); W. Lloyd Warner and Paul S. Lunt, *The Social Life of a Modern Community*, Yankee City Series, Volume 1, Yale University Press (1941), and W. Lloyd Warner and Paul S. Lunt, *The Status System of a Modern Community*, Yankee City Series, Volume 2, Yale University Press (1942).

[7] Elihu Katz and Paul F. Lazarsfeld, *Personal Influence* (Glencoe, Ill.: Free Press, 1955).

[8] For example, see R. Littell and J. J. McCarthy, "Whispers for Sale," *Harpers Magazine*, 62, 364-372, 1936, and D. J. Jacobson, *The Affairs of Dame Rumor* (New York: Rinehart, 1948).

[9] H. K. Nixon, "Notes on the Measurement of Consumer Attitudes," *Journal of Marketing*, 1 (1), 13-19 (July, 1936).

[10] H. W. Green, "Neighborhood Retail Outlets and Family Stability," *Journal of Marketing*, 1 (1), 40-45 (July, 1936).

radio.[11] Furthermore, marketing academics recognized the potential contributions of the anthropological, psychological, and sociological disciplines to the understanding of consumer demand[12] and the need for interdisciplinary approaches.

The central point is that marketers (both academicians and administrators) have not been entirely naive about the potential contribution of the behavioral sciences. Astute marketing administrators, through their sensitivity to market response and consumer behavior, have attempted to incorporate behavioral concepts into strategy, however clumsily, since the earliest hours of marketing history. In turn, researchers have attempted to profile behavioral issues and develop more effective methodology in the study of consumer behavior. Admittedly, however, these efforts have been limited to the more astute segments of the marketing community. The total commitment to the behavioral sciences during the early years of marketing's development as a discipline has been modest and the results have been fragmentary.

APPLYING THE BEHAVIORAL SCIENCES IN MARKETING: A CURRENT PROGRESS REPORT

The focus on the application of the behavioral sciences to marketing during the past decade has represented a dramatic intensification of interest among marketers rather than a discovery of a new approach to marketing problems. During the past ten years, impressive progress has been made in expanding the volume and depth of sophisticated research directed at applying behavioral science concepts in marketing, particularly in the area of consumer behavior. The conversion of the behavioral science concepts and research findings into action-oriented decision rules for guiding marketing strategies has moved more slowly. As a result, more pragmatic marketers have lost enthusiasm for mining the behavioral sciences and others have become pessimistic and occasionally critical of the actual contributions the behavioral disciplines can make to marketing.

The Problem: A Question of Objectives and Expectations

Underlying much of the criticism of the contributions of the behavioral sciences to marketing are unrealistic expectations regarding the direct

[11] J. J. Karol, "Notes on Further Psychological Research in Radio," *Journal of Marketing*, 150-153 (October, 1936).
[12] For example, see H. R. Tosdal, "Bases for the Study of Consumer Demand," *The Journal of Marketing*, 4 (1), 3-15 (July, 1939).

transfer of behavioral concepts to marketing contexts. Some marketers have expected *immediate solutions* to marketing problems with high short-run payoffs in the wake of the increased emphasis on the behavioral sciences. Immediate solutions, however, have been rare.

Realistically, the behavioral sciences can provide few hard generalizations that apply without translation to marketing issues. Most of the findings in the behavioral sciences are clearly preliminary based on limited empirical research. Nor have the emerging generalizations long stood the harsh scrutiny of time. Chronologically, the marketing discipline and the behavioral science disciplines are of the same vintage. The behavioral sciences materialized as areas of study in the late nineteenth and early twentieth centuries. Concurrently, the broad area of business administration was first identified as an area of academic interest in the late 1800's. The first courses in marketing appeared in American universities in the 1900 to 1910 era. Both marketing and the behavioral sciences are in the process of maturing. The behavioral disciplines lack the strong historical foundation that underlies mathematics and the physical sciences.

The problem of defining realistic expectations for applying the behavioral sciences in marketing is compounded by the sometimes conflicting roles that researchers in marketing frequently must assume. Is the researcher in marketing only committed to the immediate improvement of the decision-making art or does he also have a responsibility to explore the broad dimensions of the marketing process, perhaps with very limited short-term payoff?

The researcher and decision maker *within the firm* tend to be decision oriented, frequently committed to extremely short-term horizons and payoffs. The academic researcher in marketing is somewhat more ambivalent. In one role as teacher of potential marketing administrators, the academic must be aware of and empathetic with the problems of decision making under uncertainty and the immediate "action value" of information. In the role of scholar and social scientist, however, the academic researcher must adopt a broader view. The academic attempts to build a foundation of research upon which more general theories of consumer behavior and marketing may be built.

Realistically, the behavioral sciences cannot be expected to provide prescriptive models directly applicable to marketing decision making. The behavioral sciences can, however, provide hypotheses and theories about human behavior in different contexts that may be translated and tested in marketing settings. Furthermore, the behavioral sciences can provide valuable research methodologies of direct relevance to research in marketing. In turn, marketers can reciprocate in the development of an understanding of human behavior through research on consumer behavior. The generality of behavioral theory and methodology can be applied and tested in marketing settings.

Some Problems of Search, Selection, Translation, and Application

Marketers have tended to underestimate the search, selection, translation, and application problems involved in using the behavioral sciences. In terms of literature volume alone, the search problem is substantial. There are over 75 professional periodicals in the behavioral sciences written in English.[13]

Within disciplines, there are different schools of thought regarding basic dimensions of behavior. In psychology, for example, there are significantly different approaches to learning, perception, and personality widely circulated within the discipline. These intradisciplinary conflicts complicate the selection process for the marketer who would sample from the inventory of behavioral generalizations.

Nor is it an easy problem to translate behavioral findings from their context of original source to their context of marketing. Each of the behavioral disciplines has its own jargon, nomenclature, and particular methodological traditions. The marketer must be familiar with these dimensions of the disciplines to interpret fully the nuances of the research findings.

The search, selection, translation, and application of behavioral theory is further complicated by the shortage of qualified manpower in marketing. While many marketers may be "self-styled behavioral experts," the number of marketers steeped in behavioral theory, research, and methodology is limited. Although professionally trained behavioral scientists and marketers with in-depth training in the behavioral sciences are entering the marketing community in increasing numbers, they represent a relatively small segment of the total marketing fraternity.

SOME APPLICATIONS OF THE BEHAVIORAL SCIENCES IN MARKETING

Behavioral research in marketing is quite diverse. The four chapters that follow reflect that diversity. The chapters would appear to be unre-

[13] S. H. Brett (ed.), *Consumer Behavior and the Behavior Sciences* (New York: Wiley, 1966), p. 20.

lated in terms of topical content. Upon closer analysis, a common theme emerges. Each chapter draws from a relevant segment of behavioral theory and methodology and relates that block of knowledge to marketing. The chapters also reflect the breadth of topical content, the diversity of research methodology, and the heterogeneity of intellectual talent and training that pervades the movement to apply the behavioral sciences to marketing.

Chapter Seven, by James F. Engel, a marketer trained in the behavioral sciences, and M. Lawrence Light, a doctoral candidate in marketing and psychology, deals with the broad area of consumer decision making and consumer motivation. The chapter focuses specifically on the evaluation of the theory of cognitive dissonance as applied to consumer behavior. The authors set forth a general conceptual model of consumer motivation and behavior. From this base, the role of consumer commitment and the developing literature in cognitive dissonance and survey research, based on field and laboratory experimentation, are explored and related to the model of consumer behavior. The implications of consumer commitment and cognitive dissonance are developed in terms of consumer screening and distortion of communications messages. In conclusion, the authors discuss the role of commitment and cognitive dissonance in attitude change. They cite a wide range of empirical evidence encompassing field and laboratory experimentation as well as survey research techniques that have contributed to the development of dissonance theory.

Chapter Eight, by Herbert E. Krugman, Vice President of Marplan and sometime academician, deals with consumer decision making as a product of learned behavior. Krugman, a professionally trained psychologist, applies learning theory to explore the process by which consumers develop "likes, preferences, and choices." To serve as a foundation, the concepts of repetition and familiarity are discussed in the context of learning theory. The author then presents findings from an integrated series of experimental studies conducted over the past ten years that apply learning theory to consumer tastes and preferences. The research focuses on the dynamics by which consumers may "learn to like" (or not like) an item and how this learning may effect "likes" for whole categories of items. In conclusion, the author distinguishes between likes, preferences, and choices, and he outlines the implications of this conceptual framework for marketing.

Chapter Nine, by Everett M. Rogers and J. David Stanfield, discusses the broad area of the adoption and diffusion of new concepts. Rogers, a rural sociologist who expanded his research into the larger arena of communication, is a pioneering researcher and the leading synthesizer of empirical research in adoption and diffusion of new concepts in social systems. Rogers, in conjunction with J. David Stanfield (a doctoral candidate in his tutorage) presents the generalizations developed from an intensive literature survey of over 700 empirical studies reported in the field of adoption and diffusion.

Rogers and Stanfield present a conceptual framework for the discussion of the diffusion process and trace the relative volume of contributions to diffusion theory from various research traditions and the level of intertradition communications. The methodology of the Diffusion Documents Center underlying the literature survey is outlined. Building upon this base, the generalizations and methodological traditions that emerge from the cumulated empirical research are presented and criticized. In conclusion, the authors summarize the implications of these findings for marketing.

While Chapters Seven to Nine dealt with substantive behavioral theory and attempted to interpret, translate, and apply that theory to marketing, Chapter Ten, by Volney Stefflre, presents a unique methodological approach to analyzing and predicting consumer behavior. Stefflre, a social psychologist and cultural anthropologist, applies concepts from semantics and psycholinguistics to the measurement of consumer preferences for a "new" product. As a theoretical base, the author defines a "market" or "market structure." Building upon this framework, methodological procedures for "developing product similarity" estimates are discussed. The methodology for measuring preferences for new products is outlined. Finally, the author discusses how the research findings generated by the methodology can be implemented in marketing strategy.

Altogether, the four chapters that follow present an intriguing cross section of research underway within marketing directed at applying behavioral concepts. The chapters reflect the wide range of topic areas, methodology, and professional talent that is increasingly focused on developing a behavioral research tradition in the marketing discipline. The papers, however, are only suggestive of the potential contributions that may be made to the understanding of consumer behavior.

The Role of Psychological Commitment in Consumer Behavior: An Evaluation of the Theory of Cognitive Dissonance

The theory of cognitive dissonance has recently generated much research in the fields of psychology and communications. This chapter explores potential applications of the theory to marketing. The theory of cognitive dissonance offers useful insights into some of the intricacies of consumer motivation and behavior and, thus, is of conceptual value. In addition, it suggests numerous implications for marketing practice.

Cognitive dissonance refers to the consequences of commitment to an action or point of view. This is generally assumed to exist when a person ". . . has decided to do or not to do a certain thing, when he has chosen one (or more) alternatives and thereby rejected one (or more) alternatives, when he actively engages in a given behavior or has engaged in a given behavior" [Brehm and Cohen, 1962, p. 7]. Of special importance here are the consequences of an individual's commitment to a buying decision and the significance of his development of product, brand, or store preference. These and other implications are explored in the following pages.

To clarify the issues involved, the paper begins with a conceptual model of consumer motivation and behavior. This model permits a more penetrating analysis of the meaning and significance of psychological commitment. Then pertinent literature is reviewed on the nature of

* James F. Engel is Associate Professor of Business Organization and M. Lawrence Light is a Ph.D. candidate in the Departments of Psychology and Business Organization at Ohio State University. The authors gratefully acknowledge the helpful suggestions given by Professors Roger D. Blackwell and David T. Kollat.

179

cognitive dissonance, the consequences of a buying decision, and selective screening of communication messages to protect brand loyalty. It is hoped that the insights that are generated will prove useful in stimulating further research.

A MODEL OF CONSUMER MOTIVATION AND BEHAVIOR

When a biologist seeks to understand how a particular mechanism in a living organism works, he often begins by dissecting it and studying its parts. In some studies, however, this mode of analysis may be impossible, or it may be more practical to study the system as a whole. By necessity, we are forced into this position when studying human behavior. The psychologist, as a result, frequently resorts to his so-called "black box" whereby the human being is analyzed as a *system* with outputs (behavior) in response to inputs. The driving mechanisms are hidden in the "black box" and can only be identified by inference from behavior.

It is useful to conceptualize human behavior as consisting of a complex servosystem or feedback-control mechanism. A servosystem is a device that controls some variable quantity in a special way by comparing its actual value with some desired reference value [Fender, 1964]. Figure 7.1 is a model of a typical servosystem in engineering. It uses the difference between the actual and reference value (error) to drive an "actuator." This, in turn, adjusts the variable to correspond with the reference. The basic principle of the servosystem is continuous feedback from output to input. It monitors its own performance and makes alterations in output if such corrections are required.

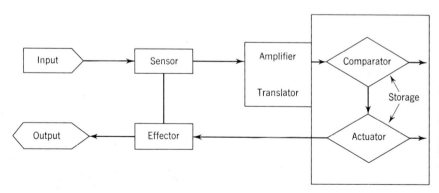

Figure 7.1. A basic servosystem model.

When human behavior is analyzed from this perspective, it is necessary to think of the system as comprising several basic components: (1) inputs; (2) predispositions and constraints; (3) a comparison process; (4) a decision-making process; and (5) feedback from outcomes. In the following discussion, each of these elements is evaluated separately and a model is constructed in step-by-step fashion.

Inputs to the System

The model begins with the inputs shown in Fig. 7.2. These are received by the five senses (the sensory receptors) and are of two basic types: (1) physical and (2) social. Howard [1963] refers to some of the physical inputs as the "state of alternatives" and discusses such relevant product variables as price, availability, quality, and distinctiveness. We also could add a great variety of other physical stimuli, such as weather and credit availability. The individual also lives in a social environment and is subject to a number of stimuli such as demands of family members, expected patterns of behavior in groups, and the behavior of friends. Of special interest in marketing are social pressures on individual attitudes, often treated in terms of the concept of reference groups [Shibutani, 1955].

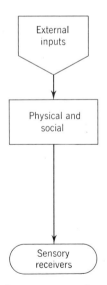

Figure 7.2.   Inputs to the system.

Predispositions and Constraints

Reference is now made to the "psychological makeup" of the individual (see Fig. 7.3). Needs, of course, have great motivational significance [Hull, 1952]. In one sense, they function to actuate the system through the process of *arousal* and the individual becomes alert, responsive, or vigilant [Hebb, 1949]. According to some researchers, the influence of arousal is exerted through physiological and biological processes. For example, the individual becomes hungry and his system is now activated to engage in need-satisfying behavior.

Needs also exert an influence in another way, because patterns of behavior which are perceived as successful in need satisfaction become learned and stored in memory. Thus, it is likely that the system will call forth this behavior in the future. Values and attitudes refer to learned orientations for or against a topic or object and also become stored in

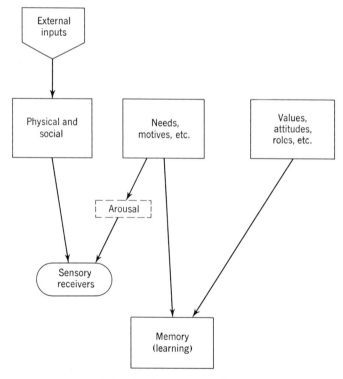

Figure 7.3. Predispositions and constraints.

memory for use in evaluating inputs when the system is aroused. In addition, roles refer to patterns of expected behavior in social contexts and are an important influence on what the system does. There is a substantial body of theory [Secord and Backman, 1964] that documents the importance of these factors.

The Comparison Process

The system now is activated and prepared to undergo need-satisfying behavior. Referring once again to the example of hunger, the individual becomes alert to those stimuli or inputs that are relevant in satisfaction of this need. Previously, the individual has been exposed to thousands of such inputs in the course of a given day, but they are not received by the five senses or acted upon until the system first becomes aroused.

Whether, in fact, the individual actually becomes aware of an input and interprets it is a function of *perception* that, in turn, involves a *process of comparison* whereby inputs are compared with those learned predispositions stored in memory. Only those stimuli that are known from past experience to be relevant to hunger satisfaction are likely to be received as actuators of the system. For example, a picture of a juicy steak on the outside of a restaurant or a huge piece of chocolate cake in an advertisement are now likely to be noticed where they previously were ignored. This process of comparison is diagrammed in Fig. 7.4.

Perception is selective in two ways: (1) attention and (2) distortion. Selective attention was described in the preceding paragraph and refers to the fact that the system attends only to stimuli which are seen to be relevant. Furthermore, those predispositions that are stored in memory can function to screen out or distort those stimuli that are seen to be inconsistent and to enhance perception of those that are relevant. For example, tomato juice from Ohio may be preferred as an appetizer when several other alternatives would do, simply because of an attitude which favors consumption of Ohio products. An equally acceptable product from another area, on the other hand, may be evaluated negatively and thereby become distorted in the comparison process.

Alternative ways to satisfy the state of arousal are, therefore, evaluated and compared with learned predispositions. The process of behavior proceeds if, in the comparison process, it is perceived that action on an alternative will improve the present state of the system and restore the balance that was disturbed when arousal occurred. Otherwise, the process halts at this point. No doubt there is some minimum level of perceived difference between the results of action and no action that

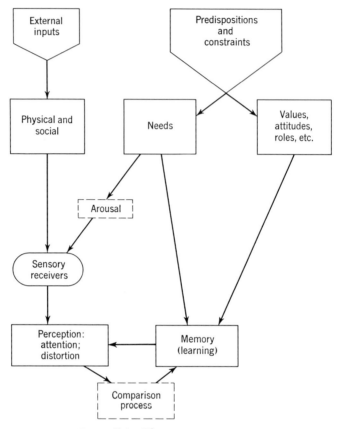

Figure 7.4. The comparison process.

must be surpassed before the "flow" proceeds through the system. It should be noted that this level, or threshold, is learned and will vary as circumstances vary. In some instances, the individual can achieve greater total satisfaction by no action at all.

The Decision-Making Process

Let us now assume that the hungry person referred to earlier perceives a greater return from behavior than from no behavior. A choice must now be made from among the kinds of action available to satisfy his aroused state, and this process is illustrated in Fig. 7.5.

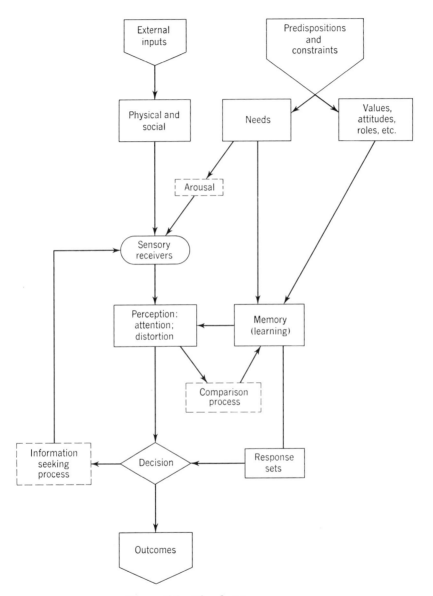

Figure 7.5.   The decision process.

A factor sometimes referred to as *response set* [Hebb, 1949] can influence the decision. This means that the individual can be oriented toward a particular pattern of response by those very predispositions that affected perception. This is shown by a direct arrow from memory to decision. For example, a strong attitude against consumption of seafood not only leads to distortion of inputs to the system relevant to this mode of consumption but also predisposes one to select some other type of entrée from a menu. Similarly, the individual can be "set" to favor or avoid particular stores or brands. Many other examples could be given of this common phenomenon.

The individual at this stage also may be unable to act because of a recognition that the risk of behavior without further information on alternatives is too great. Thus, he may decide to engage in *information search*. When this takes place, the information acquired, of course, is an external stimulus received by the sensory receivers, and it is subject to selective attention and distortion during the process of comparison. This is shown by an arrow from decision to sensory receivers.

Some persons are known to be cautious and unwilling to act under many circumstances without augmenting the information that is stored in memory. They are therefore "set" to seek information. In other instances, an alternative may be seen as satisfactory but the felt risk is too great to warrant action without additional justification. In any event, action is not taken on the existing information base and the system triggers the search process. When adequate information is procured or the costs of additional search are seen as being too great, a choice is made between alternative actions.

Information search is most likely to occur in nonroutine decisions where comparatively little is known about alternatives or where the risks of a wrong decision are seen to be great. In other situations, however, past experience with a given alternative has been so satisfactory that it is followed virtually automatically with little or no information search. Habits of this type, of course, are common in consumer buying. In addition, the individual may possess little information but reason that costs of research outweigh gains.

Feedback From Outcomes

Finally, the behavior process is completed when an alternative is chosen and the outcomes of a decision become known. Figure 7.6 shows that two additional things happen: (1) perceived doubt about the wisdom of the action can trigger a search for information to justify the

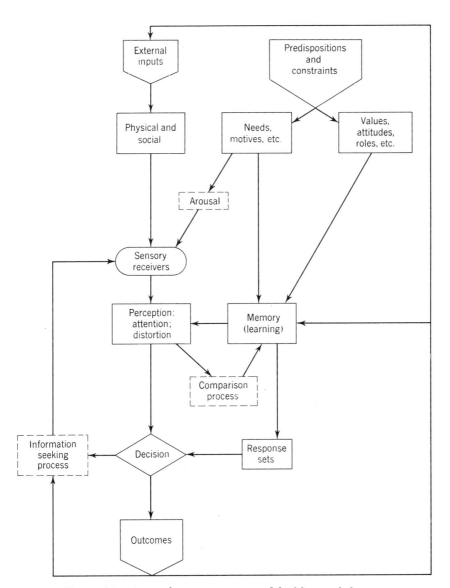

Figure 7.6.   A complete servosystem model of human behavior.

decision and (2) the outcomes become stored in memory and may change circumstances sufficiently to generate new inputs to the system. These two outcomes are shown as additional feedback loops and they complete the model of the feedback-control system.

If our hungry man, for some reason, doubts that he visited the right restaurant, he may search for additional information to prove that his choice was correct. This seems especially likely if the meal was costly, and this illustrates one possible consequence of a decision.

The results of his action then enter the system once again. If the state of arousal is fully satisfied, this information is stored in memory for possible future use. If behavior was not fully satisfactory, however, the system may trigger further action such as consumption of more food. In addition, the outcome may change the environment and, thus, give rise to a new external input that can trigger additional behavior. The waiter, for example, now appears to demand payment for the meal and hence necessitates a different type of behavior. In all these instances, the process exhibits the essential characteristics of servosystem that is continually acting, monitoring its action, and undergoing continued or modified behavior.

While this discussion has focused on the individual, it is clear that social influences constitute an important input for human behavior. The outcomes from one person's action serve as inputs for those with whom he interacts. It is useful to conceive of social behavior (for instance, in the family) as consisting of an aggregate of individual feedback-control systems, each monitoring the others.

COGNITIVE DISSONANCE AND CONSUMER BEHAVIOR

The above model provides the background necessary to assess those aspects of human behavior that dissonance theory purports to explain. Cognitive dissonance refers to nonfitting knowledges, opinions, or beliefs (cognitions) regarding some topic or event [Festinger, 1957]. If cognitions are dissonant with each other, the result is an uncomfortable state that serves as a motivational force.

This theory is confined to the *comparison process* in the above model of consumer behavior. It requires that an individual be *committed* to some belief or behavior and the theory documents the consequences when this commitment in some way becomes challenged. The attitude, belief, or action to which the individual has become committed thus is *stored in memory* and tends to resist change.

To take an example, assume that a satisfied coffee drinker reads a purportedly authoritative article alleging that coffee drinkers are prone to experience heart attacks. If he is concerned about his health, it is likely that this challenge to his coffee-drinking habit will give rise to dissonance. It might be reduced in this instance by stopping coffee consumption (changing a behavioral element), by dismissing the validity of the article, or by adding new information from other sources to downgrade the claimed relationship between coffee drinking and health. It has been documented that many strategies can be pursued to reduce dissonance and that there are wide individual differences in this respect [Steiner and Rogers, 1962; and Steiner and Johnson, 1964].

Dissonance is difficult to demonstrate and to manipulate experimentally, and, for this reason, there have been published criticisms of much of the evidence [see Chapanis and Chapanis, 1963]. First, the individual must be clearly committed to an action or point of view or dissonance will not occur [Brehm, 1960; Culbertson, 1957; Cohen, 1959; and Brehm and Cohen, 1962]. In addition, experimental evidence is invalid unless it is shown that perception and thought about contradictory information or engaging inconsistent behavior is done as a result of free choice (volition) with little applied pressure [Cohen, Terry, and Jones, 1959; Festinger and Carlsmith, 1959; Cohen, Brehm, and Fleming, 1958; and Brock, 1962]. A challenge to an existing cognition will not otherwise occur. Finally, the issues studied must be of importance or dissonance either will not arise or will be of such a low magnitude as to be negligible [Zimbardo, 1960]. Few studies have met these criteria beyond all doubts.

Commitment is the central concept of dissonance theory and it is worthwhile inquiring, before proceeding further, whether this is a useful concept in explaining aspects of consumer behavior. In other words, do consumers ever become so committed (for instance, to a brand, a product, or a store) that they will become dissonant if their preference is challenged? The authors are of the opinion that such commitment indeed *does occur* for two different reasons: (1) loyalty to a product or a store can develop because one alternative becomes ego-involved and is, in effect, an extension of the consumer's self concept; and (2) consumers establish buying routines or habits for the purpose of greater shopping efficiency. Loyalty from this latter source can represent genuine commitment.

Some products attain such importance to the consumer that considerable ego-involvement develops. A prestige brand of automobile can reach this degree of importance with some, although monetary value is not an infallible criterion of ego-involvement. Other consumers may value highly the label of a prestigious store and, as a consequence, develop a strong propensity for continued patronage at that store. The outcome is commitment to a purchasing alternative that is both extremely important to the consumer and difficult to change. A challenge to his preference can generate considerable dissonance.

Brand or store loyalty, however, also can represent a purchasing habit. Few consumers can engage in extensive problem-solving in every buying situation; for this reason, routines are developed. Commitments to specific alternatives arise from this source and resist change. This is not to say that the degree of commitment is as great as that generated by ego-involvement. Still, resistance to change may be of sufficient importance to give rise to dissonance when faced with contradictory information or behavior.

Two areas of the literature on cognitive dissonance warrant consideration here: (1) the consequences of a purchase decision; and (2) selective screening of promotional messages. The remaining research testing aspects of this theory seem to be of limited marketing use.

THE CONSEQUENCES OF A DECISION

The process of decision making by consumers has assumed growing importance in the marketing literature, as evidenced most recently by the interest shown in longitudinal analysis, the study of behavior over time [see Granbois and Engel, 1965]. Dissonance theory provides useful insights into certain aspects of this process through focusing on the consequences of a decision.

Referring once again to the model of consumer behavior discussed earlier, it will be recalled that at some point, the consumer ceases information search (if this has been initiated at all) and commits himself to an action that is signified in the model as an outcome. There are two important feedback loops from outcomes that have direct relevance for this discussion. One loop signifies a continuation of the search process and is activated when the person searches for new information to overcome dissonance arising from doubts about the wisdom of his action. This type of information search suggests some interesting marketing implications.

The other loop extends backward into memory where the results of behavior are stored; in addition, this loop is shown as providing an external input due to the fact that behavior can change the environment and, thus, provide the incentive for changed future behavior. Of special importance here is what can happen when this loop extends into memory, for two additional types of dissonance can be generated: (1) an unconfirmed expectancy regarding behavior and (2) contradiction of an important predisposition stored in memory. These types of dissonance also have marketing implications.

Post-Decision Information Search

Let us assume that a consumer has purchased a new automobile and that the purchase requires use of scarce resources and, thus, attains some importance. This purchase no doubt represents a genuine commitment and the stage is set for the possible onset of dissonance. For example, the consumer may have considered many makes prior to purchase and still be aware of their favorable attributes. This awareness, however, is dissonant with the fact that he purchased a different make. In this case, dissonance cannot be reduced by changing the behavior because of the threat of immediate financial loss. In addition, it is unlikely that it will be overcome by admitting that a wrong decision was made and living with it. It is more likely, as Cohen, Brehm, and Latane [1959, p. 63] pointed out, that "A person experiencing dissonance will avoid further inconsistent information and seek out consistent information in order to reduce his dissonance." Therefore, the *dissonant purchaser may actually seek new information in order to justify his action.*

THE PROCESS OF POST-DECISION EVALUATION.   This information-seeking tendency has been widely documented in the literature on cognitive dissonance, although much of the evidence must be regarded as tentative because of the methodological difficulties discussed earlier [Cohen, Brehm, and Latane, 1959; Mills, Aronson, and Robinson, 1959; and Adams, 1961]. It is known that the pressure for information exposure increases with the importance of a decision. The type of information sought, however, seems to vary. Some consumers seem to seek out information that challenges their action and attempt to refute it while others avoid further dissonance through exposure to information that supports their behavior.

Festinger [1964] suggested that confidence in the initial position is a major determinant of the course of action that is pursued. If an individual is relatively certain that he is correct, it is most likely that he will seek out discrepant information and reduce dissonance by refuting it. Conversely, he will seek out consonant information to the degree that he feels uncertain about the wisdom of his act. Freedman [1965a], Mills

[1965], and Mills and Ross [1964] report findings which confirm this hypothesis, although Freedman [1965b] found contradictory results in a later study.

READERSHIP OF ADVERTISEMENTS AFTER PURCHASE. The marketing implications of these findings seem to be greatest in the area of readership of advertisements after purchase to reduce dissonance. Ehrlich, Guttman, Schonbach, and Mills [1957] found an indication that new car purchasers read advertisements for their own make to a greater extent than those owning automobiles for a longer period of time. Although this study did not seem to attain the methodological requirements mentioned earlier, it was concluded that new purchasers are dissonant and, as a result, are receptive to advertisements as a means of overcoming this state of tension. Engel [1963a and 1963b], on the other hand, replicated this study with variations and found a similar tendency only on advertisements featuring price. In all other respects, new purchasers of a popular make did not appear to experience dissonance.

Although the evidence is contradictory and tentative, it does seem plausible that post-purchase readership of advertisements may serve to reduce dissonance. Indeed, certain appeals in advertisements designed for other purposes can play this role. It is doubtful, however, that entire market segments can be isolated that exhibit this tendency under normal circumstances and, unless this can be done, it is unwise to design entire advertisements for new purchasers. Moreover, dissonance is a highly individualized phenomenon and there is no universal criterion to use that would indicate those types of purchases that are most likely to generate doubts. The purchase of a new automobile may engage this tendency with some and not with others. Perhaps it is more reasonable to conclude that follow-through by personal salesmen where this is possible is the best means to help new buyers overcome dissonance where it is observed by the salesman to exist. The result otherwise may be a consumer who is dissatisfied with his action and will be unlikely to make a similar decision in the future.

It also should be pointed out that a new owner will notice advertisements for quite a different reason. The product is now a part of his life where it had not been previously. An awareness is stored in memory, and it is not surprising that external inputs that are relevant to this purchase will now be noticed where they were ignored previously. In this case, the owner is completely satisfied with his decision but still notices advertisements and other pertinent stimuli. Clearly there is no justification for appeal to new buyers under this circumstance.

Perhaps this discussion illustrates the fallacy of taking one or two studies from the literature on psychology and assuming application to marketing problems without the necessary research. This is not to say that post-decision information search does not occur. The point is that an investigator must be very cautious in assuming widespread applications unless he is clearly versed in possible methodological artifacts that can color experimental research and unless he is keenly aware of the realities of marketing management.

Unconfirmed Expectancies

A number of studies have investigated the hypothesis that performance of some sort that is inconsistent with expectations regarding the outcomes of that performance gives rise to dissonance that, in turn, is reduced through rejecting the behavior as being unsatisfactory. This hypothesis was confirmed by Carlsmith and Aronson [1963], Cottrell [1965], and was partially confirmed by Sampson and Sibley [1965]. However, Ward and Sandvold [1963] and Goldberg [1965] did not find a similar relationship, thus underscoring the need for further research. A particularly interesting finding is that dissonance occurs between expectancy and outcome even when the behavior *exceeds* expectancy. The result is that the behavior is still rejected as being unsatisfactory, as a means of reducing dissonance.

An interesting advertising implication emerges from this series of studies. A typical advertising outcome is an expectation in the consumer's mind about the product and its performance capabilities. If these expectancies are not actually confirmed by product use, the result may be dissonance that is reduced by return of the product or by brand switching. One of the authors, for example, witnessed this phenomenon recently when a new, sporty make of automobile was rejected completely during a trial because of the fact that its performance did not live up to advertising claims. This underscores the need to verify that advertisements must generate realistic expectancies if optimum results are to be attained in terms of continued repurchase and product use.

Some researchers may question whether the expectancy created by an advertisement or selling message is of sufficient importance to become committed to memory. Such a reservation is well taken but it can be dispelled by the fact that much of the experimental evidence cited above pertained to expectancies regarding taste of a bitter or sweet solution in the laboratory. An expectancy of this type could hardly be considered as of major importance to one's survival, yet disconfirmed expectancies still produced dissonance. Thus, this phenomenon seems worthy of applied investigation in marketing and advertising.

Attitude Change Following Behavior Change

It has traditionally been assumed that attitude change must *precede* behavioral change. The opposite can occur, however, when behavior that has been undertaken is seen as being dissonant with an attitude. Referring once again to the model of consumer behavior, the outcome of an action feeds back into memory and, when this knowledge is seen as being inconsistent with a strongly held attitude, dissonance is the likely result.

Generally, it is easier to reduce this type of dissonance through attitude change than it is to reverse the action that was pursued. Mills [1958], for example, reported that those opposed to cheating later became more lenient in their outlook toward this type of behavior after they had, in fact, engaged in cheating. A similar result was reported by Atkin [1962] in a purchasing situation where attitudes toward particular stores changed after shopping in the store.

If commitment to behavior can lead to attitude change, several implications emerge. Quite an assortment of promotional tactics is available for use to induce a consumer to try a given product or service. Often, devices like trading stamps, premiums, coupons, and price offers are used on the assumption that trial of a product may weaken loyalty to a competitive brand. Presumably, the dissonance created will lead to attitude change that, in this case, would be a change in brand loyalty. This may indeed occur, but it is more probable that the opposite will result because the consumer was not induced to try the product under volition. The consumer may reason that the inducement is too great to pass up for one purchase, while existing preferences remain unshaken. What has happened, of course, is that no dissonance has been generated because of the fact that the consumer is not really committed to continued use of this brand.

An interesting question is thus raised as to the manner in which to induce a consumer to try a new or competing product when he holds a commitment to an existing brand. Simply putting the product in his hands may not suffice. This problem no doubt was faced by the makers of new washing detergents to be used in cold water. One of the writers found in informal investigations during early introductions that housewives vigorously resisted the concept that a washing could be done satisfactorily in cold water. Many even stated that they would probably not give the product a fair trial if they received a sample. However, one manufacturer, in his introductory advertisements, included a price-off coupon as an inducement. This may have been a wise strategy, because the housewife still must pay the majority of the purchase price, *thereby making a real commitment* to try the product. Such a commitment might have been lacking if she had received only a free sample.

There is an interesting and largely unexpected derivation from the findings on behavioral commitment. Brehm and Cohen [1962] hypothesize that the greater the dissonance between attitude and the behavior undertaken under free choice, the greater the resulting attitude change. Normally, it is assumed that this type of discrepancy will lead to an opposite result. The implication is that dissonance will be highest when this discrepancy is large, with the result that something has to give. That "something" is usually found to be the attitude because of greater difficulty of changing behavioral commitment. Notice, then, the value of inducing some sort of genuine commitment to try a competing product in the face of strong brand preference.

It seems apparent that the dissonance literature has advanced some potentially rewarding hypotheses regarding the proper use of direct-action advertising stimuli. It is highly recommended that research be undertaken to prove or disprove their validity, because these methods may present hitherto uncapitalized-upon promotional opportunities. Of special significance is use of a new method to measure degree of commitment suggested by Sherif et al. [1965]; the implications of this approach for marketing research are explored in detail in the next section.

SELECTIVE SCREENING OF COMMUNICATION MESSAGES

The following proposition is now well established from the literature on communication and attitude change [Engel, 1964]:

Communication which contradicts or otherwise is inconsistent with the predispositions of those for whom it is intended is likely to provoke (1) a reaction of selective exposure whereby nonacceptable messages are avoided; (2) selective misperception or distortion of the message content; and (3) selective recall of those appeals which are perceived as being inconsistent.

This says that incoming communications (external inputs) can either be avoided or distorted in the comparison process as they are filtered through various predispositions stored in memory (for instance, attitudes and learned patterns of behavior).

Selective screening has long been recognized by psychologists and sociologists, but comparatively little light has been shed on *why it occurs* and under *what conditions it is to be expected*. For this reason, it is dangerous to apply the above generalization to marketing without further investigation. In fact, it may be that advertising is a form of communication that does *not* engage selective screening. These questions are the subject matter of this section.

Cognitive Dissonance and Selective Screening

Can commitment to an attitude or other predisposition give rise to dissonance when it is challenged and, thereby, generate selective screening? On a commonsense basis, an affirmative conclusion seems to be warranted. Because of the dissonance that is thereby created, an individual will be motivated to restore consonance, perhaps through attitude change, although it is more likely that selective exposure will occur to avoid dissonance in the first place.

Brehm and Cohen [1962] admit the possibility that dissonance may underlie these selective processes, but they also point out that it may be stretching a point to assume that an attitude or other type of predisposition is a true commitment. Instead, they claim that an attitude may be modified somewhat by incoming information and a new position established that represents a compromise between the previous position and that suggested by the communication. If an attitude were a true commitment, they claim, there would either be total resistance to change or a complete change in attitudinal position to that advocated by the communication. In other words, there can be no intervening degrees of change.

These reservations are well taken but they seem to have overstated the case. Truly, many of the attitude-change studies in the literature successfully meet the dissonance criteria of commitment, volition, and issue importance [for a thorough review see Klapper, 1960]. When these criteria are met under natural field conditions, selective screening, perhaps through dissonance processes, is a common result. This point was underscored by Hovland [1959] who pointed out that substantial attitude change without selective screening can be demonstrated in the laboratory. The issues used often are of little practical importance and few, if any, individuals demonstrate true commitment. Moreover, opportunity for selective exposure is seldom permitted, with the result that voluntary exposure to contradictory information under volition (a requirement if dissonance is to occur) is not allowed.

However, the issues investigated in field studies (for instance, voting, racial prejudice, and the United Nations) are likely to represent deep feelings of commitment on the part of the subjects, thus qualifying in terms of commitment and issue importance. Moreover, exposure, if it occurs, does so under genuine volition. There is, therefore, a basis to hypothesize that individuals can *avoid dissonance through selective exposure* and, if exposed, *attempt to reduce dissonance or avoid further dissonance through distortion of the message and selective forgetting of its content.*

Before reviewing the pertinent literature, it is worthwhile to state once again that product, brand, or store loyalty can represent a commitment through ego-involvement or establishment of a purchasing routine. Whether or not this type of commitment can lead to dissonance and selective screening is a function of its strength. Measurement of strength of commitment is one of the major problems to be faced later in this section.

DISSONANCE AVOIDANCE THROUGH SELECTIVE EXPOSURE. It is a logical and appealing hypothesis that individuals avoid dissonance through selective exposure in the face of strongly-held and important predispositions (for example, religious beliefs or political preferences). One study by Adams [1961] purported to demonstrate selective exposure to discrepant information, but the results are unconvincing. Other studies have found quite different results. Feather [1963] reports that smokers were *more interested* in information on the smoking-cancer relationship than non-smokers, an unexpected finding. In addition, Mills [1965] and Brock [1965] failed to find selective avoidance of dissonance-producing information.

It is possible that these contradictory findings can be explained by the presence or absence of additional cognitions that bolster a person's point of view [Brock, 1965]. If these justifying cognitions are absent, it is probable that dissonance-avoidance will be more commonplace. For example, if few of the person's other experiences are relevant to his position, it is difficult for him to justify his belief or action. Further information is then perceived as threatening and avoided for that reason.

DISSONANCE REDUCTION THROUGH MESSAGE DISTORTION. Brehm [1960] and Allyn and Festinger [1961] discovered that exposure to a communication dissonant with a strongly-held opinion leads to little or no change. In fact, it is possible that under some conditions a boomerang effect occurs in that the initial attitude is strengthened through a reaction of hostility to the point of view that is advocated [Cohen, 1962].

One of the forms of distortion that apparently is most commonplace is derogation of the credibility of the source of the dissonance-causing message. This was reported by Allyn and Festinger [1961]. If the communicator has perfect credibility, this response is not open, but under most circumstances it is logical to expect that it is easier to reject the communicator than to change the challenged attitude. This hypothesis, however, was not confirmed by Aronson et al. [1963] and Cohen et al. [1963].

SELECTIVE FORGETTING OF DISSONANT INFORMATION. Assuming that dissonance is aroused by inputs to the system, it also can be reduced by selective forgetting of that which is contradictory with existing cognitions. The experimental evidence on this point is meager and this hypothesis remains for further research. Only one study [Brehm and Cohen, 1962, pp. 94-97] has verified this possibility, but the results are not unequivocal.

The Measurement of Commitment

It seems safe to conclude that selective exposure, distortion, and forgetting can be alternative responses when a commitment stored in memory is challenged by communication that enters the system as an external input. Since brand, product, or store loyalty can be commitment, this conclusion is highly relevant to marketing. This problem, however, lies in the *measurement of commitment*. Many of the studies in the dissonance literature have failed to demonstrate such a measurement, with the result that many of the findings are suspect.

Perhaps the major problem is that most techniques for measuring strength of attitude compute only a single position on a scale of intensity (see, for example, the semantic differential scale devised by Osgood et al., 1957). It is doubtful, however, that an individual's stand toward an issue can be adequately reflected by a single alternative or position among those available. Even if two individuals have the same position on an issue (for example, they both favor Chevrolet), they may differ with respect to the other alternatives each is willing to consider as acceptable and to the range of viewpoints each considers to be definitely unacceptable. Such differences, even among persons holding similar positions, must be considered in predicting how these individuals will react to a communication aimed at persuading them to change.

Commitment, therefore, cannot be adequately measured by a single score. It is necessary to look at the range of acceptable and unacceptable positions. Sherif, et al. [1965] have devised a method of measurement that remedies these difficulties. They have introduced the concepts of *latitude of acceptance* and *latitude of rejection* [Peatman, 1960; Sherif and Hovland, 1961]. According to Sherif, the latitude of acceptance is the position on an issue or attitude toward an object that is most acceptable, and it also includes other acceptable positions. The latitude of rejection, on the other hand, embraces the most objectionable position toward the same phenomenon plus other objectionable positions.

There remains the possibility that there are some positions that the individual neither accepts nor rejects (that is, toward which he prefers to remain noncommittal). Sherif considers this possibility to be of sufficient significance to warrant introduction of the concept of *latitude of noncommitment,* defined as those positions that are regarded as neither acceptable nor objectionable.

On the basis of research summarized by Sherif et al. [1965], the following proposition was supported: the degree of commitment can be determined operationally by comparing the sizes (number of positions in) the various latitudes. Specifically, *the more involved and personally committed the individual is, the greater is the latitude of rejection in relation to the latitude of acceptance, the number of positions on which he remains noncommittal approaching zero.*

In assessing the above latitudes, the assumption is made that the individual is free to determine the number of positions he accepts or rejects or toward which he prefers to remain noncommittal [Sherif et al., 1965]. In one procedure, a subject is presented with nine statements that are consistently marked in the same order by judges with differing attitudes. The individual is asked first to indicate the one position that best represents his own stand. He also is asked to designate the one position he finds to be most unacceptable. The instructions then permit him to indicate any other positions with which he agrees or disagrees. Thus, he is free to accept or reject any remaining position or to be noncommittal.

The Sherif approach promises to be fruitful for studying attitudinal commitment for the reason that it provides the researcher with an operational tool for evaluating one of the important components of the model of consumer behavior mentioned earlier. Moreover, once commitment has been assessed, attempts to induce attitude change can be undertaken on a more realistic basis. This is the subject of the concluding part of this section.

Producing Attitude Change

It is now important to examine how attitude change can be induced under conditions of commitment. There are three possibilities to report:

(1) distraction; (2) nonovert appeals; and (3) accurate placement of appeal relative to commitment. Of these three, accurate placement of appeal is of the greatest significance, for it makes realistic use of the Sherif method discussed above.

DISTRACTION. It is interesting to note that forewarning the recipient about the intent of a forthcoming communication can arouse dissonance and engage the process of selective screening. Kiesler and Kiesler [1964] found that forewarning led to derogation of the communicator, and similar findings are reported by Freedman and Sears [1965]. This implies that an individual who is committed to a particular action or point of view (for instance, brand preference) may be "set" to reject a competing advertisement if he is aware of a forthcoming exposure.

This distortion tendency, however, can be overcome by distracting the recipient's attention while he is exposed to a persuasive message [Festinger and Maccoby, 1964]. This can be accomplished through use of a variety of competing stimuli such as background music or noise. In the above study, it was discovered that attitude change can be produced if attention is distracted sufficiently to make it difficult to counter-argue without interfering with perception of the message. In addition, these findings were verified in an unpublished experiment undertaken as part of the research program in consumer behavior at the Ohio State University.

NONOVERT APPEALS. Walster and Festinger [1962] report success in generating attitude change under conditions where recipients felt they were "overhearing" a message. Presumably it was felt that those who were speaking were making no conscious attempt to persuade. This may suggest that the "slice-of-life" commercial presumably showing real-life situations with ordinary people who normally would not be commercial spokesmen stands a better chance of success than a more overt attempt to persuade. This hypothesis, however, can only be tentative, because the Walster and Festinger study did not possess the degree of experimental control normally required for verified findings.

ACCURATE PLACEMENT OF APPEAL RELATIVE TO COMMITMENT. The literature on cognitive dissonance reveals the unexpected generalization that attitude change can be produced by *increasing dissonance* once the individual voluntarily exposes himself to information. Several studies show that increasing the discrepancy between a person's initial attitude and the point of view advocated in the communication gives rise to increased dissonance and attitude change [Cohen, Terry, and Jones, 1959; and

Cohen, 1959]. Presumably, it is easier to change the attitude under high dissonance than to distort the communication. This finding is in distinction to the usual assumption that an increase in this discrepancy reduces the probability of attitude change and serves to engage selective exposure, distortion, and forgetting.

Sherif et al. [1965] sharply qualify this conclusion, however, by pointing out that attitudes rarely change toward a position that falls far outside a person's latitude of acceptance. It is their contention that researchers in cognitive dissonance seldom have investigated issues that are ego-involved and where the latitude of acceptance is quite small. Their findings show that selective distortion is virtually certain to occur under these circumstances as the discrepancy is increased between initial position and that advocated in the communication. The problem in the dissonance studies, of course, is that commitment is erroneously estimated using only one point on a scale rather than the concepts of latitudes of acceptance, rejection, and noncommittal.

If the position of a communication does not diverge greatly from the latitude of acceptance according to Sherif's findings, there is a likelihood of an *assimilation effect* (that is, distortion of the communication will occur so that it will be seen as nearer to the subject's own position than it actually is). This is, of course, a highly favorable result. On the other hand, a *contrast effect* will occur (the communication will be seen as farther away from the subject's own stand than it really is) if the position advocated in a communication falls within the latitude of rejection. Thus, the conclusion of the literature on cognitive dissonance that *an increase in discrepancy produces greatest attitude change is valid only if the communication does not fall far outside the latitude of acceptance.* For this reason, the Sherif model is a useful extension of cognitive dissonance.

A considerable body of research shows that communication falling within the latitude of rejection is appraised unfavorably by the subject and is seen as "unfair", "biased", and "false". Research studies substantiating the above derivations and others are reported in *Attitude and Attitude Change* [Sherif et al., 1965]. This book is worthwhile reading for those interested in utilizing this approach.

The applications of this approach to marketing are highly promising, for a basis is provided for placing a communication to achieve an optimal degree of change. If it is discovered that consumers are not highly committed to a product, brand, or store (large latitude of acceptance, small latitude of rejection) then a highly divergent communication most probably would be assimilated as predicted by dissonance theory. Assume, for example, that a consumer is essentially neutral toward all brands of hair spray but one. In this case, it is likely that she will not screen out advertisements for brands other than that which she is using with the exception of the one that falls within her latitude of rejection.

On the other hand, suppose that another housewife is highly committed to one brand of hair spray (small latitude of acceptance, large latitude of rejection). She is, in other words, quite "choosy" about which items are acceptable to her. Only those communications that pertain to her product are likely to be assimilated as acceptable. An advertiser would be wary about using a highly discrepant communication in this type of situation. In fact, it is not difficult to imagine entire segments of buyers whose latitudes of acceptance are so small that competing products will not even be considered.

It is helpful, at this point, to refer once again to the findings discussed earlier on attitude change following behavioral change. This probably will take place only when the behavior that was undertaken falls close to the latitude of acceptance around the attitude. Otherwise, the behavior would be disregarded as irrelevant in order to reduce the dissonance that is aroused. For example, the housewife who feels that cold-water soap cannot get clothes clean is unlikely to change her attitude even though a trial of the product tells her otherwise.

To sum up, the Sherif approach permits an evaluation of how committed consumers are to certain products, brands, or stores; and, on this basis, it is possible to predict the probability of switching to other alternatives in the future. Furthermore, a valid practical goal is to increase loyalty over time, and a longitudinal study would permit a monitoring of whether or not the desired narrowing does indeed occur in the latitudes of acceptance of presently satisfied customers. In addition, it is possible to assess the impact of various marketing programs on changes in this latitude. Unfortunately, dissonance theorists have ignored this all-important time dimension.

CONCLUSION

Hopefully, this review has clarified the nature of cognitive dissonance and the areas of potential application to consumer behavior. Clearly, the theory is limited in scope and by no means explains the breadth of phenomena that some of its proponents have alleged; indeed, it suffers from the very real weakness that no effective method is proposed to measure its central concept—degree of commitment to a point of view or behavior. The applicability of this theory is greatly enhanced when the method of latitudes of acceptance, rejection, and noncommittal is used for this purpose. There is no question that dissonance theory has something important to say about product, brand, and store loyalty and the consequences of a decision when this methodological refinement is made. The model of consumer behavior was suggested to provide background for understanding the role of psychological commitment in consumer behavior. This model also explains and relates many other phenomena such as roles and needs, although space limitations have prevented elaboration of its many implications.

Finally, a real attempt has been made in this review to place dissonance theory in proper perspective insofar as its applications to marketing. It is high time that a halt be called to unwarranted statements about the practical implications of concepts and theories borrowed in wholesale fashion from the behavioral sciences. Thus far, the yield from such an approach has been meager indeed. Of much greater importance is identification of marketing problems where limited information plagues the practitioner (influencing brand loyalty is an example) and then experimenting with useful borrowed concepts to determine whether or not the gain in knowledge is sufficient to justify application. Frequently, the answer will be affirmative. From such an attitude of inquiry, the science of marketing is certain to advance.

BIBLIOGRAPHY

Adams, J. S. Reduction of cognitive dissonance by seeking consonant information. *Journal of Abnormal and Social Psychology*, 1961, **62**, 74-78.
Allyn, Jane and Festinger, L. The effectiveness of unanticipated persuasive communications. *Journal of Abnormal and Social Psychology*, 1961, **62**, 35-40.
Aronson, E. and Carlsmith, J. M. Effect of threat on the devaluation of forbidden behavior. *Journal of Abnormal and Social Psychology*, 1963, **66**, 584-588.
Atkin, K. Advertising and store patronage. *Journal of Advertising Research*, 1962, **2**, 18-23.
Brehm, J. W. Attitudinal consequences of commitment to unpleasant behavior. *Journal of Abnormal and Social Psychology*, 1960, **60**, 379-383.
Brehm, J. W. and Cohen, A. R. *Explorations in Cognitive Dissonance.* New York: John Wiley & Sons, Inc., 1962.
Brock, T. C. Cognitive restructuring and attitude change. *Journal of Abnormal and Social Psychology*, 1962, **4**, 264-271.
Brock, T. C. Commitment to exposure as a determinant of information receptivity. *Journal of Personality and Social Psychology*, 1965, **2**, 10-19.
Carlsmith, J. M. and Aronson, E. Some hedonic consequences of the confirmation

and disconfirmation of expectancies. *Journal of Abnormal and Social Psychology,* 1963, **66**, 151-156.

Chapanis, N. P. and Chapanis, N. Cognitive dissonance: five years later. *Psychological Bulletin,* 1964, **61**, 1-22.

Cohen, A. R. Communication discrepancy and attitude change: a dissonance theory approach. *Journal of Personality,* 1959, **27**, 386-396.

Cohen, A. R. A dissonance analysis of the boomerang effect. *Journal of Personality,* 1962, **30**, 75-88.

Cohen, A. R., Brehm, J. W., and Fleming, W. H. Attitude change and justification for compliance. *Journal of Abnormal and Social Psychology,* 1958, **56**, 276-278.

Cohen, A. R., Brehm, J. W., and Latane, B. Choice of strategy and voluntary exposure to information under public and private conditions. *Journal of Personality,* 1959, **27**, 63-73.

Cohen, A. R., Greenbaum, C. W., and Manson, H. H. Commitment to social deprivation and verbal conditioning. *Journal of Abnormal and Social Psychology,* 1963, **67**, 410-421.

Cohen, A. R., Terry, H. I., and Jones, C. B. Attitudinal effects of choice in exposure to counter-propaganda. *Journal of Abnormal and Social Psychology,* 1959, **58**, 388-391.

Cottrell, N. B. Performance expectancy as a determinant of actual performance. *Journal of Personality and Social Psychology,* 1965, **2**, 685-691.

Culbertson, Frances M. Attitude change through role playing. *Journal of Abnormal and Social Psychology,* 1957, **54**, 230-233.

Ehrlich, Danuta, Guttman, I., Schonbach, P., and Mills, J. Post decision exposure to relevant information. *Journal of Abnormal and Social Psychology,* 1957, **54**, 98-102.

Engel, J. F. The psychological consequences of a major purchase decision. W. S. Decker (ed.), *Marketing in Transition.* Chicago: American Marketing Association, 1963a, 462-475.

Engel, J. F. Are automobile purchasers dissonant consumers? *Journal of Marketing,* 1963b, **27**, 55-58.

Engel, J. F. The influence of needs and attitudes on the perception of persuasion. S. A. Greyser (ed.), *Toward Scientific Marketing.* Chicago: American Marketing Association, 1964, 18-29.

Feather, N. T. Cognitive dissonance, sensitivity, and evaluation. *Journal of Abnormal and Social Psychology,* 1963, **66**, 157-163.

Fender, D. H. Control mechanisms of the eye. *Scientific American,* 1964, **211**, 24-33.

Festinger, L. *A Theory of Cognitive Dissonance.* Evanston: Row, Peterson and Company, 1957.

Festinger, L. *Conflict, Decision, and Dissonance.* Stanford: Stanford University Press, 1964.

Festinger, L. and Carlsmith, J. M. Cognitive consequences of forced compliance. *Journal of Abnormal and Social Psychology,* 1959, **58**, 203-210.

Festinger, L. and Maccoby, N. On resistance to persuasive communications. *Journal of Abnormal and Social Psychology,* 1964, **68**, 359-366.

Freedman, J. L. Preference for dissonant information. *Journal of Personality and Social Psychology,* 1965a, **2**, 287-289.

Freedman, J. L. Confidence utility, and selective exposure. *Journal of Personality and Social Psychology,* 1965b, **2**, 778-780.

Freedman, J. L. and Sears, D. O. Warning, distraction, and resistance to influence. *Journal of Personality and Social Psychology*, 1965, 1, 262-266.

Goldberg, P. A. Expectancy, choice, and the other person. *Journal of Personality and Social Psychology*, 1965, 2, 595-597.

Granbois, D. H. and Engel, J. F. The longitudinal approach to studying marketing behavior. P. D. Bennett (ed.), *Marketing and Economic Development*. Chicago: American Marketing Association, 1965, 205-221.

Hebb, D. O. *The Organization of Behavior*. New York: John Wiley & Sons, Inc., 1949.

Hovland, C. I. Reconciling conflicting results derived from experimental and survey studies of attitude change. *American Psychologist*, 1959, 14, 8-17.

Howard, J. A. *Marketing: Executive and Buyer Behavior*. New York: Columbia University Press, 1963.

Hull, C. L. *A Behavior System*. New Haven: Yale University Press, 1952.

Kiesler, C. A. and Kiesler, S. B. Role of forewarning in persuasive communications. *Journal of Abnormal and Social Psychology*, 1964, 68, 547-549.

Klapper, J. T. *The Effects of Mass Communication*. Glencoe: The Free Press, 1960.

Mills, J. Changes in moral attitudes following temptation. *Journal of Personality*, 1958, 26, 517-531.

Mills, J. Effect of certainty about a decision upon postdecision exposure to consonant and dissonant information. *Journal of Personality and Social Psychology*, 1965, 2, 749-752.

Mills J. and Aronson, E. Opinion change as a function of the communicator's attractiveness and desire to influence. *Journal of Personality and Social Psychology*, 1965, 1, 173-177.

Mills, J., Aronson, E., and Robinson, H. Selectivity in exposure to information. *Journal of Abnormal and Social Psychology*, 1959, 59, 250-253.

Mills, J. and Ross, A. Effects of commitment and certainty upon interest in supporting information. *Journal of Abnormal and Social Psychology*, 1964, 68, 552-555.

Osgood, C. E., Suci, G. J., and Tannenbaum, P. H. *The Measurement of Meaning*. Urbana: University of Illinois Press, 1958.

Peatman, J. G. and Hartley, E. L. *Festschrift for Gardner Murphy*. New York: Harper, 1960.

Sampson, E. E. and Sibley, Linda B. A further examination of the confirmation or nonconfirmation of expectancies and desires. *Journal of Personality and Social Psychology*, 1965, 2, 133-137.

Secord, P. F. and Backman, C. W. *Social Psychology*. New York: McGraw-Hill Book Company, Inc., 1964.

Sherif, M. and Hovland, C. I. *Social Judgement: Assimilation and Contrast Effects in Communication and Attitude Change*. New Haven: Yale University Press, 1961.

Sherif, Carolyn W., Sherif, M., and Nebergall, R. E. *Attitude and Attitude Change*. Philadelphia: Saunders, 1965.

Shibutani, T. Reference groups as perspectives. *American Journal of Sociology*, 1955, 562-569.

Steiner, I. D. and Johnson, H. H. Relationships among dissonance reducing responses. *Journal of Abnormal and Social Psychology*, 1964, 68, 38-44.

Steiner, I. D. and Rogers, E. D. Alternative responses to dissonance. *Journal of Abnormal and Social Psychology*, 1963, 2, 128-136.

Walster, Elaine and Festinger, L. The effectiveness of "overheard" persuasive communications. *Journal of Abnormal and Social Psychology,* 1962, **65**, 395-402.

Ward, W. D. and Sandvold, K. D. Performance expectancy as a determinant of actual performance. *Journal of Abnormal and Social Psychology,* 1963, **67**, 293-295.

Zimbardo, P. G. Involvement and communication discrepancy as determinants of opinion change. *Journal of Abnormal and Social Psychology,* 1960, **60**, 86-94.

The Learning of Consumer Likes, Preferences, and Choices

The purpose of this chapter is to explore consumer behavior from two particular perspectives. The first perspective is to acknowledge that consumer decisions are based on *learned* behavior, and that learning is based on repeated exposures to stimuli. However, we know little about repetitious and cumulative effects on consumers and must be concerned to ask whether learning can really be demonstrated, is it like other learning, and what are its mechanisms?

The second perspective is a concern for *what* is learned. We are all aware that some products or brands elicit strong loyalties based on liking or belief, while other products are bought only as a matter of habit and can be substituted for without care. This range of response to products represents *different* behaviors, and so we must ask whether they may be learned differently. That is, is there somehow a different learning process for emotional likes, rational preferences, simple choices, and so on?

In an attempt to develop an overall view of the problem, I shall draw speculatively on a variety of small studies reported in recent years.

CONSUMER LIKES ARE LEARNED BUT ARE INFREQUENTLY STUDIED AS LEARNING

The subject of consumer likes, or what we call consumer "taste," has proved an elusive one for social scientists and businessmen alike. The social sciences have for the most part confined their interest to a broad and distant view and have only rarely descended to research on the specific processes of taste formation. For students of public opinion, the particular process of familiarization has special relevance in view of their concern with the new, if not in products then certainly in ideas. Too often

207

in the past, however, explanations for public acceptance or rejection of the new have wandered without restraint between such commonplaces as "Repetition equals reputation," and "Familiarity breeds contempt," or "It's the novelty that attracts people," and "It's too new for the public." Moreover, the sudden rise and often equally sudden fall of "fads" and fancies in the marketplace are treated as temporary aberrations not worthy of serious attention—perhaps, in part, because of the plainly trivial nature of some of the objects involved (for example, beanie caps, hula-hoops, and beards). When a fad or newly popular item becomes *generalized* into a broad acceptance for some new theme (that is, when a new "style" or "fashion" is born), then it is true that there is talk of norms and mores and the social scientists may be interested. The question of how a fad turns into a style or fashion is necessarily unanswered, however, since the antecedent fad and the whole subject of fads have been left unexplored and misunderstood. This applies equally to the new style or fashion which achieves a quiet and unobtrusive acceptance without benefit of an antecedent and much-commented-upon fad.

The subject of consumer likes is important for several reasons. To the small businessman, it represents a particularly tragic area of decision making. Too frequently, a manufacturer finds a sudden "hit" on his hands and borrows capital to expand plant and equipment, only to find, in the midst of trebled production, that the will-o'-the-wisp public has lost interest. At the other extreme, we have the manufacturer who is rightly convinced of the worth and potential of his new product, who miscalculates the time it will take for his product to catch on, and who closes his doors financially, unable to wait even in the face of mounting public interest.

For the social sciences, and especially for psychology, the subject of consumer likes is important because it concerns the question of how we learn to like objects or ideas. Although there is a great deal of research and tested knowledge concerning our ability to learn new skills or solve new problems, we do not confidently know if the principles uncovered in those areas apply to the learning of likes or dislikes and, if not, what principles do apply.

To the market or consumer researcher, the subject is also unclear. Most tests of consumer likes and dislikes involve one-time exposure procedures; for example, "Madam, how do you feel about this new product X (Like . . . . dislike . . . . or no opinion . . . .)?" No single-exposure procedure can allow for so many of the problems inherent in the learning process. Learning often implies time and repeated trials or exposures. What we like today may seem dull tomorrow. What seems uninteresting on first view may prove somewhat intriguing with a second look, and so on. Indeed, the market researchers' pretesting of television and other programs on a single-exposure basis may, in part, be responsible for the low levels of taste in much of what is presented to the public. If repeated tests rather than single-exposure tests were made, it might be demonstrated that the audience could "develop a taste" for something new and different, and the sponsor might thereby be encouraged to forego the luxury of immediate popularity for his show.

When time is taken into account, and when it is determined how well an object or idea might wear ("Will it prove popular in the long run? Will it hold up?") we encounter the problem of familiarity. At the other extreme from faddism, yet theoretically its blood brother, we find innumerable examples of manufacturers offering beautiful and superior new styles, fabrics, devices, or packages to a strange market that seems perversely to prefer going along with the older but more familiar items. The psychologist's interest may be engaged here as he identifies a familiar problem: "resistance to social change." Although it is a familiar problem in those terms, however, it may not be so familiar when linked with fads and fancies as one and the same problem. That problem concerns the beginning and the end points of learning to like. It is the problem of some new products becoming popular quickly and others slowly, of some dying out quickly and others slowly, of some fads broadening into fashions and some fashions persisting indefinitely. It concerns the question of when novelty is delightful and when familiarity outweighs all other considerations. It is the question of how we learn to like and of what is the influence of the extent of familiarity on the degree of liking.

The study of learning, especially in its relation to the phenomenon of memory, is perhaps the oldest of the classic interests of academic psychology. Indeed, it goes well back into the nineteenth century. Since that time, the world of education has created enormous pressures and opportunities for psychologists to contribute to better understanding of the learning process in the classroom situation. Out of the vast body of research and literature produced to meet this challenge, there developed several major and competing theories of learning, differing in important theoretical respects but similar in the factors of variables considered important to study, and similar also in many of the principles which later emerged as practical guides in the classroom.

The most widely accepted principles can be summarized as follows. In learning new skills, repetition or practice is effective; active practice, or recitation, is more effective than passive practice; the learning of the task as a whole is more effective than learning it piece by piece; short practice sessions spread over a longer period of time are more effective than longer practice sessions crammed into a shorter period of time; when practice is continued beyond what is required for successful accomplishment of the task at hand, there is little forgetting of what has been learned even after long periods without practice.

Now the businessman may become interested and may ask what implications there are here for how complete his advertisements should be in describing his product, how often and over how long a period his advertisements should be spaced, and the like. To some extent, practical implications do exist but, as far as we know, only in terms of product awareness. We do not know but are now asking what implications there are in terms of product liking and disliking. One difficulty lies in the difference between classroom and marketplace. In the classroom, we have motivated individuals actively coping with difficult problems, whereas, in the marketplace, we are much more involved with capturing the attention of a passive audience and creating likes for objects, forms, and ideas which, despite the manufacturers' pride, may be quite trivial in importance or consumer concern. These qualifications do not prevent us, however, from singling out the major factor in learning (that is, repetition) and putting it in terms of exposure and familiarity, to see where and how repetition can be linked to the development of likes and dislikes.

Two aspects of repetition and familiarity may be defined. One aspect concerns what is called cognitive or perceptual learning; for example, how often do we have to look at an object or hear a theme before we recognize it as "familiar"? The second aspect concerns what is called affective learning; for example, how often do we have to look or hear before we "like."

EFFECTS OF REPETITION CAN BE DEMONSTRATED

The following charming illustration is taken from Thomas Smith's *Hints to Intending Advertisers* published in London in 1885.

The first time a man looks at an advertisement, he does not see it.
The second time he does not notice it.
The third time he is conscious of its existence.
The fourth time he faintly remembers having seen it before.
The fifth time he reads it.
The sixth time he turns up his nose at it.
The seventh time he reads it through and says, 'Oh bother!'

The eighth time he says, 'Here's that confounded thing again!'
The ninth time he wonders if it amounts to anything.
The tenth time he thinks he will ask his neighbor if he has tried it.
The eleventh time he wonders how the advertiser makes it pay.
The twelfth time he thinks perhaps it may be worth something.
The thirteenth time he thinks it must be a good thing.
The fourteenth time he remembers that he has wanted such a thing for a long time.
The fifteenth time he is tantalized because he cannot afford to buy it.
The sixteenth time he thinks he will buy it some day.
The seventeenth time he makes a memorandum of it.
The eighteenth time he swears at his poverty.
The nineteenth time he counts his money carefully.
The twentieth time he sees it, he buys the article, or instructs his wife to do so.[1]

Mr. Smith was undoubtedly ahead of his time. However, we can and must determine how repetition actually works. I recently had an opportunity that provides an illustration of how a marketing decision might be reversed when initial consumer reactions are compared with repeated reactions.[2]

Two sets of packages of a washday product were prepared for separate pretesting. Each set (ACD, BCD) was tested in an eastern, midwestern, and western location (New York, Memphis, Los Angeles). The testing procedure was as follows.

1. Pairs of 35 mm color photographs of the packages were slide-projected onto a screen for an indication of preference individually from respondents. The projections were repeated five times tachistoscopically with exposure time in the first series at 1 second, in the second series at $1\frac{1}{2}$ seconds, in the third at 2 seconds, in the fourth at $2\frac{1}{2}$ seconds, and in the fifth at 3 seconds. For any one series, three pair choices were offered (A versus C, C versus D, A versus D). Thus, each package could achieve a total preference "score" from 0 to 2 per series.

2. Between each series, respondents rated actual sample packages. After exposure to the first slide-preference series, they rated the packages on familiarity; after the second, they rated them on appropriateness; after the third, on ease of use; and after the fourth, on relative size. The repeated attention given to the packages during the rating process, as well as the increasing exposure time allotted to the repeated slide-preference

[1] Thomas Smith, *Hints to Intending Advertisers*, London, 1885. Quoted by James Playsted Wood in *The Story of Advertising* (New York: Ronald, 1958), p. 241.
[2] This study was reported in H. E. Krugman, "The Learning of Consumer Preference," *Journal of Marketing*, p. 31-33 (April, 1962).

series, was meant to simulate the process of familiarization to the new packages. That is, the respondents were exposed to the packages repeatedly for longer periods of time, and evaluated the packages from several different perspectives.

As a note of caution, it should be stated that techniques of simulation require validation before being put into standard use. The purpose of the simulation technique used here was to create the same kinds of changes (if any) which respondents would experience in the normal course of events with repeated exposure to the packages. The validity of the technique depends, therefore, on these and no other changes being produced. In the absence of such validation, the present study is offered more as an illustration of what may be a new and potentially useful approach, rather than as a conclusive evaluation of the packages under study.

One set of packages (ACD) showed a significant reversal of preferences with repeated exposures when tested in the western location but not in the eastern or midwestern locations. The second set of packages (BCD) showed reversal of preferences in both western and midwestern locations but not in the eastern location (see Table 8.1).

Attention was focussed on the rank order of preferences within each series (rows), rather than the series-by-series shifts for individual packages (columns) which led to the reordering of preferences.

That is, a marketer would tend to adopt the package achieving a first-rank position, if the difference between the first and second ranks were statistically significant. Accordingly, chi-square values were computed for each series to test the proposition that differences in rank order as large as those that were obtained would have occurred on a chance basis.

In the first group in Table 8.1 (ACD, western location), differences within each series were significant at the 1 percent level. That is, differences of the magnitude indicated would have occurred on a chance basis only once in a hundred times. In this group, only two exposures were required to change the first ranking package from D to C. In this case a marketer would, on the basis of one exposure, have been justified in adopting package D. However, using the same statistical criteria he would, with a second exposure, change his selection to package C.

In the second group in Table 8.1 (BCD, western location), rank-order differences within series were also significant at the 1 percent level. Again, two exposures were all that were required to change the first ranking package from D to C.

In the third group in Table 8.1 (BCD, midwestern location), differences in rank order were not significant within the first series, but increased with each series until the fifth where they attained significance at the 5 percent level. That is, differences of the magnitude indicated would have occurred on a chance basis only 5 times out of 100. Here, therefore, all five exposures were required to place package D clearly in first rank.

This study probably represents a minimal demonstration of the importance of repeated exposure. First, familiarization was only simulated, that is, the presumed effects of time and usage were "collapsed" into about half an hour of testing. Second, none of the packages had any essentially new or unfamiliar elements per se; that is, they were only

TABLE 8.1   MEAN   PREFERENCE   SCORES   FOR   FIVE   EXPOSURE
SERIES (RANGE 0.00 LOW TO 2.00 HIGH)

Location	Series	Scores		
		A ($N = 60$)	C ($N = 60$)	D ($N = 60$)
Western				
	1	0.57	1.12	1.32
	2	0.45	1.33	1.22
	3	0.43	1.35	1.22
	4	0.47	1.30	1.23
	5	0.43	1.33	1.23
		B ($N = 30$)	C ($N = 30$)	D ($N = 30$)
Western				
	1	0.60	1.13	1.27
	2	0.57	1.50	0.93
	3	0.57	1.47	0.97
	4	0.50	1.47	1.03
	5	0.57	1.53	0.90
		B ($N = 27$)	C ($N = 27$)	D ($N = 27$)
Midwestern				
	1	1.07	1.04	0.89
	2	1.04	0.78	1.19
	3	1.04	0.78	1.19
	4	1.04	0.74	1.22
	5	0.93	0.70	1.37

"new" for the brand. Third, packaging generally does not represent a class of objects that the consumer approaches with anticipation of continual change and readiness to accommodate to that change. However, the study demonstrates that repeated exposures to a package can alter the rank order of consumer preference, and presumably a marketing decision as to which package to adopt.

It was noted that the influence of repeated exposures was manifest in some locations but not in others, thus suggesting a need to pretest in varied types of locations. Also, in two of the three cases where repetition did alter rank order of preference, two exposures of the packages were sufficient to bring about and stabilize an alternation in rank order, but more than two exposures were required in the third case.

It should also be noted that use of the term "preference" follows only from the use of that term in the literal question put to respondents. The actual respondent behavior might be more carefully described as choice behavior, the associated or underlying beliefs and attitudes being unknown.

LEARNING TO LIKE AN ITEM MAY GENERALIZE INTO A LIKING FOR THE CLASS OF ITEMS OR CATEGORY

Repetition can create learned consumer responses and these can have effects that go beyond the item being learned (to like); that is, attitudes toward an entire product category can be altered by favorable experiences with one item. This was demonstrated with popular and classical music; nine college students were chosen as subjects on the basis of an attitude questionnaire and personal interview.[3] The following is the questionnaire.

This questionnaire is presented to you in an effort to find a number of students who would be willing to serve as subjects in a psychological research project. The task of the subjects consists of listening to musical selections for approximately half an hour, once a week for the duration of the semester.

Directions: Read each item carefully and underline the phrase which best expresses your feeling about the statement. If in doubt, underline the phrase which seems most nearly to express your present feeling about the sentence.

[3] This study was reported in H. E. Krugman, "Affective Response to Music as a Function of Familiarity," *Journal of Social and Abnormal Psychology*, **38** (3), (July, 1943).

I prefer classical music to any other kind of music
strongly agree   agree   undecided   disagree   strongly disagree

I prefer popular music to any other kind of music
strongly agree   agree   undecided   disagree   strongly disagree

I listen to classical music approximately—1 hr.—3 hrs.—5 hrs.—7 hrs.—9 hrs. 11 hrs.—13 hrs.—15 hrs. a week

I listen to popular music approximately—1 hr.—3 hrs.—5 hrs.—7 hrs.—9 hrs. 11 hrs.—13 hrs.—15 hrs. a week

Three subjects, A, B, C, were chosen for their extreme preference for popular music over classical music. Their disdain for classical music was expressed in a very definite and prejudiced manner. Subjects X, Y, and Z were chosen for their similar preference for classical music. Three subjects were chosen for their indifference to all types of music but, since two of them were unable to complete the trials, we shall consider only the record of the remaining subject K.

The trials were held in a small, semisoundproofed room. The subject was seated and listened to three musical recordings played by phonograph; pitch and volume were kept constant from week to week. During the first trial, a number of recordings were played until three were found to which the subject was more or less indifferent. All were presented in the same order (that is, for this individual subject) at each weekly session over a period of eight weeks.

Affective ratings were made on a graphic rating-scale 14 centimeters in width. At the 1 centimeter line, a small VP was explained as "very pleasant," at the fourth line, P was termed "pleasant"; I, "indifference," was located at the seventh line and the "unpleasant" and "very unpleasant" at the tenth and thirteenth lines respectively.

Classical selections were played for subjects A, B, and C (the popular music fans), while popular music was played for X, Y, and Z (the classical music fans); the indifferent subject K also listened to classical music. In selecting each stimulus, we made certain that the subjects had never before heard the piece and that it reminded them of no other. All information about the selections was withheld from the subjects. All of the subjects seemed much interested and were attentive to the music. At the conclusion of the trials, the subjects repeated their attitude questionnaires, and some evidence was found that the experiment affected the ratings.

A very rough quantitative summary may be given by plotting, week by week, the algebraic mean of affective response, using all subjects and all musical selections. This curve is to be regarded as a learning curve;

that is, as a progressive trend toward enjoyment of the music. To test for the significance of the slope (that is, the genuineness of the increase in affective tone), we correlated the ordinal position of the trials with degree of positiveness in affective tone. The Pearson product moment $r = 0.91$. The music became more satisfying from the first through the sixth trial; there is a slight downward trend thereafter. It must, however, be clearly emphasized that this trend, based on averages, greatly oversimplifies the picture; there are great individual differences in affective shift, and different types of shifts in the individual subject's responses to different records. Although 18 out of 21 shifts are in the positive direction, much may have depended on our choice of records. The correlation of 0.91, based on so few subjects and so few records, is not offered as cogent evidence. By removing a single subject from the total, and averaging the rest, we could produce various changes; for example, by removing one specific subject, the drop in the seventh and eighth weeks is marked, necessitating a curvilinear graph and indicating the "waxing and waning" of positive affective responses as found in some other studies.

The individual data indicate that the positive trend is at least as marked in the case of the popular music as it is in the case of the classical music; repetition of the questionnaire suggests that most of the subjects have developed, to some degree, a liking for the type of music to which they have been experimentally exposed. All subjects agreed that they could get to like some selections from a type of music against which they had previously felt a marked prejudice.

ITEM LIKES AND ITEM DISLIKES ARE LEARNED BUT MAY OR MAY NOT GENERALIZE TO THE CATEGORY

In a recent experiment, Hartley takes a closer look at the relationship between familiarity and liking for items and categories, and he does this for different types of categories, in an attempt to discover for what categories generalization from item to category is most likely and for what categories it is least likely.[4] In his study, Hartley used "oriental," "modern," "portrait," "floral," and "landscape" as his categories, and individual paintings as his items.

Hartley had twenty-three students rate each of ten paintings on a five-point scale of familiarity, and then again on a five-point scale of liking.

[4] This study was reported in H. E. Krugman and E. L. Hartley, "The Learning of Tastes," *Public Opinion Quarterly*, **24**, 622-631 (winter 1960).

The ten paintings involved two each representing oriental, modern, portrait, floral, and landscape subjects or styles. He called these the test paintings. A week later, and five times during the three weeks thereafter, the students were shown five other paintings, one for each of the categories above, and asked to study them carefully for twenty seconds. Then the students were asked to imagine the paintings and rate them for various aspects of clarity. There were called the familiarization paintings. After the five exposures were over and these exercises in imagery completed, the original test paintings were rated again for familiarity and liking.

Comparison of the before and after ratings of the test paintings showed a general increase in familiarity for the ten items, but with different degrees of increase by category. Thus, increases in familiarity were greatest for oriental, floral, modern, and landscape paintings in that (decreasing) order, while portraits showed a decrease in familiarity (that is, exposure to portraits made them seem less familiar). Comparison also showed that there was no general change in liking for the categories, but that moderns (especially) and portraits (slightly) were more liked, while florals were less liked.

In order to discover what these differential shifts implied for the relationship between items and categories, the question was raised as to the extent to which the two orientals, two moderns, two portraits, two florals, and two landscapes were seen or treated as members of the same category. This was done by correlating the initial ratings of familiarity and of liking for each of the two paintings in the test series: did the two orientals get similar or dissimilar ratings on familiarity and on liking? Keeping the very rough $(N = 2)$ definition of category in mind, it may be reported, nevertheless, that all correlations on familiarity were significant and positive, and that this was especially true of portraits and florals; on a cognitive level these were all true categories or fell into accepted categories. As for liking, however, the correlations were both negative and positive, and only landscapes and moderns showed significant and positive correlations. In short, there were no prejudices or tendencies to like or dislike the items as a category except for landscapes and moderns. Furthermore, when familiarity and liking were correlated with each other by category, it was found that portraits and florals showed consistent and high negative correlations for the four items involved—the more familiar, the more disliked. Orientals showed a consistent positive correlation for the two items involved—the more familiar, the more liked.

What, then, are the implications of these initial reactions? First, let us summarize the results in Table 8.2 (with F = familiarity, L = liking, and D = disliking).

TABLE 8.2

Category	Intial Test of F as a Category	Initial Test of L or D as a Category	Initial Relation of L and D as Items	Retest Increase in F of the Category	Retest Shifts in L of the Category
Oriental	Yes	No	Increased $F = L$	Most	None
Floral	Especially	No	Increased $F = D$	Second	Decrease
Modern	Yes	Yes	None	Third	Increase
Landscape	Yes	Yes	None	Fourth	None
Portraits	Especially	No	Increased $F = D$	Decrease	Increase (slight)

The oriental paintings were seen as a category but were (predominantly) liked more on an item-by-item basis than on a category basis. Familiarity increased for this category more than for any other (perhaps because the category is strange to Americans), but no increase in liking for the category took place.

Floral paintings were especially seen as a category but were (predominantly) disliked more on an item-by-item than on a category basis. Familiarity with the category increased significantly and apparently produced dislike for the category as such.

Modern paintings were seen and liked or disliked as a category without much item-by-item sensitivity. Familiarity with the category increased moderately, while liking for the category increased significantly.

Landscape paintings were also seen and liked or disliked as a category without item-by-item sensitivity. Familiarity with the category increased, but liking for the category did not.

Portraits were especially seen as a category, but were (predominantly) disliked more on an item-by-item basis than on a category basis. Familiarity with the category decreased, that is, it began to be seen as different, and familiarity even produced some increase in liking for the category.

We might characterize the oriental situation as "open"; individual items can be liked, but familiarity with the category still provides room for increase without any shift in liking for the category. Florals, on the other hand, could be characterized as a dead category, where further exposure and familiarity will only broaden the dislike for individual items into a dislike for the category as a whole. Moderns and landscapes are perhaps the most popular categories of those studied here, and further familiarity with the more popular moderns increases their popularity, while further familiarity with landscapes has no further effect on their popularity. Portraits, on the other hand, represent a dead category that apparently can be resurrected or reappreciated.

In general, then, Hartley has shown that familiarity with and study of items (in this case, the exercises in imagery) for the most part increase familiarity with the category. What then happens to liking for the category may depend on what room for further familiarity still exists (as with orientals), on the relationship between familiarity and liking for individual items (as with florals), on the popularity of the category (as with moderns), or possibly on other factors not involved in the categories used in this study. The case of the portraits suggests that the students learned to see the category differently. It would have been useful, therefore, to have had a direct measure of how successful or revealing the imagery exercises were. It would seem that something was learned there about portraits that would have been measurably larger than what was learned about other categories.

LEARNING MAY NOT OCCUR AND FAMILIARITY MAY BREED INDIFFERENCE

Familiarity may affect our attitudes toward a wide variety of items from everyday life. The classic attempt to study such variety in an experimental setting was made by Maslow.[5] He recruited fifteen students for a ten-day, two-hours-a-day experiment. During each session, the students met in the same room and took the same seats. The room had large, bright pictures on the wall and a metronome ticking in the background. The sessions were devoted to looking at a series of paintings by fifteen well-known artists, trying to write down and spell correctly the names of Russian women read to them by the experimenter, copying out of a book those sentences that contained key words provided on a separate list, and marking true-false tests. Throughout the experiment, the

[5] A. H. Maslow, "The Influence of Familiarization on Preference," *Journal of Experimental Psychology*, **21**, 162-180 (1937).

students wore smocks, used grey rubber bands, large paper clips, yellow blotters, unlined 3 x 5 cards, used copies of books, yellow paper, and pens. Cookies were available for refreshment. These conditions prevailed generally throughout the sessions until the last few, when periodically the students were offered something different, without warning, or asked to make a judgment of personal preference.

The students were offered a chance to change seats, to have the pictures on the wall removed, to have the metronome stopped; they were shown a matched series of paintings by the same fifteen artists and asked which in each matched pair was more beautiful; they were read a similar series of Russian women's names and asked which in each matched pair sounded nicer; they were offered the choice of copying significant parts rather than whole sentences, and of writing original sentences rather than copying; they were offered an easier test-marking system; in addition, they were offered a chance to remove their smocks and to use red rubber bands, small paper clips, orange blotters, lined 3 x 5 cards, new books, blue writing pads, pencils, and a new kind of cookie. The results showed a general tendency to choose the "familiar," although some students were more likely to do this than others. More important, there was a great difference in what kinds of choice were affected by familiarity and what kinds were not.

Students did not care to change their seats and were no longer aware enough of the bright pictures on the wall or the metronome ticking in the background to care about these matters one way or another. These items were apparently peripheral to the tasks at hand and, while distracting at first, eventually disappeared into the background. Thus, familiarity neutralized them to the point where no liking or disliking was involved, but only indifference.

Judgments of paintings and names were clearly affected by familiarity, that is, the more familiar were preferred as more beautiful. In addition, half or more of the students preferred the familiar ways of copying sentences or marking tests even though the new methods offered were easier. It is in these two areas that familiarity seemed to have its most positive effect. These represented, of course, the focus of the students' attention. In the case of paintings and names, however, it was more surely demonstrated that familiarity was responsible for preference of the original series by showing that another group of students, not previously exposed to the original series, split their preferences more evenly between the two.

Students did not, at first, care about removing their smocks, but half of them did so with further encouragement. No preference was shown for rubber bands or blotters of one or another color, or for large or small paper clips. There were some tendencies to prefer the familiar unlined 3 x 5 cards, old books, pens, and original cookies. In one case, that of blue writing pads versus yellow paper, the new item was preferred. However, results might have been different if single sheets of blue paper had been compared with the single sheets of yellow paper.

In all, this study is a challenging demonstration of the potent and yet varied influence of familiarity. Some items were affected greatly, others less, and still others not at all. We should understand more, perhaps, if we knew how repeated exposures affected the responses of those who initially liked a picture or name as opposed to those who initially disliked a picture or name. We should also like to know which kinds of familiarized preference stood up over a long period of time and which disappeared with time.

Most important, we should want to bring more directly into play the concept of the learning process. In Maslow's study, he deals with items that are familiar and not familiar, on a cognitive level, rather than with items of a measured degree of more or less familiarity. Thus, it would be instructive to know if the influence of repeated exposures upon preference for a picture or name was greater among those students who had learned to remember the pictures more vividly or to spell the names of Russian women more correctly.

LIKES SATISFY GENERIC NEEDS ON THE BASIS OF DIRECT EXPERIENCE

Terminology in consumer research is typically quite loose. Up to now we have been talking primarily about the learning of likes and the influence of repetition and familiarization. However, the subject of preferences and of simple choices has also slipped unobtrusively into the discussion, especially in the case of the Maslow experiment. Let us therefore shift attention to a more careful distinction between likes, preferences, and choices.

Likes involve affective tone or pleasure, some of which is evident and sometimes grows or develops from learning exposure to learning exposure. That pleasure, basically physical, is provided, has suggested that affective learning involved the satisfaction by the specific stimulus of some general need. Repetition of this "solution" to the need, so to speak, progressively increases response to the stimulus. Some investigators (for example, Janet) have called this process *canalization* to distinguish it from conditioning; that is, in canalization the stimulus *itself* is satisfactory and is not becoming liked simply because it may be presented in the presence of some already liked object.[6] It is also contended that canalized likes, although they may wax and wane with temporary satiation, are never completely extinguished; for example, having once acquired a taste for olives or for beautiful paintings, this taste always remains.

From this point of view, the marketer has reason to prize consumer liking of his brand or product, since the developed loyalty may withstand counterargument from competitors quite easily. The likes, having been built upon repeated satisfaction, stand by themselves.

In the market place, it is the generic-product likes that are usually of this nature. Once the market has been so established for, let us say, olives, it is then up to the brands to compete for preference or choice. Occasionally, a marketer is lucky enough to have his brand identified with the generic category, as in the case with consumers who grew up with only one brand. More often than not, however, deep-seated likes are reserved for the category and not the item. Thus, market researchers, especially motivation researchers, can discuss product likes and dislikes with consumers and quickly tap the important attitudes towards the generic class of product. The question of individual brands, however, is harder to discuss in a reliable and meaningful way.

Much of new-product development research attempts to identify unsatisfied needs that may now be satisfied. It is a kind of research that is very satisfying to the researchers themselves because of the "real" contribution they are making to consumers, and because of the sincerely enthusiastic feedback that may be achieved from consumers. In this connection, it should be noted that the progressive satisfaction of needs and the associated learning to like is a fairly conscious phenomenon on which consumers can report. In every way, the situation is made easy for research—provided there are good new products to research.

The determined psychologist may pass up the enthusiasms of new-product research for something more complex and more common—for, after all, the really new mousetrap is a rarity. The everyday marketplace situation is more aptly described as one of a hundred better mousetraps with some better (in sales) than others. How do we account for clear differences in preference or choice when these are unrelated to true liking or perhaps even to tangible product-to-product differences? Here we move into kinds of learning that are more subtle. Here we take more account of the process of *influence* by other factors than the product

[6] P. Janet, *Psychological Healing* (New York: Macmillan, 1925), p. 683.

itself. This may be contrasted with learning to like wherein response is based more directly on the product experience itself.

PREFERENCES AND CHOICES ARE BASED ON EXTERNAL INFLUENCES AND CHOICES ARE THE LESS WELL UNDERSTOOD

Preferences are defined here as consumer decisions based on belief in the superiority of one's own (selected) item over others. It is a matter, then, of the many better mousetraps, and of the need to say so or claim so.

Marketers would like to think that their products were indeed better and that consumers believed them to be better. What is often the unrecognized case, however, is that their product is neither liked nor considered better, but chosen only because it is adequately "good" *and* for the pleasure of its recognition (that is, sheer familiarity).

Just as new-product research and true consumer liking may be more exciting to marketers and researchers, so is brand competition to be "better" more exciting than to be merely the familiar and routine choice. Nevertheless, the determined psychologist will pass up research on being better to the still more complex and common situation of research on being chosen—chosen without liking or reason. Most provocatively, to the researcher, is the fact that choices of the latter sort cannot be "explained" to the inquiring researcher and may look deceptively like random behavior.

Most of what currently passes for consumer research in popular theorizing about consumer behavior is based on the "better product" type of thinking. Thus, most advertising agencies' managements try to identify, prior to advertising campaigns, some unique selling proposition, purchase proposition, persuasion proposition, and so on, that communicates that their brand has a *reason* to offer the consumer for his preference. Those who actually produce the advertising materials may inject other strategies, but industry and client thinking tends to emphasize the "better" approach, even in the face of categories and markets where no brand loyalty can be found or in markets where loyalty persists in the face of "better" type claims.

This is not to say that "better" approach of advertising and its rational, conscious learning by consumers is inappropriate or wrong. It is indeed, however, what we rational men know best, know too well in fact, so that other equally common types of learning are not distinguished as requiring different treatment. I should like to redress this imbalance by highlighting the processes of consumer choice and the nature of the learning or advertising influences which distinguishes them from the process of consumer preference.

CHOICES ARE LEARNED WITHOUT INVOLVEMENT

The learning of consumer preference is represented by acceptance of a better product type of claim or belief. The change processes *minimally* require one-time transmission of specific new information that represents a way of perceiving the product that is in *conflict* with or different from that represented in older information, and which may lead to resolution of the difference through new decision making. While changed behavior may result as a consequence of new decisions, the behavior is not necessarily a part of the change process; that is, the change process itself may be over before the customer heads for the store, shopping list in hand.

The learning of consumer choice is quite different. It requires repeated exposure to information that the consumer recognizes as present but to which he makes no personally relevant connections; that is, he remains uninvolved. However, this repeated exposure can build a potential for the ability to see a product or brand differently. What is next required to release or trigger this potential is a behavioral opportunity such as in-store shopping; that is, to suddenly see the brand in the new manner when confronted by it on the supermarket shelf. This may also be described as recognizing the previously unconnected exposures as familiar (that is, known). Behavioral completion is *also* required to release appropriate attitudes supportive and consistent with the shift in perceptual structure; that is, if the brand is then purchased, the new way of seeing it may then for the first time be expressed in words, for example, to "explain" why it was selected.

The role of behavior in consumer choice, then, is a part of the change process that continues beyond the store. Unless behavior completion or purchase occurs, there entails an unstable condition that is characterized by a shift in perceptual structure without a corresponding shift in attitudinal structure. Without behavioral completion, therefore, the impact of a behavior opportunity is temporary only and perceptual structure reverts to its initial condition, although still carrying the potential for shift on other occasions. For example, a housewife may be repeatedly struck by some new (advertised) brand attribute each time she confronts it on the store shelf, and yet never retain this impression long enough to put it into words until one day when the actual purchase is made.

In short, with low-involvement product choices, we might look for product adoption through gradual shifts in perceptual structure, aided by repetition, activated by behavioral choice situations, and *followed* at some time by attitude change. With high-involvement product preference, we could look instead for the classic, more dramatic, and more familiar conflict of ideas at the level of conscious opinion and attitude that *precedes* changes in overt behavior.[7]

THE MOSAIC OF THE MARKET

The learning of likes is based on satisfying experience, on preferences on ideas of superiority, and on choices on recognition of familiar influences. All three types comingle, sometimes vis-à-vis the same brand and often within the same individual vis-à-vis a single brand. Sometimes a sequence develops of, first choice, then preference, and finally liking—but none need develop.

It does seem important for a particular market to find out how people are coming into and staying in that market or how many are entering it in each way. The learning of liking can be furthered by investments in forced exposures (for example, sampling and free trials). The learning of preference can be furthered by investments in research and development to make completely better products. The learning of choice can be furthered by investments in advertising to make the sales effort familiar. Each of these investment strategies may have natural proponents in the form of merchandisers, designers, and advertising personnel. The strategy for a particular market, however, should rather be based on good information about the consumer himself. If the pitfalls of terminology are avoided, and if research is based on rigorous definition and differentiation of the behaviors involved, this would seem to be an entirely feasible policy.

[7] The particular mechanisms of low-involvement learning are discussed in more detail in H. E. Krugman, "The Impact of Television Advertising: Learning without Involvement," *Public Opinion Quarterly*, **29**, 349 (1965).

NINE | *EVERETT M. ROGERS AND*
J. DAVID STANFIELD

Adoption and Diffusion of New Products: Emerging Generalizations and Hypotheses

This information crisis involves the well-being of every man, woman, and child in this country. At stake is the yield from the Nation's vast medical research effort . . . I am concerned that much of the value of this dedicated research may be lost because science's information 'arteries' are choked . . . The tragedy is that the magnificent effort to discover knowledge is not accompanied by a similar effort to make sure that the knowledge is effectively and promptly communicated.

*Hubert H. Humphrey**

The notion that scientific knowledge should be effectively and promptly communicated is widely held by those both in and out of scientific disciplines. In this chapter, we shall discuss the general problem of scientific information diffusion by looking at one specific research field which deals, ironically enough, with the diffusion of research results. We propose to see how this body of diffusion research has contributed to scientific knowledge, and how these contributions have spread through the various scientific disciplines concerned with investigating the process of diffusion. Throughout the present paper, special attention will be focused upon the implications of diffusion research for the field of marketing.

We intend to pursue the following five objectives in this chapter:

1. To discuss the conceptual elements that compose the diffusion process.

2. To examine the academic research traditions studying diffusion, and the interconnections among these research streams.

* *Congressional Record*, March 8, 1962, p. 3396.

3. To outline the methods of operation of the Diffusion Documents Center at Michigan State University, which provided the data upon which the present paper is based.

4. To summarize generalizations about the diffusion process based upon 2400 research findings.

5. To examine the methodologies utilized by researchers in obtaining those results.

We might begin by asking: what is it that diffuses? The literature that we shall review is centrally concerned with the diffusion of innovations. An *innovation* is defined as an idea that is perceived as new by an individual. Thus, innovations include the superball among teenagers, 2,4-D weed spray among Iowa farmers, a new medical drug among physicians, news of Kennedy's assassination, the IUCD birth-control technique among peasant women in India, and a new brand of coffee among United States suburban housewives. An innovation may or may not involve a new material product, as these examples illustrate, but usually does so. It is important to remember that the distinctive aspect of an innovation, as compared to other kinds of ideas, is that it is considered new by the individual who lacks previous knowledge and experience with the idea.

Many of the ideas or messages that we seek to communicate in marketing are innovations. One reason for special interest by marketing practitioners in the diffusion of innovations is because many of their new products fail. As evidence, it is estimated that 95 out of every 100 new commercial products developed today will not succeed.[1] This rate of failure implies that we do not yet completely understand how to design and introduce new products, or else that we do not fully utilize what is known.

Purchase behavior of new products is probably distinctive in many respects from habitual purchase behavior by consumers. And as the rate of new product development moves upward, our interest in understanding the diffusion of innovations likewise increases.

WHAT ARE THE CONCEPTUAL ELEMENTS IN THE DIFFUSION OF INNOVATIONS?

The crucial elements in the diffusion of innovations are (1) the new *idea* (2) that is *communicated* via certain channels (3) among the mem-

---

[1] There is some range in existing estimates of new product failure rates, perhaps due to the types of new products studied and the length of time over which success-failure is estimated. See Philip Marvin, "Why New Products Fail," in Thomas L. Berg and Abe Shuchman (eds.), *Product Strategy and Management* (New York: Holt, Rinehart and Winston, 1963).

bers of a *social system* (4) over *time*.[2] It is the element of time that marks the diffusion field as distinctive from other types of communication research. Time is involved (1) in the *innovation decision period* through which an individual moves from first knowledge of the innovation, to persuasion of its usefulness, to its adoption and continued use; (2) in the *rate of adoption* of the innovation in a social system, usually measured as the number of adopters per time period; and (3) in the *innovativeness* or the degree to which an individual is relatively earlier than other members of his social system to adopt new ideas.

The elements in diffusion differ only in nomenclature from the essential parts of most general communication models. For example, Berlo[3] posited four parts in his *S-M-C-R* model: (1) source, (2) message, (3) channel, and (4) receivers, to which might be added the effects of communication. Obviously, this *S-M-C-R-E* model corresponds to the elements of diffusion to the extent that the *receivers* are the members of a social system, the *channels* are the means by which the innovation spreads, the *message* is the new idea, the *source* is the origin of the innovation (often a commercial firm in the case of new products), and the *effects* are changes in knowledge, attitude, and behavior (adoption or rejection) regarding the innovation.

We should not forget that there are important interrelationships among these elements in the diffusion process. In fact, it is these interrelationships that constitute the main yield from a large harvest of diffusion-research studies, and which will form the corpus of the present paper. For example, the characteristics of the innovation (M) affect its rate of adoption over time (E); channel usage (C) is related to an individual's innovativeness (E) in adopting an innovation.

DIFFUSION RESEARCH TRADITIONS

In order to appreciate the breadth of research interest on the diffusion of innovations, let us consider the nature of the disciplinary environments in which this research has been conducted. A *research tradition* is a series of related studies by scientists in a field in which each previous study affects those that follow. We have identified 14 main research traditions on the diffusion of innovations that are represented by the 708 empirical

[2] For detail, see Everett M. Rogers with Floyd Shoemaker, *Diffusion of Innovations: A Cross-Cultural and Communication Approach* (New York: Free Press of Glencoe, in press).

[3] David K. Berlo, *The Process of Communication* (New York: Holt, Rinehart and Winston, 1960).

research publications gathered in the Diffusion Documents Center[4] at Michigan State University.

Table 9.1 shows the number of empirical research publications[5] from each tradition that are in the Diffusion Documents Center, classified by whether the study was done in the United States or in countries other than the United States, by ten-year time periods. The tradition producing the most publications is Rural Sociology, with roughly five times more publications than its nearest rival. If we combine all studies done by sociologists, regardless of their special area of interest (that is, rural, medical, early, and general), there are 451 publications, or over half of the total.

A second trend illustrated in Table 9.1 is the move by diffusion research to non-United States settings. During the 1960's, almost as many publications were completed outside of the United States as within. This trend reflects both the overseas migration of United States researchers as well as a growing number of non-United States scientists engaged in diffusion research. This trend toward internationalization of the field is heartening if we hope to find hypotheses about the diffusion of innovations that are generally true regardless of the geographic and cultural locale of the study. As the researchers in each of these research traditions gather data from widely varying social climates, the degree to which our findings are culture-bound should be reduced.

Unfortunately, the research traditions in the past have often acted as barriers to the complete diffusion of diffusion-research results.[6] Social scientists studying diffusion have often neglected each other's work because of differences in tradition, even where in some cases two researchers were located on the same campus. Some traditions are relatively more isolationistic than others, as is shown in Table 9.2. The index of cross-citation was computed as the average number of diffusion-research tradi-

---

[4] This documents center is one part of a research project, Diffusion of Innovations in Rural Societies, sponsored by the United States Agency for International Development and conducted by the Department of Communication, Michigan State University.

[5] In the present chapter, we are only concerned with publications reporting diffusion-research results, rather than with the several hundred publications that are bibliographies, summaries, reviews of literature, or theoretical writings without data.

[6] This is not to say that research traditions are the only barrier to better understanding of each others' work by diffusion investigators. We found a considerable number of documents in which no other diffusion studies were cited, whether in the author's own tradition or not. This tendency was most marked among the traditions of agricultural economics, medical sociology (especially in studies of family planning), anthropology, and communication and journalism (particularly in analyses of news event diffusion).

TABLE 9.1. NUMBER OF EMPIRICAL DIFFUSION PUBLICATIONS BY RESEARCH TRADITION, COMPLETED IN THE UNITED STATES AND OUTSIDE THE UNITED STATES, BY TIME PERIODS

Diffusion-Research Tradition	Number of Publications								
	United States				Non-United States				Grand Total
	1940's or before	1950's	1960's	Total	1940's or before	1950's	1960's	Total	
1. Early sociology	7	1	2	10	1	0	0	1	11
2. Rural sociology	12	115	98	225	0	18	83	101	326
3. Medical sociology	1	11	12	24	0	1	17	18	42
4. General sociology, unspecified	2	23	21	46	0	5	11	16	62
5. Anthropology	2	10	6	18	1	21	11	33	51
6. Agricultural economics	0	8	4	12	0	5	10	15	27
7. Consumer behavior, marketing, and market research	0	5	11	16	0	0	3	3	19
8. Industrial engineering	0	1	1	2	0	2	1	3	5
9. Economics (general economics and economic history)	1	3	6	10	0	0	2	2	12
10. Education	3	6	15	24	0	0	1	1	25
11. Communication	0	1	18	19	0	0	20	20	39
12. Journalism and speech	1	2	3	6	0	0	3	3	9
13. Geography	0	0	3	3	0	1	2	3	6
14. Psychology	1	3	2	6	0	4	6	10	16
15. All other traditions	4	10	8	22	0	10	26	36	58
Totals	34	199	210	443	2	67	196	265	708

TABLE 9.2. NUMBER OF CROSS-CITATIONS TO OTHER TRADITIONS MADE BY EACH DIFFUSION RESEARCH TRADITION[a]

Research Tradition (of the Diffusion Publication in Which the Citations Appear)	Total	Number of Traditions Cited[b] (Other than the Researcher's Own Tradition)										Index of Cross-Citations[c]
		0	1	2	3	4	5	6	7	8	9	
1. Geography	6	2	1	0	2	0	1	0	0	0	0	1.833
2. Education	25	9	6	6	2	1	0	0	1	0	0	1.400
3. Psychology	16	8	4	0	3	0	1	0	0	0	0	1.125
4. Journalism and speech	9	4	2	2	0	0	1	0	0	0	0	1.222
5. Communication	39	16	7	9	7	0	0	0	0	0	0	1.118
6. Consumer behavior, marketing, and market research	19	11	3	1	2	1	1	0	0	0	0	1.053
7. Economics (general economics and economic history)	12	8	1	1	2	0	0	0	0	0	0	0.750
8. Agricultural economics	27	15	7	4	0	1	0	0	0	0	0	0.704
9. Rural sociology	326	202	67	28	18	8	1	1	1	0	0	0.696
10. Medical sociology	42	33	6	1	0	1	1	0	0	0	0	0.405
11. Anthropology	51	39	9	2	1	0	0	0	0	0	0	0.314
12. Early sociology	11	9	1	1	0	0	0	0	0	0	0	0.273
13. Industrial engineering	5	5	0	0	0	0	0	0	0	0	0	0.000
14. All other traditions	120	53	18	12	11	3	4	2	0	0	1	1.067

[a] Our classification system in the present table does not include "general sociology unspecified" (which was included in Table 9.1), due to problems in identifying citations in this tradition.
[b] This index is not completely indicative of how aware the traditions are of one another, since it relies only on footnotes and bibliographic references contained in the publications. Nonetheless, it is a rough indication of the degree to which varieties of diffusion have diffused to other diffusion researchers.
[c] This index of cross-citations is the average number of citations (to other than the researcher's own tradition) made by researchers in each tradition.

232

tions (other than the author's own) cited in the footnotes and bibliography of each publication. Wc see that the Marketing tradition cites slightly more of the other research traditions than most fields, but even then, the breadth of cross-citation is quite limited as only about one non-marketing tradition is cited per publication.[7] It seems that there are severe barriers erected between our academic traditions, that sharply limit the full sharing of knowledge; in this case, a more complete "diffusion of diffusion."

Before we become too pessimistic, however, about the inadequate communication among the diffusion-research traditions, we should examine the longitudinal trends in interdisciplinary contact. Table 9.3 shows the

TABLE 9.3. AVERAGE NUMBER OF CROSS-CITATIONS PER PUBLICATION BY YEAR

Year of Publication	Average Number of Cross-Citations per Publication	Total Number of Publications Completed
Before 1940	0.083	12
1940 to 1944	0.643	14
1945 to 1949	0.300	10
1950 to 1954	0.430	79
1955 to 1959	0.522	186
1960 to 1962	0.954	173
1963 to 1964	0.975	161
1965 to 1966	1.370	73
Total	—	708

tendency over time for more adequate cross-citation of diffusion-research results, and an evident breaking down of the "paper curtains" among the traditions, especially during the 1960's.[8] Evidently, there is a growing

[7] The fact that smaller-sized traditions (such as Geography, Education, and Psychology) have more cross-citations might, in part, be due to the lack of other work to cite in the *same* tradition. Whatever the reasons, the traditions with higher cross-citation index scores have a smaller number of publications and are more recent in origin than the traditions with lower cross-citation indexes (Table 9.2).

[8] It is interesting to speculate about the specific techniques that were instrumental in causing greater interdisciplinary awareness in the diffusion field. Among the most important are probably the availability of courses on diffusion at various universities, the appearance of a general textbook on the subject (that was not tradition-bound),

awareness on the part of diffusion researchers that their findings show a general type of consistency, independent of their disciplinary affiliation, the specific type of respondents studied, the nature of the innovation, and so on. Diffusion research is thus emerging as a single body of concepts and relationships, even though the investigations are conducted by researchers in many scientific disciplines.

Where does the diffusion-research field stand today? One fact is readily apparent: the field is very rapidly growing. Figure 9.1 illustrates this rate of growth. Boulding,[9] in his discussion of the breadth of knowledge in our twentieth century, notes that in many areas of human endeavor, the turning point in terms of effort expended has occurred in fairly recent years. This event occurred in diffusion research sometime in late 1960; 50 percent of the publications now available on the diffusion of innovations have been completed since that date. There was as much research effort in the past 5 years on diffusion as in the previous 34 years. The rate of publication shown in Fig. 9.1 appears to be a logistic growth curve that has not reached its second inflection point; interestingly, this same S-shaped curve has been found to describe the rate of adoption of innovations over time.

In the remainder of the present chapter, we shall discuss the contents of this body of research in terms of the generalizations that have emerged, and the methodologies that have been used to obtain these generalizations. As background for our discussion of these generalizations and methodologies, we shall next discuss the information storage and retrieval system that we developed to synthesize the contents of the Michigan State University Diffusion Documents Center.

METHODOLOGY OF THE DIFFUSION DOCUMENTS CENTER (DDC) CONTENT ANALYSIS

The Michigan State University Diffusion Documents Center contains a total of approximately 1100 scientific publications. All of these publications are concerned with the *communication* of *new ideas* among members of a *social system* over *time*.[10]

and the activities of such scholars as Elihu Katz at the University of Chicago, Wilbur Schramm at Stanford University, and the late Paul Deutschmann at Michigan State University, all of whom promoted a more cosmopolitan view of diffusion research to their colleagues, both in their writings and in their professional activities.

[9] Kenneth E. Boulding, *The Meaning of the 20th Century* (New York: Harper and Row, 1964).

[10] These criteria exclude a great number of communication-research publications

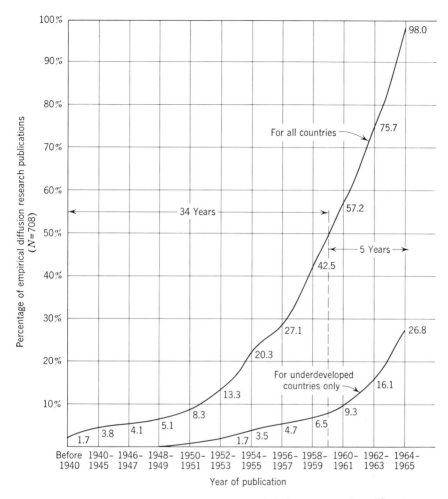

Figure 9.1.   Cumulative percentage of empirical diffusion-research publications
by year for all countries, and for underdeveloped countries only.

These four notes of our diffusion theme thus place the collection of
documents in the concert hall of social science, although exactly where in
this hall is difficult to say since the melody is played by several academic
disciplines. We attempted to listen to this cacophonous concert for two

that do not involve the time dimension. Also, a few studies on the spread of an
innovation among nonhuman "audiences" are not included in the DDC; an example
is the diffusion of a new rust disease among evergreens in New England.

reasons: (1) in order to operate the music box (our documents center) so that all might easily select and listen to those melodies most helpful in their own research compositions; and (2) in order to detect common patterns from the various scores.

Publications in the DDC are of two general types: (1) 708 empirical publications reporting data gathered about the diffusion of ideas; and (2) "non-empirical" diffusion publications in which no new data concerning the diffusion of innovations are included. The nonempirical label attached to these publications is perhaps somewhat misleading in that statements may be made in these publications that derive from empirical studies; an example would be a review of diffusion literature. Yet, since these publications deal with data that have been reported elsewhere, we do not include them in the empirical section of the DDC, and their contents are not analyzed in the present chapter.

We now turn to a discussion of the purpose and procedures of our information storage and retrieval system, the DDC. Underlying the rather extensive work that went into creating this system was the conviction that unless some rapid means was developed for handling the information available, future research would not progress as satisfactorily. Some impersonal aid for overcoming the limitations of personal memory was needed. Of course, such an information crisis is not unique to diffusion research. McLuhan[11] argued in a more general sense that "Print provided a vast new memory for past writings that made a personal memory inadequate." Our impersonal memory, the information system, was created with the idea of being able to answer two types of questions about the diffusion of innovations: (1) those of a research orientation from investigators who wished a literature search; and (2) queries concerning the reliability of statements about diffusion or, in gross terms, how often researchers of whatever academic discipline in whatever part of the world found a similar relationship between pairs of specified variables. An example of the first question is, "What research has been done on variable X?" The second asks, "How often has a relationship between variable X and Y been found and how generalizable is this relationship?"

Upon receipt of a new document in the DDC, trained coders begin their examination of its contents. The first step is the coding of the identification card, which entails the assignment of number codes to various methodological aspects of the study reported, such as the research locale, the year it was completed, and the tradition of the author. For example,

[11] Marshall McLuhan, *Understanding Media: The Extensions of Man* (New York: McGraw-Hill, 1964).

if a study is completed in the United States, it is coded "40" in columns 31 and 32 of the identification card. Other characteristics such as the type of innovation studied and the type of respondent who supplied the data (farmers, school teachers, and housewives are examples) are similarly coded by assigning numbers to these methodological categories, and punching these numbers onto the identification card. There is one of these cards per document.

The content cards contain the variables that were studied in the investigation reported in the publication. If the author gathered data on innovativeness (the relative time of adoption of a new idea), we record a four digit number code, "1300," that represents innovativeness. We consider the dependent variable of the study to be the one the author was most interested in examining and explaining. We consider the independent variables (education, for example) to be those studied in relationship to the dependent variable; these variables are used to explain variation in the dependent variable. Each relationship between a dependent and an independent variable is punched on a single IBM card with a four digit number code representing each of the variables. The linkage connecting these two variables is either positive, negative, or no relationship. Thus, a research-finding linking innovativeness and education in a positive manner is coded:

$$1300 \ 6 \ 1120$$

The number 1300 stands for innovativeness, the 6 means a positive relationship, and the 1120 stands for years of education.[12] This numerical statement may be read: innovativeness is positively associated with years of education. Similarly, a 4 code indicates a negative relationship between the independent and dependent variables, and a 5 code indicates no relationship.

We have also used another relationship code, 8, between pairs of variables that we call conditional; a relationship that may be positive or negative depending on (or conditioned by) other variables.

After the publication is coded and the data punched on IBM cards, the publication is placed in the Diffusion Documents Center for future reference. The cards associated with the publication are sorted in appropriate decks (bibliographic, identification, or content) so they may be used in future literature searches. Using IBM sorting procedures, we can produce

[12] Complete detail on the coding procedures utilized in preparing the identification and contents cards is contained in the DDC Codebook, which is available upon request.

a summary bibliography[13] of those publications that utilize certain methodologies or that consider any particular variable in which a requestor may be interested. For example, if a researcher is interested in learning of all publications dealing with the relationship of innovativeness and education in the United States after 1960 done by marketing researchers among housewives, we can obtain this set of publications for the researcher fairly easily by sorting the IBM card decks, since we have coded all the dimensions in which he is interested. The flow chart in Fig. 9.2 illustrates how publications are processed and information is stored in the DDC.

GENERALIZATIONS ABOUT INNOVATIVENESS

Now let us look at some of the generalizations that have emerged from our synthesis of the DDC materials. First, let us examine the correlates of innovativeness. From our content analysis, we have gleaned 2486 research findings relating various independent variables to innovativeness.[14] Operational measures of innovativeness were: (1) the adoption or nonadoption of one new idea or a set of new ideas, or (2) the degree to which the unit of adoption is relatively earlier (in years, months, days, or hours) in adopting new ideas than other members of his social system.[15] We counted how many times researchers have found innovativeness related to each independent variable, and in what fashion: positive, negative, conditional, or no relationship.

Table 9.4 summarizes some of the social characteristics variables correlated with innovativeness. The following social characteristics variables seem to emerge as general correlates of innovativeness: education, literacy, income, and level of living. The innovative person is likely to have more education than others in his social system, to be literate (this variable is especially important in less developed countries), to have a higher income, and to enjoy a higher level of living. We cannot give unqualified support to these relationships, yet the weight of evidence seems to in-

---

[13] In addition, an annual bibliography is published each year of all the documents in the DDC. The most recent is Everett M. Rogers, *Bibliography on the Diffusion of Innovations,* East Lansing, Michigan State University, Department of Communication, Diffusion of Innovations Research Report 4, 1966.

[14] Interestingly, almost 60 percent of the 4,197 contents cards have innovativeness as their dependent variable.

[15] The first of these two types of innovativeness is a dichotomous variable, while the second is a continuous variable.

dicate overwhelmingly a positive relationship between each of these variables and innovativeness.

The evidence in Table 9.4 does not argue for a causal relationship between the dependent and independent variables, since these findings come largely from correlational studies. Thus, neither the time order nor the "forcing quality" of causal relationships can be established. In view of the present evidence, however, researchers might next attempt to examine these correlates of innovativeness in research designs (for instance, laboratory or field experiments) that allow conclusions of a more causal nature.

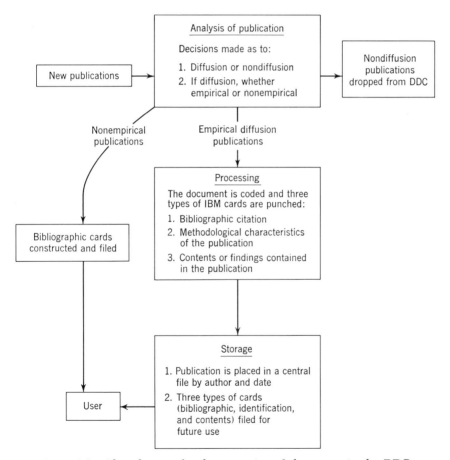

Figure 9.2. Flow diagram for the processing of documents in the DDC.

In addition, even where most evidence weighs in the direction of a positive relationship between an independent variable with innovativeness, there are findings to the contrary. A logical next step would be to retrieve the "deviant" publications, and determine what circumstances in respondents, innovations, or data-gathering methods led to the novel results. This literature review would be much easier than the usual time-consuming search, since most of the legwork could be done by machine.

TABLE 9.4.   SOCIAL CHARACTERISTICS VARIABLES RELATED TO INNOVATIVENESS

Social Character-istics of the Unit of Adoption	Number of Generalizations with Each Type of Relationship to Innovativeness (Percent)					Total Number of Generali-zations
	Positive	None	Nega-tive	Condi-tional	Total	
1. Education	75	16	5	4	100	193
2. Literacy	70	22	4	4	100	27
3. Income	80	11	6	3	100	112
4. Level of living	83	10	2	5	100	40
5. Age	32	40	18	10	100	158

At present, there appears to be little we can generalize in regard to the relationship between age and innovativeness (see Table 9.4).[16]

Some attitudinal-type variables that seem consistently correlated with innovativeness are knowledgeability,[17] attitude toward change, achievement motivation, and educational aspirations (Table 9.5). Knowledgeability seems to indicate an awareness of the external world (outside of the specific social system studied). Attitude toward change is a general predisposition to accept new ideas. If knowledgeability represents the cognitive rational aspect of change, attitude toward change refers more to the affective and emotional side. Both variables are positively related to innovativeness, although the evidence is more clearcut in the case of attitude toward change. Achievement motivation is a social value indicat-

[16] Rogers (op. cit., in press), argues that the lack of a clear-cut relationship between age and innovativeness may be due to measuring age at time of interview, rather than at time of adoption.

[17] In a strict sense, knowledgeability is more a cognitive than an attitudinal correlate of innovativeness.

ing an individual's desire for occupational excellence. Both achievement motivation and educational aspirations are motivational variables positively associated with innovativeness. Educational aspirations indicate the relative strength of the inner drive an individual feels to better the life of his family, especially in terms of his children's education and occupations.

TABLE 9.5. ATTITUDINAL-TYPE VARIABLES RELATED TO INNOVATIVENESS

Attitudinal-Type Characteristics of the Unit of Adoption	Number of Generalizations with Each Type of Relationship to Innovativeness (Percent)					Total Number of Generalizations
	Positive	None	Nega-tive	Condi-tional	Total	
1. Knowledge-ability	79	17	1	3	100	66
2. General attitude toward change	74	14	8	4	100	159
3. Achievement motivation	65	23	0	12	100	17
4. Educational aspirations	83	9	4	4	100	23
5. Business orientation	60	20	20	0	100	5
6. Satisfaction with life	29	28	43	0	100	7
7. Empathy	75	0	25	0	100	4
8. Mental rigidity	21	25	50	4	100	24

These three types of variables (knowledge, a favorable general attitude toward change, and motivation) are positively related to innovativeness. There is certainly need, however, to pursue the nature of these relationships further with careful research, and to explore the relationships of innovativeness with empathy and the other attitudinal-type variables (Table 9.5) for which we have few research studies at present.

As Table 9.6 shows, the social relationships of the unit of adoption are related to innovativeness. The more exposure to communication sources external to the social system, the more likely the individual is to be innovative. Such variables as cosmopoliteness (defined as the degree to which the individual is oriented outside of his social system), mass-media exposure, and contact with change agencies are positively associated with innovativeness. Deviancy from norms of the social system also is, in general, positively related to innovativeness.

TABLE 9.6. SOCIAL RELATIONSHIPS OF THE UNIT OF ADOPTION TO THE SOCIAL SYSTEM AS RELATED TO INNOVATIVENESS

Social Relationship of the Unit of Adoption to the Social System	Number of Generalizations with Each Type of Relationship to Innovativeness (Percent)					Total Number of Generalizations
	Positive	None	Negative	Conditional	Total	
1. Cosmopoliteness	81	11	3	5	100	73
2. Mass media exposure	86	12	0	2	100	49
3. Contact with change agencies	92	7	0	1	100	136
4. Deviancy from norms of the social system	54	14	28	4	100	28
5. Group participation	79	10	6	5	100	156
6. Interpersonal communication exposure	70	15	15	0	100	40
7. Opinion leadership	64	22	7	7	100	14

Individuals who more actively participate in the group activities of their social system are more likely to be innovative. Table 9.6 summarizes the evidence for three of these independent variables positively associated with innovativeness: group participation, interpersonal communication exposure (mostly with peers), and opinion leadership (the degree to which an individual is able to informally influence other individuals' attitudes in a desired way with relatively high frequency).

Table 9.7 shows the relationships of properties of the innovation to innovativeness. Here, we are dealing with perceptions of the innovation by the respondent; individuals are more innovative who perceive the relative advantage of the innovation (compared to other ideas) to be high, the innovation to be compatible with existing attitudes and values, and that the innovation fulfills their felt needs. Other characteristics of the innovation may also be related to innovativeness, but little research has been done to date on this score.

TABLE 9.7. CHARACTERISTICS OF THE INNOVATION RELATED TO INNOVATIVENESS

Characteristics of the Innovation	Number of Generalizations with Each Type of Relationship to Innovativeness (Percent)					Total Number of Generalizations *(published tendencies)*
	Positive	None	Nega-tive	Condi-tional	Total	
1. Relative advantage	79	15	3	3	100	66
2. Compatibility	86	14	0	0	100	50
3. Fulfillment of felt needs	92	4	4	0	100	27
4. Complexity	19	37	44	0	100	16
5. Divisibility	43	43	14	0	100	14
6. Communicability	75	25	0	0	100	8
7. Availability	56	22	17	5	100	18
8. Immediacy of benefit	57	29	14	0	100	7

Finally, Table 9.8 shows that promotional strategies of advertisers, marketers, and other professional change agents are related to innovativeness (in adoption of the new idea they are promoting) or the rate of adoption of innovations. The change agencies in this present research literature are most often rural extension services and the innovations are usually agricultural practices. Further investigation is needed to determine whether these independent variables are positively related to innovativeness among other types of clienteles. Even among the diffusion publications now at hand, there are only a total of 41 contents cards dealing with the relationships of change agents' strategies and rate of adoption; thus, it is dangerous to offer the generalizations in Table 9.8 with much degree of confidence.

X # of empirical findings Indicating relation to Innovativeness %

The need for further research on these and other independent variables related to innovativeness is obvious. We hope that the evidence reported here about the relative generality of findings will indicate the more potent variables that explain innovativeness, as well as suggest a great number of additional variables (for instance, personality dimensions) that need inquiry into their relationship to innovativeness. Further investigation and (perhaps equally important) systematic conceptual efforts to re-

TABLE 9.8. STRATEGIES OF CHANGE AGENCIES AS RELATED
TO INNOVATIVENESS (OR RATE OF ADOPTION)

Strategies of the Change Agencies	Number of Generalizations with Each Type of Relationship to Innovativeness or Rate of Adoption (Percent)					Total Number of Generalizations
	Positive	None	Negative	Conditional	Total	
1. Fitting the innovation to the culture of the clients	88	0	12	0	100	8
2. Attempt to increase competence of clients in evaluating innovations	75	0	0	25	100	4
3. Concentrate change efforts on the opinion leaders	100	0	0	0	100	6
4. Involving clients in planning the change program	100	0	0	0	100	1
5. Conducting demonstrations	79	14	0	7	100	14
6. Degree of personal communication with clients	88	0	12	0	100	8

late these variables and the conditions under which relationships hold are needed. But the first step in planning future research is assessment of the current state of empirical generalizations dealing with innovativeness. We have tried to do this with the materials in the Diffusion Documents Center.

DIFFUSION-RESEARCH METHODOLOGY

Resolving the inconsistencies found in the generalizations already reported, as well as testing new, more complex theories relating to the process of diffusion, requires a certain methodological sophistication. We hope to show in the present section how various designs, sampling procedures, and types of respondents have been utilized in past diffusion research. Moreover, we shall illustrate new and different methodologies that have been recently introduced in diffusion studies.

Design

The process of diffusion, as we have noted previously, inherently involves the notion of time. A fundamental weakness of most diffusion research has been the dependence upon recall data. As Table 9.9 indicates,

TABLE 9.9.   NUMBER OF DIFFUSION PUBLICATIONS USING
VARIOUS RESEARCH DESIGNS BY TIME PERIOD

Research Design Used in Diffusion Publications	Number of Publications by Time Period			
	1940's or Before	1950's	1960's	Total
1. Recall of previous behavior	17	197	291	505
2. Panel study over time	0	13	30	43
3. Before and after designs	3	15	32	50
4. Simulation	0	0	9	9
5. Impossible to determine	16	40	45	101
Totals	36	265	407	708

most research focused on the diffusion process at one point in time and relied for time perspective on what individuals recall they did in the past. This methodology would be adequate if respondents' memories never failed. However, recall data, while an adequate first step in this type of research, is clearly inadequate for determining the mechanisms of diffusion in a precise manner.

Unfortunately, few improvements in research design have been made in recent years in diffusion research. However, it is heartening to note (in Table 9.9) that panel studies and before-after designs have doubled in frequency since the 1950's. Yet, the majority (about three-fourths) of the diffusion research still relies on recall data, even in the 1960's.

One new research design included in Table 9.9 is simulation. The simulation approach consists essentially of expressing hypotheses in mathematical form, seeking to artificially reproduce or mimic the diffusion process, and then comparing the simulation results with reality data. Simulation can be used as a partial substitute for laboratory or field experimentation, assuming that sufficient research evidence exists to construct a simulation model consisting of mathematically-expressed rules of diffusion. This simulation experimentation, since it may be performed on a computer, removes many of the ethical and practical difficulties facing a researcher who wants to test his ideas under relatively controlled field conditions. Only during the 1960's has simulation come into its own as a diffusion-research approach, and most of that has been the property of the geography tradition (and thus stresses spatial variables).

Sampling

In order to establish some firm basis for general statements about the process of diffusion, empirical research must be conducted where innovations are diffusing in a social system. The generalizability of the relationships among variables that result from this research depend, among other factors, on the nature of the individuals examined by the researcher. The more representative the sample is of a more general population, the greater confidence we may have that the relationships hold for the entire population. Methods of statistical inference depend on sampling procedures where each unit in the population has equal probability of inclusion in the sample; this is randomness. Of course, complete census of a social system avoids the need for inference, yet data-gathering from a 100 percent sample is often too difficult and costly.

What sampling procedures are most popular in diffusion research? Table 9.10 shows that the random sample is the most popular sampling scheme used in diffusion research. The complete census was used next most frequently, while the nonprobability sample is third in frequency. The censuses are often of miniature social systems, like peasant villages,

TABLE 9.10. NUMBER OF DIFFUSION PUBLICATIONS USING
VARIOUS SAMPLING PROCEDURES BY TIME PERIOD

Sampling Procedure Utilized in Selection of Respondents	Number of Publications by Time Period			
	1940's or Before	1950's	1960's	Total
1. Complete census of a social system	8	45	68	121
2. Probability (random or stratified random sample)	8	79	159	246
3. Nonprobability (quota, structured, purposive, or judgment) sample	3	45	54	102
4. Some combinations of the above sampling techniques	3	35	50	88
5. Impossible to determine sampling procedure	14	61	76	151
Totals	36	265	407	708

which may be highly idiosyncratic and not representative of other social systems.

Nevertheless, the sampling aspects in diffusion research appear to be a relatively strong element in their methodology.

Respondents

Ideally, we should wish that diffusion research had been completed with near-equal frequency among most sections of the population. New ideas are encountered and adopted by individuals in all parts of society. Table 9.11, however, shows that farmers were the respondents in about 57 percent of the diffusion research to date.[18] Certainly, the degree to

[18] We might expect this dependence upon farmer respondents especially in less developed countries, where they usually constitute a majority of the population and where they are crucial audiences for programs of change agencies, but hardly in the United States where farmers are now a rather small share of the population. Of the 195 studies done in less developed countries, 112 (or 57 percent) centered on farmers as respondents. In developed countries, 291 (or 57 percent) of the publications reported farmers as respondents.

TABLE 9.11. NUMBER OF DIFFUSION PUBLICATIONS USING
VARIOUS TYPES OF RESPONDENTS TO
PROVIDE PRIMARY DATA

Type of Respondent from Which Data were Gathered	Number of Publications by Time Period			
	1940's or Before	1950's	1960's	Total
1. Farmers	15	146	242	403
2. School administrators, teachers, students	4	8	21	33
3. Industrial owners or managers	0	5	8	13
4. Housewives	2	12	29	43
5. Heads of villages, countries, or other political units	6	13	20	39
6. Change agents	0	6	2	8
7. Professional (for example, medical doctors)	0	11	10	21
8. Household heads (males and females)	0	27	30	57
9. Cross section of total population	4	20	23	47
10. Impossible to determine	5	17	22	44
Totals	36	265	407	708

which we can generalize present diffusion findings is severely circum-
scribed by the past dependence upon one type of respondents.

SUMMARY AND CONCLUSIONS

One of the objectives of the present chapter was to synthesize a series
of generalizations from the body of research that has been completed on
the diffusion of innovations. Essentially, this chapter is a distillation of
the methods and findings from a volume of research publications. Thus,
we have, in a sense, 708 passive co-authors.

The publications perused were the empirical materials now in the Diffusion Documents Center, an information storage and retrieval system now in operation at Michigan State University. We found that the 14 main diffusion-research traditions act as partially impermeable barriers to prevent the full diffusion of diffusion-research results, although in recent years a wider degree of interdisciplinary sophistication is apparent. The amount of diffusion research is increasing rapidly, especially in the 1960's, and is moving in international and cross-cultural directions. Methodologically, there is strong dependence upon recall data from respondents, upon random probability samples, and upon utilizing farmer respondents.

More than 2400 empirical findings from diffusion research dealing with innovativeness were summarized in terms of the following generalizations.

1. Education is positively related to innovativeness.
2. Literacy is positively related to innovativeness.
3. Income is positively related to innovativeness.
4. Level of living is positively related to innovativeness.
5. There is no consistent relationship between age and innovativeness.
6. Knowledgeability is positively related to innovativeness.
7. Attitude toward change is positively related to innovativeness.
8. Achievement motivation is positively related to innovativeness.
9. Educational aspirations are positively related to innovativeness.
10. There is not yet adequate evidence about the relationship of such attitudinal variables as business orientation, satisfaction with life, empathy, and rigidity, to innovativeness.
11. Cosmopoliteness is positively related to innovativeness.
12. Mass-media exposure is positively related to innovativeness.
13. Contract with change agencies is positively related to innovativeness.
14. Deviancy from norms (of the social system) is positively related to innovativeness.
15. Group participation is positively related to innovativeness.
16. Interpersonal-communication exposure is positively related to innovativeness.
17. Opinion leadership is positively related to innovativeness.
18. Relative advantage of the innovation is positively related to rate of adoption.
19. Compatibility of the innovation is positively related to rate of adoption.
20. Fulfillment of felt needs by the innovation is positively related to rate of adoption.

21. There is not adequate evidence about the relationship of rate of adoption to complexity, divisibility, communicability, availability, and immediacy of benefit from adopting innovations.
22. There is not adequate evidence as to the relationship of various change-agency strategies and the rate of adoption of innovations.

Implications for Marketing

Although the number of diffusion studies completed in the marketing research tradition are minute (less than 3 percent of the 708 publications),[19] one implication of the present chapter is that, at a conceptual level, the findings from other diffusion-research traditions may have useful implications for marketing practitioners. Useful steps in assessing the generalizability of diffusion results from other traditions to the marketing field would be (1) to conduct further new-product diffusion investigations among urban homemakers,[20] an audience relatively underrepresented in past research; and (2) to complete marketing studies in less developed countries, where work by rural sociologists is currently going strong, but where little marketing investigation is now reported.

Hopefully, the generalizations reported in this chapter could aid marketing planners in delineating the crucial subaudiences for their marketing strategies. For example, our present generalizations indicate that innovativeness is more characteristic of elites (those of higher income, more education, and the like). Different message strategies and communication channels should be used in communicating new products to these elites than to the nonelites in our audience.

Perhaps this chapter may serve as an invitation to marketing researchers to participate more fully in the diffusion-research club. We urge you to come on in, the water's fine.

---

[19] It must be pointed out, of course, that considerable diffusion research has been completed by commercial marketing researchers, but it is not available to the DDC.

[20] We sorted out the 42 documents in the DDC dealing with household products. Most were completed in the rural sociology and marketing traditions, with a few in psychology, general sociology, and early sociology. Independent variables most frequently correlated with innovativeness are education, income, age, attitude toward change, cosmopoliteness, and group participation. The relationships found between each of these variables and innovativeness seem to be similar to those reported earlier in this paper for all types of innovations.

Market Structure Studies: New Products for Old Markets and New Markets (Foreign) for Old Products

Research men, it is sometimes said, go armed with a set of techniques and try to fit practical problems in applied contexts to the techniques they already know, rather than trying to develop research techniques to fit the practical problems in the area in which they work. This accusation is frequently made of market researchers, and, unfortunately, not infrequently merited. The cure suggested, in view of the above diagnosis, is that researchers should be *problem* oriented rather than *technique* oriented. This chapter is *technique* oriented but it describes a family of techniques developed to solve a set of related recurrent marketing problems.

Marketing decisions of many kinds can be influenced by implicit or explicit assumptions as to (1) patterns of product-product or brand-brand substitution and competition, (2) the features of the products and brands and their advertising or distribution that lead to patterns of substitution and competition, (3) the position that a new product will occupy in an old and familiar structure of this kind, and (4) the position that an old familiar product will occupy in a new and unfamiliar market (for example, a regional or a foreign market).

The technology described below is designed to allow us (1) to estimate measures of brand-brand or product-product substitution and competition, (2) to determine the features that lead the brands or products to occupy the positions that they do in this substitution and competition structure in the market, (3) to determine the share of choices that descriptions of different new items will receive when added into the array of items currently available, and (4) to estimate where these different new items will draw their choices from when added into the array of currently available items.

Restating the above a bit more colloquially, the family of techniques allows us to estimate for brands or products that do or do not yet exist the share of choices each will receive, the patterns of substitution and competition existing between the familiar items, and the patterns that will come into existence with the introduction of specified new items. The techniques also allow estimation of the "fit" of a product to its current advertising (and vice versa), a method for prospecting the "holes" for a new product or a new brand in a particular product class, and, for the multiproduct firm, a device for developing new products that will position themselves in the market in a manner that makes them substitutable for and competitive with competitors' brands while not cannibalizing the firm's own related products.

The techniques also allow the manufacturer of an old product (1) to evaluate alternative new foreign markets for it, (2) to determine where the old item will fit vis-à-vis the products currently available in the new markets, and (3) to evaluate the demand for alternative old products in a specific new market.

These techniques are quite generally applicable. Examples described below are a synthesis of 12 studies, conducted over a five year period, ranging from light-duty liquid detergents, cigarettes, whiskey, and coffee, to automobiles and other durable goods. The techniques apply easily to very different product classes. They have also been applied to populations comprising very different markets. Studies have been made of specific cities, regions, or national probability samples of the United States. The procedures are equally applicable to United States and foreign markets, and preliminary studies have been made of market structures in Mexico and Japan.

Perhaps the oddest application of these procedures is the fact that they are currently in use in a project to study the perception of and behavior towards Peace Corps workers in Peru, on the part of both Spanish-speaking and Quechua-speaking groups. The fact that the same devices can be used with little alteration to study the markets for and behavior towards light-duty liquid detergents in the United States and Peace Corps volunteers in Peru suggests a fair range of applicability for the techniques.

DEFINING A "MARKET"

The first step in a market structure study is determining what constitutes a "market." By *market* here is meant the interrelated class of brands or products whose relations of substitution and competition are powerful enough so that the sales of each are strongly influenced by the sales of the others. In econometric language a market, for our purposes, would be the set of items whose cross-elasticities of demand exhibited sufficiently powerful substitution effects.

Economists in the United States appear, unfortunately, to have done little in the way of collecting information about the patterns of substitution and competition relating large numbers of brands or products. Schultz [1938], Telser [1962], and others have studied the relations between small sets of brands or products. Rarely, however, have American economists studied large arrays to determine the manner in which these decompose into interdependent subsets of competing products, as has, for example, Stone [1954] in England.

Businessmen, and economists too, usually make assumptions about the array of competing products based on an implicit assumption that items that are the same thing—that is, receive the same name (for example, automobiles, coffees, whiskeys, desserts)—will compete, while things that receive different names—television sets and automobiles, coffees and cola drinks, whiskeys and brandies—will not substitute or compete. While these common-sense demarcations of product classes may represent a reasonable first approximation in familiar United States markets where the executive making the decisions is also a member of the consumer culture, they will still err badly here in specific details. In foreign markets, the assumption that market structures correspond to those in the United States can be very badly misleading. An example of the first might be that, in the United States, data suggests that certain kinds of whiskey may compete more closely with brandy than they do with other kinds of whiskey. A businessman who drinks a Scotch and abhors blends may introspect and find this *obvious,* but any data on "the whiskey market" ignores this fact. Similarly, and more subtly, a specific *brand* or a product may exhibit a very different pattern of substitution and competition relations than do most of the other brands in that named product class. For a fanciful example, I have sometimes felt, with some support from relevant data, that there are some makes of automobiles whose competition for family dollars comes more from home furnishings and vacations than from other automobiles. While, in general, consideration of automobiles as representing a single large market with alternative makes and types competing for consumers' dollars may represent the situation fairly accurately, from the point of view of the manufacturer whose actual competition is nonautomotive, it would badly misrepresent the state of the world.

The problem of demarcating the major market structures—the classes of goods as those that, in fact, operate in the patterns of substitution and competition in the market and in people's usage—is usually solved in the United States by implicit assumptions. In collecting data related to product usage and purchase, only products or brands selected as relevant on the basis of judgments of this type are included. In foreign markets where the American executive's own intuitions are not transferable and, perhaps, badly misleading, and where there may be no local businessman or researcher whose knowledge of the people representing the mass of consumers is as realistic as his American counterpart's, this problem can be very important and, in appearance, quite difficult to solve.

This problem recurs in studies of the United States market in a slightly subtler way when attempts are made to demarcate the submarket structures in a particular market. For example, should we assume that all pairs of brands of light-duty liquid detergents are equally substitutable, that all pairs of brands of Scotch whiskey are equally substitutable, that all pairs of makes and brands of automobiles are equally substitutable? As a matter of empirical fact, the most similar pair of brands of light-duty liquid detergents exhibits about five times as much substitution (using the best substitution estimates currently available from purchase data) as does the most different pair. An increase in one brand's share that obtains for it an additional 10% of the total market may take away 40% of the purchases originally received by a second brand and 8% of the purchases of a third brand. On the other hand, an increase in 10% of another brand's share may take 5% away from the brand losing 40% in the case above, and 25% of the purchases received by the third brand in the example above. Among Scotch whiskeys, for example, the ratio of the nearest pair to the most different pair of Scotches among the major brands was better than 10 to 1, while among automobiles, the ratio is over 100 to 1. These data suggest that (1) demarcating major market structures is not sufficient, and that knowledge of the fine submarket structures may be necessary in making marketing decisions, and (2) this analysis into submarkets is far more necessary in some product classes than in others.

These estimates of brand-brand competition and substitution are not based on someone's intuitive judgment—as are major market structure decisions—but rather on an analysis of the data available from the Market Research Company of America's CASBAH—a Computer Analysis of the Switching Behavior of Households—from Markov matrix data on consumer brand-switching behavior, from trade-in data on automobiles, from consumers' statements as to what brand they would purchase if the brand they currently used were not available, and the like. In general, I have adopted the strategy of using the best data on substitution and competition available for the product class being studied, and this has proved to be in different forms for different products.

DEVELOPING PRODUCT SIMILARITY ESTIMATES

Except for certain simple tricks, the analysis above is much what marketing-oriented companies have been doing for some time. The next step in a market-structure study is more unorthodox, and allows us to begin a bootstrap set of operations that permit us to make inferences about the positioning of brands that do not yet exist. We can infer what positions these brands will take in familiar markets and also make inferences about substitution and competition between brands and products for markets on which we do not have available large-scale purchases or panel data (for example, foreign markets).

Small samples of consumers are asked to indicate for each of the major brands in the market (1) which other brands in the market they are "most similar to" or "most like" and (2) after completion of this task of judging similarity, what "features" of the brands they considered in making each of the judgments of similarity. For example, in a study of the regular coffee market, an interviewer might say "Ground Butternut is similar to or like" various coffees of a list of 20 or so major brands, and then, after the respondent has said for each brand on the list which of the others they are most like, the interviewer might say, "I notice that you rated Ground Butternut as 'like' Ground Yuban. In what way are these two brands similar to each other?"

This procedure gives us (1) a number for each pair of brands representing the frequency they were judged as similar to each other, and (2) a list for each brand of all the things that were said regarding the ways in which it was seen as similar to some other brand. This procedure can also be modified slightly to elicit data on the ways in which different brands are seen as different from each other.

The similarity numbers here—normalized in the computational procedure—obtained from small samples of consumers (50 to 100), have been found to correlate with patterns of brand switching from 0.50 to 0.80 in all 12 studies. Brands judged as similar exhibit more substitution and competition as estimated independently from purchase data.

The fact that such small samples of people, in their judgments of similarity, can give us back brand-brand substitution estimates comparable to those based on a four-month observation of 10,000 person panel purchase data is of some practical as well as theoretic use. That these estimates are, in fact, comparable is suggested by two facts: (1) the correlations between judged similarity and brand switching are about as high as those between brand-switching measures obtained during different time periods, and (2) the lower correlations represent the results obtained during the initial pilot studies at the beginning of this work, the higher correlations appearing with the development of improved techniques.

There appears to be a surprising amount of homogeneity in a population of people about what is similar to what, and much less homogeneity about what is good. Different samples of heterogeneous people will give back judgments of the similarity of pairs of items that correlate in the high 0.90's, while preference data obtained from samples of the same size will not be stable. This homogeneity in similarity and heterogeneity in preferences appears in much work in multidimensional scaling and is often independently discovered by different investigators.

There appear to be three major determinants of the amount of substitution and competition between brands, once a share of market is corrected for: (1) the psychological similarity of each pair of brands, (2) the overlap in availability of each pair of brands—for example, whether they are sold in the same stores, in the same regions—and (3) the overlap in media audiences in the advertising channels used by the brands—for example, two brands, both advertised in *Playboy*, will compete more than if one were advertised in *Better Homes and Gardens* and the other in *Playboy*.

The correlations described above are based solely on predictions of brand substitution from judged similarity. Multiple correlations including measures of distributional similarity should improve the correlations considerably, and in several studies the errors are quite obviously based on the fact that brands judged as similar did not exhibit much overlap in availability, and other errors were based on the fact that items judged as different were sold by the same dealers or by the same retail outlets. Data on overlap in availability are quite expensive to obtain, and for nationally available brands, if heterogeneous groups of respondents are used, a fair approximation to brand-brand substitution and competition patterns can be obtained from judged similarity data obtained from miniscule samples.

The fact that measures of brand-brand similarity have consistently allowed us to predict the patterns of brand-brand substitution and competition found in currently available data suggests that measures of psychological similarity may be used (1) to estimate major market structures in places where these currently are unknown, and (2) to find market structures more inexpensively than from large-scale purchase data, and for places where large-scale data are not available. The relevance of these two facts to international marketing research problems is, I hope, obvious.

In applying these procedures to foreign markets, or to the perception of Peace Corpsmen and their projects, the necessary first step is (1) to find out what the indigenous respondents call the items—for example, how they name or describe the items in their language; (2) to elicit from indigenous respondents the names of the things seen as similar to the word(s) or phrase(s) used as name(s) or description(s) for the item in which the investigator is currently interested—for instance, pickles, Peace Corps volunteers, and Jello; (3) to obtain judgment of the similarity of these names and descriptions to the items in which the investigator in interested; (4) to pull out the subset of items (20 or so) exhibiting the most similarity to the reference item; and (5) to give the questionnaire exhibiting these items to respondents for judgments of similarity. Following this procedure, we have (1) found out how the respondents encode—name or describe to themselves—the reference item or items by asking and observing normal usage or by introducing samples of the items, if they are not currently available in the culture being studied, and determining what names and descriptions they elicit, (2) we have found the natural set of items similar to the reference items from the point of view of the respondents, and (3) we have obtained numerical estimates of the similarity of other items in this natural subset to the reference item. From this data, we can make estimates as to item-item (for instance, brand-brand or product-product) substitution.

For example, in studying where the familiar product *Pearce's Pickles* will position itself in Eastern Slabovia, we should observe what the product is called, how it is described, and whether different varieties are named differently or described differently. We should record this fact and then begin determining what other *things* seem similar to things named in these ways to the consumers of Eastern Slabovia. For example, if one group of *Pearce's Pickles* were called *wuzguk* by our respondents, we should begin by asking the respondents to give us lists of things they thought of as similar to *wuzguk* or names of kinds of *wuzguk*, and ask them what species *wuzguk* was derived from. In this way, we should elicit the natural subset of things within which that group of *Pearce's Pickles* they call *wuzguk* nestled in the minds of Eastern Slabovia consumers. At this point, we should then begin taking this list of things (items)—or brands—and asking people to tell us which of the things on the list they felt *wuzguk* was most similar to or like, and then repeat this question with all the items on the list. Upon completion of this question, the respondent would be asked "how" those items judged like each other are like each other.

We have found this procedure quite flexible. It works well in non-Indoeuropean languages and can be run with illiterates or speakers of languages having no writing system.

The data obtained in the manner described above on item-item similarity provide numbers for each pair of items that indicate the frequency with which the items are judged similar, and respondent statements about "how" different items are similar to each other and different from each other. From these data, description lists—containing for each item a list of all the things said about it—can be obtained. These data can then be coded and provisional estimates obtained regarding (1) what features are important in determining similarities and differences among the relevant set of items, and (2) what combination of features leads each specific item to be positioned as it is in the similarity structure.

These verbal data, plus certain additional mathematical analyses of the similarity data, provide tentative hypotheses as to what features of each brand lead it to occupy the position that it does vis-à-vis the other brand or products.

From these small-scale data, we can make some provisional estimates about (1) which brands substitute for each other estimated from the judged similarity data, (2) what features of the brands lead them to be positioned as they are in the similarity structure, and (3) to the extent that judged similarity in fact predicts substitution and competition, we can estimate what features of the items lead them to be positioned as they are vis-à-vis other items in the substitution and competition structure.

MEASURING PREFERENCES FOR NEW PRODUCT DESCRIPTIONS

To test these provisional estimates—as well as to provide us with large-scale estimates as to the share of choices different new items would receive if inserted into the array containing the currently available products and with estimates as to where each of the new items would draw its choices from—a large-scale interviewing techniques has been developed that allows us to determine what would happen if a choice situation were presented to the respondent and, after his choices among the items currently available were obtained, six different new items were added into the array one at a time and the effect of each addition on the distribution of choices was calculated.

For example, if we have two items A and B and their distribution of choices is $A_{50}B_{50}$ when only the two are there, and if we then add a third item X, the outcome in the 3 element choice situation may be $X_{25}A_{25}B_{50}$. In this situation, X draws off 50% of A's choices while taking 0% of B's. This is roughly what would happen in a situation where X and A were perceived as identical or similar, and B was perceived as different by consumers. For example, if X and A were both sweet and B were sour and 1/2 the people like the sweet and 1/2 the people like the sour, the outcome in the 3 element choice situation would be approximately like this. If we took another element Y and put it into the array containing A and B, the outcome would be $Y_{34}A_{33}B_{33}$ and this is approximately similar to what would happen if Y were equally similar to both A and B. In this case, it would draw off 33% of the choices received by each. An element equally similar to both A and B could draw off 10% of each choice or 90% of each choice but it would draw off the same share of the choices of each of the original two items.

This situation is quite obvious in a single-choice situation and has been called "splitting the vote" by politicians and political observers. Similar candidates running for the same office may split the voters preferring both to the rest of the field and lead to a victory on the part of a very different candidate. In marketing, this phenomenon has been discussed by Kuehn and Day [1964] and by Benson [1963]. Similar products tend to substitute for each other and compete with each other and, thus, split the purchases of those people preferring that type of item.

What this means in practical terms is that (1) the average rating of an item may not predict its share of choices, (2) the number of times items are preferred in paired comparison to the leading brand in the market may not predict how well they will do if added one at a time into a choice array containing the items currently available.

To summarize this material succinctly: (1) average ratings will not predict the shares of choices different new items will receive when added into an array containing all the currently available items; (2) aggregate paired-comparison data will not predict how well different new items will predict when added into an array containing all the currently available items; (3) the share of choices an item will receive is a more adequate predictor of awareness/trier ratios and related market phenomena than are averages or paired comparisons; and (4) most current market research uses some variant of averages or aggregate paired-comparison data in evaluating alternative new products.

The current technology leads to a piling up of brands with particular features, while consumer demands representing larger shares of the market than those obtained by the similar brands go unmet. In my opinion, this particular idiosyncrasy of American market research technology is responsible for some depressing aspects of the consumer-goods scene.

We have built a procedure that allows us, in a fairly brief interview schedule, to insert six different new items into a choice array containing all the currently available brands and allows estimation of (1) the share of choices received by each of the new items if only it is added into the array of the currently available products or brands, (2) the manner in which each of the different new items takes its choices from the familiar brands, and (3) the patterns of substitution and competition that exist among the currently available products or brands.

These techniques are not perfect but they represent the only procedure with which I am familiar that can offer data of anything, in the course of a 15 minute telephone interview, that is suitable for inexpensive application to very large samples. These procedures are described in more detail in Stefflre [in preparation].

This information on the ways in which the different new descriptions perform in choice situations allows us to check and see if the descriptions tend to draw larger proportions of the choices previously received by the brands whose description lists are similar to the descriptions. If, for example, the description "sweet, but slightly smoky" draws 40% of the choices previously received by brand A, 20% of the choices previously received by brand B, and 10% of the choices previously received by brand C, this can be compared with the extent to which people in their judgments of similarity regarding the brands tended to say—in stating the ways in which brands were similar—that brand A was smoky and/or sweet; the same applies to brand B, and to brand C. We have, in general, found good correlations between a careful coding of brand-description lists and the patterns of draw of different new descriptions. This means, that different new descriptions tend to take a greater proportion of the choices previously received by brands whose description lists are similar to the descriptions. This has three uses: (1) it allows us independently to confirm our analysis of what features of the brands lead them to be located where they are in the substitution structure; (2) it helps us build descriptions, after careful perusal of each brand's description list, that position themselves as we want in the substitution and competition structures; and (3) consideration of each brand or product as a combination of features directs attention towards possible new combinations that would fill holes in the current market structure.

It is perhaps worth noting, at this point, that research of the type described above—(1) small-scale (n 50 to 100) similarity data and reasons for similarity, (2) large-scale choice interviews (n 1500) inserting descriptions of six new items into choice arrays containing the currently available brands, and (3) the analysis of these two types of data to determine their correspondence and to facilitate the generation of the new descriptions—can now be done routinely for a cost of approximately $25,000 for a product class containing as many as 20 major brands. This portion of the job has been done for a number of markets, and is on its way to being a routine operation. This price seems applicable to both United States and foreign studies and to studies of brand-brand and/or product-product studies.

ADVERTISING AND PRODUCT IMAGERY

Finding descriptions that perform the way that we want them to is of little help unless (1) we own an old product that matches the description we prefer, or (2) we can build a new product to match the description.

Some of the data collected in early studies compared (1) what each brand said about itself in advertising, and (2) what consumers thought about each brand as represented in its description list, and in its behavior in choice interviews. We found *negative* correlations in certain markets —that is, products advertising themselves as having certain characteristics were judged by consumers from memory to have *less* of these characteristics; other brands that did not advertise themselves in this manner were judged as having *more* of these characteristics. Some brands were, therefore, in a position of advertising product characteristics their competitors were considered to lead in, while these other brands were in a position of having their competitors do their advertising for them. It is not too surprising that the brands advertising themselves as having the desirable characteristics their competitors were seen as having were obtaining decreasing shares of the market while the brands that exhibited the characteristics were obtaining sharply increasing shares. It is necessary—in markets where repurchases are important—for the product, if it does not "fit" the advertising claims made about it, to at least not obviously contradict the claims.

In this case, the manufacturer had two strategies: (1) to develop new copy themes that would fit the products, and (2) to build new products to match the advertising themes. Both these were, in fact, adopted.

Advertising seems quite capable of shifting the salience of alternative features of different brands or products—that is, consumers can be induced to pay more attention to color and less to shape through advertising that emphasizes color and its importance—and to be quite incapable of inducing consumers to see the product as exhibiting different features than it has in certain physical dimensions—for instance, it is rather difficult to convince consumers that a green product is yellow, or that a round product is rectangular. Advertising can also allow the substitution of a slightly more flattering description for one that is less flattering, assuming that both are semantically appropriate (for example, Alford Lasker's delightful advertisements for early canned milk—previously described by people as having a "burned taste"—that suggested that the milk had an "almond taste"). This type of approach seems to consist of convincing people to call a *round* object *circular*—a description that would "fit" the object, but that would carry with it connotations its more common counterpart would not have. Advertising can also alter the positioning of products along certain more ambiguous dimensions—for example, for a product to be "rare" or "friendly" may be dependent more on advertising and packaging than on the product characteristics of the stuff in the package.

In view of the constraints in the process described above, the role of advertising in a market where repurchase rates are important is (1) to bring into greater salience the attribute dimensions along which the brand occupies a favorable position, or (2) to state as euphemistically as possible the features the brand is seen as having that are, in general, undesirable but that the product is seen unavoidably as having, (3) to attempt to move the product along those dimensions where advertising is sufficient to position the product in an advantageous position, and (4) to "fit" the product enough so that the product does not, in the consumers' eyes, contradict its advertising and play havoc with repurchase rates.

Advertising can do some jobs superbly, but it is frequently called upon to do jobs that it is not cut out for doing. This may be attributed, in part, to the generalization of research copy evaluation technology from mail-order businesses (where the best early work was done), in which repeat purchases were *not* an important factor to other types of products and to distribution systems in which repeat purchases are of key importance.

BUILDING NEW PRODUCTS TO MATCH PREFERRED DESCRIPTIONS

Attempting to build new products to match descriptions—the reverse of altering the advertising to fit the product—can be an exciting business. We need (1) techniques to develop hypotheses as to which aspects of the product and its packaging lead it to receive specific descriptions, and then (2) hypothesis-testing techniques that allow us to take the new products that have been built and check to see if, in fact, people describe them as the products were supposed to be described. Several cycles of this process of hypothesis generation and hypothesis testing, using consumers as evaluators, may be necessary before a new product is developed that matches the desired descriptions. This has been done, at present, for several different product classes and for several products in each product class.

Working with skilled technicians familiar with the product classes, the procedure was somewhat as follows. Assume that we wished to build an image of "a happy tasting pickle" because this description had functioned in the large-scale choice situation just as the manufacturer (Pearce) wanted his product to perform in the market. We might ask people to list the "happiest tasting things" they could remember tasting and from this list try to develop hypotheses about how to build an image of a pickle that exhibited comparable characteristics. People exhibit remarkable unanimity in answering questions like this; a large number, for example, might say that "a birthday cake" was the happiest tasting thing they could remember eating. The problem, then, is "How do we make a pickle that is more similar to birthday cakes than are other competing pickles?" After we have tried this, we can then have consumers freely describe our new "happy pickle 1" and other competing pickles after tasting them and observe how often our pickle was described as happy, in comparison with the frequency with which others were so described. A more straight-forward approach would be simply to have consumers rate the new pickles and competitors' brands on scales ranging from *very happy* to *not at all happy*. If our new pickle is the happiest we have done our job. If some competitor's pickle is happier, we can then look at it and see how it is different from our own sadder pickle, and then try to build a pickle that will be even happier than our competitor's. By the time we have arrived at "happy pickle 7," we should have a pickle happier than any competing brand; for what manufacturer, after all, had ever previously tried to build a happy pickle.

The next test of our new pickle is a more stringent one. We have now shown that it elicits the description it is supposed to elicit but have not yet demonstrated that it performs in a quasi-purchase situation as did the description it was built to match and as the manufacturer desires the new product to perform. Design of this purchase situation is fairly straightforward. We simply obtain an estimate of the distribution of purchases across the array of products that is currently available, and then we add our new product to the array and calculate how many purchases it receives and where it takes them from.

If the product does not perform as desired—back to the drawing board or laboratory. If it does perform in this manner, the problem is then to take care of the packaging, advertising, naming, pricing, and the like, in a manner that is consonant with the *happy pickle* image we are trying to induce. A test market or quasi-test market of the new pickle then lets us check out and see if the new item performs as it should when all the trimmings are added.

If the example above strikes the reader as trivial, he is probably right. This same research strategy, however, can be applied to major product innovations and the creation of new things. For example, if we consider a large class of kinds of things—vehicles, ranging from roller skates, submarines, and housetrailers, to jet air planes—new combinations of features can emerge from consideration of the ways in which things are similar and different. Superficial examination of vehicles and the ways in which each kind of vehicle is like and unlike an ideal vehicle leads to the following description of an object:

1. It is easily carried when not in use like roller skates, or better yet, it can be folded up and put in your pocket.

2. It is operable on land with and without roads, and on and under sea.

3. It will allow six people to live aboard for six months using its own water, fuel, food, and air supply.

. . . .

n. It is quite inexpensive, perhaps used once then thrown away to avoid maintenance costs.

Building a new vehicle consumers would see as meeting the specifications for our new object would be more difficult than building "a happy pickle" but several things should be borne in mind in this context. First, the new vehicle would *not* have to absolutely measure up to the criteria —only meet them better than competing products. A relative rather than absolute criterion for success greatly reduces the order of magnitude of the difficulty of the task. Second, the new item does not have to satisfy all criteria at once. Different members of the population give different weight to the various listed criteria, and some combination of these criteria put into a description may produce an item that performs more than adequately from a marketing point of view, and is several orders of magnitude simpler from the point of view of engineering and production. Third, the extensive list of requirements, even if unworkable mechanically, can give interesting new directions to product development. For example, in view of the list above, the closest "vehicle" appears to be a general-purpose *credit card* like the Diners Club or American Express credit cards. Inclusion of this card in the class of vehicles and redoing of the similarities and differences procedures can lead to exotic new classes of objects that serve to illuminate possibilities for new items that consideration from more conventional aspects would leave in the dark.

There are, after all, an infinite number of new brands and new products that can be built and the selection among these represents an interesting problem in screening and prospecting.

The similarities and differences procedure for the development of new combinations, the screening of descriptions by their performance in choice situations, and then the building of new items to match the descriptions that perform appropriately and the test of these in purchase situations can be done for all levels of new-item development from "a happy pickle" to an exotic vehicle. The procedures involved are much the same with the major shifts being in the arrays of items considered (brands versus things) and in the procedures for generating new descriptions (go-for-broke versus aiming for a specific share of the market).

A QUESTION OF STRATEGY

The manufacturer putting a familiar product into an unfamiliar market or markets is in a slightly different position than the manufacturer trying to build a new product for a familiar market. In the first case, the manufacturer is trying to predict how an unfamiliar group will behave toward a new thing that has specific features (for example, the familiar product) while in the second case, the manufacturer is trying to ascertain what features to give a new item so that people will behave toward it in a given way (for example, it will receive a given share of choices and will position itself in the competition and substitution structure in a given way). Underlying both of these problems is a familiar state of affairs, however; in both situations, the people will behave toward the new item in a manner that is similar to the way in which they behave toward items that they perceive as similar to the new item (Stefflre, 1956).

The problem of the manufacturer going into an unfamiliar market is that the people there may (1) see the familiar item—for instance, pickles—as similar to different things than the people in the manufacturer's familiar market see the product as similar to, and (2) they may behave differently toward things than do the consumers in the familiar market. Our pickle manufacturer is attempting to decide whether to go into the pickle business in Eastern Slobovia. Several important problems occur: (1) he may think he is going into the pickle business but actually, in terms of consumers' perceptions, he will be going into the snack business (competitive with candy, fresh berries, and certain fruits) with all of his sweet pickles and certain of his other pickles—those exhibiting such and such a degree of wartyness of skin texture—and into the dessert business with his nonwarty sour pickles; (2) he may be accustomed to the products being evaluated in certain ways due to certain characteristics in addition to expecting them to have certain natural sources of competition and substitution and certain patterns of usage; and (3) his marketing information system and the marketing research facilities available in the new market may be such that it will take him a considerable time and expense to realize that he is not in the pickle business in this new market but rather in the *wuzguk* and *umphal* business. In one of these it is important that an item be seen as healthful (for which wartyness of skin is a high salience cue), and in the other it is, in general, important that the food be seen as a slight dissipation (though a small segment of the market has a desire, currently unmet, for an extremely evil and lascivious *umphal*).

Case histories in international business seem to be full of stories in which products succeed or fail dramatically for reasons that seem to an outsider as bizarre, and to an insider in the consuming culture as obvious; for instance, Pearce's Pickles' failure in the *wuzguk* market and success in the *umphal* market. At some later point, an observer may comment that it is particularly surprising that Pearce's *umphals* succeeded, as Americans were seen at this time in Eastern Slobovia as "evil and lascivious."

The point of the somewhat fanciful example above will, I hope, be clear to the reader. That is, (1) trying a familiar product in a new and unfamiliar market is actually attempting to introduce a new product or a new set of products; (2) in addition to the standard legal and financial risks in entering unfamiliar markets, the introduction of an old product into a new market includes also all the gambles of the introduction of a new product into a familiar market; and (3) the procedures I described above are as applicable to the old product in a new market problem as they are to the new product in an old market problem—if not more so. The reason for the "if not more so" is simply this. Research techniques of the type I described above can do on the order of 20% better than an experienced executive familiar with marketing in a particular product class in the United States; they can, I believe, do 200% better than these same executives could if they attempted to transfer their United States experience to the foreign, unfamiliar market. Due to the rather less egalitarian social structures found in certain areas outside the United States, and the fairly recent emphasis on marketing and market research, urban businessmen's intuitions regarding how village consumers see the market may be only slightly better than an attempt to naively apply American traditional knowledge.

SUMMARY

In the above, I have considered the problem of (1) designing a new product for a familiar market, (2) determining where a familiar product —or products—may go when introduced into an unfamiliar market, and I leave (3) the problem of designing a new product for an unfamiliar market for the reader as an exercise. *Hint:* the techniques to be applied are exactly the same as those relevant to problems 1 and 2 described above.

As I said at the beginning, this is a technique-oriented rather than a problem-oriented chapter. The techniques consist in (1) determining what is seen as similar to what, and why, through studying small samples of consumers' judgments of similarity and difference, (2) determining patterns of brand-brand and/or product-product substitution and competition through use of large-scale purchase data when these are available or through large-scale interview procedures where these are not available, (3) development of descriptions of new brands or products for testing of new unfamiliar items in familiar markets or determination of how new and unfamiliar consumers will describe familiar products, (4) insertion of these descriptions into large-scale choice situations to see how they do and where they get their choices from, (5) building new products to fit successful descriptions for new products in old markets or finding successful marketing strategies for old products in new markets, and (6) then testing these new products and/or new places through quasi-purchase situations introducing the new or old things.

I have argued that this type of procedure is applicable to a multitude of superficially different marketing problems ranging from evaluation of advertising copy to the development of new brands and products for familiar markets to determining where an old product will fit when introduced into a new market. There are a set of problems to which this family of techniques is not applicable—for instance, optimization of resource allocation in advertising media—but there seems to be a group of hoary hardy perennials for which this approach to the problem can serve as an alpenstock.

BIBLIOGRAPHY

P. Benson, "A Short Method for Estimating a Distribution of Consumer Preferences," *Journal of Applied Psychology,* **46** (**5**), 375-381 (1962).

P. Benson, "Consumer Preference Distributions in the Analysis of Market Segmentation," *Emerging Concepts in Marketing,* W. S. Decker (editor), A. M. A. (1963).

A. A. Kuehn and R. L. Day, "Strategy of Product Quality," *Harvard Business Review,* 100-110 (1962).

H. Schultz, *The Theory and Measurement of Demand* (Chicago: University of Chicago Press, 1938).

V. Stefflre, "Simulation of People's Behavior to New Items and Events," *American Behavioral Scientists,* **8** (**9**), (1956).

V. Stefflre, *Language and Behavior,* Addison-Wesley (in preparation).

R. Stone, *The Measurement of Consumers' Expenditure and Behavior in the United Kingdom 1920-1938,* Volume 1 (Cambridge University Press, 1954).

L. G. Telser, "The Demand for Branded Goods as Estimated from Consumer Panel Data," *Review of Economics and Statistics,* **64** (**3**), 300-324 (1962).

PART THREE

Experimental Methods and Simulation Models in Marketing Management

The chapters in Part Three illustrate a variety of theoretical concepts of interest to the marketing manager. Chapter Eleven, by Professor Kotler, examines the critical planning problems management faces when dealing with new-product decisions. The models that he reviews span many levels of complexity and analytical techniques. The need to quantify subjective information, evaluate uncertainty, and revise estimates on the basis of new data are noted. Chapter Twelve, by Professor Green and his co-authors, Peter FitzRoy and Patrick Robinson, discusses the response of decision makers to situations in which uncertainty surrounds the available alternatives. By using a gaming situation, the subjects' skill in buying and processing information was studied at close range. The controlled experimental setting of the game proved useful in examining dynamic estimates of subjective probability and models of sequential, adoptive choice-behavior. Chapter Thirteen, by Professor Peters, complements the preceding papers by outlining the historical development of utility theory and decision-making experiments under risk and uncertainty. The last part of his chapter contains an imaginative list of significant problems in marketing management to which experimental methods and extant theoretical concepts can be applied. Professor Peters' chapter also serves as an introduction to Chapter Fourteen by Robert Holloway. This chapter focuses on the relatively recent experimental studies related directly to marketing. Although Holloway finds it impossible to provide summaries of all of the current work in this rapidly expanding field, a relatively wide range of experimental procedures and problem areas has been covered. Finally, Chapter Fifteen, by Professor Hess, and Chapter Sixteen, by F. J. Van Bortel, introduce pioneering efforts in the growing field of pupillometric research and its potential applications in the study of consumer attitudes. In a sense, this book ends in the same vein in which it began, emphasizing how the sciences can make a significant contribution to the solution of particular types of marketing problems. In the case of the chapter by Professor Kotler, the decision area related to new-product opportunities, and in the chapter by Mr. Van Bortel, it related to the selection of persuasive advertising messages.

In general, the chapters of Part Three provide both a historical perspective and an analysis of the likely directions of future work. In many cases, extensive bibliographic references have been included that can prove valuable to the research worker interested in a deeper understanding of the relevant literature. As further background, the remainder of this introduction will discuss some general theoretical, methodological, and managerial issues surrounding the topics treated by the individual chapters.

BROADENING THE MARKETING MANAGER'S RANGE OF ANALYTICAL TECHNIQUES FOR DECISION MAKING

The areas related to new-product development serve as a convenient point of focus for discussing the contributions of the sciences to managerial decision making in marketing. New-product development underlines the importance of continuously monitoring the social and scientific environment to discover new needs and means to satisfy them. The firm's capabilities in this field show up in how well it is able to guide a research and development effort, an acquisition and mergers activity, and the general search conducted for new ways to serve its consumers and provide for profitable growth. Particularly in the research and development arena, we find a growing interest in forecasting the rate of scientific discovery, technological innovation, and social change.[1] It has

[1] Raymond Isenson, "Technological Forecasting in Perspective," *Management Sciences,* pp. 70-83 (October, 1966).

become more common to study the economic consequences of allocating funds to long-run, scientific, and technical endeavors. Searching questions are being asked about the value of objectives, the probabilities of success, and the cost of programs. Even in the field of military and space programs, attention is being devoted to the potential indirect benefits achieved by better serving man's more mundane social and economic needs. Clearly, unless a firm or not-for-profit institution is willing to study the ultimate outcomes in terms of consumer goods and services, however broadly defined, decision makers cannot produce reasonable allocations of effort to alternative scientific, technical, educational, and social developments. In a very real sense, allocations of resources to these purposes are shaping the future of the economy. The wise use of resources will effectively generate scientific, technical, and social advances that will yield the kinds of products and services consumers and society need. Ill-advised efforts will produce limited new opportunities which are too costly, too late, and too low in value.

At the other end of the new-product process, social scientists have been giving increasing attention to the elements that produce social change and modify its rate. Chapters in earlier sections of this book deal directly with selected aspects of this general problem. The point is, a major effort is underway designed to acquire a better understanding of how industrial buyers and consumers will view new products and what must be done to gain acceptance of useful new innovations. The availability of improved products, services, and social organizations does not assure their ultimate use or optimal rates of adoption. In the words of Paul Mazur, "Marketing is the creation and delivery of a standard of living."[2] Making good on delivery requires a deep understanding of social change; its objects, agents, and processes.

In this light, the new-product activity in the firm is a key bridge from science and technology to the aesthetic, social, and economic aspects of the consumer's world. Occupying this key position, it is useful to study the data and conceptual schemes managers should employ in making new-product decisions. Naturally, data about the firm's environment occupy a central role. Setting aside political issues, the principal subdivisions concerned are: (1) the rate and nature of scientific and technical development, (2) the projected behavior of customers, and (3) the response of competitors to the common environment posed by 1 and 2.

An unusually dramatic example of the complex set of influences which

[2] Paul Mazur, "Progress in Distribution: An Appraisal After Thirty Years," *Thirtieth Annual Boston Conference on Distribution*, p. 22 (1958).

must be handled in a new-product decision can be found in IBM's decision to back the 360 product line.[3] For a decade prior to the time at which the subject was a matter of central concern to the organization, scientific and technical advances surrounding the computer field had been explosive. Some of the advances revolved around memory and logical elements and others around programming languages and concepts. Further, the rate of change during the next decade promised to be fully as breathtaking as those of the immediate past. In this environment, two key technical decisions were made: (1) to proceed with hybrid circuits instead of pushing for monolithic elements, and (2) to make the line compatible in terms of programming and peripheral equipment. But these decisions were not made purely on scientific and technical grounds. If they had been, there would have been far less emphasis on compatibility and a strong tendency to attempt the full jump to monolithic elements. Threats to the firm's market position were clearly visible in a time span that would place great pressures on the firm's ability to design and build monolithic elements. And, on the manufacturing side, less could be said about the costs and time tables for delivery under the more advanced technology. Therefore, the perceived market needs for a wide, modern, integrated product line, and the desire to contain risks that would be very large under the best conditions, led to the ultimate decision to proceed with a wide, compatible line based on the better-understood technology. As the physical characteristics of the line began to take shape, a further set of interactions was going on related to pricing. For each significant piece of equipment, marketing selected a lease-price structure and estimated volume under a hypothesized set of market conditions related to consumers and competition. Then they asked for estimates of manufacturing costs at this level of volume. These estimates led to further pricing patterns, volume estimates and cost estimates until one or more reasonable lease-price strategies became evident.

The deliberations can be displayed in a flow diagram (Fig. 1) to expose the central nature of the new-product planning activity.

When the new-product decision process is viewed in the light of the above example and flow diagram, it becomes clear that the demands for information are high and that much of the information required is, by its nature, imprecise and difficult to quantify. Furthermore, the number and types of variables that must be accounted for make the relevant

---

[3] T. A. Wise, "IBM's $5,000,000,000 Gamble," *Fortune*, pp. 118 ff. (September, 1966), and "The Rock Road to the Marketplace," *Fortune*, pp. 138 ff. (October, 1966).

decision model very complex. To be most fruitful, the model must identify the risks and the expected rewards, suggest potential productive new alternatives, and point out opportunities to gather new information that will clarify or reduce the uncertainty surrounding each alternative. It is here that the more modern stochastic models outlined by Professor Kotler have their greatest utility. For example, these models permit management to investigate the economic consequences of the alternatives representing each product-specification price-volume-cost cycle in the above flow diagram. The consequences will be stated in a form that allows quantitative measures of the expected return, the allied risks, and the expected value of various types of additional information. And when the project reaches the stage where relatively detailed promotional strategies can be defined, the effect of each one can be investigated with similar tools of analysis.

An often overlooked advantage of the more formal methods of gathering and processing relevant data is the extent to which communication between various segments of the organization can be enhanced. Each function — research and development, manufacturing, marketing, and finance — can see what information they must provide and how it fits into the whole of the analysis. Sponsors can more readily see what factors

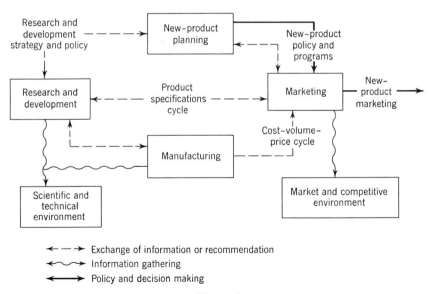

Figure 1

influence the judged effectiveness of the project or new-product proposal. Furthermore, they will typically provide only a limited proportion of the inputs to the analysis. This fact reduces the data bias and obtains a wider acceptance of the responsibility for the various elements that will ultimately produce success or failure. And finally, a great variety of benchmarks for success are established against which project performance can be compared. In addition to the customary overall measures of effectiveness, year-by-year forecasts are produced that relate to various functional areas or fields of responsibility.[4]

There are several significant data-related elements about the above type of decision models that warrant further comment. It is convenient to discuss them in the new-product decision frame of reference. These data problems, like the decision models that have been described, apply to a very wide range of decisions, spanning both marketing and nonmarketing problems. The first element concerns man's ability to provide the initial subjective inputs required to evaluate alternatives and to make reasonable choices. For example, it is typically necessary to estimate the period-by-period response of consumers and competitors to a particular product-price-promotion strategy. Even when test-market data can be gathered, subjective estimates of the product's full-life market behavior will be needed to assess the strategy. Although management may be fortunate enough to face relatively well-defined conditions, a good deal of uncertainty about the reliability of estimates typically remains.

A difficult and at least partially unsolved question concerns how to keep managers fully informed and how best to extract their expert judgments. Ideally, judgmental data would be based on available facts, weighted to account for the judges' skill, and would be free of personal and organizational bias. The Delphi technique is one imaginative attempt to accomplish this difficult task.[5] It integrates the judgments of experts by feeding back to each individual the estimates made by the other experts together with the data and rationales that they employed. By repeated interrogation and feedback cycles, during which the anonymity of the experts is preserved, several objectives can be served. Personal conflict and face-saving behavior is minimized, estimates with supporting data and logic are diffused, and a movement toward consensus is obtained by reducing disagreements and misunderstandings. Although strong consensus may result from the activity, it is not the objective of the procedure. Rather, the individual differences which remain are clari-

[4] Edgar Pessemier, *New-Product Decisions: An Analytical Approach* (New York: McGraw-Hill, 1966), pp. 141-158.
[5] Norman Dalkey and Olaf Helmer, "An Experimental Application of the Delphi Method to the Use of Experts," *Management Science,* 9 (3) (April, 1963).

fied with respect to assumptions, values, and the like. Although the Delphi technique has been employed by military and not-for-profit organizations, it has not been extensively tested in industrial circles. The cost of employing this type of analysis may be a factor but, in the case of important new-product decisions, it should not be a real barrier.

Work by Ward Edwards concerned with the early-warning defense effort, and work by a number of researchers concerned with applied industrial problems, has offered procedures for representing subjective uncertainty about estimates in the form of probability mass functions. Perhaps the greatest short-run barrier to more widespread use of these techniques is the degree to which individuals providing data are unfamiliar with or opposed to the proper use of the techniques. At one extreme, the individuals may not understand the task and, therefore, provide estimates that do not reflect their judgment. At the other extreme, individuals may clearly see the nature and implications of the data that they are generating but for one reason or another intentionally misrepresent their true judgments. A third difficulty can arise if the techniques employed are not properly designed. In this case, the estimator finds the data required are not in an appropriate format for his use in expressing his judgments. For example, one individual may find it easy to cast part of his judgments in terms of the mode and the range of a distribution, as in the case of procedures used in PERT. Other individuals may find it much easier to use the mean and quantiles. The analyst must be continually on guard against letting his desire for analytical convenience undesirably influence the quality of the data.

The second major data problem concerns extracting individual preferences for risky alternatives. Here, the analyst and manager must cope with measuring subjective utility and studying choice behavior under risk and uncertainty. The difficulties are due in large part to three basic conditions, the multidimensional character of most choice situations, the shift in the types and importance of the relevant dimensions at various levels in the organizations, and the definition and quantification of utility for individuals and groups. Although the theoretical literature in this area is very large, few studies have focused on decision makers in the firm. Grayson has studied the behavior of executives in artificial situations closely allied to the executives' normal area of decision making, and Swalm studied the effects of the individual's location in the organization on utility and choice behavior.[6] The chapter by Paul Green and his

[6] C. J. Grayson, *Decisions Under Uncertainty* (Boston: Harvard University, 1960) and Ralph Swalm, "Utility Theory—Insights Into Risk Taking," *Harvard Business Review*, pp. 123-136 (November to December, 1966).

co-authors sheds some light on personality factors as they relate to choosing among risky alternatives in a contrived but realistic environment. Clearly, much more work needs to be done before enough is understood about the executive's decision process in relation to realistic, static situations. In general, it appears likely that theoretical work performed under limited environmental conditions is well ahead of our ability to analyze and recommend action in common, relatively simple, real-world decision problems.

The third data gathering and processing problem of considerable import is the man and man-machine capacity to assimilate new information. Here, dynamic decision processes are the dominant problem. To perform well, the decision maker is confronted with the task of appraising the cost of uncertainty and the expected value of additional information. Furthermore, the decision maker must be able to continually up-date his estimates by integrating the new and old evidence bearing on the problem. The chapter by Paul Green and his co-authors covers the general literature in this area and directly treats the question of whether there is a tendency to overpurchase or underpurchase information in light of the calculated worth of the information.

THE EXPANDING RANGE OF DATA COLLECTION TECHNIQUES APPLICABLE TO DECISION MAKING IN MARKETING

In the preceding section, the usefulness of Monte Carlo and gaming simulations has been noted. Their value is found principally in the degree to which they can represent the essential elements of real-world phenomenon in a well-defined artificial environment. Typically, these conditions permit the research worker to replicate his experiment. This replication capability is a hallmark of research in the pure sciences. The nature of research in the management sciences frequently prohibits transferring this characteristic of data gathered in physical and biological investigations. Current experimental research in the behavioral sciences as it applies to marketing, however, offers real hope of gaining many of the benefits that can be obtained from carefully planned and tightly controlled experiments, including the possibility of replicating results.

The history of these attempts is long and honorable, having its foundations principally in the early work of psychologists. More recently, scientists from a wider range of disciplines have participated, particularly economists and organization theorists. In the space available, it would be foolhardy to attempt to review this massive literature. Very helpful background data and bibliographic materials can be found in the chapters by Peters and Holloway. Some of the work noted by Peters applies to the general problem of subjective probability estimation and the utility of uncertain outcomes. More directly, however, he opens up a second significant issue, the use of experimental procedures for the study of consumer choice behavior. Advances in both these areas of research promise an increasing yield of scientific findings of value to the marketing manager. Brief comments have already been made about the thorny theoretical issues related to casting estimates in usable form for managerial decision making. Here, it is valuable to consider how experimental work regarding the behavior of customers can contribute to a better understanding of the consumer-buyer and to better estimates about their responses to marketing actions.

Returning to the area of new-product analysis, part of management's on-going task is monitoring the changing environment and assessing how it will respond to potential new products. A central phase of this work must be a continuing analysis of market structure, brand performances, competitive activity, and the like. Statistical analyses of accounting records, panel data, and survey results represent the backbone of these efforts. By their nature, these analyses tend to limit extrapolations to conditions similar to those previously encountered. They may offer little aid concerning responses to novel new conditions.

Occasionally, management can rely on clearly analogous situations that permit confident predictions of the outcomes in question. And in other situations, slow adaption to new conditions based on repeated trials and analyses of feedback data will yield effective results. More commonly in a new-product introduction, management must make major decisions that cannot be easily modified, decisions concerning environmental and behavioral factors about which it has little relevant knowledge on hand. To permit the study of likely responses of buyers and competitors to genuinely new circumstances, it is often desirable or necessary to place the buyer in an environment that approximates one of interest. For example, it may be important to know something of the likely source of new customers if a particular type of new product is introduced. In this case, test-market data may be of real assistance but the number of variables explored and their range will be sharply limited by both time and cost. As a result, seldom can management learn how loyal were the customers who did not switch to the new brand or what inducements must be employed to attain the given level or type of brand-switching behavior. By studying the degree of brand loyalty to existing brands and the reactions of the buyer of various extant brands to the new brand in carefully designed, simulated purchase situations, these elements are subject to study. In a similar manner, demand may be observed over a range of price changes not often feasible in a test market.[7] At the sacrifice of some aspects of the real-market situation, the phemonemon of interest may be studied in depth in a relatively short time span. Experiments of the types outlined have been conducted for consumer convenience goods, automobiles, and some industrial goods.

In comparison to most test-marketing studies, these studies also offer wider opportunities to study the differential behavior for various types of customers. For example, do older buyers require larger or special incentives to try a new product? Are the brand-loyal customers of a selected brand largely drawn from a distinct socioeconomic group? Do the trial-prone buyers possess certain personality characteristics? Do potential new users have different media habits? Gathering the relevant data in a test market is difficult, but experimental procedures performed under either laboratory conditions or in a tightly controlled field study can shed light on these and other questions that may assume importance in formulating a marketing strategy. Unlike most panel or survey work where the types and ranges of variables may be confined to those encountered under past and present conditions, in experimental work the consumer-subject can respond to an entirely new product, a new copy theme, or a new set of prices.

The most serious limitation to the use of experimental methods is the persistent, general difficulty associated with inferring long-run effects from relatively short periods of observation or experimentation. An enriched understanding of the consumer and the buying process will aid the prediction of long-run phenomenon on the basis of short periods of experimentation. Naturally, longitudinal studies of behavior will enhance the researcher's understanding of the time flow of effects and his ability to predict. Another problem that is currently troublesome but more readily subject to solution concerns transforming experimental results in a way that will permit confident prediction of market behavior. For example, in a bidding experiment or gaming situation, the researcher may not know to what degree subjects are influenced by the experimental conditions; for instance, surveillance and small stakes. Often, he can safely assume that the variables will influence subjects in the proper direction but that the magnitude of this influence is open to serious question. Monetary gain may be viewed as desirable in both the game

[7] Edgar Pessemier, *Experimental Methods of Analyzing Demand For Branded Consumer Goods* (Pullman, Wash.: Washington State University Press, 1963).

and the allied real-world situation, but the size or type of the payoff encountered may differ so much that predictions will be tenuous, at best.

In a sense, experimental work is also plagued with many of the same general problems of response error and bias familiar to survey research workers. The stimulus may elicit responses that are not directly related to the issue at hand or that reflect the subject's inability or unwillingness to provide the needed information in a suitable form. The problem becomes especially acute when information is sought about behavior or attitudes whose wellsprings are deep in the subjects' mental or emotional character. A partial solution to the problem can be found in motivational research but difficult problems of quantification and analysis have hobbled this methodology. To mitigate some of these difficulties, recent efforts in psychophysical research and pupillometrics offer new hope of obtaining involuntary responses to stimuli. If these responses can be readily linked to market-related emotions and behavior, current work by Dr. Hess and his associates will have provided a strong new link in the methodological chain.

Although most of the broad field of psychometrics lies beyond the scope of this discussion, it is worth underlining the present and potential value of developments in this field to marketing management. The paper by Volney Stefflre in an earlier section is illustrative. So is the early work by Thurstone and his associates that is briefly noted in the chapter by Peters. Additional procedures of potential value to marketing managers would include the scaling methods employing similarity data. The multidimensional technique by Kruskal, that can be applied to single subjects, is an important example.[8] For groups of subjects, the method due to Scheffé is valuable.[9] In regard to the more widely employed rank-order and paired-comparison data, the measures of consistency, concordance, and agreement reported by Kendall can provide useful insights into consumer behavior.[10] In each case, data can be processed in a manner that will produce scale values for objects of interest to the marketing manager or will reveal elements related to preference and choice behavior. Although the data used by these procedures are often gathered in an experimental setting, in some cases it is practical to use relatively straightforward survey instruments.

[8] J. B. Kruskal, "Multidimensional Scaling by Optimizing Goodness of Fit to a Nonmetric Hypothesis," *Psychometrika*, pp. 1-27 (March, 1964).
[9] Henry Scheffé, "An Analysis of Variance For Paired Comparisons," *American Statistical Association Journal*, pp. 381-400 (September, 1952).
[10] M. G. Kendall, *Rank Correlation Methods* (London: Charles Griffin, 1948).

SOME GENERAL ASPECTS OF RESEARCH STRATEGIES

Returning to the more general problem of establishing a research strategy designed to support managerial action, several additional points should be noted. The first deals with the types of models that are most relevant. Generally, the research questions are relatively unique and transient. The manager wants to know more about *his* action possibilities in the time frame in which *he* must act and evaluate the results. This means that the analyst needs flexible models that can be adapted readily to new conditions. As new data become available, it is often desirable to modify the model and the value assigned to various types of additional data that may be gathered. Furthermore, the model's predictive ability is far more important than its demonstrated power to cope with the past. To be explicit, it is easy to imagine a firm developing a simulation model of a particular market that would produce excellent, detailed predictions of behavior over some extended past period. If the market had been for a product with no close substitute and the current task is to predict the markets after several firms introduce a new type of good that will be an adequate substitute for many end uses, the model must be changed to account for this fact. Here, the analyst or manager may be in need of expert opinion about (1) the variables that apply to the new market conditions, (2) how they are related, (3) the values they are likely to assume in the future. In other words, we need a new model and data that can be used to explore alternative plans of action.

The second major point can also be discussed using the same illustration. Note that the manager now needs a series of descriptions of plausible strategies and competitive responses that apply to the new market conditions. These can take the form of scenarios that describe in meaningful detail the possible actions and reactions. But since it is impossible to consider all possible scenarios, those are sought that are plausible and productive. Again, expert opinion will be helpful but so will a well-constructed model because it can produce simplified scenarios. The likely outcomes of any strategy management may consider employing may be produced rapidly in the environments described by competitive and general economic conditions. The dominated strategies for the firm can be discarded so that a smaller useful set of strategy-response pairs will be the only set ultimately considered. This activity has the additional advantage of providing contingency plans that will guide action in the face of a change in the competitive or economic environment.

Third, the above activity may lead to an analysis of the degree to which the model represents real-market behavior and the levels of uncertainty surrounding the data. Here, the questions directly concern the cost of errors in the assessments that lead to plausible scenarios. In turn, this may lead to the collection of additional statistical data, expanded use of expert opinion, further pseudo-experimentation with the model, or controlled experimentation in the laboratory or field. In each case, an effort is being made to sharpen understanding in those areas in which the expected payoff is high enough to warrant the cost in time, manpower, and money. Finally, it is worth observing that the activity is not passive, or does not involve simply a passive response to the inevitable. Rather, the activity entails understanding each possibility well enough so that the firm, by its actions, to the largest extent possible makes its own wishes come true. The firm acts to make its most desirable future possibilities come true.[11]

[11] Olaf Helmer, "Social Technology," RAND publication P-3063, pp. 37-40 (1965).

ELEVEN | *PHILIP KOTLER*

Computer Simulation in the Analysis of New-Product Decisions

Under modern conditions of competition, it is becoming increasingly risky not to innovate. Consumers and industrial customers want and expect a stream of new and improved products. Competition will certainly do its best to meet these desires. Continuous innovation is the only way to avoid obsolescence of the company's product line.

At the same time, it is extremely expensive and risky to innovate. Many product ideas that go through product development never reach the market; many of those that are introduced in the market are not successful; and many of the successful ideas tend to have a shorter life than new products once had.[1] New product development can be as risky a course as doing nothing.

Thus, management finds itself in a dilemma; it must develop new products, yet the odds weigh heavily against their success. The answer must still lie in new-product development, but that development must be conducted in a way that reduces the risk of failure.

The risk can never be completely taken out of new-product development, but specific practices may increase the likelihood of successful innovation. The risks of innovating are reduced through the development of effective organizational arrangements for new-product research and development, staffing with professional and experienced executives, company willingness to make adequate investments in marketing studies, and the use of conceptually refined models for new-product decision making.

This chapter will focus on the last ingredient. As a new product proposal passes through the stages of screening, business analysis, product development, market testing, and commercialization, management has the option of continuing the project, terminating the project, or gathering

[1] For some background and statistics, see [5].

additional information before deciding. The critical factor is estimates of the expected payoff and risk characterizing the alternative decisions. These estimates depend not only on the available information but, indeed, on the types of information sought in the first place. Stated differently, there are different conceptions or models for the best way to estimate the merits of alternative courses of action regarding new products.

Two different types of evaluation take place in considering the new product. The first type is called a *compatibility* evaluation and usually precedes the second, a *profit* evaluation.

The compatibility evaluation raises the question whether the product proposal is possible and desirable considering the various company objectives and resources. A good product proposal may have to be stopped or dropped if it is recognized, for example, that the company could not gain access to the needed distribution channels, lacked the financial resources, or had an image that was incompatible. Many factors have to be looked at in this connection. The major device for formally considering and weighing these factors was suggested over a decade ago and has been modified several times since then [16, 27, and 29].

This chapter will not consider further the compatibility evaluation. It will assume that good instruments exist for determining whether the firm can logically undertake development of a new product in terms of company objectives and resources. There remains the question of whether it would, in fact, be worthwhile to do so. That question can be answered by a profit evaluation. The kinds of instruments available for making the profit evaluation will be discussed at length.

The earliest profit model proposed a straightforward breakeven analysis of a new product proposal in terms of its total expected sales and costs. More recent models have introduced additional factors; for instance, product life-cycle considerations, cash-flow discounting, the sales effect of marketing-mix variations, and the explicit consideration of uncertainty. The extant models differ considerably in mathematical character and substantive focus. Nowhere is any extensive review and comparison of new-product decision models available, although in other important marketing-decision areas (for example, physical distribution [21] and mathematical media selection [17]) critical comparisons of different models have been made. The following section presents a general critique. In turn, a number of aspects of the profit-evaluation problem are exposed that need further research. Two of these aspects (the formulation of a satisfactory demand function and the handling of competitors' marketing strategies) are selected for specific discussion in a second section.

A major issue facing contemporary model builders in the area of new-product decision making is whether to go the route of building optimization models or simulation models. Casting the new-product decision problem in the framework of an optimization model typically requires a number of simplifications. The decision maker is able to identify the optimal solution to the stated problem, although the statement of the problem may contain serious omissions. Going the simulation route enables the model builder to construct a more realistic and complex model at the price of foregoing an algorithm for finding the best solution. The issues raised by these conditions and the meaning of simulation are considered at various points.

NEW-PRODUCT PROFIT EVALUATION MODELS

A new-product profit evaluation may be made at various stages in the development of a new product. A preliminary forecast of sales and costs can be made at the screening stage, to consider whether the product promises at least a minimum rate of return on the required effort. The model used at this stage may be a very simple breakeven model, although even here a more advanced model might prove desirable. If the product moves into development and emerges successfully, another profit evaluation is likely to take place. The analysis should be more extensive because the company is now facing the prospect of launching the product with all the attendant costs and risks. Better information about the product and the market is available at this stage. In the evaluation, all the unrecoverable expenses incurred up-to-date must be left out. They are sunk costs and as such have no bearing on the decision. The issue is whether the further development of the product would produce sufficient additional revenues over costs. At this point, the company also faces some expensive options in the further study of demand (for instance, in-home tests or test marketing) and must know how to allocate wisely its limited study funds. Guidance in making the allocation should also be provided by the profit model. Some time later, after the company has gathered further market information and has assembled appropriate cost data, it will face the ultimate decision about adding or dropping the product. Here the firm will make the most meticulous forecast of the future flow of revenues and costs extending over the economic life of the product, if possible. The particular marketing program contemplated for the new product as well as expectations about competitive behavior must be explicity introduced.

Profit evaluation is therefore a task that is likely to be repeated several times in the course of developing a new product. At successive points, the available information increases; at the same time, the number of factors that must be considered increase. This change in the complexity of the required analysis may account for the existence of different models, all dealing with the evaluation of future profits.

At the same time, part of the differences in the existing models must be attributable to the ordinary evolution that formal models go through. One of the chief benefits of formal model building is that each effort reveals its weaknesses as clearly as its strengths, and these weaknesses spark new refinements leading to a cumulative development, the end product of which may have been impossible to formulate full-blown without the preceding painstaking steps.

This section selects and contrasts seven profit-evaluation models for the new-product problem ranging from the simple to the highly complex. A summary of these models and their contrasting characteristics is presented in Fig. 11.7. The discussion on which Fig. 11.7 is based now follows.

Breakeven Model

The traditional approach to evaluating a new-product proposal is to determine the breakeven volume and whether company sales are likely to exceed or fall short of this breakeven volume. The breakeven volume is the sales volume (in units) that would have to be sold in order to cover all the costs involved in developing and producing the product, including the company's opportunity cost of capital.

The formula for computing breakeven volume seems straightforward. At the breakeven volume (Q_B), total revenue (R) equals total cost (C).[2] Total revenue is price (P) times the breakeven volume, and total cost is fixed cost (F) plus the product of unit variable cost (V) and breakeven volume. In symbols:

$$R = C$$

$$PQ_B = F + VQ_B$$

$$Q_B = \frac{F}{P - V} \qquad \text{(simple breakeven volume equation)} \quad (11.1)$$

[2] Consistent symbols are used in this paper to compare models. A glossary of symbols is found in Appendix A.

The breakeven volume represents an anchor estimate based on cost against which the more difficult estimate of demand (Q) is considered. The question is whether management thinks the firm can sell enough units to at least break even. The greater the probable excess of expected sales over breakeven sales, that is, $(Q-Q_B)$, the greater is management's confidence in the ultimate profitability of the new product.

This seemingly straightforward model is not without ambiguity. One source of ambiguity is the time period. There are two aternative interpretations. The first interpretation holds that the formula is set up to evaluate annual sales and to ascertain whether they would be sufficient to cover annual costs. Unfortunately, this interpretation is not a natural one for new-product commercialization decisions because, typically, product sales are expected to initially grow through time and ultimately decline rather than remain at a constant level from the first year on. If the model is used under this interpretation, then management is called upon to consider not sales growth but the average level of sales over the product life cycle.

The other interpretation holds that the formula is set up to determine whether a point in time will be reached when cumulative sales revenue equals cumulative costs. If management can foresee cumulative revenue reaching cumulative costs in a reasonably short time, then it would be more strongly disposed to introduce the product. The shorter the payback period, the greater management's confidence, in view of the competitive uncertainties that plague planning in the long run.

The payback period (m) is given by the condition that

$$
m = \frac{F}{\displaystyle\sum_{i=1}^{m} (P - V)Q_i} = 1 \quad \text{(payback period equation)}
$$

$$(11.2)$$

where Q_i is the expected sales in year i and i goes from year 1 to year m. This interpretation is more flexible for new-product decision making because it does not assume a constant level of sales each year.

Both breakeven interpretations have another ambiguity related to the treatment of costs. A new-product involves all kinds of costs, some of which cannot be classified simply as a fixed cost or a constant unit variable cost. There are difficult questions in the treatment of start-up costs, opportunity costs, and semivariable costs, and an extended version of Eq. 11.1 or Eq. 11.2 would be required for practical implementation.

In addition to these ambiguities, the breakeven model fails to grapple with several substantive issues in the estimation of new-product profitability. Among its chief shortcomings are the following:

1. It assumes that P and V remain constant over the planning horizon, whereas new-product marketing usually is characterized by a falling price over time due to changing market conditions and a falling unit variable cost because of a production learning curve.

2. It fails to consider the opportunity costs of different timing patterns of future revenues and costs.

3. It fails to consider the effect of different marketing programs on the level and timing of future sales and costs.

4. It fails to consider the effect of different facilities strategies on the level and timing of future revenues and costs.

5. It fails to consider explicitly the uncertain nature of the data entering the estimation process. As a result, the model fails to produce an estimate of risk alongside the estimate of return. Lacking an estimate of risk, there is no way to measure the value of additional information.

6. It fails to consider possible profit interaction effects between the new product and the company's existing products.

It should be clear by now that formal breakeven analysis is much too simple a device to guide decision making in this costly and vital area. It is this realization that has led to the development of more advanced models, each overcoming one or more of the shortcomings of the simple breakeven model.

Cash-Flow Model

The realization that new-product revenues and costs typically change during the product life cycle sparked interest in the use of a cash-flow model for estimating new-product profits. Cash-flow models are used to evaluate any investment whose proceeds vary over time.

Two different methods are available for finding the value of a proposed investment. *The present value method* involves discounting the future expected net income stream by the company's cost of capital; this yields the present value of the income stream. This present value is compared against the estimated investment required to develop and support this product. If the present value exceeds the investment, the company would earn a rate of return on its investment exceeding its cost of capital.

Present value is given by the following formula:

$$W = \frac{R_1 - C_1}{(1+c)^1} + \frac{R_2 - C_2}{(1+c)^2} + \cdots + \frac{R_i - C_i}{(1+c)^i} + \cdots + \frac{R_n - C_n}{(1+c)^n}$$

$$W = \sum_{i=1}^{n} \frac{R_i - C_i}{(1+c)^i} \qquad \text{(present value equation)} \qquad (11.3)$$

where

W = present value of investment.
R_i = expected total revenue in year i.
C_i = expected total cost in year i.
c = company opportunity cost of capital.
n = the last year for which R and C are estimated; the length of the planning horizon.

After calculating W, it is compared to the required investment (I) and the following decision rule is used:

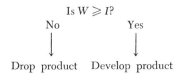

If the company must choose among a number of new-product ideas where $W > I$, and lacks the resources to develop them all, it may choose the subset with the highest ratios (W/I) that is within the budget.

Alternatively, the value of an investment may be analyzed by *the rate-of-return* (*or yield*) *method*. It calls for estimating the discount rate (r) that would cause the value of the future income stream to just equal the required investment. This amounts to solving the following formula for r:[3]

$$I = \frac{R_1 - C_1}{(1+r)^1} + \frac{R_2 - C_2}{(1+r)^2} + \cdots + \frac{R_i - C_i}{(1+r)^i} + \cdots + \frac{R_n - C_n}{(1+r)^n}$$

$$I = \sum_{i=1}^{n} \frac{R_i - C_i}{(1+r)^i} \qquad \text{(rate-of-return equation)} \qquad (11.4)$$

[3] The equilibrating rate-of-return (r) is usually found by the method of successive approximation. The results of trying a few different r's usually reveals the neighborhood of the solution that can then be approached as finely as desired.

The decision rule is then:

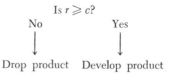

Is $r \geq c$?

No   Yes

Drop product   Develop product

The present value method and the yield method lead to the same decision in the case where one product is being considered. If several product proposals are being simultaneously ranked in order of desirability, these criteria can sometimes produce a different ranking for the same product, thereby leading to advocates of one or the other criterion. But this issue need not concern us here.[4]

An early adaption of the cash-flow model to the new-product profit evaluation problem was developed by Solomon Disman of Abbott Laboratories [12]. His method is reportedly used in a number of companies [3]. The executive concerned with a new-product decision makes an estimate of probable revenues and costs from the time of product introduction to some number of years later (the period known as the planning horizon). The resulting income stream is discounted at the company's opportunity cost of capital to yield the present value (W) of the product proposal. To allow for risk, Disman introduced a special factor into the calculation. He recommended that the estimated present value be scaled down by the subjective probability (Pr) that the company would achieve technical and commercial success. He called the result $Pr \cdot W$, the proposal's *maximum economic justification*. It represents the maximum amount the company should be willing to invest in developing the new product. The proposal's $Pr \cdot W$ would be compared to the estimated investment, I. A GO decision would be indicated whenever $Pr \cdot W \geq I$. If several product proposals were being compared, and not all could be developed, their relative attractiveness would be indicated by the ratio $Pr \cdot W / I$.

The use of a scaling factor for the probability of technical and commercial success is one of several ways to handle the problem of uncertainty. According to Disman, the confidence of those working on new-product proposals varies with each project and can be quantified. In fact, he suggested that separate probabilities be estimated for the likelihood of technical success (Pr_t) and commercial success (Pr_c). A problem does arise if different company estimators make widely different esti-

[4] See [34], Chapter Three. The two methods may lead to different rankings if the economic lives of the various projects differ, or if quite different size capital outlays are involved.

mates of these probabilities.[5] Although a weighted mean of the estimates could be used (weighted by the relative accuracy of the estimators in the past) a measure of dispersion is needed to effectively indicate the uncertainty in estimates. Another problem is that some of the risk must already be implicitly reflected in the estimate of future revenues and costs, but the connection between the explicit and implicit risk evaluation is not made clear. While it overcomes a few weaknesses of the simple breakeven model, considering the approach as a whole, it fails to grapple with many important issues.

Simple Marketing Mix Model

The two previous models failed to consider explicitly the profit effect of different marketing programs for launching the product. It is hardly debatable that alternative programs for pricing, promoting, and distributing the product will differentially affect product sales and costs. Yet, there is little evidence that current profit-analysis practices give formal consideration to this factor. This factor can be incorporated into the breakeven model or cash-flow model in a straightforward fashion.

For ease of exposition, assume that a company's proposed marketing program for a new product can be summarized by the vector (P,A,D), where

$$P = \text{Price}$$
$$A = \text{Advertising budget}$$
$$D = \text{Distribution budget}$$

Now these marketing factors can be introduced explicitly into the breakeven formula in the following way [20]. Assume that the company is planning to spend a constant annual amount A and D on advertising and distribution, respectively. These can be treated as fixed costs and shown in the breakeven formula in the following way:

$$Q_B = \frac{F + A + D}{P - V} \qquad \begin{array}{l} \text{(breakeven volume equation} \\ \text{showing marketing factors)} \end{array} \qquad (11.5)$$

where F is assumed to be nonmarketing fixed costs.

The expenditures on advertising and distribution and the price charged are marketing factors that will affect the quantity sold; that is,

$$Q = f(P, A, D) \qquad \text{(demand function)} \qquad (11.6)$$

[5] For alternative methods of handling this, see [28], pp. 107-11, or [11].

The addition of a demand equation to the breakeven equation allows us, for the first time, to solve for the optimal marketing mix *and* the consequent expected profits. We have only to note that profits are given by the following formula:

$$Z = (P - V)(Q - Q_B) \quad \text{(profit equation)} \quad (11.7)$$

where Z is defined as dollar profits from sales in excess of the breakeven level. In view of this profit equation, it is possible to insert Eq. 11.6 for Q and Eq. 11.5 for Q_B into Eq. 11.7 and solve for the marketing mix that maximizes it. This involves finding the first partial derivatives of Z with respect to P, A, and D, setting the three partial derivatives equal to zero, and solving the three equations simultaneously for the three unknowns (P, A, D). The solution (P, A, D) represents the optimum marketing mix and its substitution into the profit equation (Eq. 11.7) yields the expected profitability of launching the product with the given marketing mix.

Although it does lead to a defined optimum, there is much that is unsatisfactory about this approach. One fault is the assumption of a constant (P, A, D) throughout the product life cycle. One of the characteristics of marketing a new product is that a more dynamic marketing strategy is contemplated, including the possibility of a falling price over time and a rising budget for marketing. A second fault, thinking in terms of breakeven, is that the rate of return on the investment is not explicitly estimated (the index Z/I does not really give the true yield). For these and other reasons, it is desirable to recall the marketing analysis in cash-flow terms.

We can start with the rate-of-return version of the cash-flow approach:

$$I = \sum_{i=1}^{n} \frac{R_i - C_i}{(1+r)^i} \quad \text{(rate-of-return equation)} \quad (11.8)$$

But $R_i = P_i Q_i$ (that is, revenue in period i) is the product of the price and quantity sold in period i. And $C_i = \overline{C}_i + A_i + D_i$, that is, total cost in period i; C_i is made up of total nonmarketing cost $(\overline{C}_i)$ and of total advertising (A_i) and distribution (D_i) costs. Therefore Eq. 11.8 becomes:

$$I = \sum_{i=1}^{n} \frac{P_i Q_i - \overline{C}_i - A_i - D_i}{(1+r)^i} \quad (11.9)$$

But $Q_i = f(P_i, A_i, D_i)$; that is, the quantity sold in period i is a function of the price, advertising, and distribution in period i:

$$I = \sum_{i=1}^{n} \frac{P_i \, [f(P_i, A_i, D_i)] - \overline{C}_i - A_i - D_i}{(1 + r)^i} \qquad \begin{array}{l} \text{(rate-of-return} \\ \text{equation showing} \\ \text{marketing factors)} \end{array} \quad (11.10)$$

How is Eq. 11.10 used? Marketing management spells out a dynamic marketing program for the new product covering the planning horizon. The program may be represented by a $3 \times n$ matrix (M), where 3 stands for the number of marketing factors being planned, here (P, A, D), and n for the number of periods being planned. The marketing program matrix looks like this:

$$M = \begin{pmatrix} P_1 & P_2 & \ldots & P_i & \ldots & P_n \\ A_1 & A_2 & \ldots & A_i & \ldots & A_n \\ D_1 & D_2 & \ldots & D_i & \ldots & D_n \end{pmatrix} \qquad \begin{array}{l} \text{(marketing program matrix)} \\ (11.11) \end{array}$$

This marketing program will lead to a certain pattern of future sales (Q) for the company over time, indicated by some demand function, $Q_i = f(P_i, A_i, D_i)$. This pattern can be presented by the $(1 \times n)$ vector Q:

$$Q = (Q_1 Q_2 \ldots Q_i \ldots Q_n) \qquad \text{(sales time series vector)} \quad (11.12)$$

Given the marketing program matrix (M) and the sales time series vector (Q), the corresponding figures are inserted into the rate-of-return equation (Eq. 11.10). The numerator for each year is determined. The size of the investment (I) on the left-hand side is also determined.[6] Then the equation is solved for r. The r represents the expected rate of return on the new product conditional upon the given marketing program matrix.

Logically, the next question is whether a procedure exists for determining the optimal dynamic marketing program, given some specific demand equation. A procedure is certainly possible in principle, although the analytical task is formidable. For a $3 \times n$ marketing program matrix, there are $3 n$ variables to be determined. The demand function is likely

---

[6] It will probably be necessary to treat investment as a flow just as income is a flow. The "I" used on the left-hand side of Eq. 11.10 should therefore be the present value of the expected investment flow, discounted by the company's cost of capital. The problem is further complicated because different marketing programs will result in different levels and time patterns of demand toward which investment has to be adjusted. In other words, $I_i = f(Q_i) = f(P_i, A_i, D_i)$. The left-hand side is therefore not only a discounted flow but a conditional discounted flow as well.

to be so intractable analytically that it would seem better to hunt for a satisfactory solution through simulation techniques. Specifically, management could prepare a small set of alternative hypothetical marketing programs and solve the r for each. If the r seems to improve with certain types of programs, a few more could be developed and their r computed. When a satisfactory program and r is found, the search can stop. The computer program for this approach is quite straightforward and could yield solutions quickly.

Bayesian Decision Model

Quite a different approach to the profit-evaluation problem is provided by the Bayesian decision model. It is an approach that allows a more flexible, detailed model to be built of the specific decision problem and it uses explicit probabilities to reflect uncertainty. The approach allows an estimate to be made of the value of buying additional information to reduce the uncertainty.

The Bayesian decision model, reduced to its simplest elements, calls for executives to define the company's objective(s), possible alternative strategies, major events affecting the outcomes of each strategy, the probabilities of these events, and the profit value of different outcomes. These data allow a calculation to be made of the expected profit of each strategy, including the strategy of gathering more information before acting.

Paul E. Green recently described a specific application of the Bayesian decision model to a new-product problem at a large chemical company [1]. The new product had been under development for several years. It was estimated to have approximately twenty major end uses. The personnel responsible for making the commercialization decision felt great uncertainty regarding the product's potential profitability. They were uncertain about the size of the market and the effect of different pricing strategies. They were uncertain about the best size plant to build if they introduced the product nationally.

To analyze this problem formally, the company's operations research director met with the product manager and marketing personnel. This committee agreed on the following ground rules:

1. The executives would consider three alternative pricing policies: a skimming price policy, a penetration price policy, and an intermediate price policy.

2. The executives would consider two alternative initial plant sizes,

with capacities of 10 million pounds and 25 million pounds, respectively. They also agreed that if demand exceeded capacity, there could be up to three years delay before the capacity could be developed.

3. The analysis would be limited to a 13-year planning horizon.

4. The executives would judge among the alternative possible decisions on the basis of which appeared to have the highest expected present value.

Using these ground rules, the executives prepared three different forecasts of annual sales covering the thirteen years, representing respectively a pessimistic, optimistic, and most-likely outlook.

The next step involved computing the expected present values of 72 different possible developments (2 initial plant sizes, 3 pricing policies, 3 sales forecasts, and 4 capacity addition delay levels). An illustration of 18 of these developments (based on the first 3 variables and assuming a zero capacity addition delay) is shown in Fig. 11.1. The dollar figure at the end of each of the 18 branches represents an estimate of the present value of the expected cash flow during the 13-year period. For example, management expects a cash flow whose present value is $30.4 million if it employs a skimming pricing policy, builds a small plant of 10 million pounds annual capacity, and meets up with very good sales.

The numbers in parentheses preceding the present value estimates are the probabilities assigned by management to the optimistic, most probable, and pessimistic forecasts, respectively (0.3, 0.5, 0.2). The next step calls for computing the expected present value for each alternative facing management. This is found by multiplying each of the three present values by their respective probabilities as outcomes. Thus, the expected present value of the skimming price, small-plant alternative is $11.04 (0.3 × $30.4 + 0.5 ×$14.2 + 0.2 × −$28.9).

Examining Fig. 11.1, it turns out that the large plant size yields the highest expected present value under all pricing policies and sales forecasts; the skimming pricing policy dominates the others under all conditions. Thus, if the company decided to introduce the product commercially, it should build a 25 million pound plant initially and use a skimming pricing policy. In fact, the analysis leads to the conclusion that the company *should* introduce the product commercially under the aforementioned strategy. This move has an expected present value of $14.15 million whereas dropping the product has an expected present value of $0.0.

At the same time, the company has to recognize that this decision involves some risk of a large loss. Specifically, there is a 20 percent proba-

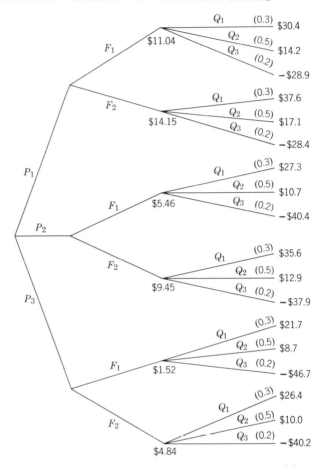

Figure 11.1   Illustration of Bayesian decision model.

P_1, skimming pricing policy; P_2, intermediate pricing policy; P_3, penetration pricing policy; F_1, small plant; F_2, large plant; Q_1, optimistic demand forecast; Q_2, most probable demand forecast; and Q_3, pessimistic demand forecast.

Source: Tree diagram was developed from information in the text of Green [1].

bility (in the executives' minds) of the company losing as much as minus $28.4 million. This piece of information proves to be quite useful and, in fact, is the basis for making an assessment of the value of purchasing further information before acting. Suppose the company is able to buy a perfect forecast of future sales. What is the most it should be willing to pay for this forecast? The answer is $5.68 million. Why? Because if the company acted without buying this information there is a

20 percent probability that it would incur a loss of $28.4 million; that is, a conditional expected loss of $5.68 million. Therefore, it should not be willing to pay more than $5.68 million for information to save itself from a possibly incorrect decision.[7]

In practice, the company will not be able to buy a perfect forecast, but the calculation provides an upper limit to reasonable expenditures on marketing studies. In this example, the upper limit is quite high. The company could now proceed to consider alternative possible studies and choose among them on the basis of which would have the highest expected present value. This involves making judgments as to the prior probabilities of different findings turning up with each study. The details need not concern us here [4].

The following two characteristics summarize the main features of the Bayesian approach to evaluating new product profitability.

1. The Bayesian model allows considerable flexibility in modelling the problem with all the alternative moves and outcomes that are possible, including their timing.

2. Usually, one of the decision alternatives involves delaying the decision and buying information. The value of this alternative can be calculated and compared to the value of immediate action.

Monte Carlo Simulation Model

One of the contributions of the Bayesian model is that it introduced explicitly the probabilistic nature of rate-of-return estimation. It recognized that the value of a particular strategy is affected by the unknown states of nature. It called for distinguishing possible outcomes of each strategy, and estimating their respective probabilities. As a result, the value of a strategy could be portrayed by a probability distribution of possible returns. The probability distribution for the skimming pricing-large plant strategy in Fig. 11.1 is reproduced in Fig. 11.2.

The Bayesian model did not compare the probability distributions of the different strategies but, instead, the means of these distributions. The means are the expected present values, and it is typical of Bayesian

---

[7] The analysis has been simplified here in relation to the example developed in Green [1]. Green assumes that buying information would delay the decision for one year with attendant costs, and he also assumes that if the company introduced the product and met with poor sales, it would cut short its losses to something less than $28.4 million. His calculation under the new assumptions indicated that the preferred alternative would be to delay the decision if the company could acquire highly reliable information within a year at a cost not exceeding $1.6 million.

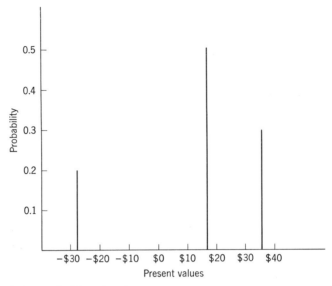

Figure 11.2. Probability distribution of present values for skimming pricing—large plant strategy. (*Source:* see Figure 11.1.)

analysis that the decision criterion is to choose the strategy with the largest expected present value. However, there are cases where the expected values are not a sufficient criterion. Consider, for example, the two continuous probability distributions shown in Fig. 11.3. Each dis-

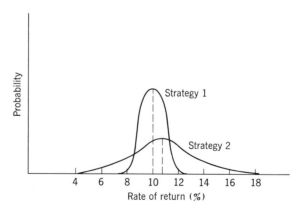

Figure 11.3. Estimated probability distributions of rate of return for two alternative new-product strategies.

tribution is estimated for a different introductory marketing strategy for a new product. The second strategy has a higher mean rate of return than the first strategy but also a higher variance of return. Here lies the reason for the desirability of estimating the whole distribution and not only the mean. If management were to receive an estimate of only the mean return, it would favor the second marketing strategy. However, the choice is less clear when the two distributions are compared. A conservative management may decide on strategy 1 because of the very high probability that the rate-of-return will be between 8 and 12 percent; under strategy 2, the rate-of-return could turn out to be as low as 4 percent. An adventurous management would prefer strategy 2 because the mean expectation is higher and, even more importantly, because there is chance for high gains. The distribution of the whole range of possible returns helps remind us of a very important thing about "risk." While it means the firm could do very poorly, it also means that there is a chance that the firm might do very well. The right half of risk means opportunity [6]. Not every firm, therefore, will discount for risk.[8]

Granting the desirability of new-product models that produce profit probability distributions, two things should be noted about the Bayesian model. In the example, only three sales forecast levels were prepared and therefore the probability distribution was highly discrete. There is nothing about the model that prevents the use of a continuous probability distribution for sales and therefore the derivation of a continuous probability distribution for each strategy; the mathematics simply get a little more complex. Second, present value was used as the random variable in the example; it is equally possible to make the random variable the internal rate-of-return.

An extension of the Bayesian decision model has been formulated by Edgar Pessemier that yields probability distributions of rates-of-return [28]. This approach calls for the executives to supply not only expected values for several of the variables in the model, but also the 0.1 and 0.9 decile values. These data permit the derivation of a probability distribution for each of the key variables. Among the variables treated in this stochastic fashion are unit sales, price, unit cost, and investment. There-

[8] In one formulation of the return-risk tradeoff problem, the value of each strategy is represented by a "certainty equivalent" ($\bar{Z}$) equal to the expected profits (Z) less some multiple (k) of the profit variance (σ_z):

$$\bar{Z} = Z - k\,\sigma_z$$

See Eq. 11.13. The point made above is that companies with a gambling propensity may choose a zero k, or even a negative k.

fore, the final outcome of any strategy is stated in probabilistic terms. It is not possible to derive analytically the final probability distribution for a strategy from the input probability distributions. Pessemier resorts to the technique of Monte Carlo simulation to estimate the final distribution. In other words, he generates annual values for the various key variables by drawing simulated observations from probability distributions with the required characteristics.

The entire model is represented in flow diagram form in Fig. 11.4. Its major features are summarized below.

Figure 11.4. Monte Carlo Simulation Model (Pessemier). *Source*: this flow diagram has been developed by the author from Pessemier's discussion [28].

Flow Diagram

Ⓐ
↓

Informed company executives spell out:

    I. a specific marketing strategy, s

    II. a specific marketing environment, e

Ⓑ
↓

The executives then estimate the annual expected values of the following variables over the i years in the new-product planning horizon:

    1. unit sales (Q_i)

    2. unit price (P_i)

    3. unit cost (V_i) implies a·specific

    4. investment (I_i) facilities strategy, f

In addition to the expected values of these variables, the executives estimate the respective 0.1 and 0.9 decile values. The decile values enable the analyst to treat each variable as subject to a lognormal probability distribution with a known mean and variance. (These will be used later.) Finally, the executives estimate annual expected values, but not quantile values, for the following three variables:

    5. depreciation (g_i)

    6. opportunity costs in dollars (h_i)

    7. nonrecurring start-up costs (u_i)

Ⓒ
↓

The analyst now generates through Monte Carlo methods a sample value for each variable (Q_i, P_i, V_i and I_i) for each year during the product-planning horizon. (A device is used to permit serial correlation of successively generated values of unit sales.)

These values enable a computation to be made of the positive cash flows (Z_i) each year. The formula is:

$$Z_i = T\{Q_i(P_i - V_i) - h_i - u_i\} + g_i$$

where T stands for one minus the tax rate. In other words, the profit contribution in year i is found by first taking the difference in year i between price (P_i) and unit cost (V_i) times unit sales (Q_i). This gives the unadjusted before-tax profit. Then opportunity costs (h_i) and nonrecurring start-up costs are subtracted (u_i). The after-tax profit is found by applying the profit retention rate. Depreciation (g_i) is then added back to the cash flow to cancel the effect of its being subtracted implicitly as part of V_i.

(E)
↓

The investment cash-flow stream is discounted back to the present by the firm's opportunity cost of capital to yield the present value of the firm's investment flow (I).

(F)
↓

Successive approximation is used to find the rate-of-return (r) that will discount the profit flow to an amount equal to the discounted investment (I).

(G)
↓

Have enough r's been generated yet?

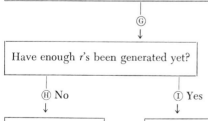

(H) No
↓

Return to Step C

(I) Yes
↓

Order the r's in a frequency distribution and show graphically. This is the approximate probability distribution of rates-of-return for marketing strategy s, marketing environment e, facilities strategy f, and various expected values and quantile estimates.

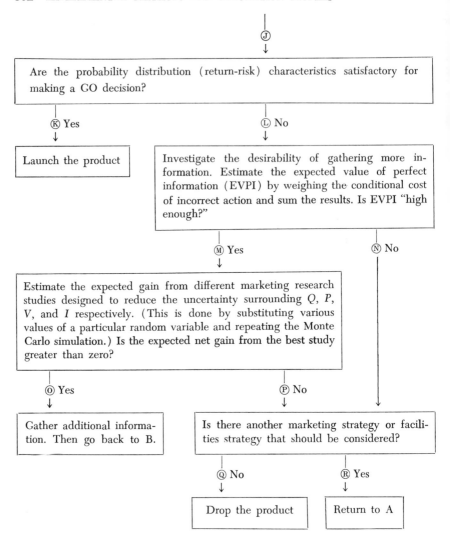

1. It requires executives to spell out a marketing strategy, a facilities strategy, and assumptions about the marketing environment.

2. It requires them to estimate, on the basis of the given strategies, sales, costs, and investments for each year of the planning horizon.

3. It requires executives to reflect their uncertainty regarding their estimates of sales, prices, costs, and investment. These uncertainties lead to a probability distribution for each variable. By drawing simulated observations representing prices, sales, costs, and investment, it is possible to derive the earnings and the investment cash flows.

4. The cash flows are discounted to find the rate of return (r) for the particular simulation. The simulation is repeated many times to derive a probability distribution of r's.

5. The model allows the calculation of the value of additional information.

Thus, the model has many features that are desirable in a refined analysis of the new-product decision. Forms that executives may fill out and a computer program to perform the calculations have been developed. Further refinements of the model and field tests on major product decisions are in progress.

At the same time, some weaknesses are apparent. First, Pessemier's procedure for determining the value of additional information is not altogether satisfactory (see Box M); it involves a great deal of computation. A different approach to this problem is worked out in the DEMON model that will be described shortly. Second, except through the recognition of opportunity costs, the model does not contain an explicit procedure for considering interactions between the new product and the existing products in the line. This type of difficulty is considered in the SPRINTER model that will be examined later. Third, the treatment of price, unit costs, and investment as independent random variables within narrow strategy-marketing environment limits is theoretically weak. It would seem that if a high annual price is drawn by Monte Carlo methods, this should lead to a lower sales level than expected that year, a higher unit cost than expected (assuming unit costs decline with output), and possibly a lower annual investment than expected. In other words, these variables in principle are functionally related. In more recent versions of the model, these relations are handled directly but at the cost of obtaining additional estimates relating to the price elasticity of demand.

Finally, the model unfortunately does not provide an algorithm for determining the best marketing and facilities strategy. Like many simulation approaches, the model basically offers a way of generating the dynamic results of a particular strategy. Comparison of the Monte Carlo results of employing various strategies often suggest potentially fruitful new strategies that can be tested but functional relationships are not sufficiently simple to permit the direct computation of an optimal strategy.

GO-ON-NO Information Network Model (DEMON)

As a new product moves through development and testing, information is continuously needed to determine the desirability of introducing the product and the best manner to introduce it. The information is expensive to buy and there are many options. DEMON (*DE*cision *M*apping *V*ia

Optimum GO-NO Networks) is the name of a new model for making optimal sequential information purchase decisions in connection with trying to reach the best terminal decision on introducing or dropping the product. DEMON was developed by the advertising agency, Batten, Barton, Durstine, and Osborn, and appears to be used by a growing number of client companies [6, 7, and 23].

The model is oriented toward the idea that the company testing a new product will have to evaluate where it stands after each test. Each evaluation can result in one of three decisions:

GO: The company should begin national marketing because the accumulated evidence indicates that the stated company objectives and requirements will all be met.

NO: The company should discontinue testing and should not market the product.

ON: The company should continue testing because the accumulated evidence is not sufficient to warrant a GO or NO decision.

An ON decision means that the company undertakes to make a particular market study or sequence of studies (the "best" one(s)) and then will make another evaluation of whether to choose GO, ON, or NO. It is likely that the company, in retrospect, will have made a sequence of ON decisions before reaching a GO or NO decision. A picture of the information network is illustrated in Fig. 11.5a.

In principle, the company would want to move through the information network in the optimum way. Presumably, the study team has a fixed total budget B for making various marketing research studies as they are needed (product-use tests, TV commercial tests, economic analyses, test markets, and so on). Each alternative study has a certain cost C and is expected to yield a certain improved estimate of demand, Q. The problem is seen as that of plotting an optimal path through the total information network subject to the budget and other constraints.

How is this path discovered? The DEMON model requires management to specify several constraints that help direct it through the network. Among the guiding constraints are the following:

m: payback period.
n: horizon planning period.
Z_G: minimum acceptable profits for a GO decision.
Z_O: minimum acceptable profits for an ON decision.
B: total marketing research budget.
Pr_G: minimum degree of confidence (probability) needed for a GO decision, a chance constraint on Z_G.

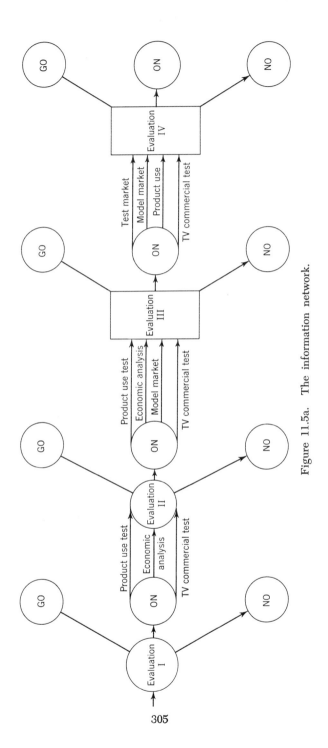

Figure 11.5a. The information network.

305

Pr_0: minimum degree of confidence (probability) needed for an ON decision, a chance constraint on Z_0.

These constraints enable the determination of GO-ON-NO boundaries on the decision grid illustrated in Fig. 11.5b. Consider the GO decision. Suppose one constraint is that the expected profit by the end of the payback period should exceed the minimum level for a GO decision; that is,

$$Z_m > Z_G \quad \text{(condition 1 for GO)} \tag{11.13}$$

Suppose a second condition is that the probability of achieving this profit within the payback period should exceed the minimum degree of required confidence for a GO decision; that is,

$$P_r \{Z_m > Z_G\} > P_{r_G} \quad \text{(condition 2 for GO)} \tag{11.14}$$

These constraints lead to the tracing of a specific boundary for the GO constraint on the decision grid. Similar constraints lead to the tracing of a specific boundary for the ON decision.

The model permits an evaluation to be made of every possible path through alternative marketing studies to reach a GO decision. Each possible sequence of marketing studies involves an estimated cost and an estimated result in terms of the demand estimate. These two can be netted to yield an expected profit and risk for that sequence. The sequence with the best hypothetical profit and risk is found. It may be the sequence ON (product-use test) → ON (test market) → GO. This may appear to be better than an immediate GO decision. The company decides on ON and makes the product-use test. Now it does not make

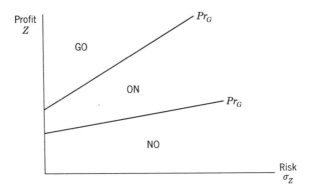

Figure 11.5b. The decision grid.

another ON decision (test market) automatically but uses the result of the product-use test to reevaluate the best decision. It may be an immediate GO, NO, or some sequence of ON's.

Suffice it to say that the model for demand determination is crucial in DEMON. A pictorial view of the model is given in Fig. 11.5c. Demand is shown to be affected by advertising, sales promotion, and distribution. The links between advertising and the number of triers are particularly spelled out. Market studies are used to estimate any of the magnitudes or relationships shown, for instance:

1. The relationship between the number of dollars spent on advertising and the number of gross impressions created.

2. The number of gross impressions created and the reach and frequency.

3. The reach and frequency and the percentage of advertising awareness achieved.

4. The percentage of advertising awareness achieved and the number of triers.

5. The number of triers and the number who became users.

6. The typical usage rate of a user.

The various marketing studies are evaluated in terms of how well they promise to increase the accuracy of the respective data inputs into the final demand estimate. An optimum path through the information network is determined on the basis of a chance-constrained programming format.

The DEMON model shows some differences from other models that should be noted.

1. It calls for developing a marketing program through time and estimating the likely year-to-year progress of sales and costs. It does not directly employ discounting to find a rate of return but cash-flow data information from the model can be used for this purpose. A payback period is used as a policy constraint.

2. The competitive effects of delaying the GO decision by a sequence of ON decisions can be studied by an extended application of the model. These competitive costs vary with the particular sequencing through the information network. Each sequencing through the network involves a different reduction in competitive lead time.

3. It does not explicitly consider the effect of the new product on the existing products' profits, in common with the previous models. However, policy constraints can be introduced to limit the adverse effects on the profits from related products.

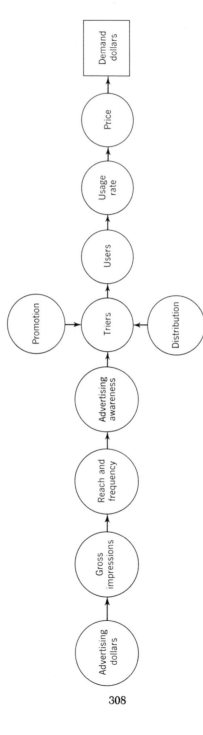

Figure 11.5c. The demand model. (*Source:* Adapted from various DEMON papers [6, 7, 23].)

308

Product Interaction Model (SPRINTER)

The one factor to which all the previous models have neglected to give full formal treatment is the product-interaction problem. When a new product is related on the demand and cost side to some current company products, the deciding factor should not be the direct new product's profits but the differential profits on the whole product line with and without the new product. The estimated profits for the new product must be adjusted downward if it reduces the profits on the company's current products, and upwards if it enhances the profits on the company's current products.

SPRINTER (Specification of *PR*ofits with *IN*teractions under *T*rial and *E*rror *R*esponse) was developed by Glen Urban and, like DEMON, is oriented toward yielding a GO, ON, or NO decision [33]. However, SPRINTER gives explicit consideration to the dynamic marketing programs planned over the new product's economic life for both the new product and any existing products in the line having profit interactions with the new product. In addition, variations in competitive response during the product life cycle are considered explicitly. Estimates of demand and costs are derived functionally from marketing plans, competitive actions, and product trend, cyclical, and seasonal characteristics.

The two pivotal measures in the model are discounted differential profit and differential uncertainty. *Discounted differential profit* is the present value of the annual differences in the profits on the whole line with and without the new product. *Differential uncertainty* is the difference in total uncertainty (as measured by the variance of profit) with and without the new product. These two measures form the axes of the decision grid used to decide between GO, ON, and NO.

The mathematical structure of the model is too difficult to solve analytically for the best marketing plan. Consequently, Urban developed a simulation approach to approximate the best solution. This approach involves trying out gross variations in the marketing program to approach the neighborhood of the maximum, and then approaching optimal values more closely through finer variations. This technique is efficient if the profit function is well behaved. The overall model is described in flow-diagram terms in Fig. 11.6.

Urban tried out his model on data supplied to him by a large chemical company that had just introduced nationally a new nylon compound that had significant demand and cost interactions with two current products in its line. His purpose was to determine whether the model would lead to the same decision made by the executives on the basis of the data

Figure 11.6.   Flow Diagram of SPRINTER Model. *Source*: Adapted and
modified for this paper from Glen Urban [33].

Flow Diagram

Informed executives supply estimates and data on:

1. A reference marketing program matrix (P_i, A_i, D_i) over the planning period for the new product and for any interacting products.
2. Estimate of probable time of competitive entry and marketing program of competitors. (Also high and low estimates.)
3. Estimates of market share of competitors in new-product market over planning period and effect of industry marketing effort on demand. (Also high and low estimates.)
4. Planned plant capacity for each year in the planning period.
5. Estimate of the reference life cycle demand for the new and interacting products on the basis of the marketing programs. (Also high and low estimates.)
6. Executive estimates of the demand response of the new and old products to systematic variations in (P_i, A_i, D_i), including cross-product response functions. Also needed is an estimate of the shift in the reference life cycle in response variations to the marketing program. (Also high and low estimates.)
7. New-product development costs and production for new and existing products.
8. Management constraints on advertising budget, plant output capacity, technical service, and price.
9. Management requirements regarding the minimum profit necessary for a GO decision (Z_G), the minimum profit for an ON decision (Z_0), the minimum probability necessary for a GO decision (Pr_G), and the minimum probability necessary for an ON decision (Pr_0).
10. A reference marketing program matrix for the old line (on the assumption that the new product is not introduced).

Calculate the total discounted profits for the new line and the old line under the new reference marketing program and the old reference marketing program. (All constraints must be satisfied.) Subtract old line discounted profit from new line discounted profit to find total discounted differential profit.

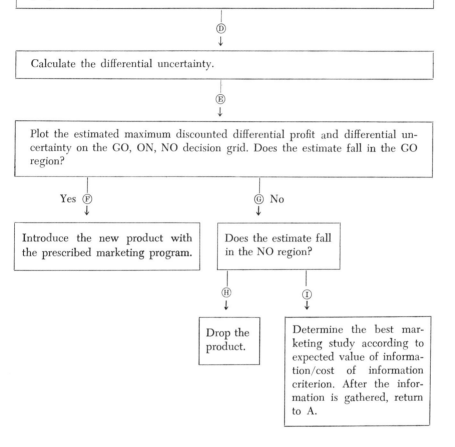

Specify alternative values for price, advertising, and distribution and for each combination find total discounted differential profit. Select the marketing program that yields the maximum total discounted differential profit.

Ⓓ

Calculate the differential uncertainty.

Ⓔ

Plot the estimated maximum discounted differential profit and differential uncertainty on the GO, ON, NO decision grid. Does the estimate fall in the GO region?

Yes Ⓕ   Ⓖ No

Introduce the new product with the prescribed marketing program.

Does the estimate fall in the NO region?

Ⓗ   Ⓘ

Drop the product.

Determine the best marketing study according to expected value of information/cost of information criterion. After the information is gathered, return to A.

known to them at the time. Urban's model quite surprisingly led to a NO decision, in view of the company's planned marketing program.[9] Urban's model then proceeded to search for other configurations of the marketing program that might lead to an ON decision and perhaps a GO decision.

[9] Urban was later told by a company executive that his NO decision, instead of casting doubt on his model, increased their confidence in it. The reason was that they had given him their best estimates of all the data and response functions except one: they gave him a significantly lower estimate of market size than was expected. The fact that his model produced a NO decision was in its favor.

After considerable search, a marketing strategy and a facilities strategy were found that just managed to lead to a GO decision.

To summarize, the central features of the SPRINTER model are as follows:

1. Profits and uncertainty are estimated for the new-product line versus the old-product line.

2. A demand equation is formulated that incorporates life cycle, seasonal, industry marketing, competitive and product interaction effects.

3. The model uses the GO, ON, NO framework, based on rate-of-return measures.

Simulation is used to solve for an approximately good marketing program because of the impossibility of determining the optimal solution analytically. However, results from testing proposed strategies may lead to formulating new improved alternatives that can be tested.

Summary Comparison of Models

As noted, models differ in terms of their structure, complexity, and the basic mathematical format used to process or solve them. Of the models, three are algebraic, one involves chance-constrained programming to arrive at an optimum, and three use simulation in some sense. Note, however, that simulation may mean different things in the respective models.

SIMULATION AS A COMPUTATIONAL TECHNIQUE FOR MEASURING PARA-METRIC SENSITIVITY. The Bayesian decision model often involves so many branches that the job of computing their respective expected values is typically accomplished on a computer. Very often the analyst will want to see how sensitive the solution is to a change in some parameter(s) such as the company cost of capital or the assumed rate of sales growth. Frequently, the model is too complicated to solve analytically for extended parametric sensitivity. The analyst resorts to simulation to determine the effect of hypothetical alterations in assumptions.

SIMULATION AS A WAY OF GENERATING STOCHASTIC OUTCOMES. The Monte Carlo simulation model is, to a large extent, a stochastic version of the Bayesian decision model. Instead of simply using the prescribed probabilities directly in the calculations, the Monte Carlo model uses the probabilities to generate events with the same chance structures, and it is these events that enter the calculation. Thus, the model creates a hypothetical simulation of a possible event sequence following the introduction of a new product. Since any one event sequence may not be typical, many simulations are carried out to help discern average and distributional characteristics. The only justification for this time-consuming exercise is that the model is too complicated to solve in a more efficient fashion. When various input events are subject to different probability distributions (some not even representable by standard equations), there is clearly no other way to estimate the final probability distribution than through simulation.[10]

SIMULATION AS A HEURISTIC SEARCH TECHNIQUE FOR AN APPROXIMATELY OPTIMUM SOLUTION. The SPRINTER model involves so many non-linearities that it is virtually impossible to solve it analytically for the best marketing program matrix. This led its author to create a routine for the model to evaluate the effects of systematic, discrete changes in the marketing program. SPRINTER investigates the payoff characteristics of different marketing programs and examines the neighborhood of the best solution through a finer probing interval.

AREAS OF FURTHER RESEARCH

This review of existing models makes it clear that profit models for the new-product decision area are still evolving and that there is considerable room for further development and synthesis. No one model excels in all characteristics. It may be that different partial models will thrive, the choice always resting on the strengths needed for the particular problem. If the issue is one of efficiently managing the large costs of market studies, then DEMON seems to be tailor-made, although we must accept other limitations in the process. If the issue is that of carefully evaluating product interactions between the new product and the old ones, then SPRINTER is more appropriate.

On the other hand, a different hope is that the good characteristics of the various partial models will eventually be synthesized into a single comprehensive model that is strong in all respects. We have already seen how newer models incorporated useful characteristics of previous models, how (for example) the Monte Carlo simulation model evolved from the simple Bayesian model, and how SPRINTER employs the GO-ON-NO framework of DEMON. One of the benefits of formal model building is just this tendency of models to improve with time.

---

[10] Pessemier [28] fits a lognormal probability distribution to all stochastic variables. This raises the question whether it is possible to solve for the final distribution of r analytically without the apparatus of Monte Carlo simulation.

Whether separate models continue to flourish in this field or converge into one comprehensive model, it will be necessary to continue to refine the method of handling particular characteristics of the total model. This section will discuss two particular characteristics on which the author is currently working: (1) the demand function and (2) the treatment of competitors' strategy.

Models of Demand

The demand function is perhaps the key component in any profit model for the new-product decision. The surveyed models treat the determination of demand in a number of different ways. There are at least five conceptually different ways to handle demand. They are discussed below.

EXOGENOUS DETERMINATION. The simplest way to handle demand is to estimate some figures directly. The executives may be asked to spell out a certain marketing program and marketing environment and then specify expected product sales over the life cycle. For another marketing strategy and environment, a different sales curve will be estimated. The estimates of sales are *not* mathematically derived from the marketing assumptions through a formal demand function. This is the essential demand-estimating technique in the Bayesian decision model and the Monte Carlo model. The current version of the Monte Carlo model does include direct estimates of this relationship between price and volume.

TRADITIONAL DEMAND FUNCTION. The traditional demand function developed by economists seeks the relationship between sales and such variables as per capital income (Y), population (N), and price (P); that is,

$$Q = f(Y, N, P, \ldots)$$

In its limited way, it combines explicitly the effect of some environmental variables (Y,N) and a marketing variable (P). Other marketing variables are typically left out and assumed to underlie some of the unexplained variance. For this function to be used, forecasts must be made of income and population, as well as of intended prices, in order to forecast future sales [25].

PURE MARKETING DEMAND FUNCTION. To provide a more formal statement of the estimated effects of marketing factors on demand, I experimented with a function consisting only of marketing factors and used it to evaluate a new-product decision [20]. The function had the following form:

$$Q = kP^p A^a D^d \qquad \text{(marketing mix demand equation)} \quad (11.15)$$

where

$Q =$ quantity demanded per time period

$k =$ a scale factor

$P,A,D =$ price, advertising, and distribution expenditures

$p,a,d =$ elasticities of price, advertising, and distribution

This equation type, known as a multiple exponential equation,[11] has at least three desirable properties. First, it provides that the effect of a specific marketing variable depends not only upon its own level but also on the levels of the other marketing variables. This arises out of the multiplicative relationship among the variables. Second, the exponential equation is flexible enough to show increasing, constant, or diminishing marginal returns to increases in the advertising and distribution budgets, depending upon the exponent (exp). (Increasing marginal returns, exp > 1; constant marginal returns, exp $= 1$; diminishing marginal returns, exp < 1.) Finally, the measured exponents represent the respective elasticities of the marketing variables, provided that strong multicollinearity does not exist among the independent variables.

At the same time, this equation for demand determination errs as much in one direction as the traditional demand equation erred in the other. It leaves environmental factors out entirely. This treatment implies that relevant environmental factors stay at some specific and constant level during the planning horizon, a hardly tenable assumption.

Other weaknesses exist. In its present form, this demand equation says that if advertising or distribution expenditures are set at zero, demand will be zero. The equation could easily be modified, however, to avoid this weakness.

Another problem is that the equation imputes constant elasticities to all the marketing factors. This is a highly restrictive assumption. It can only be overcome by more advanced equation forms.

LIFE CYCLE PLUS MARKETING DEMAND FUNCTION. The deficiencies of the previous demand formulations led the author to develop a more comprehensive expression for demand determination in a recent study

---

[11] This equation type was first applied in economics by Charles W. Cobb and Paul H. Douglas in 1928 to represent the production function, where Q was national output and the three independent variables were land, labor, and capital. The exponents represented the respective elasticities of these three factors. The fitted equation provided a measure of the respective contribution to national output of a one percent increase in land, labor, or capital [8].

of competitive marketing strategy [19]. The demand formulation gave expression to product life cycle factors, seasonal factors, marketing mix factors, and competitive marketing factors; that is,

$$Q = f(\text{product life cycle, seasonal variation,}$$
$$\text{industry marketing effects, competitive effects})$$

Each factor has a different reason for being included and is represented by a different but appropriate mathematical function; all the functions are related in a multiplicative fashion. An example of this function is shown in Fig. 11.7. The product life cycle factor represents the normal type of sales growth exhibited by new products as increasing knowledge and usage take place. In this case, it is fitted by a Gompertz equation, one of several equation forms capable of yielding an S-curve growth pattern and one which has yielded an especially good fit to many product case histories [10 and 14].

Seasonal variation is represented by a sine curve. This is a useful curve for expositional purposes, but it is inadequate for describing irregular seasonal patterns. For this purpose, it would be better to use the direct executive estimates of the seasonal pattern. A more fundamental point, however, is that the seasonal factor generally need not be considered in the analysis of the profitability of a new product. The basic need is for annual cash-flow estimates over the planning period. The seasonal factor was inserted in the particular application to make possible the testing of different advertising strategies regarding the seasonal timing of advertising.

The industry marketing factor describes the fact that total demand may grow faster or slower than indicated by the product life cycle factor if the industry spends more or less on marketing than the reference amount. In the particular form used, as long as the industry charges an average of $20 for the product, and spends an average per month of $2500 on advertising and distribution respectively, sales will grow at the rate prescribed by the product life cycle. But if price is drawn down, or marketing expenditures per period increase, sales will grow faster. This is accomplished by stating the current period's marketing mix and level as a ratio to the "normal" level: the higher the ratio, the greater the sales above the product life cycle level. However, an exponential term, $2(1.05)^{-i}$, produces two interesting and desirable effects. The first effect is that, as the new market matures, total industry marketing expenditures have a diminishing influence on total product demand. By period 60, for example, the industry marketing factor virtually no longer influences total demand because the exponent approaches zero. The second effect is that the term reduces the cross-elasticity of brand promotion from

$$Q_{ij} = [4000(0.20)^{0.9^i}]\,\{1 + 0.1[\sin(30i + 180)]\}\left[\frac{\displaystyle\sum_{j=1}^{w} P_{ij}^{-2} A_{ij}^{\frac{1}{8}} D_{ij}^{\frac{1}{4}}}{w\,(20^{-2}\,2500^{\frac{1}{8}}\,2500^{\frac{1}{4}})}\right]\,2(1.05)^{-i}\left[\frac{P_{ij}^{-2} A_{ij}^{\frac{1}{8}} D_{ij}^{\frac{1}{4}}}{\displaystyle\sum_{j=1}^{w} P_{ij}^{-2} A_{ij}^{\frac{1}{8}} D_{ij}^{\frac{1}{4}}}\right]$$

$$\binom{\text{Sales at time}}{i \text{ of company } j} = \binom{\text{Product life cycle:}}{\text{Gompertz curve}}\binom{\text{Seasonal variation:}}{\text{sine curve}}\binom{\text{Total industry marketing effect:}}{\text{normalizing ratio}}\binom{\text{Competitive marketing share effect:}}{\text{proportionate ratio}}$$

Figure 11.7. Example of a life cycle plus marketing demand function. (*Source*, Kotler [19].)

positive to negative as the market matures. In a new market, increases in one company's promotional expenditures tend to increase the sales of other firms as well, although not proportionately. Eventually, further increases in company promotion begin to affect other companies' sales negatively.

The last factor in the equation shows how total demand is divided among the competing firms. The market share of a particular company is assumed to be in the same ratio as its marketing effort is to the total industry marketing effort. This is quite plausible in the long run. It says that companies are about equally capable of getting the same marketing effect for their dollars. However, it does leave out short-run effects, such as the fact that the first firm in a market often enjoys a disproportionate share of the market long afterwards because its reputation is capitalized.

To use this demand formulation for the purpose of estimating sales and profits over time for a new product, it is necessary to ask the executives to make estimates of life cycle demand under a reference marketing program, and also to estimate the magnitudes of demand responses (the elasticities) to systematic variations in the marketing factors. They must also estimate the likely marketing programs of individual competitors. (It is not necessary to assume that all the competitors enter the industry at the same time. The competitive factor can be reformulated in a way to take care of delayed entry and lagged effects.)

PRODUCT INTERACTION DEMAND EQUATION. Urban extended the previous formulation of demand in two significant directions. The first was his addition to demand function [15] of terms for *product interaction*. In one version, Urban employed cross-elasticity terms to represent the product interactions. This is shown below:

$$Q_{ij1} = f(\ldots, P_{ijq}{}^{cp_{1q}}, A_{ijq}{}^{ca_{1q}}, D_{ijq}{}^{cd_{1q}}, \ldots) \qquad (11.16)$$

where

Q_{ij1} = quantity sold in period i by company j of product 1

P_{ijq} = price charged in period i by company j for product q

cp_{1q} = cross price elasticity on product 1 of price charged for product q

A_{ijq} = advertising budget in period i of company j for product q

ca_{1q} = cross-advertising elasticity on product 1 of advertising budget for product q

D_{ijq} = distribution budget in period i of company j for product q

cd_{1q} = cross-distribution elasticity on product 1 of distribution budget for product q

The second significant change was to increase the flexibility of the demand function by dropping the constant elasticity assumption. Under the constant elasticity assumption, the response of demand to variations in a marketing factor is represented by a single constant used as an exponent to the particular factor. While the use of constant elasticities makes for mathematical tractability, it is highly restrictive. Urban replaced each factor and its constant exponent by an actual response function. The response function is defined in terms of the reference marketing program. For example, suppose the reference price in a particular year is $250, and the executives are asked to estimate the "scale effect" of changes in price on the quantity sold in this period. At a price of $200, they might estimate that twice as much would be sold: a response of 2. Their "scale" responses to a few other hypothetical prices will form a curve like that shown in Fig. 11.8, and an equation can be fitted to this curve. The equation is used to describe price response in the demand function. Since all marketing responses are determined in a similar way, the level of demand is the product of these response functions and the product life cycle estimate. The reference marketing program will yield a demand estimate equal to the product life cycle estimate, because in this special case all the response levels will be 1.

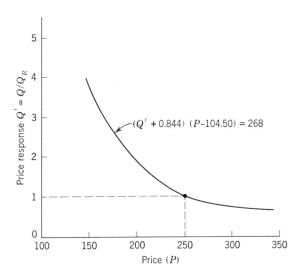

Figure 11.8.   An estimated price-response curve. Q = estimated demand at price P; Q_R = estimated demand at reference P; $Q' = Q/Q_R$.
(*Source:* Urban [33], p.136.)

Microanalytic Demand Model

The previous demand models produced a forecast of total demand as a function of gross variables such as advertising expenditures and national income. They can be classified as *macroanalytic demand models* in that they deal with relationships among aggregates. They link up variables without suggesting the specified mechanisms at work. A *microanalytic demand model*, on the other hand, is a model that specifies the intervening behavioral variables and sequences occurring between the reception of stimuli and its crystallization in action. Here interest centers in explicating exactly what transpires when customers are exposed to particular marketing and environmental stimuli.

DEMON is the only new-product profit model reviewed here that approaches the use of a formal microanalytic demand model (see Fig. 11.5c). Instead of using a gross association between dollar advertising expenditures and sales, DEMON uses a causative chain of events between advertising dollars, gross impressions, reach and frequency, and level of awareness. Instead of talking about total sales, DEMON spells this out as the number of triers, users, and the usage rate. These intervening variables are introduced because the direct relationships among them are often more measurable through marketing studies than the ultimate relationship between advertising expenditures and sales. Since DEMON is set up to help the firm choose an efficient set of marketing studies, the intervening demand variables are spelled out carefully.

Microanalytic models of demand take other forms as well. There is a long history of verbal models that would qualify loosely as primitive microanalytic demand models. One of these is known as AIDA, and holds that customers must pass through the following series of states in reacting to a product or promotion [15]:

Attention → Interest → Desire → Action

Lavidge and Steiner suggested the passage of the buyer through the following sequence [22]:

Awareness → Knowledge → Liking → Preference → Conviction → Purchase

A model that is formulated specifically for the new-product area distinguishes five stages in the consumer adoption process for any new innovation. These stages are [31]:

Awareness → Interest → Evaluation → Trial → Adoption

Various factors are known to operate at the various stages with different degrees of effectiveness, among them carefully chosen marketing stimuli by change agents. Particular marketing programs will affect the rate at which any individual may move through this process. For example, an electric-dishwasher manufacturer may provide a trial-use-with-option-to-buy plan to increase the number of people willing to move from the evaluation stage to the trial stage.

Another finding coming out of consumer adoption studies is that there are strong individual differences in the rate at which persons move through the stages in the adoption process. Individual differences in "innovativeness" has led to persons being classified as innovators (the first $2\frac{1}{2}\%$ of the individuals who adopt a new idea), early adopters (the next $13\frac{1}{2}\%$), early majority (next 34%), late majority (next 34%), and the laggards (last 16%). It is hoped that by studying the characteristics of these different adopters, information and theory will eventually enable early prediction of the rate of growth of demand for a new product from the first signs of adoption. Monitoring the test-market performance of a new product may provide just this sort of guidance.

The dynamics of the consumer adoption process are just beginning to be studied through the device of computer simulation [32]. This allows study of how fast demand may grow as a result of complex social relationships in a community, geographical adjacency, particular distributions of characteristics, and so on. Computer simulation may represent a new and hypothesis-rich way to investigate demand formation.

Akin to this is the recent development of simulated consumer populations to represent the market for a product. The simulated consumers represent a well-researched cross-section of the American population stratified by sex, age, type of community, employment status, education, and whatever other characteristics are deemed relevant. The population could be clustered at different sampling points in the United States. The consumers would differ in their present product choices and habits, propensities to try new products, psychological characteristics, media habits, susceptibility to price, advertising and distribution variations, and so forth. The technology of developing these microanalytic behavioral simulations is developing rapidly [18 and 2].

A main use of microanalytic simulation models is to predict demand more carefully under different possible marketing programs. Instead of executives developing direct gross estimates of demand for different marketing programs, or instead of demand being estimated from a macroanalytic mathematical function, a microanalytic simulation model permits more testable relationships between marketing variables and demand to be specified, and a more concrete estimate to be made of the number of people who buy, the rate at which they buy, and so forth.

Because microanalytic behavioral simulations involve a large investment, they are only likely to be built if they are multipurpose both in terms of the number of new products that can be examined on them, and in the continuity of their usefulness over the product life cycle. It is hoped that increasing research will be done on the theory and technology of micro-analytic behavioral simulations as one of the most powerful and promising ways to study demand determination.

Models of Competitive Strategy

Any estimate of profits from the introduction of a new product must incorporate assumptions about competitors' behavior. Some questions that must be answered are the following:

1. Will other competitors enter this market?
2. When will they enter?
3. What will their product and their marketing program be like?
4. How will the market be split?

Each of these questions has specific implications for estimating the profits on the company's new product.

EXISTENCE OF COMPETITION. There are a few sheltered markets where competition is not a real or substantial problem. When A.T.T. made its profit calculations regarding the introduction of the touch-tone telephone, it did not have to worry about whether a competitor would introduce a superior telephone design in a few months. However, the vast majority of firms have to worry about this issue. Sometimes they may not even know where the competition may come from, but feel sure it will come. Typically, however, they know who their competitors will be. Whether the competitors will introduce a version of the new product is the question. Sometimes it is obvious that they will, because they would not be serving their self-interest otherwise. In these cases, the company can put a probability of one that the competitors will introduce a version of the product. If the company is not sure, it can put a smaller probability on this occurrence and enter it as a possible state of the marketing environment.

TIMING. Unless competitors have been developing the new product concurrently (a question that marketing intelligence may answer), they will not be able to introduce their versions until later. The competitors must make an investment in product development and testing, manufacturing facilities, channel arrangements, and so forth, and all this takes time. However, there have been many episodes of competitors who skipped some normal phase in the product development process in order to get into the market at the same time.[12] Generally speaking, the company can make some reasonable estimate, based on its own experience and marketing intelligence, of the approximate time when the first competitor and later competitors will enter the market.

COMPETITORS' MARKETING PROGRAM. The particular impact of the competitors' entry on the company's sales and profits will also depend upon how the competitors come in. Do they charge a lower price, go after a different market target, use different distribution channels, spend more on advertising? These are some of the questions that must be answered and yet this is the hardest area in which to find information. The company can try to place itself in the competitors' position to develop a view of a plausible strategy. The conjectured strategy, however developed, may be represented in one of two ways for the purpose of formal analysis. The conjectured strategy may be represented in a marketing-program matrix similar to the one discussed in the early part of the paper. The likely annual values of the competitors' price, advertising, and distribution over the planning horizon may be described in matrix form. Alternatively, the conjectured strategy may be expressed in the form of marketing-decision rules that the competitor(s) is(are) expected to use. For example, it may be assumed that a particular competitor will set his marketing mix in the following way:

$P_{i,y} = 0.95\,P_{i-1,j}$ (Competitor y sets his price at time i at 95 percent of company j's last price.)

$A_{i,y} = 1.02\,A_{i-1,j}$ (Competitor y sets his advertising expenditures at time i at 102 percent of company j's expenditures in the previous period.)

$D_{i,y} = 1.03\,D_{i-1,y}$ (Competitor y increases his distribution expenditures 3 percent each period.)

This is one of many possible strategies [19]. In view of the competitors' conjectured strategies and those of the company, they can be tested on

12 For example, Alberto-Culver was so eager to beat a new Procter & Gamble shampoo to market that it developed a name and filmed a TV commercial before it even developed its own product (*Time*, March 29, 1963, p. 8). S. C. Johnson & Son, Inc. cut short its test marketing of an aerosol room deodorant when it learned that Colgate was entering its product on the market that month [Neil H. Borden and Martin V. Marshall, "S. C. Johnson & Son, Inc. (A)," *Advertising Management: Text and Cases* (Homewood, Ill.: Richard D. Irwin, 1959), pp. 533-547.]

the computer to see what they logically imply about the behavior of prices, advertising, and distribution, and the implications of all this for demand.

MARKET SHARE. The conception of the marketing program of the company and of the competitors becomes the basis of estimating how the market will be shared. The estimate can be made formally through the appropriate factor in the demand equation. For example, the demand equation in SPRINTER provides an estimate of demand based both on the timing of the competitors' entry and on their marketing programs relative to those of the company.

There is need for further research on the methodology of measuring competitive behavior and estimating its effect on demand. The classic models of competitive behavior (for instance, oligopoly, monopolistic competition, and duopoly) provide some insights into interfirm competitive behavior but often are not dynamic or rich enough for real application.

SUMMARY

One of the major factors in successful innovation is the correct estimation of returns and risks on new-product proposals and new products under development. The estimation depends upon having good information and also upon processing the information in the right way. This chapter deals mainly with the second question.

The history of new-product profit evaluation models is that of evolution from simple to complex models.[13] Seven different profit models are compared in this paper: breakeven model, cash-flow model, simple marketing mix model, Bayesian decision model, Monte Carlo simulation model, GO-ON-NO information network model, and product-interaction model. The models vary in complexity, substantive emphasis, and mathematical character. Some of them are built with mathematical optimization in mind, while other rely on simulation for sensitivity testing, creating a dynamic picture of stochastic outcomes, or searching for improved marketing programs where mathematical analysis fails. Computer simulation is undoubtedly a fruitful format for future model building in this area.

Two particular needs are the development of better demand models

---

[13] For other models and approaches not reviewed here, see references 9, 24, 26, and 30.

and better competitive models. There is a movement away from the traditional demand function toward a demand function that reflects product life cycle characteristics, total industry marketing effects, market-share effects, and product-interaction effects. There is an attempt to move beyond the use of a single equation model into the development of a full-scale microanalytic simulation model for the purposes of testing competitive marketing strategies and estimating demand.

There are additional problem areas not specifically considered in this chapter. One of these is the problem of how to get good subjective estimates from executives and how to combine them optimally when they differ substantially. Improved procedures would be helpful in this area. Another problem is how the company might evaluate several products under development at the same time. These products will compete for the company's resources and may have demand and cost interactions. Another problem is the evaluation of the best marketing studies to undertake. Although considerable progress has been made in several of these areas, more work is needed.

An important question concerns the cost versus the value of model building in the new-product decision area. The more advanced models require extensive model formulation, data, and computer running time. It may be argued that they do not produce enough net gain over simple breakeven analysis. This depends upon how many new products a company introduces each year and the degree to which its markets are sheltered or competitive. Where uncertainty is great enough to make the difference between GO and NO, even small increments of accuracy may be desirable. The cost of building and using an advanced model is typically very small in relation to the possible costs of a wrong decision. An advanced model stimulates more careful consideration of marketing plans, competitive interactions, product interactions, and the quality of information. For many reasons, executives should not be satisfied to entrust the future of a new product to evaluation by an undesirably simple model.

BREAKEVEN MODELS

Breakeven volume version

$$Q_B = \frac{F}{P - V}$$

Payback period version

$$m = \frac{F}{\displaystyle\sum_{i=1}^{m}(P - V)\,Q_i} = 1$$

Q_B = breakeven volume
F = total fixed costs
V = unit variable costs

m = payback period

CASH-FLOW MODELS

Present value version

$$W = \sum_{i=1}^{n} \frac{R_i - C_i}{(1 + c)^i}$$

W = present worth
R_i = total revenue in year i
C_i = total cost in year i
c = cost of capital

Rate-of-return version

$$I = \sum_{i=1}^{n} \frac{R_i - C_i}{(1 + r)^i}$$

Disman model

$$P_r\,W \geqslant I \rightarrow \mathrm{GO}$$

I = total investment
r = internal rate of return
P_r = probability of success

SIMPLE MARKETING MIX MODELS

Breakeven version

$$Z = (P - V)\,(Q - Q_B)$$

$$Q_B = \frac{F + A + D}{P - V}$$

$$Q = F\,(P, A, D)$$

Z = total profits
Q = expected sales
P = price
A = total advertising expenditures
D = total distribution
expenditures

326

Cash-flow version

$$I = \sum_{i=1}^{h} \frac{P_i [F (P_i, A_i, D_i)] - \overline{C}_i - A_i - D_i}{(1+r)^i}$$

$$M = \begin{pmatrix} P_1 P_2 \ldots P_i \ldots P_n \\ A_1 A_2 \ldots A_i \ldots A_n \\ D_1 D_2 \ldots D_i \ldots D_n \end{pmatrix}$$

$$Q = (Q_1 Q_2 \ldots Q_i \ldots Q_n)$$

$\overline{C}_i$ = total nonmarketing costs
M = marketing program matrix
Q = sales time series vector

MODELS OF DEMAND

Exogeneous determination $Q = (Q_1, Q_2, \ldots Q_i \ldots Q_n)$

Traditional demand function $Q = F (Y, N, P \ldots)$

Pure marketing demand function $Q = k P^B A^a D^d$

Life cycle plus marketing demand function $Q = F$ (product life cycle, seasonal variation, industry marketing effects, competitive effects)

Microanalytic behavioral demand model

327

APPENDIX A

Glossary of Symbols[a]

A	advertising expenditures
a	advertising elasticity of demand
B	budget for market research
C	total cost
$\overline{C}$	nonmarketing total cost
c	company opportunity cost of capital
ca	cross-advertising elasticity of demand
cd	cross-distribution elasticity of demand
cp	cross-price elasticity of demand
D	distribution expenditures
d	distribution elasticity of demand
e	a subscript for marketing environment
exp	abbreviation for the word "exponent"
EVPI	expected value of perfect information
F	total fixed cost
f	a subscript for facilities strategy
$f()$	states ". . . is a function of . . ."
G	subscript for GO decision
g	depreciation in dollars
h	opportunity costs in dollars
I	total investment
i	subscript for time
j	subscript for company
k	a scale value
M	marketing program matrix
1	subscript for a product
m	payback period (in years)
n	the length of the planning period (in years)
N	population in millions of people
O	subscript for ON decision
P	price
p	price elasticity of demand
Pr	the probability of an event
Pr_c	probability of commercial success in developing a new product
Pr_G	minimum degree of confidence (probability) needed for a GO decision

[a] Uniform symbols are used in this text to facilitate the comparison of different models. In several cases, this has required departing from the symbols used by the original source of the model.

Pr_O minimum degree of confidence (probability) needed for an ON decision

Pr_t probability of technical success in developing a new product

Q expected sales per time period

Q' Q/Q_R

Q vector of expected sales over time

Q_R estimated demand at reference P

Q_B breakeven volume

q subscript for an interacting product

R total revenue

r internal rate of return (yield of an investment in percent)

s a subscript for marketing strategy

σ_z profit variance

T tax rate on corporate earnings

u nonrecurring start-up costs

W present value of investment

w number of competitors

Y national income in dollars

y subscript for competitor

Z dollar profits

Z_G minimal acceptable profits for a GO decision

Z_O minimal acceptable profits for an ON decision

$\bar{Z}$ dollar profits adjusted for variance ("certainty equivalent")

REFERENCES

1. Wroe Alderson and Paul E. Green, *Planning and Problem Solving in Marketing* (Homewood, Ill.: Richard D. Irwin, 1964), pp. 216-233.

2. Arnold E. Amstutz, "Management Use of Computerized Micro-Analytic Behavioral Simulations," Working Paper 169-66, Alfred P. Sloan School of Management, M.I.T., Cambridge, Massachusetts (1966).

3. Norman R. Baker and William H. Pound, "R&D Project Selection: Where We Stand," *IEEE Transactions on Engineering Management* (December, 1964).

4. Frank M. Bass, "Marketing Research Expenditures: A Decision Model," *Journal of Business*, pp. 77-90 (January, 1963).

5. Booz, Allen, and Hamilton, Inc., *Management of New Products*, 4th ed., 1965.

6. A. Charnes, W. W. Cooper, J. K. DeVoe, and D. B. Learner, "DEMON: Decision Mapping via Optimum GO-NO Networks—A Model for Marketing New Products," a paper presented at the Tenth International Meeting of the Institute of Management Sciences held at the Palace Hotel, Tokyo, Japan, on August 24, 1963.

7. A. Charnes, et al., "DEMON: Decision Mapping via Optimum GO-NO Networks—A Model for Marketing New Products," *Management Science*, pp. 865-887 (July, 1966).

8. Charles W. Cobb and Paul H. Douglas, "A Theory of Production," *American Economic Review*, pp. 139-165 (March, 1928).

9. C. Merle Crawford, "The Trajectory Theory of Goal Setting for New Products," *Journal of Marketing Research*, pp. 117-126 (May, 1966).

10. Frederick E. Croxton and Dudley J. Cowden, *Applied General Statistics* (Englewood Cliffs, N. J.: Prentice-Hall, 2nd ed., 1955), Chapter 13.

11. Norman Dalkey, "An Experimental Application of the Delphi Method to the Use of Experts," *Management Science*, pp. 458-467 (April, 1963).

12. Solomon Disman, "Selecting R & D Projects for Profit," *Chemical Engineering*, pp. 87-90 (December 24, 1962).

13. Donald Farrar, *The Investment Decision Under Uncertainty* (Englewood Cliffs, N. J.: Prentice-Hall, 1962).

14. *Growth Patterns in Industry*, National Industrial Conference Board, New York, 1952.

15. M. S. Heidingfield and A. B. Blankenship, *Marketing* (New York: Barnes and Noble, 1957), p. 149.

16. Charles H. Kline, "The Strategy of Product Policy," *Harvard Business Review*, pp. 91-100 (July-August, 1955).

17. Philip Kotler, "Computerized Media Selection: Some Notes on the State of the Art," *Occasional Papers in Advertising* (Babson Park, Mass.: American Academy of Advertising, the Babson Institute, January, 1966), pp. 45-52.

18. Philip Kotler, "The Competitive Marketing Simulator—A New Management Tool," *California Management Review*, pp. 49-60 (spring 1965).

19. Philip Kotler, "Competitive Strategies for New-Product Marketing Over the Life Cycle," *Management Science*, pp. 104-119 (December, 1965).

20. Philip Kotler, "Marketing Mix Decisions for New Products," *Journal of Marketing Research*, pp. 43-49 (February, 1964).

21. Alfred A. Kuehn and Michael J. Hamburger, "A Heuristic Program for Locating Warehouses," *Management Science*, pp. 643-666 (July, 1963).

22. Robert J. Lavidge and Gary A. Steiner, "A Model for Predictive Measurements of Advertising Effectiveness," *Journal of Marketing*, p. 61 (October, 1961).

23. David B. Learner, "DEMON New Product Planning: A Case History," *New Directions in Marketing*, ed. Frederick E. Webster, Jr. (Chicago: American Marketing Association, 1965).

24. Harlan D. Mills, "Dynamics of New Products Campaigns," *Journal of Marketing*, pp. 60-68 (October, 1964).

25. Erwin Nemmers, *Managerial Economics* (New York: John Wiley, 1962), 96 ff.

26. Ole C. Nord, *Growth of a New Product: Effects of Capacity Acquisition Policies* (Cambridge, Mass.: M.I.T. Press, 1963).

27. John T. O'Meara, Jr., "Selecting Profitable Products," *Harvard Business Review*, pp. 83-89 (January-February, 1961).

28. Edgar Pessemier, *New Product Decisions: An Analytical Approach* (New York: McGraw-Hill, 1966).

29. Barry Richman, "A Rating Scale for Product Innovation," *Business Horizons*, pp. 37-42 (summer 1962).

30. Edward B. Roberts, *The Dynamics of Research and Development* (New York: Harper & Row, 1964).

31. Everett M. Rogers, *Diffusion of Innovations* (New York: Free Press of Glencoe, 1962), p. 81 ff.

32. J. David Stanfield, James A. Clark, Nan Lin, and Everett M. Rogers, "Computer Simulation of Innovation Diffusion: An Illustration from a Latin American Village," a paper presented at a joint session of the American Sociological Association and the Rural Sociological Society, Chicago, August 30 to September 1, 1965.

33. Glenn Lee Urban, *A Quantitative Model of Product Planning with Special Emphasis on Product Interdependence*, an unpublished doctoral dissertation, Northwestern University, 1966.

34. Harold Bierman, Jr. and Seymour Smidt, *The Capital Budgeting Decision* (New York: Macmillan, 1960).

TWELVE | *PAUL E. GREEN, PETER T.*
FITZROY, AND PATRICK J.
ROBINSON

Experimental Gaming in the
Economics of Information*

The broad question to which this chapter is addressed is: How do people acquire and use information in dealing with decision making under uncertainty?

Conceptual problems underlying this deceptively simple question are myriad. Research efforts that have been directed toward answering it are extensive and variegated. The objectives of this paper are twofold:

1. To summarize the current state-of-the-art regarding certain behavioral aspects of individual decision making under uncertainty.

2. To discuss the highlights of a recently completed series of experiments—utilizing marketing executive and student subjects—and to relate these findings to the mainstream of research in behavioral information processing.

THE EVOLUTION OF BEHAVIORAL RESEARCH
IN CHOICE MAKING

A significant segment of the entire literature of the behavioral sciences has been concerned with how people make choices. The large volume of studies on descriptive decision theory alone precludes any attempt at an exhaustive review.[1] Rather, our purpose is to highlight key

* The complete study on which this chapter is based will appear in a future technical monograph to be published by the Marketing Science Institute.

[1] Some appreciation of the diversity of the field of behavioral decision theory may be obtained from perusing *Decision Making: An Annotated Bibliography* by P. Wasserman and F. S. Silander (Ithaca, N. Y.: Graduate School of Business and Public Administration, Cornell University, 1958; 1964).

papers that are directly related to the subject of how people acquire and process information and to point out pertinent trends in the direction of this research.

General Research in Behavioral Decision Theory

For our purposes, two papers—both by Ward Edwards—stand out as key references. In 1961, Edwards published a review of the literature of behavioral decision theory over the period 1954 to 1960.[2] During this period, the predominant choice model involved subjectively expected utility, either of a deterministic or stochastic nature (the stochastic nature illustrated by R. D. Luce's model).[3] In each case, however, the models were essentially static. That is, they referred to one-shot choice situations and neglected predecisional and postdecisional processes (that is, activities preceding and following terminal choice).

A host of experiments have been performed on the measurement of subjective probabilities and utilities, and it is fair to say that most of the choice models being studied today still involve some aspect of expected utility maximization. This is not to say, however, that inadequacies in the model have not been found. For example, the work by Coombs and Pruitt[4] suggests that variance preferences may also be an influencing factor on choice.

In the second section of his review article, Edwards discusses a new direction in research—so-called "dynamic" decision making. Models of these processes deal with *sequences* of decisions, including information acquisition and processing. Pioneering studies by Frank Irwin and his colleagues[5] and Gordon Becker[6] suggest that in *simple* situations human beings are pretty fair statisticians—at least qualitatively—both with regard to direct probability estimation and simple inference problems.

Edwards' second article[7] is of even closer relevance to our studies. In

[2] W. Edwards, "Behavioral Decision Theory," *Annual Review of Psychology*, 12, 473-498 (1961).

[3] R. D. Luce, *Individual Choice Behavior* (New York: John Wiley, 1959).

[4] C. H. Coombs and D. G. Pruitt, "A Study of Decision Making Under Risk," Report No. 2900-33-T, Willow Run Laboratories (Ann Arbor, Michigan: University of Michigan, April, 1960).

[5] F. W. Irwin and W. A. Smith, "Value, Cost, and Information As Determiners of Decision," *Journal of Experimental Psychology*, 54, 229-232 (1957).

[6] G. M. Becker, "Sequential Decision Making: Wald's Model and Estimates of Parameters," *Journal of Experimental Psychology*, 55, 628-636 (1958).

[7] W. Edwards, "Dynamic Decision Theory and Probabilistic Information Processing," *Human Factors*, 4, 59-73 (April, 1962).

this article, Edwards describes dynamic decision situations more fully, including information processing and sequential choice models. He speculates that Bayesian information processing and concepts from dynamic programming may be useful models for comparing real behavior with "optimal" behavior. In psychology, it is not unusual to define an "ideal" decision maker as a starting place for the study of actual behavior.[8]

Edwards suggests that information-seeking activity is sensitive to differences in costs, payoffs, and probabilities, but that there is a general tendency for subjects to seek too much information relative to the Bayesian model. Furthermore, the basic concept of randomness appears difficult for many subjects to grasp. For example, in sequential prediction experiments, subjects with modest training were able to predict the next character of extremely complicated, but deterministic, numerical sequences. As soon as a little "noise" was introduced into the system, however, their performance decreased markedly.

As illustrated by these two articles, there appears to be growing interest on the part of some experimental psychologists in the following.

1. The extension of static subjective utility models to deal with sequential and adaptive choice, including information acquisition and processing.

2. The use of the Bayesian model as a first approximation to behavioral choices involving predecisional processes.

We say "first approximation" because human beings naturally have limitations with regard to computational capability and, moreover, there is cost associated with "thinking." While we could (rather drastically) alter the subjective utility model to account, for instance, for Simon's contention that individuals "satisfice" rather than "maximize," it seems to us that a more fruitful approach might be to see how individuals depart from the utility idealization a step at a time.[9] After all, interest in a prescriptive model should relate to the fact that a normative formulation does purport to represent "*efficient*" behavior. We should be niggardly with regard to the number of "free" parameters that we introduce in the model in order to explain actual choice; otherwise, the tautological character of utility maximization would be about all that remained.

---

[8] As an illustration, see W. P. Tanner and J. A. Swets, "A Decision-Making Theory of Visual Detection," *Psychological Review*, 61, 401-409 (1954). Also, see A. Rapoport, "Human Control in a Decision Task," *Behavioral Science*, 11, 18-32 (January, 1966).

[9] H. A. Simon, "Rational Choice and the Structure of the Environment," *Psychological Review*, 63, 129-138 (1956).

These earlier efforts in the development and test of behavioral choice models appear to lend some support to a Bayesian formulation as an interesting starting point for the study of "dynamic" decision making. We might next inquire as to the relevance of this model for the researcher in marketing.

Relevance of the Bayesian Model to Marketing

For some time now, we have felt that a Bayesian choice model may represent a useful approach to the descriptive study of consumer and managerial information acquistion and processing. Bauer,[10] for example, has proposed the view that consumers make product choices as responses to risk-taking situations where information exists (at a cost) for reducing perceived risk. It seems to us that his theory could be explicated in terms of a Bayesian model. Elsewhere, one of us has tried to point out this correspondence and also the relationship of the Bayesian model to Rogers' innovation theory.[11]

Managerial decision making, as well, is characterized by uncertainty and the possibility of risk reduction through information acquisition. It remains to be seen, of course, if at least some types of choice behavior are consistent with a subjective "counterpart" of the Bayesian model and, if so, what this behavioral model may look like.

This type of research would also seem to have relevance for *prescriptive* decision theory in marketing. Clearly, expanded application of management science techniques will face problems attendant with the education and training of those who will use the techniques. Behavioral research can help to establish the limitations of managers' capabilities for using quantitative tools and suggest strategies for the modification and implementation of prescriptive models in a manner consistent with human constraints. Edwards, for example, has conjectured that information systems of the future may be essentially probabilistic where human beings supply appropriate conditional probabilities, but a computer is used to process and update this information.[12] Thus, behavioral research

[10] R. A. Bauer, "Consumer Behavior as Risk Taking," *Proceedings of the 43rd National Conference of the American Marketing Association* (June, 1950), 389-398.
[11] P. E. Green, "Consumer Use of Information," *On Knowing the Consumer*, J. W. Newman (editor), (New York: John Wiley, 1966), 67-80. Also see R. E. Quandt, "A Probabilistic Theory of Consumer Behavior," *Quarterly Journal of Economics*, 70, 507-536.
[12] W. Edwards, "Man as Transducers for Probabilities in Bayesian Command and Control Systems," *Human Judgments and Optimality*, M. W. Shelly and G. L. Bryan (editors), (New York: John Wiley, 1964), 360-401.

may help the researcher determine the roles of man versus machine in complex planning and control systems of the future and what the implications of normative models are for selection and training of systems' users.

Recent Research in Bayesian Information Processing

During the past few years, several experiments have been undertaken on the adequacy of the Bayesian model as a means for describing subjects' actual choice behavior under uncertainty. As is usually the case, the student population has been over-sampled in the conduct of these experiments.

Edwards has reported several experiments dealing with information acquisition and use that compare "real-with-ideal" performance as based on a Bayesian model.[13] He found that student subjects tend to exhibit qualitative correspondence with the Bayesian model (that is, their behavior is sensitive to changes in monetary values, probabilities, and costs) but, generally, are unable to extract all of the "information" in the data. As a result, subjects tend—for motivational and cognitive reasons —to "buy too much information."

E. H. Shuford[14] and V. R. Cane[15] are other researchers who feel that the Bayesian model represents a useful "ideal" for describing learning processes. Shuford suggests that successive degradation of the Bayesian model can be helpful in the design of decision-making experiments in which various assumptions about informational inputs are sequentially relaxed.

Cane's article represents a persuasive critique on the naivete of linear learning models and their inability to describe adequately such behavior as extinction responses. Cane proposes a Bayesian type of learning model and presents the results of some simple learning experiments that are consistent with this critique.

[13] W. Edwards, "Man as Transducers for Probabilities in Bayesian Command and Control Systems," op. cit., 395-397. Also see "Information-Seeking to Reduce the Risk of Decision," Predecisional Processes in Decision Making: Proceedings of a Symposium, AMRL-TDR-64-77 (Ohio: Wright-Patterson Air Force Base, December, 1964).

[14] E. H. Shuford, "Some Bayesian Learning Processes," Optimality and Human Judgments, op. cit., 127-152. Also see R. A. Weisen and E. H. Shuford, "Bayes Strategies as Adaptive Behavior," Biological Prototypes and Synthetic Systems (New York: Plenum Press, 1963), 303-310.

[15] V. R. Cane, "Learning and Inference," Journal of the Royal Statistical Society, Series A., 125, Part 2, 183-200 (1962).

Our own work in experimental games has tended to support findings by Edwards and others but raises some tantalizing questions.[16] Briefly, in past experiments we have found that subjects—students, for the most part—are sensitive to differences in prior probabilities but, within the range of the variables included in our experiments, their responses were not highly sensitive to payoff differences and information reliability. On the positive side, they did tend to chose consistently with the Bayesian model when no conflict arose between prior and sample evidence. However, conflict situations were resolved in accordance with a Bayes' criterion in only about two-thirds of the cases. Moreover, subjects generally tend to overbuy information (assuming the criterion of expected *monetary* value maximization) and experience difficulty in extracting all of the information in the data. Putting it bluntly, while it is difficult to refute the qualitative evidence in support of the Bayesian model, quantitative correspondence is something else again.

What about competing models as explanations of how people search, acquire, and process information? Aside from the Simon model mentioned earlier, D. E. Berlyne has proposed a model from behavior theory that does not embody the normative flavor of Bayesian theory.[17] He suggests that the degree of internal conflict is an antecedent of search behavior and that the amount of search is partially dependent on the extent of this conflict. He proposes an uncertainty measure (from Shannon's communications theory) as a way of measuring the degree of internal conflict. A second variable—the "importance" of the problem—is also proposed as a partial explanation of the amount of search behavior.

J. T. Lanzetta and his colleagues have performed a number of experiments that are based on the Berlyne model.[18] Lanzetta's research leads him to the conclusion that a subject's cognitive structure and capacity

[16] P. E. Green, M. H. Halbert, and J. S. Minas, "An Experiment in Information Buying," *Journal of Advertising Research*, 4, 17-23 (September, 1964); P. E. Green, M. H. Halbert, and P. J. Robinson, "An Experiment in Probability Estimation," *Journal of Marketing Research*, 2, 266-273 (August, 1965); P. E. Green, M. H. Halbert, and P. J. Robinson, "Experimental Gaming in Consumer Brand Choice Behavior," *The Business Quarterly*, 49-56 (fall 1965). Also see P. E. Green, "Consumer Use of Information," *op. cit.*, 73-78.

[17] D. E. Berlyne, "Attention, Curiosity, and Decision," *Predecisional Processes in Decision Making: Proceedings of a Symposium, op. cit.*, 101-115.

[18] J. T. Lanzetta and V. T. Kanareff, "Information Cost, Amount of Payoff and Level of Aspiration as Determinants of Information-Seeking in Decision Making," *Behavioral Science*, 47, 208-214 (1962). Also see J. T. Lanzetta and J. Sieber, "Predecisional Information Processes: Some Determinants of Information Acquisition Prior to Decision Making," *Predecisional Processes in Decision Making: Proceedings of a Symposium, op. cit.*, 125-171.

for abstract thinking also influence the amount of information sought and his rule for terminating research.

This comment, of course, raises the question of *individual differences* in decision making and their relationship to personality and cognitive variables. Some work has been done along these lines but, again, the results are mixed. D. G. Pruitt found that in sequential decision problems, highly dogmatic subjects—as measured on an attitudinal test—consistently took less information than their more open-minded counterparts.[19] His data also indicated that high-anxiety subjects and low-academic achievers took less information. Other researchers have suggested a variety of personality characteristics—high versus low tolerance for ambiguity, abstract versus concrete conceptualization, inner-versus other-directedness—as being related to the degree of information acquisition.

Kogan and Wallach,[20] in a monumental study of the relationship of risk taking and cognitive-judgmental situations to personality variables, suggest that test anxiety and defensiveness are important enough characteristics to serve as moderator variables in the examination of all correlative data. When subjects exhibit both high anxiety and defensiveness, these researchers found that risk taking or conservatism, whichever may be the case, tends to "swamp" the effects of situational variables. Subjects low in anxiety and defensiveness, however, show much more sensitive behavior to task differences and higher adaptability for task learning. Moreover, these two groups of subjects evidence different behavior with regard to postdecisional dissonance reduction. Highly anxious and defensive subjects do not appear to be sensitive to the negative effects of using poor decision strategies. Rather, they insist all the more strongly that they are satisfied with their choice of strategy.

Our own research findings on the relationship of information acquisition to personality variables appear more equivocal. In an early set of experiments, we administered seven personality tests to all game participants.[21] Only two of these tests—the Gough-Sanford rigidity test and the Rotter social-reaction test—showed both high and invariant statistical significance over succeeding experiments. Even at that, the intersubject variance explained by these personality test scores was quite low,

[19] D. G. Pruitt, *An Exploratory Study of Individual Differences in Sequential Decision Making*, unpublished Doctoral Dissertation, Yale University, 1957.

[20] N. Kogan and M. A. Wallach, *Risk Taking* (New York: Holt, Rinehart and Winston, 1964).

[21] P. E. Green, M. H. Halbert, and P. J. Robinson, "Canonical Analysis: An Exposition and Illustrative Application," *Journal of Marketing Research*, 3, 32-39 (February, 1966).

in our work at least. Encouraged by Kogan and Wallach's results, we recently undertook a replication of part of their overall study. Unfortunately, our results did *not* corroborate their findings with regard to the high predictive efficacy of the test-anxiety and defensiveness variables.

Where Do We Stand on Experimental Findings?

At this juncture, our brief and selective review of the literature on information-acquisition-and-use models and experiments discloses many unsolved problems. On the optimistic side, it does appear that the Bayesian model offers several advantages as a starting point for the development of a behavioral model. As a matter of fact, the Berlyne "conflict" model seems, to us at least, to embody concepts which are operationally similar to the Bayesian model. Moreover, subjects' choice behavior does appear to be sensitive to certain components of the model—prior probabilities, payoffs, and costs—as long as the range of these variables is sufficiently great to be perceived by the subject. The closeness of actual behavior to "optimality," however, has varied markedly from experiment to experiment.

Edwards[22] feels that the static approach to decision theory has provided a legacy of three important concepts that will be useful to the study of dynamic choice making: (1) trade-off relationships among inconsistent value dimensions (as manifested in utility theory) are essential to the conception of decision making; (2) people do impute probabilities to events (whether they agree with "objective" probabilities is, of course, another matter); and (3) people do combine utilities and probabilities according to a principle that, at least, resembles expected value, and choose according to an ordering of such values.

Our own, more limited, work suggests that the notion of subjectively expected utility is difficult to reject (even on nontautological grounds) but that present theory does *not* account satisfactorily for the "noise level" of the subject, his limited computational abilities, and his subjective "cost of thinking." After all, in reasonably complex exercises, how many of us—even with training—can perceive small differences in expected value? It seems to us that a *subjective* counterpart of the Bayesian model of information acquisition and use will require a *stochastic formulation of the model where the experimenter's prediction refers to the probability of choice as a function of several arguments that represent perceived components of the Bayesian model.* That is, in this formulation

---

[22] W. Edwards, "Information-Seeking to Reduce the Risk of Decision," *op. cit.*, p. 7.

the subject is *not* required to choose the highest utility act with a probability of one. We are even less sanguine about our ability to explain individual differences in behavior in terms of "standard" personality-test scores, the Kogan and Wallach experiments notwithstanding. It is one thing to get statistically significant results; it is quite another to be able to explain much of the variance in the appropriate dependent variable. Perhaps we are using the wrong personality "measures." Perhaps personality theory itself could be fruitfully *redefined* in terms of the classes of behavior observed in the experiments themselves, in a manner not unlike Rapoport's recent work in Prisoner's Dilemma games.[23]

Luce[24] has most succinctly described the difficulties attendant with choice-model validation by his comment that, in past experiments, observations about an individual's decision process have been confounded with the effects of his sensory process. Perhaps future experiments can be designed to disentangle these effects. This major difficulty in experimental design would seem to strengthen the advisability of formulating choice models based on expected utility in probabilistic terms. In this way, small differences in utility would be considered to fall within the subject's "noise" level.

OVERVIEW OF THE PRESENT STUDY

All of the experiments discussed above utilized student (and, in some cases, housewife) subjects. Few experiments—based on a Bayesian information processing model—have dealt with managerial subjects, although Starbuck and Bass[25] have recently reported the results of a study in information processing that involved, in addition to college students, a professorial group and a group of county agricultural agents as subjects. We shall comment later on these findings and their relationship to the results of our own experiments.

In this section of the chapter, we discuss the highlights of a series of four information-buying experiments that utilized marketing-executive

[23] A. Rapoport and A. M. Chammah, *Prisoner's Dilemma* (Ann Arbor, Michigan: The University of Michigan Press, 1965).
[24] R. D. Luce, "Learned Versus Optimizing Behavior in Simple Situations," *Optimality and Human Judgments, op. cit.,* 101-115.
[25] W. H. Starbuck and F. M. Bass, "An Experimental Study of Risk-Taking and the Value of Information in a New Product Context," Institute Paper 117, H. C. Krannert Graduate School of Administration, Purdue University, 1965.

and student (control) subjects. One of the four exercises has, in summarized form, already appeared in print.[26] In addition to the authors, M. H. Halbert, of the Marketing Science Institute, W. S. Peters, of Arizona State University and J. S. Minas, of the University of Waterloo, have been associated with various phases of this study.[27]

Within the confines of this chapter, only a brief overview of the study will be undertaken. After a short description of each exercise, the principal research questions will be listed. Principal results over all four experiments will then be discussed, followed by some comments on their implications for future behavioral research and prescriptive decision making.

The Experiments

Each exercise was characterized as a decision problem under uncertainty, placed within a marketing context involving the selection of alternative advertising campaigns. Approximately 30 marketing-executive subjects and 30 student subjects played each game, no subject playing more than one exercise. In each game, subjects were given "full information" (in a Bayesian sense). Student subjects were paid at the end of the exercise, proportionate to their correspondence with Bayesian solutions. Executives received a critique of the exercise. Each game lasted about one hour, including instructional time; subjects were not time paced and were permitted to use pencil and paper for any computations. Insofar as the experimenters could tell, no subject had received training in statistical decision theory. All subjects who participated in the first two exercises also took two pencil-and-paper tests—the California F-Scale test and the Rotter Social Reaction test.

Exercise 1 consisted of a set of eight two-act, two-state conditions. The subject could purchase, at a cost, perfectly reliable information before choosing a terminal act. The eight conditions reflected a full factorial design in which (1) prior probabilities, (2) an additive constant applied to the original payoff matrix, and (3) a multiplicative constant applied to the original payoff matrix were each set at two levels.

For each of the eight conditions, the task to be performed by the subject was: (1) given a set of ten survey costs, to choose that survey cost that was, to him, "break-even" (that is, for any lower survey cost, he

[26] P. E. Green, W. S. Peters, and P. J. Robinson, "A Behavioral Experiment in Decision-Making Under Uncertainty," *Journal of Purchasing*, **2**, 18-31 (February, 1966).

[27] Financial support of this study was provided by the Marketing Science Institute.

would always purchase the perfect information before choosing a terminal act, while for any higher cost, he would forego survey purchase). After receiving survey outcomes from the umpire, where appropriate, (2) the subject had to choose a terminal act. After each block of ten subtrials within condition, the subject received the state outcomes from the umpire and then proceeded to the next set of experimental conditions.

For each subject, the data set consisted of 80 responses indicating: (1) whether or not he chose the survey at the stated cost, and (2) his choice of terminal act, with or without the survey results. Survey results were designed according to a prespecified random sequence in accordance with the probabilities assigned to each condition.

Exercise 2 represented various modifications of exercise 1, but the task was similar. In exercise 2, the subject was presented with a series of twelve three-act, three-state conditions, each with ten subtrials. A full factorial design was used involving prior probabilities at four levels and payoff matrices at three levels. Moreover, in four of the twelve conditions, a dominant strategy existed. The survey opportunity provided only 80 percent reliability, however. Again the subject had to specify for each condition: (1) his "break-even" survey cost, and (2) his choice of terminal act, with (or without) the survey results.

For each subject, the data set consisted of 120 responses, indicating: (1) whether or not he chose the survey at the stated cost, and (2) his choice of terminal act, with or without survey results. This exercise, however, was considerably more complex than game 1.

Exercise 3 differed somewhat in format from the two preceding games. In this exercise, prior probabilities and payoff matrices remained constant over all conditions. A two-act, two-state payoff matrix was used. Each of the twelve conditions consisted of subtrials in which the subject had to choose among the following options: (1) no survey, (2) a perfectly reliable survey, and (3) a partially reliable survey. In the latter option, survey reliability was, respectively, 90 percent, 70 percent, and 50 percent, constituting three subtrials for each condition. The experimental variables in this problem involved the survey costs associated with the perfectly reliable and partially reliable surveys.

The data set consisted of 36 responses, indicating: (1) the information-buying option chosen on each subtrial, and (2) the subject's choice of terminal act. Again survey outcomes, where appropriate, were selected in accordance with the probability characteristics of the stated problem.

Exercise 4 was a more complex version of game 3. Again a two-act, two-state payoff matrix, in which prior probabilities and payoff entries remained constant over conditions, was used. In this game, however, the subject had the opportunity to purchase one (or both) stages of a two-stage survey. That is, for each of the twelve conditions he could choose: (1) no survey, (2) a 90 percent reliable single-stage survey, or (3) one (or both) stages of a two-stage survey, depending upon first-stage survey outcomes. The reliabilities of this two-stage survey were 70 percent and 80 percent, respectively, for the first and second stage. After choosing an information-buying option, the subject was then required to choose a terminal act, with or without survey results, as the case might be. Again the experimental stimuli involved varying the costs associated with the single-stage, highly reliable survey and the two-stage, "less reliable" survey.

The data set consisted of twelve responses indicating: (1) the information-buying option chosen on each condition, and (2) choice of terminal acts.

General Comments on the Exercises

As might be understood from the above description, exercises 1 and 3 appeared to represent simpler games, while exercises 2 and 4 represented more complex versions. A limited series of pretests of each game in which individual subjects were asked to "think out loud" to establish their protocols tended to support this judgment.

It should also be mentioned that, in the instructions, subjects were told that state outcomes would be determined *randomly* in accordance with the probability characteristics of each problem; in this way, the subjects could not predict a specific state outcome on the basis of previous outcomes.

Principal Research Questions

While the results of each exercise could be (and were) analyzed as individual entities, our primary attention was centered on generalizations that might be drawn over all four exercises. Principal research questions were as follows:

1. How well do subjects perform in comparison with the "ideal" (Bayesian) model, assuming maximization of expected monetary value?

2. What insights can be gathered regarding the situational variables that influence performance in various segments of the task?

3. What differences in play exist between the executive and student groups?

4. What differences in play exist among various subsets of subjects within each group taken separately?

5. Can personality test scores predict intersubject variation?

While many additional questions arose in the analysis of game results, we shall concentrate our attention on the above, introducing subsidiary questions where appropriate.

STUDY RESULTS

Information Biases by Subject Group

The most consistent finding over all four exercises was that both subject groups—executives and students—purchased more information than prescribed by the Bayesian model. This result is in accord with the findings of earlier experiments by ourselves and others.

It does appear, however, that as game complexity increased, *differences* between subject groups narrowed. For example, in the "qualitatively similar" exercises, games 1 and 2, executive subjects displayed a lower information bias in (the less complex) exercise 1 than did students. This difference disappeared in (the more complex) exercise 2.

Similarly, in comparing executive versus student performance between exercises 3 and 4, we note similar results. In this case, exercise 3 represented the less complex game. In this exercise, executive subjects exhibited a lower bias for highly reliable surveys than did student subjects. This difference disappeared in (the more complex) exercise 4.

How can these tendencies be explained? One (intuitively appealing) explanation involves the notion of subjects' "preprior" information and attitudes. In the simpler games, exercises 1 and 3, subject behavior appears to be less "game bound." That is, there seems to be greater opportunity for the employment (consciously or unconsciously) of outside knowledge, attitudes and experience. In the more complex games, exercises 2 and 4, the experimental context is more "self-contained." We should conjecture that executive subjects are more used to "living with uncertainty" (and, thus, less prone to seek perfect information) than student subjects. As the *task* itself becomes more complex, however, the influence of external attitudes and experience might play a less important role.

As the exercises become more complex (for example, game 2 versus game 1; game 4 versus game 3) it is possible that the subject's propensity for information reflects a desire to reduce complexity *within* the game setting. That is, some subjects may wish to reduce the mental labor of trying to cope with less information within the game setting itself.

In the Starbuck and Bass experiment, differences in play were found between the high school-county agent group and the student-professorial group. We should speculate that a similar phenomenon was operating in their experiment, at least with regard to the county agent subset. In our postgame interviews, many of the executives evinced disbelief that survey findings could be as "reliable" as stated in the instructions. But the complex exercises, games 2 and 4, tended to be viewed more as "puzzles" than reproductions of real-world situations; it seems likely that the question of real-world correspondence did not even arise.

Integration of Sample and Prior Information

Another question of interest concerns how subjects, compared to the Bayesian model, combined (possibly conflicting) sample information with prior information. In the perfect-information case of exercise 1, both groups of subjects, given purchase of the survey information, almost invariably chose terminal acts in accordance with the Bayesian model. The very few exceptions to this practice might be explained in terms of oversight, checking on the experimenter's "veracity," and so forth.

In exercise 2, the integration of survey results with prior information was much more complex. Generally, students displayed a higher percentage of terminal-act selection in accord with the Bayesian model than executive subjects. This difference is partly explained by the fact that, in this game, executives were more prone to adopt an "event-matching" strategy of terminal-act selection. That is, they chose courses of action according to a relative frequency that would be implied by attempts to predict specific state occurrences.

In exercise 3, the prior probabilities were noninformative (0.5:0.5 for states 1 and 2, respectively). In this case, no conflict existed in prior versus sample information and subjects should choose terminal acts in accordance with the survey information. Almost all executive subjects behaved in accordance with the Bayesian model in this phase of the exercise. A somewhat smaller proportion of student subjects followed the Bayesian model. For both groups of subjects, correspondence with this phase of the model declined slightly as survey reliability decreased.

In exercise 4, both subject groups behaved closely according to the Bayesian model when survey information was highly reliable, but tended to overvalue the *most recent information* when prior-survey and first stage-second stage survey conflicts existed. This finding would seem to have interesting implications for the construction of behavioral models. That is, we may have to introduce "weights" (a subject parameter) for prior and sample evidence.

Summarizing results over *all* four games, it did not appear that consistent intergroup differences existed in the combination of prior and survey sample evidence.

Terminal Act Selection Given Nonpurchase
of Survey Information

In each exercise, a variety of models appeared to be employed by both subject groups in making terminal-act selections, given nonpurchase of the survey information. In exercise 1, both groups of subjects performed about the same and chose terminal acts in accordance with the Bayesian prescription about three-quarters of the time. Again, for each subject group, two major classes of terminal-act selection were observed; that is, "Bayesian type" selection and "event matching." The incidence of each type of behavior did not appear to vary between subject groups nor to be affected by the experimental variables.

In exercise 2, it appeared as though student subjects were more prone to adopt single-act selection; a higher proportion of executive subjects event matched on this game.

In exercise 3, executive and student subjects appeared to behave similarly. The major typologies of play were, again, "Bayesian" type and "event matching" (or combinations). Few subjects chose in accordance with the (ultraconservative) "maximin" principle in this or in any of the other three games.

In exercise 4, executive and student subjects also appeared to perform similarly. Only about half of each subject group, however, behaved in accordance with the Bayesian choice model, despite the fact that "probability maximization," in this game, would also entail selection of the same act. Event matching was somewhat more common in this exercise than in exercise 3.

What are the implications of these results? First, it appears that both subject groups behave rather similarly in this phase of each game. Very possibly, differences in real-world experiences do not affect this type of behavior. There is some indication that executive subjects are more likely to employ event matching, but the difference is not significant when considered over all four games.

Perhaps of most interest is the fact that neither group appeared to utilize the "maximin" principle. Its use would be tantamount to ignoring the stated prior probabilities and choosing terminal acts in accordance with the assumption that the most pessimistic set of conditions would always prevail. While a variety of models appeared to be employed—expected monetary value, probability maximization, event matching—all of these models utilized the prior probabilities in one way or another.

Behavior of Consistent versus Inconsistent Subjects

In each exercise, a set of ground rules was set up for identifying consistent versus nonconsistent subjects with regard to terminal-act selection. In addition, in each exercise, a subset of "optimal" information buyers was identified.

The purpose of the above screening was to see if "optimal" behavior in one phase of the exercise "carried over" to other phases of the game.

In no case was this "carryover" effect noted. That is, consistent terminal selectors did not make significantly better information-purchasing decisions than nonconsistent terminal-act selectors. Optimal survey purchasers did not make significantly better terminal-act selections than nonoptimal survey purchasers.

Moreover, with the exception of exercise 2, it appeared that no significant differences among executive groups versus student groups were noted with regard to the proportion of total subjects who were classified as "consistent," either with regard to terminal act selection or (where appropriate) to survey selection.

Personality Test Scores and Intersubject Behavior

As indicated earlier, all subjects who played the first two exercises were given two personality tests—the California F-Scale and Social Reaction tests. In previous experiments, these tests had discriminated rather well between information-sensitive and nonsensitive subjects.

The results of this phase can be summarized succinctly. No significant results were found on each test for each subject group. As far as we are concerned, the question of personality correlates with information-acquisition behavior is still wide open.

A Tentative Behavioral Model

Our discussion of each exercise has been, by necessity, general and brief. Two central questions arise, however, that are believed to be quite general in scope.

1. With regard to terminal-act selection, why do some subjects choose consistently with the expectation principle while others try to predict specific outcomes; that is, what we have called "event matching"?

2. Can a *general* behavioral model be suggested that accounts for information-option selection over a variety of experimental situations?

With regard to the first question, we are still perplexed. We could speculate that "event-matching" behavior is more deeply inculcated in our culture and reflects attitudes in which the world is viewed as essentially deterministic. But it also reflects subjective probability and utility considerations. By trying to predict *specific* state outcomes—despite the instructions that stated that events were independently chosen—subjects could "pit their wits" against nature (or against the experimenter). This game-within-a-game might provide higher motivation for play.

Furthermore, if the subject attaches a high utility to a "perfect score" (or wishes to check on the experimenter's veracity), the phenomenon may be explained on fairly reasonable grounds. But we could also speculate that attempts at *specific* predictions raise the player's subjective probability of the occurrence of the event. Event matching versus expected-value maximization represents an intriguing area for further study, both with respect to subject-specific variables and situational variables.

The second question of general interest—development of a general model for predicting information-option selections—is also an interesting one and we believe that a start has been made on this problem. As stated earlier, one of the difficulties associated with the expected-utility criterion is that options that are "close to each other" with respect to expected values may well fall within the "noise" level of the subject. However, as the "stimuli" become farther apart, we might expect that the *probability* of choosing an inferior information-buying alternative would decline.

Suppose we were to view each information-buying alternative as a "large" stimulus, the "strength" of which is the expected monetary value yielded by the Bayesian model. The "ideal" discriminator would, of course, always choose the option carrying the highest expected monetary value (assuming a linear utility function and subjective probabilities equal to the objectively stated ones). Our real decision maker, however, would be presumed to exhibit only some probability of choosing the optimal information-buying act.

Continue to assume, for the moment, that all subjects did wish to maximize expected monetary value but, through perceptual and computational limitations, could not distinguish among those stimuli whose expected monetary values were close together. One way to compare intergame performance is to compute, for each trial, the expected monetary value for each information-buying alternative. Assuming no ties, one option will be optimal and inferior alternatives can be expressed in terms of Relative Expected Opportunity Loss (REOL):

$$\text{REOL}_i = \frac{\text{EMV}_{i^*} - \text{EMV}_i}{\text{EMV}_{i^*}}; \text{EMV}_{i^*} > 0$$

That is, for each trial, one information-buying option will offer the highest expected monetary value; call the option i^*. For any ith option not i^*, we can compute the relative degree of "inferiority." The lower limit of this measure will, of course, be zero.

Now, suppose we identify each information-buying option and tabulate the proportion of all subject trials on which this option was selected as a function of its relative expected opportunity loss, again over all trials. This was done for each subject group separately for each of the four

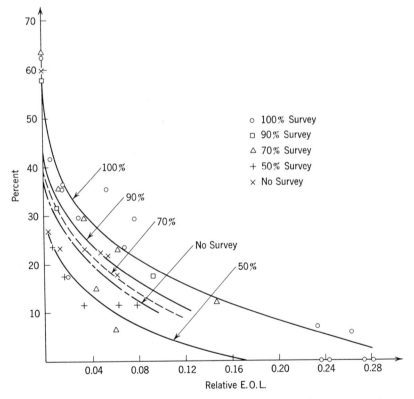

Figure 12.1. Percent choosing each survey versus relative expected opportunity loss (executive subjects).

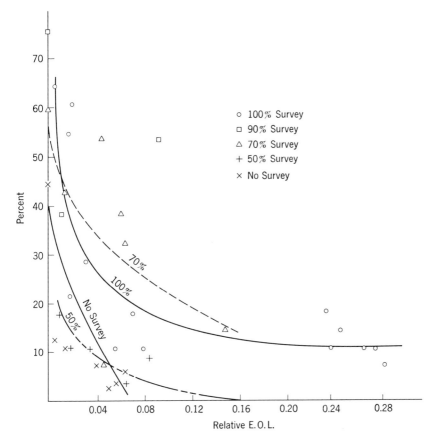

Figure 12.2. Percent choosing each survey versus relative
expected opportunity loss (student subjects).

exercises. For illustrative purposes, we show only the results for exercise
3 (Figs. 12.1 and 12.2).

It will be recalled that, on any given condition in exercise 3, the subject had a choice of: (1) a perfectly reliable survey, (2) a partially reliable survey (where reliability was varied at 90 percent, 70 percent, and 50
percent), or (3) no survey.

Figure 12.1 shows the results for executive subjects only. Notice, first,
that all curves decline as the "inferiority" of each option increases. We
next note that the vertical distance between the curves can be viewed as
labeling bias. If executive subjects had acted in a pure Bayesian fashion,

the graphs would show a spike when the REOL was zero (that is, when the survey actually selected was, in fact, optimal) and be zero along the abscissa elsewhere. If no "labeling" bias existed, we should expect all graphs to be superimposed. For a given REOL, there would be no reason why the subject should elect one survey over another; both are nonoptimal to the same degree.

However, the graphs do not demonstrate this; indeed they show quite the opposite. As noted from Fig. 12.1, if executive subjects select a non-optimal survey, they are much more likely to take the 100 percent survey than a partially reliable survey. We see that the graphs lie in the sequence 100, 90, 70 percent, indicating that executive subjects are indeed consistent in this behavior, although they are not acting in a purely "Bayesian" fashion. The 50 percent reliable survey provides *no* information for the decision maker, and this is generally recognized by the subjects, with fewer executive subjects selecting this survey than the no-survey option. (Notice that no intercept has been drawn for this survey.)

The *intercept* of the graph indicates the percentage of subject trials at which each survey was selected when it was indeed optimal. For executive subjects, these intercepts are grouped very closely to one another, ranging from 57 percent to 63 percent. We can say that about 60 percent of the time an executive subject selected the optimal survey, and this percentage was relatively insensitive to which survey was optimal.

When we observe Fig. 12.2 for student subjects, we notice some marked differences, compared to executive behavior. First, the intercepts of the curves with the ordinate axis show wide variations:

84 percent for the 100 percent survey option.
75 percent for the 90 percent survey option.
60 percent for the 70 percent survey option.
45 percent for the no survey option.

For example, 84 percent of the time, student subjects elected to purchase the 100 percent survey when it was optimal, but they only chose the no-survey option 45 percent of the time when it was optimal.

The probable explanation for this is that student subjects were more prone to overbuy information in this game, as has already been pointed out. Thus, students are buying the 100 percent survey much of the time and consequently, are buying it a large fraction of the times when it is indeed optimal. If we evaluated these results "in vacuo," we might be inclined to say that students can tell when the 100 percent survey is optimal and cannot tell when the no-survey option is optimal. However, in the context of other data, the conclusion that students just buy the 100 percent survey more often—that is, exhibit a stronger tendency toward certainty—is much more tenable.

The second point we notice from Fig. 12.2 is that, while the students do exhibit a labeling bias, they are less consistent in this respect than are the executive subjects.

For both groups of subjects, we notice that the percentage of subject trials decreases as REOL increases; this is true for each survey. Students, however, continued to purchase a survey even when it was far from optimal, particularly with the 100 percent reliable survey. Again, this indicates that students were prepared to incur higher costs in order to avoid uncertainty, in this game at least.

Similar curves were plotted for the other three exercises. Their general appearance was similar to Figs. 12.1 and 12.2, suggesting that both groups evince choice behavior as a function of relative expected opportunity loss, but that biases for highly reliable information show up in the positioning of the curves.

We are currently working on a "psychophysics" type of model with which we shall try to predict choice probability in future games as a function of relative expected opportunity loss. Of course, what is required is the *subjective* equivalents of the components making up the stimulus; that is, prior probabilities, survey reliability, payoffs, and survey costs.

IMPLICATIONS FOR FUTURE RESEARCH

The preciding remarks represent a rather stark summary of a quite detailed study. Many problems, both methodological and substantive, remain for future research. A few of these problems are noted here.

Methodological Problems

One of the central problems of this research, and experimental gaming in general, is the question of *aggregation of responses*. In the exercises previously described, each subject, on each trial, had to do the following:

1. Choose an information-buying act (including the "null" case of foregoing purchase of a survey).
2. Choose a terminal act, with (or without) the information provided by the survey result.

Questions arise regarding aggregation of responses over subjects, over trials and over components of the subject's total response.

In our detailed analysis of this set of experimental games, we elected to show subject responses in various degrees of aggregation. Our first concern was with the "gross behavior" of each exercise. This suggested aggregation over subjects and trials. Accordingly, the results of each experiment were summarized in very gross terms while maintaining group (executive versus student) identity.

We then looked at trial-dependent behavior in order to see if gross differences could be found over trials, still maintaining aggregation over groups.

Next, we set up a list of "screening" criteria wherein subjects were segregated according to their performance on these criteria. This device enabled us to probe, on a more selective basis, for systematic differences among subsets of subjects regarding various aspects of the decision exercises. In this way, we could identify relatively homogeneous subsets of subjects and compare behavior among subsets on other phases of the decision exercise.

As might be suggested by the preceding remarks, serious data-analysis problems arise in attempting to develop certain measures of aggregative behavior. For example, the valuation of information presupposes some type of choice model, assuming the receipt of the information.

Here, again, we started out with an aggregation of data over subjects, conditions, and subtrials, where appropriate. We then disaggregated responses into terminal acts, with and without information, ultimately arriving at subsets of subjects who exhibited similar behavior on various subphases of the game. We then examined the behavior of these (more or less) homogeneous subsets in other phases of the exercise.

In summary, our strategy for analyzing the response data utilized *both* aggregated and disaggregated data, the disaggregation being made according to certain criteria that had been set up to agree with the postulates of the decision model. We rather like this methodological approach (although our defense for it is largely pragmatic) and have summarized it here for other researchers who have been plagued with the same type of problem.

A second type of methodological problem concerns the *design of the experiment* itself. In a model as complex as the Bayesian formulation, it is, of course, highly probable that *several* alternative behavioral rules could lead to similar responses, even assuming that a subject's choice behavior remained stable over trials. That is, when the experiment is all done, we still have alternative hypotheses that could explain at least part of the data. In the design of the experiment, of course, one set of alternatives is typically selected as *presuppositions* in order to be able to isolate the variables that are being tested. Again, this problem is common in behavioral experimentation.

Although we have no satisfactory answer for it, we are seriously considering the possibility of sequentially designed experiments in which the output of the first experiment becomes an input for the determination of what experiment to do next. Moreover, by making a conscious effort to separate presuppositions from hypotheses, we feel that we can design a sequential set of experiments in which this partition is changed in a systematic and efficient manner. We believe that this approach may be fruitful in designing games that get "closer to the real world" without forsaking the value of experimental control.

Substantive Problems

As might be understood from our earlier comments, the development of behavioral models of information acquisition and use is only just beginning. We are planning to investigate the two general problems described earlier: (1) situational variables affecting the incidence of single-act selection versus event matching; and (2) the predictive efficacy of our "psychophysics" model. While in the second case we have found some invariance in functional form over all four experiments, ideally we should like the probability of option selection to be a function of a set of "general" arguments involving the subjective counterpart of the (current) expected monetary value stimulus.

With regard to the former problem, we should conjecture that event matching is much more "subject centered" and "organic" than single-act selection based on expected utility. If so, we believe it is possible to design experiments to test this hypothesis and also to find out the condition under which "learned" responses of the single-act type may revert to event matching.

What are the implications of such research for consumer and managerial behavioral theory? We still believe firmly in the strategy of comparing "real-with-ideal" performance for the development of descriptive theory. Although we could make our experiments more and more complicated—and, hopefully, closer to the real world—our intuition tells us that this would be less fruitful than "cycling back" and working intensively with some simple decision exercises. Then, through sequential design, we should like to move to more complex tasks.

As far as we know, so little is known about the *strategy* of behavioral research that it would be foolhardy to say that higher priority should be given to complex, closer-to-the-real-world research than to "simpler," more artificial exercises. About all we can say with some conviction at this point is that we continue to believe in the basic *intended* rationality of human behavior. A recent remark made by Ward Edwards succinctly summarizes our feelings on this subject:

Question: What is he doing?
Answer: He's doing the best he can!

In our judgment, this remark cannot be improved upon as a basic presupposition for the investigation of human choice behavior.

Experimental Research in Marketing: Historical Perspective

In his "research agenda for functionalism" at the end of his book, *Dynamic Marketing Behavior*, Wroe Alderson includes the following hypothesis.

A product is selected to replenish or expand the assortment in the hands of a household by taking account of expected value.[1]

Alderson indicates that the research problems connected with this rather innocent sounding statement are many and difficult. But the consumer viewed as a Bayesian decision maker makes a fascinating topic for investigation. Our task is to review the historical development of this idea and related research findings. This review is not concerned with the technical problems connected with utility theory and measurement but, instead, is an introduction to the principal lines of theory and experimentation connected with utility theory. The hope is that the perspective afforded will be of some assistance in the discussion of applications in the marketing field.

EXPECTED VALUE

Applications of Bayesian decision theory to marketing management have become quite fashionable in recent years. One of the participants in this conference, Paul Green, has, through his writing, been especially instrumental in this movement. And, as you know, Bayes was not a statistician, but an English Unitarian minister whose famous work, "Essay Towards Solving a Problem in the Doctrine of Chance," was edited and

[1] Wroe Alderson, *Dynamic Marketing Behavior* (Homewood, Ill.: Richard D. Irwin, 1965), p. 348.

published posthumously by Dr. Richard Price in 1763. Dr. Price, also a minister, was a consultant on actuarial matters to the Equitable Life Insurance Corporation, one of the first corporations formed for the express purpose of insuring individual lives. During this era, population and life expectancies were increasing rapidly, a circumstance that drew the Reverend Malthus to write his famous essay. In this environment, we can see how a person would be concerned about changing probabilities of death, and of the distinction or relation between prior probabilities, current experience, and posterior or predictive probabilities. It is interesting that this intrusion of a business problem into a field formerly concerned only with the gaming table produced a controversy in statistics that continues even to the present day.

The aspect of Bayesian decision making that we wish to start with is not the determination of probabilities, but the criterion for decision:— expected value. Use of expected monetary value as a criterion for decision making assumes (1) that the desirability of an incremental dollar of net proceeds is independent of the number of dollars already held or earned and (2) that the desirability of a given expected dollar amount does not depend on the particular probability-payoff combination that produces the expected value. The decision maker is assumed to be indifferent between alternatives with equal expected value. As is well known, these two assumptions do not necessarily describe how decision makers feel about different alternatives under uncertainty. If we grant the second assumption, we may question the first, and we come up against an old problem: the marginal utility of money. If we grant the first assumption but question the second, two sometimes related problems arise. The first is the problem of what kind of probabilities the decision maker is operating with. Here we encounter distinctions between objective and subjective probabilities. If there are no known or given probabilities, the decision maker will perforce be operating with personal probabilities. If there are probabilities given, they may not be believed, and the decision maker may be operating with "his own" probabilities. Further, the decision maker may have probability preferences. As between equal expected values, in view of whatever kind of probability is employed, the decision maker may prefer to gamble with one set of odds rather than with another.

UTILITY AND UNCERTAINTY

The first of these problems—the question of whether the attractiveness of money gain is independent of the amount already held, or gained—

was recognized in 1738 by Bernoulli in the famous St. Petersburg paradox. In this problem, A agrees to pay B the sum of 2^n dollars where n is the serial number of the throw of a fair coin that first shows a head. What is the game worth to B? There is a 0.50 chance of B's winning $2, a 0.25 chance of winning $4, and a 0.125 chance of winning $8, and so on. There is a small chance of winning a very large amount; in fact, the expected value of the series is infinite. But few persons will pay more than $15 or $20 for a chance. The problem must have been around for some time, because the mathematician, Gabriel Cramer, speaks of having been acquainted with the problem from a letter written by Nicolas Bernoulli, a cousin of Daniel's, in 1713. Cramer states:

I believe that it (the paradox) results from the fact that, in their theory, mathematicians evaluate money in proportion to its quantity while, in practice, people with common sense evaluate money in proportion to the utility they can obtain from it.[2]

Cramer goes on to suppose a case where an individual deems any sum greater than 2^{24} dollars to be equal in value to 2^{24}, and derives an expected value of 2^{13}, which he declares to be "a result which seems much more reasonable than rendering it infinite."[3] He then tries out a square root law, and comes up with an expected value of 2.9, observing that this is a "trifling amount, but nevertheless, I believe, closer than is 13 to the vulgar evaluation."[4] Bernoulli's solution was a logarithmic utility function—from the assumption that the marginal utility of gain is proportional to the amount already gained, or possessed. From this, it follows that the utility of a gamble will equal the geometric mean of the probability distribution of states that the decision maker could find himself in after the gamble. His expected monetary position is the arithmetic mean, or common expectancy, of the same probability distribution. The geometric mean is always a lower value than the arithmetic mean, and the difference represents an inevitable loss in utility to the gambler. By the same token, however, a gain can be made in utility terms by insuring against loss, and the gain will be greater the larger the loss insured in relation to the current level of assets. Bernoulli goes on to show how small a fortune a man must have to make it rational for him to pay a given amount to insure against a specified loss, and how large a fortune another man must have in order for him to underwrite the insurance.

[2] Daniel Bernoulli, "Exposition of a New Theory on the Measurement of Risk," reprinted (in translation) in George A. Miller (editor), Mathematics and Psychology (New York: John Wiley, 1964), p. 50.
[3] Ibid., p. 50.
[4] Ibid., p. 51.

Although he did not mention it, it is an excellent example of the mutual gain in utility through exchange and, incidentally, of the difference between gambling and insurance. Bernoulli does not raise the question of why people, despite an alleged loss in utility, nevertheless engage in fair games of chance. He says that ". . . indeed, this is Nature's admonition to avoid the dice altogether."[5] He does work out, however, how much of an advantage a gambler must possess over his opponent in order to avoid any expected (utility) loss.

While Bernoulli was prompted by empirical considerations to question the assumption of constant marginal utility, there was no empirical support for the logarithmic function he proposed. More than 200 years later, Von Neumann and Morgenstern introduced an operational method of measuring the degree of preference (or utility) of alternative payoffs.[6] Given payoffs A, B, and C, where A certain is preferred to B certain that is preferred to C certain, they say that utility of B to a subject is numerically equal to a probability $(\bar{p})$ such that the choice between the expected gain $\bar{p}(A) + (1 - \bar{p})C$ and the certain payoff of B is a matter of indifference to him.

Mosteller and Nogee determined in a related manner the utility attached to indifferent money prizes by players in an experimental situation.[7] In their experiments, A represents a gain, C a loss, and B zero gain or loss. Again A certain is preferred to B certain and B certain is preferred to C certain. But there is some probability combination of A and C for which the subject is indifferent to A and C versus B. Fixing arbitrarily the utility of B and C and the probability combination, the experimental problem is to find the money value of A that satisfies the utility equation. This is the money prize for A, which in the given probability combination with C, will be chosen by the subject neither more or less frequently than the certain no gain-no loss alternative, B. When this money value of A is found, we have the predetermined figure for A to associate with it, and many such pairs of values will determine a curve of utility for varying money prizes.

It is evident that strict adherence of choice behavior to the traditional expected-value criterion presupposes a constant marginal utility of money gain to the decision maker. Utility is assured to be strictly proportional to money gain, so that expected money gain can be used in

[5] *Ibid.*, p. 43.

[6] John Von Neumann and Oscar Morgenstern, *Theory of Games and Economic Behavior* (Princeton: Princeton University Press, 1944).

[7] Frederik Mosteller and Phillip Nogee, "An Experimental Measurement of Utility," *Journal of Political Economy*, **59**, 371-404 (October, 1951).

place of expected utility as a norm of behavior. Friedman and Savage deduced, from the behavior of individuals in purchasing insurance and lottery tickets, that the utility of money curve might, typically, have a generalized reserve "S" shape.[8] If individuals will pay more than the fair value for a sweepstakes ticket, the marginal utility of large money gains must be high. Similarly, if persons pay more than the actuarial value for the protection from large money losses afforded by insurance, the marginal disutility of large losses must be high.

Friedman and Savage further assert that the individuals also display a preference for a high probability of small gain—that it is the intermediate probability of intermediate gain that will be resisted. If this also prevails on the "loss" side, the resultant money utility curve would have to have inflection points above and below the current money level. The resulting series of plateaus have been identified with different aspiration levels of the individual. Such a pattern of changing marginal utility suggests that not all kinds of insurance will be purchased nor will an individual see fit to take small chances on all kinds of drawings. Where the marginal utility curve assumes this more complex shape, only a limited amount of certain money will be given up in exchange for probable gain and protection against probable loss. The Friedman-Savage form of the utility function accords with the common behavior of purchase of some insurance against loss simultaneous with the taking of some chances on lotteries.

PROBABILITY PREFERENCES AND SUBJECTIVE PROBABILITY

Implicit in the utility approach introduced above is the notion that choices are a function of expected utility or, more precisely, that choices reflect expected utility that, in turn, is a function of money value. Probabilities serve only to discount utilities of uncertain prizes so that expected utility may be compared with the cost (fair money value or expected value) of the prize. Preference for an uncertain gain over a certain gain reflects a personal valuation of the prize, not a preference for the uncertain over the certain. Probability serves as a mechanism for equating alternatives with varying risk, but that is all. Individuals are not assumed to have a different attitude toward varying probabilities. And, where probabilities must be evaluated from experience, individuals must be assumed capable of correctly assessing them.

[8] Milton Friedman and L. J. Savage, "The Utility Analysis of Choices Involving Risk," *Journal of Political Economy*, **56**, 279-304 (1948).

A classical experiment on probability preferences was conducted by Preston and Barrata.[9] In their experiment, two or four contestants bid for the opportunity of participating in 42 gambles representing exhaustive combinations of six prizes offered at seven different odds. The prizes ranged from 5 to 1000 points and the probabilities from 0.01 to 0.99. The highest bidder won the opportunity to participate in the gamble and put up the bid amount from an original "endowment." The endowment received by each player equalled two-thirds of the expected value of the 42 gambles. The participants included sets of women undergraduates, male undergraduates, and faculty members with a knowledge of probability theory. The player with the most points at the end of the game received a trivial prize.

Preston and Barrata found consistent overevaluation of long odds and underevaluation of short odds. That is, the winning bids on probabilities below 0.25 tended to exceed expected value and winning bids on probabilities over 0.25 failed to equal the expected values on balance. This was true of the sophisticated as well as of the unsophisticated subjects.

The Preston-Barrata results have since been corroborated in similar experiments conducted by others. Some of the explanations offered for the consistent overevaluation of gambles involving long odds center not on the valuation of the prizes but on the perception of probabilities and attitudes towards them. Irwin offers an interpretation, supported by experiments conducted by him and by others,[10] that favorable events are assigned a higher subjective probability than are unfavorable ones. The individual really believes the likelihood of a large gain at low odds is greater for him than objective or relative frequency indicates. Subjective probability theory suggests that gambles involving long objective odds would be overvalued even if the individual's marginal utility for money were strictly proportional to money value.

Evidence also exists that individuals faced with experience data tend to overestimate the relative frequency of occurrence of rare events and underestimate the relative frequency of common events. Attneave, for example, found this tendency in estimates made by ninety subjects on the relative frequency of various letters in passages of English text.[11]

[9] M. G. Preston and P. Baratta, "An Experimental Study of the Auction-Value of an Uncertain Outcome," *American Journal of Psychology*, 61, 183-193 (1948).
[10] Francis W. Irwin, "Relation Between Value and Expectation as Mediated by Belief in Ability to Control Uncertain Behavior," paper read before the *Annual Meeting of the American Psychological Association*, Chicago, 1960.
[11] F. Attneave, "Psychological Probability as a Function of Experienced Frequency," *Journal of Experimental Psychology*, 46, 81-86 (1953).

"The breaking point" comes at roughly the mean frequency, or the reciprocal of the number of letters in the alphabet. Thus, where probabilities must be found from experience, both perception and attitude (or subjective probability) work in the direction of overevaluation of choices involving long odds.

Griffith provides an interesting example in horse-race betting behavior.[12] He studied the percentage of winners among horses placed by betting in various odds groups in American horse races. The odds groups represent aggregate psychological probabilities while the associated winning experience represents objective probability. Griffith finds a systematic underevaluation of the chances of short-odded horses and an overevaluation of the chances of horses at long odds. The breaking point occurs at odds of 6 to 1 or 5 to 1 which, Griffith points out, are approximately the same as the indifference points found in the Preston-Barrata experiments. Griffith offers his evidence merely as an addition to knowledge of the psychology of probability. At this point, we should seem to have three alternate explanations of preference for gambles at long odds: (1) increasing marginal utility of larger money gains, (2) persistent overestimates of the frequency of winning at long odds, and (3) psychological overestimation of personal chances of winning.

Application of the Von Neumann-Morgenstern technique for the determination of utility assumes that subjective probabilities are equal to objective probabilities, and that there is no utility as such attached to the alternative of a gamble as opposed to a certain option. In 1931, Frank Ramsey had proposed a method for measurement of subjective value that did not employ objective probabilities,[13] and this approach was adopted by Davidson, Seigel, and Suppes in their experiments in the mid-1950's. In this method, a pair of options are offered, each containing two payoffs that depend on the outcome of an uncertain event with subjective probability 1/2. The method of finding an event with subjective probability 1/2 was the contribution of Ramsey, who was concerned with the interpretation of probability as a degree of belief. Ramsey defines degree of belief 1/2 in an ethically neutral proposition (X), an indifference between the options A if X is true and the options B if X is false, and A if X is false and B if X is true. He also gives the following interpretation of the term "degree of belief."[14]

[12] R. M. Griffith, "Odds Adjustments by American Horse-Race Betters," *American Journal of Psychology*, 62, 290-294 (1949).
[13] F. P. Ramsey, "Truth and Probability," reprinted in George A. Miller (editor), *Mathematics and Psychology* (New York: John Wiley, 1964), pp. 67-76.
[14] *Ibid.*, p. 69.

I am at a cross-roads and do not know the way; but I rather think one of the two ways is right. I propose therefore to go that way but keep my eyes open for someone to ask; if I now see someone half a mile over the fields, whether I turn aside to ask him will depend on the relative inconvenience of going out of my way to cross the fields or of continuing on the wrong road if it is the wrong road. But it will also depend on how confident I am that I am right; and clearly the more confident I am of this the less distance I should be willing to go from the road to check my opinion. I propose therefore to use the distance I would be prepared to go to ask, as a measure of the confidence of my opinion.

For fifteen subjects whose utility curves could be determined, Davidson-Seigel-Suppes found none who were consistently conservative in that they would accept an alternative with a smaller actuarial value provided it was less risky.[15] Most of the subjects had utility curves that looked "like a miniature version of the curve hypothesized by Friedman-Savage."[16] Comparing their results with earlier results of the Mosteller-Nogee experiments, the authors find that "considering the very different methods used to arrive at the utility curves, the degree of similarity in the results is fairly striking."[17] In contrast to this, Ward Edwards has asserted that where independent measurements have been derived for utility and subjective probability, the experiments tend to suggest that they are proportional to objective (money) value and objective probability, respectively.[18] This suggests that individuals can assess value and likelihood correctly, but they deliberately operate with some decision rule other than maximizing expected value.

Elsewhere, Edwards presents some data tending generally to support the Irwin hypothesis of subjective probabilities that overstate the objective probability of favorable events. However, he finds choices quite consistent with objective probability expectations when the alternative decisions involve expected losses. From this, Edwards suggests that the sign (gain versus loss) rather than the value of the payoff may be the critical factor associated with the subjective probability phenomenon.

The descriptions of choice behavior under differential risks discussed thus far can be summarized. Excepting the viewpoint of constantly di-

[15] Donald Davidson and Patrick Suppes, *Decision Making: An Experimental Approach*, Stanford, California, Stanford University Press, 1957.
[16] *Ibid.*, p. 75.
[17] *Ibid.*, p. 72.
[18] Ward Edwards, "Interactions between Utility and Subjective Probability and the Variance Preference Problem," paper presented to the *American Psychological Association Meetings*, Chicago, September 1, 1960, Engineering Psychology Group, University of Michigan.

minishing marginal utility of money, the most general agreement is found in observed preference for low probability of large gain. Some question seems to exist whether patterns that might persist with respect to gains repeat themselves in connection with loss avoidance. However, let us now consider some possible marketing applications suggested by some of the theory and experimentation in choices under risk and uncertainty.

SOME MARKETING APPLICATIONS

Consider the adoption of new products and brands by consumers. From past experience the consumer-buyer is familiar with the performance of certain products or brands. However, he has no personal experience of the merits of untried products and brands and must rely on advertising statements or information provided by salesmen, relatives, friends, and so on. An advertising claim to which the buyer attaches quite low credibility may nevertheless represent an advantage with greater subjective expected value to the consumer than more modest, highly credible claims. Both an increasing marginal utility at higher payoffs and overestimation of the magnitude of the low probability may predispose the buyer to prefer the small chance of a large gain.

A related application from lotteries is of interest. Sprowls suggested that if buyers of lottery tickets undervalue smaller prizes at the same time that they overvalue the large prize, then they may not grossly overvalue the lottery ticket as a whole.[19] His interviews with buyers suggested that they do not consider the smaller prizes important, but rather, a kind of consolation prize as an inducement to participate in the lottery another time. This suggests that, if a product lives up to some minimal expectation regarding its more mundane uses, it may be bought again on the chance of the large payoff. Even if the 007 hair cream did not produce a James Bond style affair, it may have produced a comment from mother about good grooming.

Friedman and Savage noted that if the marginal utility of money gain for individuals were monotonically increasing, a lottery operator would maximize his gain by offering a single large prize. The fact that such is not the case in lotteries was used by Friedman and Savage as evidence that the utility curve has an inflection point (or perhaps several) above

[19] R. C. Sprowls, "Psychological-Mathematical Probability in Relationships of Lottery Gambles," American Journal of Psychology, 66, 126-130 (1953).

the current money level. These they take to represent various levels of aspiration. Now a multiple prize offering is optimal. To return to the advertising analogy, the problem then becomes not one of finding the most profitable appeal, but of finding an assortment of claims or advantages, some credible and some not so credible, that will in some way have a maximum subjective expected value.

A related application is suggested by the higher subjective probabilities attached to favorable as opposed to unfavorable outcomes of objective probability. The analogy here is the relative effectiveness of positive as against negative advertising appeals. It may follow that negative appeals must have relatively greater credibility than positive appeals. The objective probability of the event to which the product is related must be high, and the argument for the remedy must have high credibility. We wonder about the difficulties with health and safety campaigns (for example, those dealing with smoking or safe driving) in this connection.

Thus far, the context in which decision behavior has been discussed is that of a series of similar decisions. The personal and environmental determinants of decision behavior have been regarded as homogeneous from occasion to occasion. Herrmann and Stewart, from experiments involving gambling preferences of the kind already discussed, observe that individuals are more willing to take speculative long odds when losing than when winning a game.[20] Many persons will agree with this tendency, based on their own observations of amateur gamblers. Simon discusses another phenomenon related to cumulative performance.[21] He considers what happens when an individual's performance fails to measure up to his own expectation or aspiration level. Search for new alternatives for action (perhaps new rules for decision) ensues, and at the same time there is a tendency for adjusting the level of aspiration downward in accordance with more readily attainable goals. Where performance and aspiration are not sufficiently adjusted, irrational rather than rational adaptive behavior may well ensue. It is quite possible that the taking of increasingly long chances when losing a game represents just such a shift of behavior—a shift to action patterns that the individual, in retrospect, would agree departed from his best judgment. On the other hand, if it is important to recoup one's stake in a limited amount of time, the behavior may be quite reasonable. If, as Alderson says, the

[20] Cyril Herrmann and John B. Stewart, "The Experimental Game," *Journal of Marketing*, 22(1), 12-20 (July, 1957).
[21] Herbert A. Simon, "Theories of Decision Making in Economics and Behavioral Science," *American Economic Review*, 49(3), 253-284 (June, 1959).

consumer is quite conscious of his level of performance as a buyer,[22] behavior under performance-aspiration discrepancy may be a fruitful area to study experimentally.

Littig introduces into differential risk calculations the decision maker's motivation for success and anxiety over failure.[23] He suggests that, where outcomes depend on the skill of the decision maker, these motivational elements operate as coefficients that modify the subjective probability times payoff criterion discussed previously. The result is that an individual with a high motivation for success and a low anxiety over failure will prefer alternatives involving intermediate probabilities of success. On the other hand, high failure anxiety combined with low motivation for success will produce more extreme behavior. The individual will prefer either relatively sure modest gains or low chances of great gain. Either of these will present the decision maker with a low chance of ego damage through failure. In the first instance, assurance of success is high and, in the second, failure can be easily explained away by reference to the long odds involved. It is tempting to speculate about the validity of these psychological determinants in such diverse fields as the behavior of chronic gamblers, the selection of occupational endeavors, and risk choices in business. In the area of shopping behavior, the extent and character of experimentation with alternative products and brands may be closely related to perception of performance and attitudes toward achievement of success and avoidance of failure.

Feather brings out the point that the attainment attractiveness or utility of various goal objects may influence the subjective probability held by an individual that he can attain the object.[24] Lacking any other information, we tend to feel that the more valuable prizes are less attainable. This view stems originally from Kurt Lewin,[25] and constitutes an explanation of subjective-probability choices that reverses the cause-effect direction suggested by the explanation of overestimation of low probabilities. Feather reports on experiments in which the prizes were

[22] Wroe Alderson, *Marketing Behavior and Executive Action* (Homewood, Ill.: Richard D. Irwin, 1957), p. 167.
[23] L. W. Littig, "Motivation, Probability Preferences, and Subjective Probability," paper read before the *Annual Meeting of the American Psychological Association*, Chicago, 1960.
[24] N. T. Feather, "Success Probability and Choice Behavior," *Journal of Experimental Psychology*, **58**(4), 257-266 (October, 1959).
[25] Kurt Lewin, "Group Decision and Social Change," in T. M. Newcomb, E. J. Hartley and others, *Readings in Social Psychology*, edited by the Society in the Psychological Study of Social Issues. (New York: Henry Holt, 1947).

payoffs of candy to school children. Preferences for alternative prizes as well as subjective probabilities of their attainment were obtained from the subjects. Subsequently, in games where the outcomes were perceived as chance determined, the subjects elected to play for prizes that were more obtainable (higher subjective probability) than were the cases in skill-oriented situations. In the skill-oriented situations, there was a definite tendency for selection of prizes with low subjective probabilities of attainment.

INFORMATION AND LEARNING

The consumer's quest for information can be interpreted in the Bayesian sense as the postponing of a current terminal decision in favor of further sampling. Current uncertainties are high, so that the value of information that may reduce the uncertainty is correspondingly high. Ellsberg's question [26] of whether individuals would prefer to bet on "red" in an urn of 50 percent red balls or bet on "red" in an urn of unknown proportion of red balls points up the difference between positive knowledge and "pseudoknowledge" based on insufficient reason. This is related to quantity and adequacy of information in a shopping decision. We might suppose that individuals would be willing to give up certain amounts of payoff in return for increased credibility or confidence as well as for increased probability, and that trades are possible between probability and confidence, given a stated payoff. Either of these may be the means of assessing the value of information to the decision maker. It is in ambiguity and inadequacy of information that real uncertainty as opposed to risk lies.[27] Trade-offs between pure risk and uncertainty may be a potentially valuable avenue of experimentation in consumer decision making.

In experiments involving choices under risk, the probabilities of outcomes or payoffs are known. There is a considerable body of experimentation, however, on learning in a probabilistic environment. Learning theory has always occupied a central role in psychological thought, and

[26] Daniel Ellsberg, "Risk and Ambiguity, and the Savage Axioms," *Quarterly Journal of Economics*, 75(4), 643-669 (November, 1961).

[27] See also, for example, Nicholais Georgescu-Roegen, "Choice, Expectations, and Measurability," *Quarterly Journal of Economics*, 68(4), 503-534 (November, 1954), and Martin Shubik, "Information, Risk, Ignorance, and Indeterminacy," *Quarterly Journal of Economics*, 68(4), 629-640 (November, 1954).

it should not be surprising to find in this area some materials of use in the field of consumer decision making under uncertainty. A classic experiment in this field is the binary choice experiment under conditions of probabilistic reward reinforcement. In these experiments, at a given cue a subject makes one of two choices, a or b. Choice a is rewarded with probability p_1 and choice b with probability p_2. Sometimes b is simply "not a," and $p_2 = -p_1$; for instance, when light A goes on (cue), the subject predicts that light B will then go on (a) or it will not (b). Light B then goes on with relative frequency p_1 in an appropriately selected random sequence. The reward may be simply the satisfaction of having guessed correctly; it may involve a punishment of incorrect responses, or may involve a monetary incentive. A common pattern of response, termed asymptotic matching behavior, has been observed in the binary-choice learning experiment. After a period of learning, the subjects tend to choose alternative "a" with relative frequency p_1 and alternative "b" with relative frequency p_2. Where this happens, it appears that we must conclude that the subjects estimate objective probabilities correctly but do not maximize expected value. Parenthetically, it is interesting to note that experiments have been recorded in which monkeys and rats consistently chose the more frequently reinforced alternative when $p_1 > 0.7$ and $p_2 < 0.30$.[28] Apparently, human behavior is more complex than animal behavior and some explanations of asymptotic matching behavior proceed along these lines. Refusal of human subjects to believe that the reward series is random and resultant search for pattern in the reward sequence is a popular interpretation of the event-matching behavior.[29] Examination of choice sequences in the binary learning situation has shown a tendency for the relative frequency of a given response to first increase and then decrease after the response was found to be correct on several occasions in succession.[30] Apparently, subjects will try to capitalize on perceived trends and also to anticipate some kind of compensation mechanism in the sequences.

Event-matching behavior seems to be another example of failure of individuals to maximize expected gain in the classical sense. Estes notes

[28] Ward Edwards, "Reward Probability, Amount, and Information as Determiners of Sequential Two-Alternative Decisions," *Journal of Experimental Psychology,* 52(3), 177-187 (September, 1956).
[29] See Herbert A. Simon (cited in footnote 21).
[30] R. C. Atkinson, G. R. Somner, and M. B. Sterman, "Decision Making by Children as a Function of Amount of Reinforcement," *Psychological Reports,* 6, 299-306 (1960).

that a strategy of always choosing the more frequently rewarded response would not permit discovery and adaptation should the reinforcement probabilities be subject to change.[31] We had better try our second favorite brand once in a while to check on our earlier assessment of its merits compared to the favorite brand. It has also been observed that differential monetary incentives (rewards) and risks in the binary-choice situation lead to relative frequencies of choice that overshoot the matching values.[32] The extent of departure from matching behavior is apparently greater as differentials in risks or payoffs increase. Edwards suggests that, if the rewards are trivial, the subject will not really care if he is right, and the choice probabilities will tend toward the reinforcement probabilities.[33] The subject sees the trials as a game, and tries to outguess the experimenter on each choice. As the reward or the desire for it increases, choice behavior deviates from event matching toward consistently choosing the favored alternative. However, this tendency stops short of always choosing that alternative. Precisely because some desire or motivation is present, the subject becomes distressed over the inevitable occasions when his favored choice is unrewarded, and directs some proportion of his choices to the unfavored alternative.

By changing some of the environmental conditions of learning-choice experiments with probabilistic reward it may be possible to simulate brand-choice behavior in a useful way. Some of the directions that such simulation may take are suggested by other work in learning experiments. For example, a number of researchers have experimented with extinguishing response patterns in binary-choice experiments.[34] The rapidity of extinction of prior response appears to vary inversely with the original probabilities of reward and, thus, with learned response. It takes longer to extinguish a 50 percent response pattern than a 75 percent response pattern. The effects of changes in reward pattern in the analogous brand-purchase situation could merit investigation. We could introduce

[31] W. K. Estes, "Individual Behavior in Uncertain Situations: An Interpretation in Terms of Statistical Association Theory," Decision Processes, edited by R. M. Thrall, C. H. Coombs, and R. L. Davis (New York: John Wiley, 1954), 127-137.
[32] W. K. Estes, "A Descriptive Approach to the Dynamics of Choice Behavior," Behavioral Science, 6(3), 177-184 (July, 1961).
[33] See Ward Edwards (cited in footnote 28).
[34] See, for example, D. A. Grant, H. W. Hake, and J. P. Hornseth, "Acquisition and Extinction of Verbal Conditioned Response with Differing Percentages of Reinforcement," Journal of Experimental Psychology, 42, 1-5 (1951), and L. G. Humphreys, "The Effect of Random Alternation of Reinforcement of the Acquisition and Extinction of Conditioned Eyelid Reactions," Journal of Experimental Psychology, 25, 141-158 (1939).

sudden changes in probability of reward that correspond to product innovation and gradual changes that resemble steady comparative quality improvement. The effect of information of varying reliability could also be studied in this context. Information could be made available, prior to each decision, about the occurrence of reinforcement. If this information were reliable, and if this were perceived by the "shopper" through experimentation, then presumably it would be used, even at some cost. But if the information is not perfectly reliable, would it be used? What degree of inaccuracy will be tolerated, and how much value is put upon increments of accuracy? The possibilities for experimentation related to buying decisions are considerable.

Some further investigations in the realm of learning deserve attention because they focus on environmental conditions that affect learning. Phares finds, for example, that expectancies regarding future reinforcement show greater changes following reinforcement when the reward is viewed by the subject as a consequence of skill rather than as a result of chance.[35] Where the consumer-buyer is performance oriented, changes of this kind might be found even in the repetitive purchasing of so-called convenience and impulse items, whose purchase is regarded by some researchers as habit determined.

Lewin reports that informal learning produced faster results in changing the food-consumption habits of a group than did formal lecture methods.[36] The informal method provided a greater involvement for the individual. In interrupted task situations, investigators have looked for factors associated with subsequent recall of completed and incompleted tasks. Rosenweig, Alper, and Glixman were unable to find significant personality factors (for instance, repression, pride, and ambition), but Alper finds a significant environmental effect—that is, that a preponderance of incompleted tasks are recalled when the task situation is informal, while recall of completed tasks predominates in formal settings.[37] Motivation is more positive in the informal setting. In general, Atkinson feels that the greater the motivation to achieve, the greater will be the tendency to recall incompleted rather than completed tasks.[38]

It will be recalled that Atkinson felt that the motivation differential

[35] E. Jerry Phares, "Expectance Changes in Skill and Chance Situations," *Journal of Abnormal and Social Psychology*, **54(3)**, 339-342 (May, 1957).
[36] See Kurt Lewin (cited in footnote 25).
[37] T. G. Alper, "The Interrupted Task Method in Studies of Selective Recall: a Reevaluation of Some Recent Experiments," *Psychological Review*, **59**, 71-88 (1952).
[38] J. W. Atkinson, "The Achievement Motive and Recall of Interrupted and Completed Tasks," *Journal of Experimental Psychology*, **46**, 381-390 (1953).

between achievement of success and avoidance of failure influenced the kinds of risks that individuals prefer. Here we find that motivation may affect recall of incompleted tasks. Again, the connection with Alderson's performance-conscious consumer-buyer is evident. Many shopping tasks are interrupted. Time runs out without enough opportunity to view alternative choices, or a few out of a set of related items may have been purchased, leaving until later the purchases required to round out the assortment. Both of these phenomena appear to be susceptible to incorporation in shopping games in which the shopper is faced with a sequence of decision about acquisition of "products" to fill a set of programmed needs.

FURTHER SUGGESTIONS FOR EXPERIMENTATION

In an experimental game that he designed in the mid-1950's, Alderson found evidence of a low level of search by consumer-buyers.[39] The shopping game is an intriguing one. Ten envelopes containing small slips of paper with a number written on each paper were used. Respondents were instructed to look for the highest possible number, with an incentive to open only a few envelopes. The envelopes are analogous to stores with assortments of goods (numbers), and the objective is to find the best value (highest number) where some cost is attached to shopping or information seeking. Over ten trials per respondent, Alderson found a tendency for subjects not to search further than the first envelope by the fourth trial. This tendency paralleled actual shopping-trip results based on a survey panel. The account is not completely clear on how costly further search was made, and how varied were the assortments of numbers among the various envelopes. However, it is evident that these parameters could be varied, and that the resulting activity could be studied to determine the response in terms of search behavior. The structure of the game could be shifted in various ways. For example, the objective might be to achieve some experience with or to estimate the range of numbers rather than to find the largest number. This would correspond to finding the range or assortment of offerings present in a market. The completeness of the assortment offered by the alternative

[39] Wroe Alderson and Robert E. Sessions, "Consumer Information and Rational Choice," *Cost and Profit Outlook*, 9(3), (March, 1956). See also, Wroe Alderson and Robert E. Sessions, "Basic Research Report on Consumer Behavior," unpublished report on the study of shopping behavior and methods for its investigation, Philadelphia (April, 1957), (mimeographed).

sources could be varied, and the change in search behavior could be studied. There seem to be many possible extensions of this experiment. Another area for study is the influence that group decision making may have on probability choice behavior. Does group participation lead to more conservative behavior in probability choice experiments? What effect would the group have, for example, on individual disposition to overvalue long odds and on the tendency to extreme behavior motivated by individual success and failure attitudes and by position in a game? With a proper design, much might be learned by comparing shopping-game decisions made by husbands and wives separately with decisions made jointly. Other "teams" appropriate to differing situations could be formed by various members of a family.

In studying the characteristics and motivation of subscribers to consumer product-rating publications, Sargent finds readers are more interested in information about comparative consumption merits of products and brands than in discussions of price.[40] This suggests that some buyers may be greatly concerned with payoff and its probability and relatively indifferent to the cost of bets. A promising avenue of investigation may be found in gambling choice and simulated shopping experiments in which costs are subject to some indeterminateness, either random or purposive. How much variation in cost (which need not change expected value) will be tolerated without some change in decision behavior? When variation is recognized and acted upon, what changes in choice behavior occur? In purchase experiments involving coincident information seeking, realism would dictate that information or shopping costs be subject to some random variation. Indeed, we might find some buying situations in which product price or information costs were subject to more uncertainty than payoff. How the consumer-buyer behaves in the face of various sources of uncertainty could prove a fruitful investigation.

Guarantees are a traditional method of reducing consumer uncertainty over the workmanship or functioning of a product. They insure the purchaser against losses arising from failure of the product to meet stipulated conditions or specifications. It is as if near certainty were offered with respect to minimal performance at the same time that the purchaser has to evaluate the probability that other claims made for the product will, in fact, prove valid. The guarantee insures against maximum loss without, apparently, detracting materially from possible gain. Studies of analogous choice problems ought to be capable of casting some light

---

[40] Hugh W. Sargent, *Consumer Product Rating Publications and Buying Behavior*, Urbana, Ill.: Bureau of Economics and Business Research, University of Illinois (December, 1959).

on the kinds of decision problems in which a virtual guarantee of minimal partial payoff has a real attraction for the decision maker. This needs to be supplemented by consumer surveys to determine how guarantees are viewed by prospective purchasers.

The role of information is counted heavily by students of innovation adoption.[41] Innovators have been described as members of active, high-status families who employ technical sources of information and are moved to adopt an innovation by abstract argument. The recognized leaders of the community are not found among these earliest adopters and are moved to accept new practices by demonstration rather than by the abstract scientific arguments that influence the innovators and early adopters. Although the earlier adopters tend to trust expert evidence, the sources of information regarded by later adopters as trustworthy are different from those sources they regard as expert. These are all fairly specific hypotheses about differential acceptance of change among various elements of the population. The verification of these hypotheses in controlled choice experiments would add to their significance.

Particular contributors to this same field have offered generalizations whose content might be incorporated as part of a program of experimentation in consumer decision making. Eisenstadt feels that the specialization of roles that develops in a complex society favors the rise of different sets of opinion leaders and the use of mass media as an information source.[42] Fanelli finds a lack of relation between communicativeness and position in the social structure.[43] Lionberger and Coughenor find that persons seek information from other persons who have a moderately higher prestige rating than themselves.[44] In the adoption of new drugs by physicians, Coleman, Katz, and Menzel find greater personal influence of associates when the performance of the product is regarded as uncertain.[45]

We might expect to find that brand-preference studies have been conducted along lines similar to the innovation-adoption studies. The

[41] See, for example, Everett M. Rogers, *Diffusion of Innovations* (New York: The Free Press of Glencoe, 1962).

[42] S. W. Eisenstadt, "Communication Systems and Social Structures: An Exploratory Comparative Study," *Public Opinion Quarterly*, 19(2), 153-167 (summer 1955).

[43] A. A. Fanelli, "Extensiveness of Communication Contacts and Perceptions of the Community," *American Sociological Review*, 21 (1956).

[44] Herbert F. Lionberger and Milton C. Coughenor, *Social Structure and Diffusion of Farm Information*, Agricultural Experiment Station, College of Agriculture, University of Missouri, Research Bulletin 631, Agriculture Service (April, 1957).

[45] James Coleman, Elihu Katz, and Herbert Menzel, "The Diffusion of an Innovation Among Physicians," *Sociometry*, 20(4), 253-270 (December, 1957).

search for distinguishing characteristics of brand-faithful, brand-adopting, and brand-switching consumers would seem to parallel the attempts to classify various groups of adopters. The marketing literature does not reveal many studies of this kind.[46] It is difficult to believe that sociological and psychological determinants of behavior in the adoption of innovations would be completely without influence in the area of brand-purchase behavior.

Pessemier has reported some work in the measurement of brand preference that is in sympathy with experimental studies advocated here.[47] He used simulated shopping trips in which the price of each subject's favorite brand of toothpaste or cigarettes was persistently increased in relation to other available brands. He also used a choice series in which the alternative brand was simply "a new brand." The results appeared to indicate which members of the groups tested could be most easily swayed from their favorite brands and, also, which of the brands possessed the strongest loyalties. It would be most interesting to supplement this type of experimentation with the administering of some standard personality-measurement tests to see if the early switchers have a different set of psychological traits than those with strong preferences. Experimental research that will permit examination of the personal characteristics of loyalty-prone groups is currently being conducted at Purdue by Pessemier and his associates.

Finally, the probability choice experiment suggests a measure of brand preference that could be compared with the results of relative price variation. The framework would be a brand-preference experiment offering alternative brands as prizes with varying probabilities. The brand chosen with lowest probability is the preferred brand, and the strength of preference can be measured by the extent of further reduction in probability of payoff that will be endured by the choice maker without shifting his choice.

George Katona, through research and writing over a period of years, has been preeminently forceful in calling attention to the importance and frequent neglect of the psychological bases of economic decisions. The

[46] See, however, Ross M. Cunningham, "Brand Loyalty—What, Where, How Much?," *Harvard Business Review*, 34(1), 116-128 (January-February, 1956). The results are rather negative, owing perhaps to the retrospective nature of the study.

[47] Edgar A. Pessemier, "A New Way to Determine Buying Decisions," *Journal of Marketing*, 24(2), 41-46 (October, 1959). For a more complete exposition, see Edgar A. Pessemier, *Experimental Methods of Analyzing Demand for Branded Consumer Goods with Applications to Problems in Marketing Strategy* (Pullman, Wash.: Washington State University Press, 1963).

attitude and anticipations surveys of the Survey Research Center embody this fundamental viewpoint. In *The Powerful Consumer*, Katona presented a summary of insights gained from the work of the Center.[48] He finds that the consumer is fairly rational and not capable of being excessively manipulated because he has a fairly complete knowledge of the economy. His attitudes and anticipations, having an essentially rational basis, do not, on balance, tend to aggravate the cyclical fluctuations of the economy. Katona is concerned with the role of psychological variables on the behavior of the total economy over time. It is conceivable that dynamic aspects could be programmed into simulated sequential decision experiments. Budgets decisions involving the allocation of income over time to consumption goods, durable-goods acquisition, and saving could be studied. Decision behavior over stages of the life cycle could be telescoped through simulation. Although such experimental studies would admittedly be several stages removed from the ongoing complexities of "real world" decision making, they might provide a basis both for generation and confirmation of hypotheses relevant to consumer decision making. The following generalizations from Katona serve to suggest the directions that such work could take.

1. Uniform learning influences opinions and attitudes and causes behavior changes in the same direction for most people.

2. Only under the influence of powerful motivational and attitudinal forces will established principles, rules of thumb, and habitual practices in decision making be abandoned.

3. Orientation toward achievement, in contrast with security, is related to satisfaction with current conditions, and tends to produce higher levels of durable goods consumption and discretionary saving than does an orientation toward security.

Other students have been concerned with the effects of personal differences on risk behavior. Wallach and Kogan studied the effects of age and sex on probability estimates placed on events.[49] They were concerned with extremity of judgment, or the deviation from a 50-50 judgment of the probability of an event, and the confidence expressed by the subject in his probability judgment. They concluded that the young were more disposed to venture extreme judgments with high confidence. Women appeared to make more extreme judgments with high confidence than did men.

[48] George Katona, *The Powerful Consumer* (New York: McGraw-Hill, 1960).
[49] Michael A. Wallach and Nathanial Kogan, "Aspects of Judgment and Decision Making: Interrelationships and Changes with Age," *Behavioral Science*, 6(1), 23-36 (January, 1961).

Wallach and Kogan also devised an index of disutility of failure based on twelve situations in which the respondent indicated the lowest probability that he felt justified undertaking the riskier of the two alternative propositions. A high critical probability level here represents high disutility of failure. Generally speaking, disutility of failure was found to increase with age. If the more elderly are less inclined to extreme probability judgments, less confident in their judgments, and more concerned with consequences of failure than are the young, then we should expect their patterns of response to purchase decisions carrying disparate risks to be quite different from those of the young.

In a number of sociological studies, attitude toward risk has been included. Bohlen and Beal, for example, rated farmers based on responses to ten questions.[50] They found that renters had higher risk propensities than owners, and that those farmers with higher credit outstanding, in general, ranked higher on the risk-preference scale. From an internal analysis of the risk-preference items, they conclude that farmers' goals are more oriented toward improvement of existing land and buildings and the accumulation of savings than toward expanding the farm operation, increasing production, and the like. The typical farmer respondent preferred a smaller farm with less debt to a larger operation requiring debt financing. Bohlen and Beals feel that this reflects a conservative attitude toward risk bearing—that debt financing as a means to the goal of expansion is not acceptable and leads to abandonment of the expansion goal. Nearly 90 percent of the farmers surveyed agreed to the statement that it is desirable for every farm family to get out of debt as soon as possible.

Martineau draws psychological portraits of middle- and lower-status groups that have implications for decision making involving risk and uncertainty.[51] He finds middle-class persons future oriented, possessed of a sense of rationality and awareness of purposive choice making, willing to tolerate risk, and capable of abstract thinking. In contrast, lower-status individuals are more concerned with the past and present, have a more limited sense of rational choice making, are concerned more with security, and are inclined to think concretely and perceptively rather than abstractly. The relevance of these factors to choice behavior indicates the importance of using social class as a control variable in any experimental program in consumer decision making.

[50] Joe Bohlen and George M. Beal, "Sociological and Social Psychological Factors Related to Credit Use Patterns," paper presented at Annual Convention of T. V. A. Cooperators, Knoxville, Tennessee (March 27-29, 1960).
[51] Pierre Martineau, "Social Classes and Spending Behavior," *Journal of Marketing,* 23(2), 121-129 (October, 1958).

CHOICE AS PSYCHOPHYSICS

In psychophysical terms, choice experiments deal with three fundamental variables. First is the stimulus magnitude, R. In classical psychophysics, this is a physically measurable variable such as weight, pressure, brightness of light, and so on. In a money-utility relationship, this would be the amount of money. In an experiment involving money gambles, it is the probability-prize offer. Where there is an objective probability we might say that the stimulus magnitude is the expected value of the gamble; that is, its objective expected value. Second, there is the psychological or subjective sensation, S. In a money-utility relationship, this is the utility. In an experiment involving money gambles, it is the subjective expected utility. If the experiment involves choices among goods, the psychological sensation is still subjective expected utility, although the stimulus magnitude is multidimensional, involving all the product attributes or qualities. The stimulus magnitudes mentioned above were either one dimensional (money amounts for certain) or, possibly, two dimensional (probability-payoff combinations). Finally, the third variable is consistency of choice. In classical psychophysics, this is the confusion of the stimulus, and one measure of this is the proportion of judgments or preference of one stimulus over another. Let us identify this as P.

Three famous psychophysical relationships deal with various pairs of these variables, R, S, and P.[52] Weber's law states that the proportion of judgments that R is greater than $K(R)$, where K is a constant, is itself a constant. Translated into a gambling-choice experiment, this would assert that the proportion of times a subject chooses an alternative with, for instance, 1.2 times the expected value of a competing alternative, is a constant, regardless of the levels of expected values involved.

The second relationship is the R versus S, or stimulus versus subjective sensation relationship. Fechner asserted that this takes a logarithmic form $S = K$ (log R), or that a psychological magnitude (for example, utility) varies with the logarithm of the objective stimulus (for example, money). This is the relationship that Bernoulli posited.

The third relationship, that between the proportion of judgments, P, and the subjective sensation, S, is involved in Thurstone's "law of comparative judgment." This is a method for determining an interval scale for the psychological sensation—a necessity for empirical investigations

[52] See "Three Psychophysical Laws," in L. L. Thurstone, *The Measurement of Values* (Chicago: University of Chicago Press, 1959), 61-66.

concerned with the other two relationships. The central concept here is the discriminal dispersion, or variance of the judgments rendered in conjunction with a particular choice experiment or decision environment. The discriminal dispersion becomes the scale unit, and the psychological distances are measured as so many of these units. This allows us to compare distances between the psychological sensations—as, for example, to say that the preference for A over B is twice the preference for B over C. But we cannot compare absolute magnitudes, as would be required if we wanted to go from the above to saying that A is twice as desirable as B and three times as desirable as C.

In 1931, Thurstone published a paper on "The Indifference Function."[53] He credits his colleague, Professor Henry Schultz of the University of Chicago, for the suggestion that psychophysical methods be applied to this problem in economics. Using variations from a "standard combination" of eight hats and eight right shoes, he elicited from a subject indications of preference, or lack of preference, for other combinations on the indifference map. These form a topographic map of plus and minus points. Then an equation, derived by assuming that Fechner's law holds for the utility function for hats and for shoes, is fitted to this map. This is the indifference curve. Thurstone constructs also an indifference curve for hats versus overcoats from indicated preferences, and then uses this in conjunction with the curve for hats and shoes to predict the indifference curve for shoes versus overcoats. The predicted indifference curves appear to agree well with the observational curve for shoes versus overcoats. In deriving his model, Thurstone speaks of what we call the marginal utility as "motivation." In his words, "motivation is defined quantitatively as the anticipated increment in satisfaction per unit increase in the commodity."[54] On the economic and psychological aspects of the measurement of values, Thurstone comments:[55]

In the measurement of utility the psychologist and the economist are dealing with overlapping problems. The utility concept is essentially the same as that of mean affective value for the individual. The addition of a parameter for dispersion could lead to interesting results for psychological and economic theory. Consider, for example, a surface whose base coordinates represent the amount of two commodities and whose ordinates represent the associated utility of affective value for the individual. Horizontal sections of the surface

[53] See L. L. Thurstone, "The Indifference Function," in L. L. Thurstone, Reference (52), 123-144.
[54] Ibid., p. 125.
[55] L. L. Thurstone, "The Prediction of Choice," in L. L. Thurstone, The Measurement of Values (Chicago: University of Chicago Press, 1954), p. 156.

give a family of indifference curves whereas vertical sections, parallel to either base give satisfaction curves which are interpreted as Fechner's law. Now, if dispersions in affective values among individuals are introduced as new parameters, we have the possibility of summing the effects for individuals to that of the group. Further, the first derivative of the satisfaction curve at any point is the motivation of the individual with reference to the commodity concerned.

At the time of Thurstone's encounter with economics, economists were little concerned with the measurement of utility beyond an ordinal scale. There appear to be four methods that can lead to an interval scale, or ordered metric scale of utility.[56] The first method is to assume that the difference in utility between pairs of alternatives is a function of the difficulty of choosing between them. If I prefer A over B and B over C but have a harder time deciding between B and C, then the utility distance between A and B is greater than that between B and C. We have already mentioned the idea of determining comparative differences in utilities through a measure of consistency of choice or judgments. This is the method that appears most directly related to classical psychophysical methods. The third method is to assume that the utilities are additive, and to observe preferences for various composite offerings made up of combinations of elemental offerings. Regarding additivity of utilities, E. W. Adams states that "the abandonment of this hypothesis, due to the general recognition of the fact that it is obviously false if applied in full generality led directly to the rise of the ordinalist school of economic theorists and the belief that the only observable consequences of statements about utility are simple preferences."[57] The fourth approach to deriving an interval scale of utility is Von Neuman's standard gamble technique.

While Thurstone is best known for his contributions to multifactor analysis, he regarded as more important his contributions to psychophysics. One of his last studies, completed by Lyle V. Jones after Thurstone's death in 1955,[58] was concerned with a rational origin for the scale of measurement of subjective values. In the paper as finally published, reference is made to earlier work of Horst in 1932 on the same problem. Horst asked his subjects to consider if they would be willing to accept a

[56] See Ernest W. Adams, "Survey of Bernoullian Utility Theory," in Herbert Solomon (editor), *Mathematical Thinking in the Measurement of Behavior* (Glencoe, Ill.: The Free Press, 1960), 155-264.

[57] *Ibid.*, p. 164.

[58] L. L. Thurstone and Lyle V. Jones, "The Rational Origin for Measuring Subjective Values," L. L. Thurstone (editor), *The Measurement of Values* (Chicago: University of Chicago Press, 1959), 195-212.

given negatively valued proposal in order to obtain a particular positively valued proposal. An example would be "sit through a boring lecture and attend the world series." If the proportion of subjects accepting the proposal is greater than 0.50, then the positive affective value of the advantage exceeds the negative affective value of the disadvantage. The law of comparative judgment will not only scale the distance between the proposals, but can be used to locate the zero or indifference level of affective value between them. If a number of these comparisons are made, and the calculated zero points cluster at a particular location, Horst would take this point as the rational origin of subjective scale. Thurstone and Jones use a similar procedure to calculate implied zero points when the items compared are all of positive affective value. They feel that, in some contexts, it is difficult to find objects, propositions, and the like, with negative affective value.

For Thurstone and Jones, derivation of a cardinal scale of utility has several advantages. It would make combinations of utilities more amenable to study, and it would permit studies of the relation between utility and price. The choices in their experiments, conducted with business administration students at North Carolina University, were a briefcase, a dictionary, a record player, a desk lamp, and a pen and pencil set. A rational origin is found for the utility scale. According to the results, we should predict that the record player would be preferred to the dictionary, briefcase, and desk lamp combined, despite the fact that the price of the dictionary alone exceeded that of the record player.

The method used by Thurstone and Jones assumes that utilities are additive. It is possible to check this assumption within the context of the experimental data. They appear to feel that this assumption would not be seriously violated when the choices involved are among a limited number of pairs of objects that are not dependent in their functions and not substitutes for one another.

CONCLUSION

Regarding the consumer-buyer as a Bayesian decision maker may seem, at first glance, to be an unworkable abstraction. Joseph Clawson once assembled a list of twenty-four problem-solving functions connected with a buying decision.[59] These ranged through transporting and storing,

59 J. C. Clawson, "Problem-Solving Functions in the Behavior of Households," *Cost and Profit Outlook*, Philadelphia, Alderson and Sessions, (September, 1957).

communicating with users and assessing results, repair and maintenance, and disposal of used resources. There are uncertainties about consumption occasions, about the relevance and credibility of advertising claims. Nevertheless, decisions are made, and it may be useful to assume that a value scale for equating differing benefits at different future times and with differing probabilities exists. This Bayesian formulation, supported by tools from the fields of scaling and modern psychophysics, may offer a promising field for experimental research in consumer decision making.

Experimental Work in Marketing: Current Research and New Developments

The purpose of this chapter is to report on current experimental research in marketing and to suggest some of the new developments that are taking place. The scope of the chapter is restricted by my own limitations concerning my awareness or lack of awareness of research projects that utilize some variety of experimental technique. Published articles represent the primary source, although there are included several reports of unpublished research. Undoubtedly there are omissions that may be obvious to many of you, but there has been an attempt made to be as inclusive as possible under the existing time and resource restraints. A bibliography of materials used is included at the end of this chapter.[1]

The scope and the coverage of this chapter include the following.

1. What is an experiment?
2. Subject areas in marketing experimental research.
3. The laboratory, field, simulation, and other experiments.
4. Ingredients of the experiment.
   a. Statement of problem and hypotheses.
   b. Independent variables.
   c. Manipulations.
   d. Dependent variables.
   e. Controlling the variables.
   f. Randomization.
   g. Experimental design.
5. Concluding comments.

[1] Both Robert Ferber of the *JMR* and Steuart H. Britt of the *Journal of Marketing* are to be credited with including many experimentally oriented articles in the two journals.

WHAT IS AN EXPERIMENT?

Prior to examining the literature, the question "What is an experiment?" was not seriously considered. However, the literature includes a wide variety of research studies under the heading of experimentation. Those who have written on research methodology tend to reflect a degree of precision in defining terms that has not always been carried out by those conducting experiments. Thus, the literature includes reports that range from simple testing of two alternatives to extremely sophisticated research efforts that utilize the best available experimental designs.

Because it was the purpose of this chapter to report on experimentation in a general way, it was decided to follow a loose kind of definition: "An experiment is what the researcher defines as an experiment." Included, therefore, are studies that did not have randomization of treatments, some that gave little evidence of any control of extraneous variables, some that are simple tests, and some that are experiments by any definition.

Experimentation has become a familiar technique and a potentially more important method of conducting research than it was a few years ago. Experimentation is not a new technique for many academic and applied areas of research and, indeed, there were marketing experiments reported half a century or so ago. However, the experiment is now being tried by many researchers in marketing and it is being considered by others.

Universities have constructed laboratories for experiments in business fields and the laboratory here at Purdue is undoubtedly one of the best of these developments. University courses have been added to the curriculum in order to expose the new business student to experimentation. These courses are in various fields, including quantitative analysis and marketing.

Marketing research firms are now advertising their availability for research involving the use of the experimental design. Businesses are conducting experiments. It is safe to conjecture that although the literature contains a good number of experimental research studies, there are many, many more unreported studies.

This chapter is based on an examination of over one hundred reported experiments in marketing. A few early studies reported in the 1920's and 1930's have been included but, for the most part, the studies have been reported during the last decade. Approximately one hundred experimental studies have been reported (plus any omissions made here) since 1955.

1966: 10	1959: 5
1965: 18	1958: 5
1964: 17	1957: 4
1963: 11	1956: 2
1962: 8	1955: 1
1961: 11	Earlier: 10-20
1960: 6	

The increasing use of experimentation is characteristic of most marketing subject areas. Whether the topic is pricing, marketing research technique, or simulation, there has been an increasing number of experiments reported.

SUBJECT AREAS IN MARKETING EXPERIMENTAL RESEARCH

The experiments reported cover a rather wide range of marketing activities. They include the very theoretical and the practical everyday kind of marketing activity. The following list of subjects has been arranged arbitrarily, although hopefully it will prove an adequate way in which to illustrate the subject range of experiments.

Persuasion	Simulation games
Merchandising	Taste
Theoretical	Communications
Marketing research	Perception
Pricing	Social-ethical

The area in which the largest number of experiments have been reported is that of *persuasion*. In this category are included experiments dealing with advertisements shown in the various media. Sales, profit, recall, recognition, preference, and other ways to measure impact have been used as the dependent variables. The role of the *Journal of Advertising Research* is very evident since approximately half the articles in this category have appeared in that journal.

Persuasion

Value of repeat exposures
Success of television commercials
Measuring advertising effect
Effects of television
Television:
  Night versus Day

Spot versus Network
Frequency of commercial
Effect of blank space in ads
Promotion expenditures and sales
Advertising and brand preference
Effect of "local color" in ads
Effect of color in ads
Effects of product, appeal and program on commercials
Size of advertisement
Recall versus projection
Source effects
Value of advertising a television show
Promotion and test marketing

We shall look at one or two examples in each of the various fields. In persuasion, Schrimper and Peeler [35] point out that, in 1965, twelve hundred farm groups spent over $90 million for promotional efforts. Their own study of the effectiveness of promotion was undertaken to assess the value of promotion on egg purchases (Fig. 14.1). Three groups of consumers were selected from the North Carolina state consumer panel.

Group A received three promotional pieces at two-week intervals.

Group B (Control) received no promotional pieces during the six months' study.

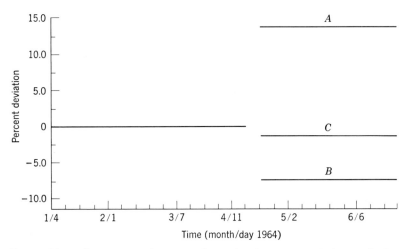

Figure 14.1. Comparison of egg purchases for three groups before and after mail-outs after adjusting for other factors affecting purchases including separate price response for each group.

Group C received a single letter (identical to the first one for A). Group A purchase records showed an increase of 13.5 percent above their previous level of purchases. Group C had a small decline and the control group B showed a 7.4 percent decline. The study indicated, however, that between 21 and 72 weeks (depending upon egg prices) of sustained higher purchasing rate of eggs would be necessary to break even on the promotional costs.

Becknell [12] has reported on a number of experiments, including one on the influence of newspaper tune-in advertising. That is, does it pay the sponsor to advertise in the local newspaper about his special TV program? Becknell selected 21 cities that were randomly assigned to groups receiving normal, double and no tune-in advertising for a special TV program. The ad appeared on April 21, the day of the show. That evening, 375 telephone calls were made in an effort to determine the percentage of viewers. The percentage of viewers in April as compared with four previous viewings is shown in Table 14.1.

TABLE 14.1

Mean Percent Claimed Viewing		
City Group	April	Four Shows' Average
B (none)	13.7	16.5
A (normal)	13.8	18.3
C (double)	15.6	19.1

The differences among the experimental groups were not significant but the differences between the April (advertised) viewing and the previous (normal-advertised) viewing were significant and in favor of the normal-advertised viewing. The study showed, however, that the audience may have been less variable (that is, more homogeneous) when advertising was used.

The general area of *merchandising* has been the focal point for many experiments. Agricultural marketing personnel have examined a number of variables in connection with eggs, fruit, and milk. Most of these studies have been in-store studies. The Latin-square design has been rather popular with these experiments, probably due to the influence of the agricultural researchers who have performed some fine experimental research studies.

Merchandising

The stocking of shelves and profitability.
Promotion, display, package, quality, price.
Size of package and pricing unit.
Location, size, and use of pictures in displays.
Branded versus unbranded products.
Shopping cart displays.
Merchandising factors and retail sales.
Changes in window trim.
Shelf space and product sales.
Number of brands.
Package design.
Point-of-sale promotion.

An early merchandising experiment was reported in 1950 [98]. In this study, the manager of a New England supermarket discovered that small, hard-to-stack, high-margin items could be displayed in a shopping cart with the effect of getting increased sales. Twenty-eight items ranging from popping corn to scouring pads were displayed in shopping carts and a simple hand-printed sign was affixed to each. Normal movement of the 28 items was watched the previous week and was used as a base for the experimental period when the items were placed into the carts. Sample results of this experiment are shown in Table 14.2.

TABLE 14.2

Items	I Sales During Week Preceding Cart Display	II Sales During Week of Cart Display	Percent of Change, I to II
Pillsbury Pie Crust	36	176	+ 390
General Mills Pie Crust	8	6	− 25
Duffy-Matt Jellies	17	108	+ 535
Borden Cheese	3	83	+2666
Nestle Toll House Morsels	24	207	+ 762
Overall, including items not listed here			+ 118

A more recent study that related merchandising decisions to profitability is the Buzzell-Salmon-Vancil study [87]. The purpose of the study was to develop and evaluate a method of measuring the performance of individual products. Research was conducted in 16 supermarkets with four "product families" in which changes in product assortments and space allocation were introduced. One of the hypotheses that was supported by the study was the following:

If an item with a relatively low DPP/CF is eliminated, and if the space released by the elimination is assigned to a relatively high-profit item, then total profit for the product family will increase. (DPP/CF = direct product profit per cubic foot.)

This merchandising experiment involved many of the research problems that confront the experimenter. The selection of stores (8 Stop & Shop stores and 8 Hannaford Brothers stores) represented a major decision in the research procedure. The product families chosen represented another. The method of reallocating and eliminating space had to be worked out carefully. As the authors indicated, the imperfect conditions reduced their 64 conditions to 17. Still, the results are valuable for those handling space allocation for products, since profit is clearly related to that decision (Table 14.3).

Field-type marketing experiments are typically of an applied nature whereas the *theoretical* studies tend to be run in a laboratory, usually a university facility where the subjects are college students. There are examples, however, of a theory being taken later to the field for a "real" test. The following list is heavy with studies of dissonance, one of the more applicable psychological theories.

Theoretical Studies
Dissonance and the purchasing of automobiles.
Dissonance and the selection of information.
Reevaluating purchasing alternatives.
Number of choices facing the buyer.
Preferences before and after purchase.
Familiarity and dissonance.
Self-confidence and exposure to information.
Regret following the purchase.
Decision making among imperfect alternatives.
Anticipating dissonance.
Interactions among dissonance factors.
Personality and the type of advertisement.
Attitude change.
Customer effort, expectation, and satisfaction.
Group influences upon consumer brand preferences.
Conformity and reactance in purchase situations.

TABLE 14.3 RESULTS OF ITEM ELIMINATION EXPERIMENTS.
(SS—STOP & SHOP; H—HANNAFORD BROTHERS
AFFILIATE)

	Direct Product Profit (Dollars) Per Cubic Foot in Base Period		Percentage Change from Base Period to Experimental Period			
						Product Family Total
Product Family and Store (1)	Elimi- nated Item (2)	Replace- ment Item (3)	Replacement Item		Direct Product Profit (6)	Direct Product Profit per Cubic Foot (7)
			Shelf Space (4)	Sales (5)		
Family A:						
H–1	0.02[a]	0.11	+ 47	+ 23	+33	+41
Family B:						
SS–1	0.36	0.65	+ 55	− 32	−17	−10
SS–2[b]	0.97	0.67	+ 33	− 8	−45	−38
SS–3[b]	0.15	0.80	+100	+101	− 5	+81
H–1	0.84	0.50	+ 34	+ 88	+ 8	+ 4
Family C:						
SS–1	1.17	0.41	+ 52	+ 9	−45	−45
H–1	0.48	0.63	+ 19	+ 51	− 9	+ 2
Family D:						
SS–1	0.55	1.18	+ 55	+ 41	+ 8	+11
H–1	0.99	0.43	+ 67	+ 9	−13	−17

[a] Loss.
[b] Discount supermarket.

Cardozo [107] performed a laboratory experiment in which he tested the effects of effort and expectation on satisfaction. He worked with inexpensive ball-point pens as the product. He converted a classroom into a laboratory by fashioning booths made from several yards of wrapping paper held in place by cellophane tape. Effort was developed by using blinking overhead lights, small soft-lead pencils, a boring and, in some ways, difficult task. Expectation was manipulated through catalogs of ball-point pens wherein the prices differed according to the condition desired. Two branches of psychological theory (contrast theory and dis-

sonance theory) were used as the basis for hypothesizing the relationships between effort and expectations, on the one hand, and satisfaction
on the other. The theoretical study was set up as follows:

	Expectation	
Effort	Low	High
Low	A	B
High	C	D

After running 107 students through the various conditions, Cardozo
concluded that satisfaction may be higher when customers expend considerable effort to obtain the product than when they use only modest
effort. Satisfaction is lower when the product does not come up to expectations than when the product meets expectations. Since these factors
are involved in most consumer buying situations, implications for marketing are somewhat intriguing.

In another theoretical study, Stafford [115] used the group-influence
theory in relation to brand preferences of group members. Stafford used
ten informal groups in one census tract in Austin, Texas. Preferences were
given for four slices of white bread, identical, of course. The results indicated that consumers are influenced by informal groups and that the
extent and degree of brand-loyalty behavior within a group is more
closely related to the behavior of the informal leader than to the cohesive-
ness of the group.

Researchers are continually checking their techniques and it is helpful
to them to have the experimental method to examine the relative efficiency of alternative *marketing research* techniques. It is quite certain
that many experiments have been conducted along these lines although
only a few are included here.

Marketing Research

Alternative methods of paying interviewers.
Effects of interviewing designated respondents.
Interviewer bias in selecting households.
Comparisons among coders.
Increasing the rate of return in mail surveys.
A study of paired comparisons.
Product-testing alternatives.

A rather unusual kind of study was performed by Carter, Troldahl, and
Schuneman [41]. They wanted to determine if interviewers who were
assigned sex and age quotas in small block clusters exhibited bias in their

selections of households. To check this, the researchers had the interviewers select houses for a study that the interviewers supposed was a
regular marketing survey. Pictures were taken of the chosen house and of
the rejected house on either the right or left of the chosen. These pairs
of pictures were then shown to a class of students who, in turn, made a
choice as they played the role of interviewers who were selecting respondents. The results indicated that interviewers do utilize nonrandom
bases for selecting sample households, and that there is consistency in
these biases across interviewers. Interviewers tended to select households
that they "liked" and that they perceived as having a relatively high
income.

Perhaps a more typical kind of technique research is illustrated by
Kimball [45]. Seeking to increase the rate of return in mail surveys, he
set up a single experiment to examine the drawing power of three incentives. He used a very large sample: 3000 randomly selected names
that were subsequently separated into six subsamples of 500 each. Results were highly significant (Table 14.4).

TABLE 14.4 NUMBERS OF RETURNS FOR TESTED INCENTIVE
VARIATIONS

Group	Number of Sample	Number of Returns		Incentive Variations	
A	500	174	No coin	Dear Sir	Airmail stamp
B	500	130	No coin	Dear Sir	Airmail permit
C	500	169	No coin	Personal address	Airmail stamp
D	500	134	No coin	Personal address	Airmail permit
E	500	223	10¢ coin	Dear Sir	Airmail stamp
F	500	191	10¢ coin	Dear Sir	Airmail permit

Groups A versus B, C versus D, and E versus F provided the information on postage. The airmail stamp provided increased returns of 34, 26,
and 17 percent over the airmail permit. Groups A versus C and B versus D
varied on the address detail and here the respondent's name on the
cover letter did not help very much. Groups A versus E and B versus F
indicated that a 10-cent coin increased returns of 28 and 47 percent. This
rather straightfoward test of three incentives could be used with other
kinds of alternatives (for instance, follow-ups, art work, promises of
results, and premiums).

Pricing research has been primarily of three types: price and demand, psychological pricing, and the relationship between price and quality. The effect of price on demand is clearly one of the important problems facing most businesses and it would seem that pricing research would be reported more frequently in the journals than it actually has been.

Pricing Experiments

Price and demand (frozen orange juice).
Price and demand (skim milk).
Odd-even pricing.
Pricing of a new product.
Price and quality relationship.
Price and quality and demand.
Learning prices.

The reluctance of managers to experiment with prices is perhaps understandable, in part, but it is difficult entirely to condone this hands-off attitude. In 1936, Ginsberg [49] developed an experiment with mail-order catalogs (six million copies of the spring edition). The experiment revealed conflicting information, and the manager's zeal, according to Ginsberg, was held in check when he found that a change of one cent a yard on one item led to a loss of $50,000. Apparently, the manager was not interested in $50,000 gains.

A frequent complaint made of marketing studies is that they are shallow, one-shot varieties of research. However, Baker and Berry [47] reported on the price elasticity of demand for fluid skim milk, a study that lasted four years! The University of Connecticut Dairy supplied one community with its milk and, therefore, the experimenters had some control over price and "competition." At the time of reporting, the study was only one year old and so the results were not available. However, the design is interesting since it was a Latin-square that assigned skim and whole milk price differentials over a four-year period with each yearly period itself being divided into four bimonthly subperiods, summer months excluded but "controlled" (Table 14.5).

In recent years, there has been a tendency to delve into the psychological aspects of pricing. At the University of Minnesota, we have attempted to learn more about some of the psychological aspects of pricing. The first question asked concerned the relative merits of odd versus even pricing. Nothing could be found in the literature to prove that odd pricing was superior, but surveys of retailers certainly indicated that they believed in psychological pricing. The psychological price may or may not be an odd price, as it depends upon a number of factors. That is, retailers

TABLE 14.5

	Year I	Year II	Year III	Year IV
Preperiod	A	B	D	C
Subperiods				
1	A_a	B_b	D_d	C_c
2	B_a	D_b	C_d	A_c
3	C_b	A_d	B_c	D_a
4	D_c	C_a	A_b	B_d

Key. A, 6¢ differential; B, 2¢ differential; C, 4¢ differential; and D, 8¢ differential.

felt that, if they wanted to sell a prestige item, they could round off the price to give the right effect but, if they wanted to imply a bargain, they should use one of the odd prices, even $24,999 for a home.

The literature did reveal that studies of frequencies of pricing did clearly show that retailers have favorite prices which (according to some of the articles) means that the retailers knew how to use psychological pricing. Here, however, is where the experiment should be able to provide a cause-and-effect relationship, if one exists. A survey of the frequency of each advertised price offers no such cause-and-effect relationship.

It was decided first to test the concepts of "bargain" and "quality." The initial study in the program was an attempt to determine if perceptions of product "quality" and "bargain" exist and, further, to determine the extent to which these perceptions would be affected by prices. It was hypothesized that, for a particular product, an "even" price (zero final digit) would elicit perceptions of higher product quality than the same product carrying an "odd" price (nonzero final digit). It was also predicted that odd prices would be perceived as greater "bargains" than would even prices. Responses, elicited for twenty-four products ranging in price from less than one dollar to more than two hundred dollars (from two independent groups of subjects), produced these findings:

1. Averaged over the twenty-four products, the "even" priced items were perceived as being of higher quality than the same product carrying an "odd" price.

2. Averaged over the twenty-four products, the "odd" priced items were seen as being greater bargains than the same item carrying an "even" price.

3. As the absolute level of price increased there was an increase in the perception of product quality and a decrease in the perception of the product's being a bargain.

In an attempt to explore more explicitly the relationship apparent from the initial study, three other studies were run.

The second study was intended as a modified replication of the first study as well as an attempt to assess the effects of a number of different "odd" prices within a product class. Using male subjects, ratings of three white dress shirts (cotton, cotton/polyester blend, and polyester) were obtained on "bargain" and "quality" dimensions. The results confirmed the inverse relationship between perceptions of quality and bargain when averaged over the three shirts. Within shirt types, however, the relationship was not uniformly upheld. Further analysis of the data and the experimental procedure suggested that a halo effect was unintentionally created in describing one of the shirts, thus biasing perceptions of that particular item.

A third study was run in order to investigate differences in the accuracy with which a price of a product was recalled. Within nine products of three price levels ($15.00, $5.00, and $1.00), systematic manipulation of the last two digits of the price yielded no significant difference in accuracy of recall for any of the price variations. The trend of the data indicate, however, that the absolute error or price recall increased as the price varied from the zero-zero ending digits. The interpretation given to these findings is that there may be a tendency to recall only the first two digits (the dollar digits) of the price.

The final study utilized a milk-shake mix product that was in test-marketing status. Four experimental groups saw the product priced at either five, ten, fifteen, or nineteen cents. Two control groups saw the product but were not given its price. A semantic differential scale was used to measure subjects' associations with the product. Contrary to expectation, it was found that, as price level increased, evaluation of the product decreased. The two control groups evaluated the product in a manner almost identical to the ten-cent price group, although, as might be expected, the variation in responses of the controls was much greater than that of the experimental groups. Prices may affect expectation that, in turn, may affect satisfaction.

A fairly recent type of experiment in marketing is that of *simulation*, a situation in which subjects simulate buying activities under certain conditions. Pessemier has contributed much to this type of experiment through his own work and through the work of his students.

Simulation Games

Shopping-behavior game with stores.
Product line selection.
Brand switching.

Choices in a game situation.
Competitive market behavior.
Risk and innovation.

This kind of experiment is in between the laboratory and the real market place. It permits the manipulation of price or other variables in a simulated buying situation and, hopefully, the subject responds as if he were actually purchasing the item. Let us examine three different studies in this category.

Alderson and Sessions [55] developed a shopping game that utilized envelopes for retail stores. The contents of the envelope were descriptions of items of merchandise. In this way, the independent variables of merchandise lines and price ranges could be manipulated. The consumer could tell by the envelope whether he was "in" a store that had wide, narrow, or medium price and product lines. Decisions on buying reflected his preferences of width of product and price lines (Table 14.6).

TABLE 14.6 CHARACTERISTICS OF THE FIRST SET OF GAME "STORES"

Store Name	Number of Merchandise Lines	Number of Items per Line	Total Number of Items	Price Range (Dollars)
Brown	2	8	16	$6.00–$ 8.00
Davis	2	8	16	5.00– 9.00
Green	2	8	16	3.50– 10.50
Hoffman	4	4	16	6.00– 8.00
Johnson	4	4	16	5.00– 9.00
Miller	4	4	16	3.50– 10.50
Smith	8	2	16	6.00– 8.00
Williams	8	2	16	5.00– 9.00
Wood	8	2	16	3.50– 10.50

An interesting aspect of the Alderson and Sessions study was that the researchers also had a panel of housewives and the panel results were compared to the experimental results.

Pessemier [58] simulated market conditions and explored brand-switching and brand-loyalty patterns. He found that 53 percent of all buyers could be switched to a second-choice brand of toothpaste with a $0.03 increase in the price of their first choice. In some instances, the less popu-

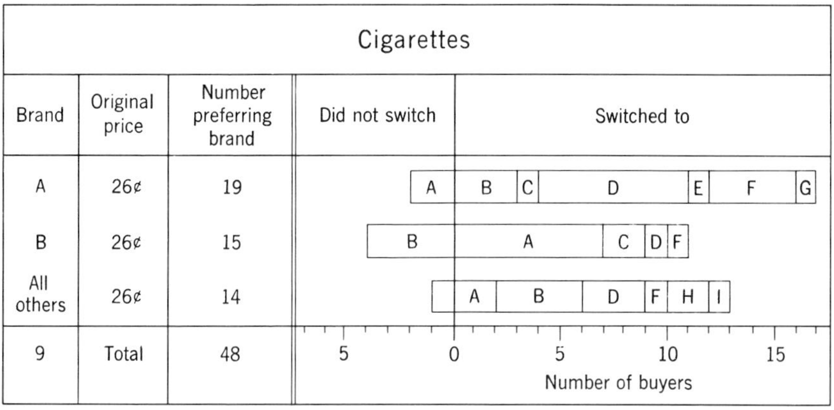

Cigarettes				
Brand	Original price	Number preferring brand	Did not switch	Switched to
A	26¢	19		A B C D E F G
B	26¢	15		B A C D F
All others	26¢	14		A B D F H I
9	Total	48		5 0 5 10 15 Number of buyers

Figure 14.2. Comparison of brand-switching patterns for individual brands of cigarettes.

lar brands had strong brand loyalties. The amount of brand switching varied considerably among products and among brands. In the case of cigarettes, the leading brand was not able to hold many of its customers through the full $0.10 range that its prices increased during the manipulation (Fig. 14.2).

A slightly different kind of simulation or game is that suggested by A. J. Wood [57]. Charts can be used to offer the subjects the alternatives or alternatives can be given in the form of multiple-choice questions. An example of one combination follows in Table 14.7.

TABLE 14.7

Brand	Store Type	Distance
Brand S	Candy Store	1 block
Brand B	Drug Store	2 blocks
Brand A	Supermarket	3 blocks
Brand S	Drug Store	1 block
Brand B	Supermarket	2 blocks
Brand A	Candy Store	3 blocks
Brand S	Supermarket	1 block
Brand B	Candy Store	2 blocks
Brand A	Drug Store	3 blocks

TABLE 14.8

	Preference		
Product	First	Second	Third
Aspirin	Convenience	Price	Brand
Toothpaste	Ingredient	Convenience	Price
Ball-point pens	Price	Retailer	Brand
Sporting events	Team	Price	Convenience
Cigarettes	Convenience	Brand	Price
Gasoline	Price	Brand	Convenience
Magazines	Brand	Price	Retailer
Haircuts	Convenience	Price	Barber shop
Lipstick (girls only)	Brand	Price	Convenience

Variations of this technique were used for a marketing class at the University of Minnesota with the results shown in Table 14.8.

One of the areas of experimentation that is between the technical and the marketing fields is that of *taste* testing. Usually there is a preference aspect involved, although sometimes it is a matter of identification or quality.

Taste Tests

Amount of information given.
Identification of a flavor.
Perceived taste and brand preference.
Sucrose versus glucose.
Taste sensitivity: time of day.

Thousands of taste experiments are run annually by the many food companies in the United States. Instead of examining a conventional type of comparison test, we have selected two less ordinary experiments. The first was performed by Makens [64] who wanted to determine the effect of brand information on taste preferences. Makens had a sample of 150 consumers who were drawn from a Michigan State University consumer preference panel of Detroit area consumers. One turkey was roasted and similar size samples were cut from one section of the breast and evenly divided on two ceramic plates. Behind one plate was a plastic bag that identified a brand well known in the Detroit area while behind the second plate was a plastic bag bearing an unknown brand. Consumers were told the samples came from two turkeys of the brands shown behind the plates. They were asked to compare the taste and texture of the two samples and to rank them on a scale. The consumers also indicated their preferences, if they had any. The results clearly showed the influence of the known brand. Only 15 subjects indicated that the samples tasted alike; the preference for the known versus the unknown brand was 56% to 34%.

A second experiment in this area of food preferences is that performed by Kamen and Eindhoven [63]. They wanted to determine if the amount of information given to persons would affect their ratings of unfamiliar foods. Three types of instructional sets were given to people tasting both familiar and unfamiliar foods. *Set I* was the normal set usually given to tastetesters in their laboratory: "Indicate how much you like or dislike each food." *Set II* indicated that the foods were intended as a short-term dietary or ration and that these would be used only in an emergency. *Set III* indicated that the foods would be used as part of a long-term austere dietary, by men living at isolated radar outposts where the work is routine and nonhazardous but may last for months at a time. Familiar foods were a vanilla-cream bar and a chocolate-fudge bar. Unfamiliar foods were specially prepared 7 gram tablets of compressed cheddar cheese and dehydrated cottage cheese and 8.5 gram tablets consisting mainly of compressed sausage. Twenty-four testers were assigned to each of the three sets of instructions. Presentation was randomized, rinse charcoal-filtered distilled water was provided, and adequate quantities were given to the testers. The results indicated that the instructional sets had no effect for familiar foods but, for unfamiliar foods, minimal instructions yielded the greatest difference in preference ratings, less with the short-term instructions and almost none for the long-term set.

New-product research is one of the most common types of marketing research but the literature does not include vast numbers of experiments with new products. There is, of course, a great deal of test marketing and certainly many of these studies could be classed as types of experimental efforts.

Two studies are cited here because they illustrate the usual and the unusual in new-product experiments. The first has to do with the testing of Crest toothpaste [75]. On the basis of tests, the Council on Dental Therapeutics of the American Dental Association accepted the claims made by Proctor & Gamble for Crest and permitted the company to quote the Council. Crest's laboratory tests began in 1945 and continued for 7 years. Clinical tests then began and by 1960 the Council recognized Crest's efficacy.

Dr. Joseph C. Muhler of Indiana University conducted many of the tests. He had run these tests on thirty-six hundred Bloomington children and Indiana University students, half using the new toothpaste and half using a nonfluoride exactly the same except for the absence of the fluoride. Students were handed plain white tubes of toothpaste, each marked only with a small symbol: a cross, a square, a triangle. Neither Muhler nor any of his associates knew the key to these markets; only an independent statistician had the answers to the code. The results indicated statistically significant differences and the rest of the story is well known. Incidentally, dentists err considerably in their identification of cavities and procedures had to be set up to check on their detection work.

A very different kind of new-product study was performed in a laboratory by Walter Gruen [77]. Gruen wanted to determine if some people prefer new styles and new exteriors regardless of the type of product. He prepared thirty slides that included ten groups of three each of different styles or patterns. The products were all contemporary, but it was known that they had existed for some time. For example, one group of slides consisted of three pictures of living room furniture, one labeled as a 1950 to 1956 pattern of so-and-so company. A second slide was labeled as a 1957 to 1959 product of the same company, and a third slide was labeled as a product of a different company without the benefit of a date. Thus, there were ten slides of relatively new products, ten of products several years older, and ten so-called neutral slides. They were scrambled and presented in a random order. A fairly elaborate disguise was used and a number of dependent measures were obtained.

The results indicated the following:

66 subjects or 58% showed no particular preference for either older or newer products.
31 subjects or 27% showed some preference for newer products.
17 subjects or 15% showed particular preferences for older products.
114   100%

Although *communications* experiments might be included under persuasion, they have been classified separately because they are somewhat basic types of experiments as contrasted to the applied experiments discussed under persuasion.

Communications

Effects of competing messages.
Effect of overheard message.
Warnings and attitude change.
Buying adequate information.
The value of information.

This area of research has developed substantially during the past two decades. The work of Hovland and his colleagues certainly did much to further the development of communications work.

Cox [79] studied information in a consumer decision-making situation. He was more concerned as to how consumers utilized information about a product. His experiment was designed to isolate the dimensions on which consumers evaluate information, measure the value assigned to information, and relate information value to the probability of information utilization in evaluating a certain product. (Cox cited the Laird [1932] study in which 50 percent of a group of housewives preferred one of four brands of stockings despite the fact that they were identical except for a faint narcissus scent.)

Cox first decided upon a dimension of information value called the predictive value of a cue. He also defined a confidence value of a cue. His hypothesis was that consumers assign value to information or cues on these two dimensions: predictive and confidence value. Three groups, totaling 414 housewives, participated in the experiment. They evaluated "two brands" of nylon stockings and indicated how confident they were about their evaluation. After evaluating, the housewives heard a tape-recorded salesgirl's opinion that brand R stockings were better on six attributes. Subjects then reevaluated the nylons, evaluated the salesgirl, and indicated how confident they were about their evaluations of the salesgirl. The results of the experiment confirmed the hypothesis as it was found that subjects who were equally confident in their evaluations of the nylons and the salesgirl, and who rated the salesgirl high on experience, were most likely to utilize the salesgirl cue. The information value of a cue seems to be a function of the predictive value and the confidence value assigned to the cue.

Psychologists have long performed experiments having to do with *perception*. In recent years, marketing researchers have also conducted experiments that relate perception to the buying process. Recognizing that what is important is what the consumer perceives rather than what may actually be, the marketers are anxious to understand the implications for marketing.

Perception Experiments

Perception and acceleration.
Accentuation and perception.
Effect of color of product on acceptance.
Perception of pictures.
Taste perception and identification.

The cooperation of the Florida Citrus Commission, United States Department of Agriculture, Kroger Company, and Penn Fruit Company made one perception experiment possible [74]. The color of an orange was thought to be important to the housewife. (Color is actually added to the orange to make the orange visibly more attractive to the buyer. The Florida citrus code requires that color-added oranges yield a minimum of 5 gallons of juice per standard box, whereas for natural-color oranges the minimum is 4½ gallons.)

The experiment was conducted in Cleveland and Philadelphia. Nine stores were used in Philadelphia and 15 were used in Cleveland. A Latin-square design was used to assign treatments to stores and time periods in both cities. Prices were identical in all stores within each city for like sizes of natural-color and color-added oranges in any specific week of the experiment. The same United States grade was used and, to the extent possible, the same grove was used for each experiment!

Results showed that consumers in the two cities differed in their perception of color or in the value they placed on color. Cleveland buyers purchased more color-added oranges whereas Philadelphia buyers purchased the two kinds in about equal amounts. Combination displays sold more in both cities than did natural or color-added oranges alone (Table 14.9).

TABLE 14.9   SALES OF FLORIDA ORANGES; THREE TEST
METHODS OF DISPLAY

	Sales, by Test Methods		
	Color Added	Natural Color	Combination
	Pounds	Pounds	Pounds
Cleveland			
1959, fall	17,402	14,874	23,189
1960, fall	12,372	8,671	13,254
1961, spring	4,165	3,443	5,066
Total	33,939	26,988	41,509
Philadelphia			
1959, fall	21,156	20,601	25,820
1960, fall	8,080	8,360	10,445
1961, spring	6,365	6,245	6,340
Total	35,601	35,206	42,605

Stayton and Wiener [73] conducted a test that involved the relationship between size estimation and value. Previous studies had shown an overestimation of the valued object. Thus, if a person likes a big car, he may overestimate the size of the Lincoln. Stayton and Wiener wondered if accentuation could work in different ways. Their directions were as follows.

Below are six lines, three marked X-Y and three unlabeled. The lines, measured by the distance from X to Y, represent the length, width, and height of a Chevrolet, drawn to scale. The task is to mark off on the lines below the X-Y lines the length, width, and height of the Volkswagen in relative proportion to the length, width, and height of the Chevrolet.

There were other tasks to perform and there were several different kinds of dependent measures. Results showed that most subjects underestimated the size of the Volkswagen. Further, the greater the desire to own the Volkswagen, the greater the deviation was in the size estimate from the true size of the Volkswagen. Hence, the experiment indicated that it is conceivable that most any attribute dimension may be correlated with value.

At the University of Minnesota, subjects were administered a similar kind of test. Among the questions asked was a question concerning the way that they traversed the one-quarter mile bridge that joins the East and West campuses. Those subjects who walked judged the bridge to be shorter than those who usually rode across the bridge.

Most marketing research is undertaken to improve the efficiency of a company's marketing operations, to give the firm a competitive advantage, and to sell consumers more of a particular product. However, the literature does contain several examples that might be called *social-ethical* studies in marketing.

Social-Ethical Experiments

Viewing business risks.
Buying decisions and ethics.
Deceptive packaging.
Subliminal persuasion.

A fascinating experiment was undertaken by Naylor [102] of Ohio State University. Naylor was able to differentiate between consumption and purchase deception. Purchase deception takes place at the point of sale but consumption deception takes place during the period of consumption. Thus, a person might be deceived at the point of sale but he may or may not detect that something is wrong during consumption.

To examine the effects of deceptive packaging, Naylor secured the cooperation of a potato chip manufacturer and two supermarket managers. Certain restraints were placed on the study by these individuals and these are understandable in the real market place. The normal package of chips weighed 9 ounces. Experimental packages weighed 9 (control pack), 8, or 7 ounces. All packages used chips from the same batch. The procedure was for the experimenter to give one of the experimental packs free of charge to each person who purchased a normal package of chips. 144 packs were distributed during the course of the study. A buyer

TABLE 14.10   SAMPLE QUESTIONNAIRE USED IN THE INTERVIEW

AGE _____
SEX _____   SAMPLE _____

1. Was this the first time you have purchased this brand? Yes _____ No _____
2. Do you usually purchase this brand?   Yes _____ No _____
3. Do you expect to purchase this brand again?   Yes _____ No _____
4. What did you like most about this brand? _____
5. What (if anything) did you like least about this brand? _____
6. Please circle the point on the scale that expresses your reaction to each pack.
   a. How well did you like the contents of the regular pack?

   | 1 | 2 | 3 | 4 | 5 | 6 | 7 | 8 | 9 |

   terrible   poor   average   good   excellent
   b. How well did you like the contents of the sample pack?

   | 1 | 2 | 3 | 4 | 5 | 6 | 7 | 8 | 9 |

   terrible   poor   average   good   excellent
7. If both were available for purchase the next time you went to the store, which would you buy?
   _____ sample pack
   _____ regular pack
   _____ either
   _____ neither
8. List three words that describe the two packs.
   a. Sample pack: _____
   b. Regular pack: _____
9. Which pack had the most in it?
   _____ regular pack
   _____ sample pack
   _____ same

---

of a normal 9 ounce pack then received either a 7, 8, or 9 ounce experimental pack. The buyer was told that the free pack was an experimental effort and that the experimenter would follow up on the study within 3 days. At that time, the experimenter called on the customer and determined his preferences between the normal and the experimental packages (Table 14.10).

The results indicated that the majority of the respondents (118 consumers) thought the two packs were equal in weight. When the experimental pack was equal to the normal, a marked preference was indicated for the experimental. When the experimental pack was 1 ounce less, however, the preference for the experimental was only slight, and when there was a 2 ounce difference the regular pack was substantially preferred (see Fig. 14.3).

Thus, a seller who deceives a consumer at the point of sale may not be able to deceive this buyer all through the consumption period. Although the consumer may not realize why he rejects the product, it is possible that he senses a difference.

Up to this point, we have examined a number of marketing experiments. They have come from a variety of marketing operations. They have included the work with a consumer before the product is developed and have proceeded to cover the marketing functions through promotion and point of sale and even during consumption. These experiments have obvious relevance to the marketing processes. Though many are explora-

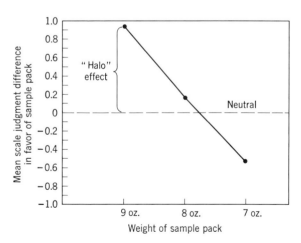

Figure 14.3.   Preference in favor of the contents of the experimental
pack as a function of experimental pack weight.

tory, they suggest a number of findings that might be developed into generalizations that, in turn, could further improve our marketing efficiency.

IMPLICATIONS FOR MARKETING. As briefly as possible and, hopefully, without changing the meaning of the experimental evidence, we are selecting a number of findings that have relevance to the marketing operation. These have been taken from the studies cited in this chapter.

Overheard persuasive communications are more effective than purposely directed communications.

Although an information cue may be a very good predictor of product quality, it will not be used if the buyer is not confident or experienced in the use of the cue.

Brand loyalty among members of a social group is determined primarily by the leader's brand loyalty.

Satisfaction with a product may be higher when customers expend considerable effort to obtain the product than when they use only modest effort.

The prestige of the medium and the sponsoring company affect consumer attitudes toward unbranded advertised products.

There is no general preference for "newer" products.

Subliminal forms of communication are ineffective means of persuasion.

While consumers may say that they do not perceive differences between products (for example, package weight) these differences are reflected in purchase behavior.

The greater the advertising space and proximity to other eye-stopping items, the greater the probability of attracting viewers' attention.

There is a general similarity in Negro-white responses to promotional stimuli.

In a purchase decision, the dissonance-producing elements can interact to create results different from what one of these elements would create by itself.

While the geographic locale of a news event is important to the average reader, the geographic locale of the person or thing featured in an advertisement is of much less importance than the subject matter.

Pre-TV show advertising (newspaper) has the effect of creating a more homogeneous viewer audience in terms of program interest.

Color ads evoke more positive reactions to merchandise and are more often identified with high quality stores than is true with black-and-white ads.

Liking or interest in a product can cause a change in the respondent's pupil dilation.

When consumers cannot detect actual quality differences in competing products, indirect indicators (brand name, image) are used as indications of quality differences.

Price changes from "odd" to "even" and vice versa can have dramatic effects on the sale of an item.

"Goodwill" collection letters that contain a high proportion of goodwill talk are more effective in collecting delinquent accounts than are letters with low proportions of goodwill talk.

At least two-thirds of normally reported exposure to advertising may be false.

Significant relationships exist between promotional expenditures and sales of fluid milk.

Demand curves may not invariably be negatively sloped. If there is a perception of quality differences among brands, a higher priced alternative is often chosen. Price imputes quality.

Both whites and Negroes responded better to package designs prepared for whites than to designs prepared for Negroes.

Simple incentives (airmail stamp, enclosed money, and so on) increase the rate of return in mail surveys.

There is a differential preference for mass communication appeals based on whether the person is inner- or other-directed.

The value of repeat exposure becomes greater with the passing of time after exposure.

THE LABORATORY, FIELD, SIMULATION, AND OTHER EXPERIMENTS

The illustrations cited previously have included experiments performed in different environments. Of the experiments examined in this chapter, almost half (or 50) have been field experiments. Approximately 25 have been laboratory studies, and about 25 have been simulation-game and in-between the laboratory and field studies. Panels, church groups, and setups in homes are examples of the in-between study. Approximately 25 of the field studies took place in retail stores, mostly food stores. Nearly all laboratory studies were conducted in universities.

The laboratory is not meant to duplicate real-life conditions but there may be the desire on the part of the experimenter to be able to take his study from the laboratory to the field in order that the results may have some meaning for marketing. Laboratory studies are concerned with more than basic research where the main concern is with the development of a theory. Controlling the conditions is obviously easier in the laboratory because the experimenter does not have to worry about public relations, competition, price changes, new products, changes in the economy, and lack of cooperation. If the experimenter attempts generalization, however, he is proceeding from evidence gathered in an artificial situation. There is a need for planned research that would start with a theoretical concept in a laboratory and would proceed systematically to the real-market test situation.

LABORATORY EXPERIMENTS. In an effort to provide some of the flavor of laboratory research, several brief examples will be given. Attention will be focused on the laboratory setup rather than on the substantive aspects of the research.

The Lennen and Newell [96] advertising agency conducted laboratory and field tests with Stokely and competing labels. From among hundreds of label designs, the company established the optimum. A tachistoscopic technique was used in this process in order to establish the relative visibility of elements. The results of this laboratory test were subsequently taken to housewives in order to determine the best colors. Finally, the labels were subjected to a controlled sales test. The new labels did well as sales climbed 44 percent. This three-stage experiment began in the laboratory with controlled conditions and with an instrument designed to measure one specific element.

A second laboratory experiment reported here was selected because it utilized the one-way laboratory screen or mirror. It is even more interesting because it utilized the one-way screen in reverse! Festinger and Walster [83] examined the assertion that overheard communications are especially effective. (Think of the possibilities of planting "overheard communications.")

As part of the course work in a psychology class, students were asked to tour the laboratory's observation room. Half the students made the tour and half were told the tour would be arranged later: this second half of the class served as a control group. The experimental group was divided into two groups. One of these groups was led to believe that graduate students frequently used the laboratories as a lounge and that the experimental students could go into the observation room and just listen so that they could see how the laboratory was operated. The second experimental group of subjects was led to believe that the graduate students in the laboratory were aware that students would be coming into the observation room. The experimental subjects actually heard a six-minute persuasive communication that concerned the common "misconception" that smoking causes lung cancer. A week later a question-naire purporting to be from the National Institute of Health was given to all students in the regular class. This included questions about smok-ing and lung cancer and these questions furnished the basis for evaluat-ing the effect of overheard persuasive communications.

The results showed that the persuasive communications were effective in that those subjects who had heard the message differed significantly from the control group. Further, the overheard communication was more effective than the regular communication. Unexpectedly, smokers were more influenced than were nonsmokers.

The laboratory is an extremely valuable setting for marketing experi-ments. The limit of our research is probably set by the lack of our imagi-nation.

FIELD EXPERIMENTS. More than 50 field experiments are included in the bibliography at the end of this chapter. These range from household experiments to vast studies involving newspaper readership and tele-vision viewing.

Keith Cox [88] has conducted a number of in-store studies and the operation is briefly reviewed here. Cox's hypotheses were: (1) additional shelf space given to a grocery product will increase the sale of the product, and (2) the sales of different grocer-product commodities respond in different patterns to changes in shelf space. He used a Latin-square design to measure the relationship between shelf space and sales. (It is interesting to note that sales is a common dependent measure in field experiments but not in laboratory research.)

Cox selected four products: baking soda, hominy, Tang, and powdered coffee cream. He faced the usual difficulties in setting up an in-store experiment such as price changes, new products, and the like. His selec-tion of Austin was made because of cost and time considerations, two factors that influence much marketing research. Six stores were used and one supermarket chain was selected because of the problem of get-ting cooperation with six different managers. This is not to criticize the study but rather to point out the practical limitations with which the field experimenter must deal.

The treatments were spaced at equidistant intervals in order to simplify the analysis. The differences among shelf treatments were made as large as possible in order to make the test more powerful. Cox then counted the weekly sales of the four product lines.

Time of testing had to be decided: July 9 to August 27, 1962, excluding the holiday weeks of July 4th and Labor Day. Shelf levels had to be

14.11   SUMMARY OF FIVE-WEEK EXPERIMENTAL PROGRAM

Experimental Condition	Hypothesis	Test of Effect
First Experimental Week		
Subliminal suggestion to "Buy Product A" broadcast for five nights during feature film.	Subliminal persuasion *alone* will increase sales of the food product in the area reached by the TV signal.	The amount of increase in the sale of Product A in the area.
Second Experimental Week		
Subliminal suggestion to "Buy Product A" broadcast for another five nights during feature film, followed by TV Special sale on Product A on the following news program.	Subliminal persuasion in combination with ordinary advertising of product at reduced price will increase the sale of Product A to a greater degree than ordinary advertising alone.	The amount of increase in the sale of Product A during the second week, checked against the effect of ordinary advertising as a control.
Third Experimental Week		
Subliminal suggestion to "Watch Frank Edwards" broadcast during feature film for five nights. Also, TV Special on Product B broadcast during news program.	The increase in size of audience watching Frank Edwards as a result of subliminal suggestion will increase exposure to the TV Special on Product B and thereby increase the sale of Product B to a greater degree than if there were no subliminal suggestion.	The amount of increase in the sale of Product B during this experimental week, checked against the effect of the TV Special alone, as a control.

TABLE 14.11 (*Continued*)

Experimental Condition	Hypothesis	Test of Effect
Fourth Experimental Week		
Subliminal suggestion to "Watch Frank Edwards" continued for another five days during feature film. Also, TV Special on Product C broadcast during news program.	The audience size of the Frank Edwards program will significantly increase because of the ten two-hour broadcasts of the subliminal message during the third and fourth weeks. The effect will be to increase exposure to the TV Special on Product C, and thereby increase sale of Product C to a greater degree than by a TV Special alone.	A comparison of regular audience surveys made three months before the fourth experimental week and at the end of the fourth experimental week. The amount of increase in the sales of Product C during the experimental week checked against the effect of a TV Special alone, as a control.
Fifth Experimental Week		
Subliminal suggestion to "Buy Product D" broadcast during the two-hour feature film for a five-day period. Also, TV Special on Product D broadcast during news program.	The combination of (1) the increased audience size from the conditions of the third and fourth weeks, (2) the subliminal suggestion to buy Product D, plus (3) the TV Special on Product D will increase the sales of Product D to a significantly greater degree than the increase due to a TV Special alone.	The amount of increase in the sale of Product D during the experimental week, checked against the effect of a TV Special alone, as a control.

maintained at the pretest level. Store personnel had to be restrained from changing the shelf space. Adequate inventory had to be maintained and this required warehouse cooperation.

This illustration gives a good picture of in-store experimenting. Cox's results indicated that a significant relationship existed between the amount of shelf space given to hominy but not for the other three products.

For an elaborate field study, we have selected the DeFleur and Petranoff [100] experiment that examined the matter of subliminal persuasion (Table 14.11). Laboratory experiments with carefully controlled conditions first established that communication is possible with subliminal messages. Subliminal persuasion was then examined in a field experiment. The authors decided upon two forms of behavior: (1) viewing a particular program as a result of subliminal suggestion; and (2) buying certain food products as a result of exposure to subliminal stimuli.

This was an elaborate field study that required a good deal of cooperation of the radio station. The results of this experiment indicated that subliminal persuasion failed (see Table 14.12). At best, it would be a very inefficient way to persuade people to buy a product; simply telling them to buy proved more efficient. Selected results of the experiments are shown.

Many of the experiments are neither laboratory nor field experiments but are somehow in-between the two. Simulation studies such as Tucker's [60] would fall into this category, and so would the study of Leavitt's [52] on pricing in which he used a captive audience that he had available—sixty Air Force officers and graduate students. He took four products—cooking sherry and moth flakes (all look-alike), razor blades and floor wax (considerable difference)—and had the subjects imagine that they were at a supermarket to buy, for example, a pint of floor wax. The subject was given a choice such as Brand A at $0.68 versus Brand B at $0.72, according to the modified Latin-square used. The results of this study indicated that people would often choose the higher priced of two alternative brands when their only differential information was price. This suggests that demand curves may not invariably be negatively sloped, that price itself may have more than one meaning to a consumer, and that a higher price may sometimes increase, rather than decrease, his readiness to buy.

SELECTED INGREDIENTS OF THE EXPERIMENT

Like any other research method, there are phases, pieces, or parts to the experiment. It has been my experience that students can grasp these

TABLE 14.12 EFFECTS OF SUBLIMINAL PERSUASION, AND COM-
BINATIONS OF SUBLIMINAL PERSUASION AND MORE
ORDINARY PERSUASIVE TECHNIQUES

Experimental Condition	Average Number of Units Sold per Week for Normal 6-week Period	Number of Units Sold during Experimental Week	Range[a]	Percent Increase above Normal Sales
1 week of subliminal promotion of Product A	6,143	6,204	6,026	1
2 weeks of subliminal promotion of Product A, with TV Special on Product A during second week	6,143	17,304	6,026	282
1 week of subliminal suggestion to "Watch Frank Edwards," with TV Special on Product B during same week	2,073	9,418	741	454
2 weeks of subliminal suggestion to "Watch Frank Edwards," with TV Special on Product C during second week	4,451	24,120	5,364	542
2 weeks of subliminal suggestion to "Watch Frank Edwards," followed by 1 week of subliminal promotion of Product D, with TV Special on Product D during same week	5,413	27,510	6,400	508

[a] Computed by determining the difference between the greatest and smallest number of units sold per week for the 6-week period of normal sales.

different ingredients more easily than they can grasp the important several parts of the survey. Something about the experimental method makes them more conscious of hypotheses and variables than is true of the survey. Further, students seem to become more analytical after examining several experiments than has been the case with similar examinations of surveys. These are simply personal observations and may not be good generalizations.

Nevertheless, we might, at this point, examine the ingredients of the experiment.

PROBLEM STATEMENT AND HYPOTHESES.   Although there was not a clear statement of the problem in every experiment examined, there was no trouble in locating the problem that was being investigated. Only about one-third of the studies had clearly stated hypotheses, however. The clear statement of the problem and the suggested hypotheses certainly facilitates the reading and understanding of the experiment.

As an example of a hypothesis, Venkatesan [116] proposed the following in his study of conformity and reactance:

In a consumer decision-making situation, where no objective standards are present, individuals who are exposed to a group norm will tend to conform to that group norm.

Allison and Uhl [71] stated their experimental hypothesis as follows:

Beer drinkers cannot distinguish among major brands of unlabeled beer either on an overall basis or on selected characteristics.

Junker and Urban [56] stated that:

. . . no distinguishable difference by sight and/or taste exists between butter and margarine.

Gardner and Cohen [23] stated:

Social Research, Inc. tried to answer these questions:

1. Does the addition of color significantly change the reaction to an ad?
2. Is this change favorable to the advertiser?

Regardless of the manner in which the problem and hypotheses were stated, each of the experiments reviewed did have some objective.

INDEPENDENT VARIABLES.   The aspect of the problem or environment which is being studied is of course the independent variable. The purpose of this section is to list some of the independent variables in marketing that have been investigated through the experimental method.

Commitment to a decision	Type of store
Design of a label	Effect of Negro in ad
Size of display	Width of merchandise line
Display location	Location of store
Carton with picture versus no picture	Brand identification
	Number of product alternatives
Ease of depressing gas pedal	Familiarization
Amount of color	Amount of time to make decision
Imperfect alternatives in choice	Inducement to buy
Anticipated dissonance	Amount of information
Kind of information available	Cognitive overlap
Amount of effort in buying	Expectation with purchase
Group influences	Flavor of products
Effect of a warning	Cues for buying
Effect of subliminal persuasion	Degree of ethics
Magnitude of gain: probability of gain	Ad selection
	Method of selecting products
Interviewer bias	Increasing mail response
Coder biases	Effectiveness of salesmen
Order of presentation	Quality of sales presentation
Source effect	Day versus night television
Collection letters, type of	Frequency of advertising
Spot versus network advertising	Amount of promotional expenditures
Amount of blank space in ads	
Size of an ad	Ad recognition
Advertising television shows	Position of the ad
Point of sales promotion	Number items to carry in inventory
Amount of shelf space	Window trim
Equipment in store	Effect of branded merchandise
Bulk packaging	Type and size of package

While this is, essentially, a repetition of subject matter covered in the experiments, it does emphasize that a problem was stated and that an independent variable was identified. All kinds of marketing situations were obviously included in these experiments and the examination of the independent variables drives home the point that experimentation is a technique that is applicable to marketing problems.

MANIPULATIONS. The little experience we have had at Minnesota suggests that the manipulation is a crucial part of the experiment. Some manipulations may come very easily but others are extremely difficult to develop. The psychological pricing study appears easy on the surface but we have not yet developed a good manipulation or, perhaps, a good experimental situation. Some manipulations are most ingenious, for instance, the reversal of the one-way screen in the overheard persuasion experiment previously mentioned. Another manipulation is the gearing up or down of a clock to make the subject believe he has been at a task for a certain length of time.

Many of the experiments examined used only a system of comparing two alternatives. Others, however, were much more complicated. Let us examine a few of the manipulations reported in the marketing literature.

The amount of shelf space in a store was varied.
The type of collection letter sent to overdue accounts was varied.
The source effect of a company and its products was varied.
Displays were changed from branded goods to unbranded goods.
Window trim was added and eliminated.
Advertising was increased and decreased.
Blank space was inserted in ads and changed about in the ads.
Color was used in some ads and black and white was used with other ads.
Size of the package was changed.
Contents in the package were changed by weight.
Group pressure was changed according to the condition desired.
Brand identification was used in one case and removed in another.
The amount of effort was varied.

Instructions are used in the manipulation process. An example of this has been taken from a study of inducement as it applies to dissonance [111] in a battery purchasing situation.

High Inducement

You have been in northern Minnesota for the weekend and are driving back to the Twin Cities. After a stop for coffee, you find that you cannot start the engine of your car. You return to the cafe and locate the phone number of a nearby garage. The attendant arrives in a few minutes, checks your car, and reports that your battery probably has a leaky cell which is shorting out.

The attendant tows your car into his garage and determines that your battery is dead and cannot be recharged. The long winter has apparently taken its toll.

Low Inducement

You were planning on running several errands today. After the first stop, however, your car will not start. After several attempts to start it, you give up and call the nearest garage. The attendant arrives in a few minutes and starts your car with the aid of his booster battery.

You follow him to his garage where he checks over your engine and battery. He believes that you may have a leaky cell in the battery and that, with a little luck, it may be possible for you to get along for a few weeks.

Venkatesan [116] developed the desired effect for conformity and reactance in a group-pressure situation as he told the confederates the responses they should give.

Conformity: Confederate 1: "It is B."
               Confederate 2: "B is the *best* suit."
               Confederate 3: "It is B."
               Subject: "_____"
Reactance: Confederate 1: "I am not sure if there is a difference—it is not great; but if I have to choose, then B is the *best* suit."
               Confederate 2: "(Looking at Confederate 1) You say B . . . Well, I cannot see any difference either—I will *go along with you*—B is the *best* suit for me."
               Confederate 3: "Well, you guys choose B. Although I am not sure, I am *just going along* to be a good guy. I choose B, too."
               Subject: "_____"

The manipulations should be powerful in their effect. Fortunately, they can be pilot tested until they have been developed to the point of "working." Gardner's [80] distraction experiment underwent several changes until he developed three levels of distraction. He manipulated distraction (or divided attention) by having subjects operate slot racing cars while they heard a radio commercial. His "high-distraction" condition was effected by having subjects keep two cars side by side as they went around the track at a high speed. His "low-distraction" condition had subjects operate one car that was set at a fairly low speed.

DEPENDENT VARIABLES. The dependent variables show the resultant change in behavior as a result of the experiment or manipulations of the independent variable. Some of the independent measures used in the experiments reviewed are as follows.

Recall of ad	Profits
Sales	Semantic differential
Estimate of magnitude	Choice of store
Choice of product	Magnitude of dissonance reduction
Amount of regret	Various kinds of scales
Changes in attitude	Degree of satisfaction

Degree of confidence

Exposure to information

Amount of pupil dilation

Changes in standards

Tabulation by coders

Amount of bad debts collected

Ranking of preferences

Ability to identify

Decision to repurchase

Brand choice

Change in awareness of product attributes

Rating of salesmen

Filmed eye movements

Frequently, the experiments utilized several dependent measures. The researchers may have been measuring different effects or they may have had different ways of measuring the same effects. In the field, as in a store experiment, the measure was often the amount of sales. Sales or profits is the ultimate measure of success but much worthwhile marketing experimentation will not be so directly measured.

CONTROLLING THE VARIABLES. Control is one of the keys in experimentation. If sales reflect a variety of factors that cannot be measured, let alone controlled, the experiment is so confounded that the results may be meaningless. Care was taken in most of the experiments to provide an adequate amount of control.

You may have seen the one-minute Shell commercials for their gasoline with Platformate. These are pretty well-performed experiments, yet in one class where these were shown, the students listed 25 variables that may not have been controlled. Some writers in marketing have stressed the difficulty of controlling the variables to the extent that readers may not believe experimentation possible. We can learn to do a better job of controlling the variables and it is conceivable that, as experiments become more common, there will be improved cooperation between the researcher and the store manager, television station, or newspaper. It takes a good deal of cooperation to black out one-half of a city while another half is receiving a commercial on television, but it is possible to do just this.

Engel [109] reported that a full-page advertisement for Chevrolet was run in the newspaper while he was conducting his experiment. This he had not anticipated. Many of the other experiments included reports of unexpected developments that caused problems in conducting the experiment or in analyzing the data. Many of the extraneous variables are almost humorous, often remembered long after the experiment has been conducted, but the need to control as much as possible is certainly a most serious matter.

RANDOMIZATION. The majority of the experiments reported some attempt to randomize treatments. Compromises were made frequently but for good reasons. Students in laboratory experiments were generally exposed in random fashion. Stores frequently were chosen randomly, although not always.

Some examples of the randomization process follow:

Seventy overdue accounts in a department store in Prairie Grove, Arkansas were divided into two groups, using a table of random numbers to select comparable accounts for each group [125].

Forty-two women participated in the experiment. They were selected by two-stage random sampling from a single census tract in order to minimize delivery problems [60].

THE EXPERIMENTAL DESIGN. Many of the experiments examined for this paper have been tests of alternatives that have not been strict experiments in the statistical sense. A few have been experimental only in that they tried something new, that is, "experimental." At the other extreme have been those carefully designed experiments that utilized an accepted design. It should be pointed out that the design has to do with the efficiency of the experiment. While it is not the purpose of this chapter to touch upon this aspect, brief examples of several different kinds of studies are included.

For his Master's degree, Popielarz [114] tested for a relationship between "category-width" and consumer risk-taking behavior. The first phase of the study consisted of determining the subject's category width. This was accomplished by having the subject indicate his estimates on a number of measurement problems. The subject then indicated his willingness to try products of varying degrees of newness within six product classes. It was hypothesized that the breadth of categorization would be linearly related to willingness to try new products: broad categorizers would be associated with expressions of greater willingness to try new products than would narrow categorizers. There was no manipulation of any independent variable but, instead, a hypothesis was tested by selecting subjects along one dimension and then testing them on their willingness to accept new products.

Another Minnesota student, Gardner [80], designed a *before-after* study. One aspect of the experiment was the measure of desire on the part of subjects to see certain movies. This same measure was administered at the conclusion of the study in order that the before-after comparison could be made. The independent variables were handled between the before-after measures, of course.

A number of *Latin-square* designs have been mentioned. In this kind of study, the treatments are assigned to the cells of the table randomly

TABLE 14.13   3 × 3 LATIN-SQUARE FOR THREE TREATMENTS

	Square I		
Time Period	Chattanooga	Knoxville	Rochester
1	A	B	C
2	B	C	A
3	C	A	B

Key: Expenditure levels: A: Normal promotion (approximately 2¢ per capita annually); B: Medium promotion (15¢ per capita annually above normal); and C: Heavy promotion (30¢ per capita annually above normal).

except that each treatment will appear once in a row and once in a column. For example, consider the design, in Table 14.13, for a study involving levels of promotion for milk in three different time periods and with three different stores [17].

There are variations of the basic Latin-square. For example, because of the *carry-over* effects of advertising, a reverse Latin-square is added. As is shown in the following study (Table 14.14) of apple themes in advertising, a fourth time period was added to the original three time periods in order to increase the precision of the estimation of carry-over effects. Again, the design takes us into efficiency.

One other design that will be mentioned here is the *factorial* design. This design permits the experimenter to handle several variables simultaneously instead of varying them one at a time. Main effects of the study

TABLE 14.14   EXTRA-PERIOD LATIN-SQUARE CHANGE-OVER EXPERIMENTAL DESIGN USED IN APPLE ADVERTISING STUDY OF 72 SUPERMARKETS IN 6 MIDWESTERN CITIES [25]

	Sequence (Cities)					
Four-Week	Square I			Square II		
Time Periods	City 1	City 2	City 3	City 4	City 5	City 6
1	A	B	C	A	B	C
2	B	C	A	C	A	B
3	C	A	B	B	C	A
4	C	A	B	B	C	A

Key: Treatment A: general health theme; Treatment B: apple use theme; and Treatment C: no advertising and promotion (control group).

are examined but, in addition, the interaction between the variables can be statistically measured. A University of Minnesota study [111] of dissonance was undertaken in an effort to determine whether we could perform a factorially designed experiment. We selected four dissonance producing factors:

(1) Inducement to buy: (a) high inducement; (b) low inducement.

(2) Anticipated dissonance: (a) high anticipated dissonance; (b) low anticipated dissonance.

(3) Information: (a) no additional information given; (b) additional information given.

(4) Cognitive overlap: (a) high cognitive overlap; (b) low cognitive overlap.

The resulting design is shown in Table 14.15. A study with 2 conditions for each of 4 factors means that there will be 16 cells as shown in the bottom row of the design. Hypotheses were developed for each of the main effects since previous dissonance studies had given us a good idea of what could be expected. Interaction effects were more difficult to predict.

Automobile batteries were used as the product for this experiment. Subjects were given a before-test to determine their preferences of batteries. Later, they were put into the buying situation in which the first two variables were manipulated through written and oral directions. Information and cognitive overlap were manipulated by placing information on the display rack. Subjects were administered an after-test that was compared to the before-test in order to determine the amount of dissonance reduction. Results are shown in Table 14.16.

The interaction of information with high inducement proved to be significant. Apparently, when the buyer is provided with high inducement to buy, the use of information becomes important to him. By contrast, the interaction of the information variable with the high anticipated dissonance condition produced no significant interaction. Three-way interactions and even the four-way interaction were readily available but these are extremely difficult to comprehend. This kind of variable mixing is unlike the mixing of paint pigments.

CONCLUDING AND MISCELLANEOUS COMMENTS

Experiments have definitely found a place in marketing research. I hope that they will not become a fad so that they will be misused and serve to disillusion marketing management and researchers. By proceed-

TABLE 14.15 THE EXPERIMENTAL DESIGN

	High inducement								Low inducement							
	High anticipated dissonance				Low anticipated dissonance				High anticipated dissonance				Low anticipated dissonance			
	No additional information		Additional information		No additional information		Additional information		No additional information		Additional information		No additional information		Additional information	
	High	Low	High	Low	High	Low	High	Low	High	Low	High	Low	High	Low	High	Low
No additional information																
Cognitive overlap High																
Cognitive overlap Low																

Example of one condition: High inducement, Low anticipated dissonance, Additional information, Low cognitive overlap.

TABLE 14.16 DISSONANCE SCORES: CHANGES BETWEEN PRE- AND POST-RATINGS

| | Main Effects (n = 40 for each score) | Interaction Effects (n = 20 for each cell score) | | | | | |
| | | Anticipated Dissonance | | Information | | Cognitive Overlap | |
		High	Low	Additional	No Additional	High	Low
Inducement	Hyp: low > high						
High	2.30	2.40	2.20	1.35[a]	3.25[a]	2.05	2.55
Low	2.72	2.45	3.00	2.90	2.55	3.45	2.00
Anticipated dissonance	Hyp: high > low						
High	2.42	—	—	2.40	2.45	2.10	2.75
Low	2.60	—	—	1.85	3.35	3.40[a]	1.80
Information	Hyp: none > additional						
Additional	2.12	—	—	—	—	2.65	1.60
No additional	2.90	—	—	—	—	2.85	2.95
Cognitive overlap	Hyp: high > low						
High	2.75	—	—	—	—	—	—
Low	2.27	—	—	—	—	—	—

Overall mean change: 2.51

[a] Significant at 0.05 level.

ing carefully, experimenters should be able to supplement marketing research work by adding the experimental method to ascertain cause and effect relationships in a number of instances. The experiment is another method: it is not *THE* method.

It is a method that offers definite advantages to the researcher, as the literature has shown. For example, the experimental method makes "detective" work possible since it is relatively easy to follow up clues and to go to a second or third study. It is possible to undertake a series of studies, tightening up here and there, modifying, changing the manipulation, improving the dependent measure, and adding more realism to the experimental setting.

Recent experiments have included a number of research techniques that combine effectively with the experiment. This makes the experimental method a flexible one for researchers.

There remains much to be tried and much to be accomplished. With encouragement from business, the experimental method can be applied to many marketing problems. There will be costs but there will be rewards. The ultimate benefits from using the experimental methodology will probably depend upon the ingenuity of the researcher as he applies another research technique to marketing problems.

BIBLIOGRAPHY

General References
1. Seymour Banks, "Designing Marketing Research to Increase Validity," *Journal of Marketing*, **28**(4), 32-40 (October, 1964).
2. Seymour Banks, *Experimentation in Marketing* (New York: McGraw-Hill, 1965).
3. Seymour Banks, "Marketing Experiments," *Journal of Advertising Research*, 3(1), 34-41 (March, 1963).
4. James C. Becknell, Jr., "Utilizing Pre-Testing Devices to Reduce Variance in Advertising Experiments," paper presented at the 11th Annual Conference of the Advertising Research Foundation (October 5, 1965).
5. Max E. Brunk and Walter T. Federer, "Experimental Designs and Probability Sampling in Marketing Research," *American Statistical Association Journal*, 440-452 (September, 1953).
6. C. West Churchman, "The Philosophy of Experimentation," Chapter 12 in Oscar Kempthorne, Theodore A. Bancroft, John W. Gowen, and Jay L. Lush (editors), *Statistics and Mathematics in Biology* (Ames, Iowa: The Iowa State College Press, 1954), 159-172. Also reprinted by Case Institute of Technology, Cleveland 6, Ohio.
7. William E. Cox, Jr., "Experimental Designs for Marketing Analysis," mimeographed paper, 1965.

8. "The Experimental Method in Marketing Research," *Wood Chips*, 4(7) (October, 1960).
9. Benjamin Lipstein, "The Design of Test Marketing Experiments," *Journal of Advertising Research*, 5(4), 2-7 (1965).
10. James H. Lorie and Harry V. Roberts, "Some Comments on Experimentation in Business Research," *The Journal of Business*, 23, 94-102 (April, 1950).
11. Stanley L. Payne, "The Ideal Model for Controlled Experiments," *Public Opinion Quarterly*, 25, 557-562 (fall 1961).
Persuasion
12. James C. Becknell, Jr., "The Influence of Newspaper Tune-In Advertising on the Size of a TV Show's Audience," *Journal of Advertising Research*, 1(3), 23-26 (1961).
13. James C. Becknell, Jr., "Media Effectiveness," *Media/Scope*, 46-49 (August, 1962).
14. James C. Becknell, Jr., and Robert W. McIsaac, "Test Marketing Cookware Coated with 'Teflon'," *Journal of Advertising Research*, 3(3), 2-8 (September, 1963).
15. Leo Bogart and B. Stuart Tolley, "The Impact of Blank Space: An Experiment in Advertising Readership," *Journal of Advertising Research*, 4(2), 21-27 (June, 1964).
16. Stanley D. Canter, "The Evaluation of Media Through Empirical Experiments," paper presented at the 11th Annual Conferences of the Advertising Research Foundation (October 5, 1965).
17. Wendell E. Clement, Peter L. Henderson, and Cleveland P. Eley, "The Effect of Promotional Expenditures on Sales of Fluid Milk" (Washington, D.C.: United States Department of Agriculture; October, 1965).
18. Thomas E. Coffin, "A Pioneering Experiment in Assessing Advertising Effectiveness," *Journal of Marketing*, 27(3), 1-10 (July, 1963).
19. Gwyn Collins, "Advertising Experimentation," speech delivered to American Marketing Association National Conference on Research Design (March 6, 1964).
20. Lauren E. Crane, "How Product, Appeal, and Program Affect Attitudes Toward Commercials," *Journal of Advertising Research*, 4(1), 15-18 (1964).
21. Alan S. Donnahoe, "A New Direction for Media Research," *Richmond Times-Dispatch* (January 17, 1961).
22. Douglas A. Fuchs, "Two Source Effects in Magazine Advertising," *Journal of Marketing Research*, 1, 59-62 (August, 1964).
23. Burleigh B. Gardner and Yehudi A. Cohen, "The Effect of ROP Color on Newspaper Advertising," *Journal of Marketing Research*, 1, 68-70 (May, 1964).
24. William R. Hazard, "Responses to News Pictures: A Study in Perceptual Unity," *Journalism Quarterly*, 37(4), 515-524 (autumn 1960).
25. Peter L. Henderson, James F. Hind, and Sidney E. Brown, "Sales Effects of Two Campaign Themes," *Journal of Advertising Research*, 1(6), 2-11 (December, 1961).
26. William S. Hoofnagle, "Experimental Designs in Measuring the Effectiveness of Promotion," *Journal of Marketing Research*, 2, 154-162 (May, 1965).
27. Ward J. Jensen, "Sales Effects of TV, Radio and Print Advertising," *Journal of Advertising Research*, 6(2), 2-7 (June, 1966).

28. R. J. Jessen, "A Switch-Over Experimental Design to Measure Advertising Effect," *Journal of Advertising Research*, 1(3), 15-22 (March, 1961).
29. Herbert Kay and Dan E. Clark, II, "Effects of Injecting 'Local Color' into Advertisements," *Journal of Marketing*, 23(1), 56-58 (July, 1958).
30. Richard B. Maffei, "Can the Effect of Advertising on Brand Preference be Predicted?," *Journal of Retailing*, 17-24 (spring 1961).
31. Eric Marder and Mort David, "Recognition of Ad Elements: Recall or Projection?," *Journal of Advertising Research*, 1(6), 23-35 (1961).
32. D. Morgan Neu, "Measuring Advertisement Recognition," *Journal of Advertising Research*, 1(6), 17-22 (1961).
33. Charles K. Ramond, "Using the Experimental Method to Measure the Sales Effectiveness of Advertising," a talk to the National Shoe Manufacturers Association Market Research Institute (January 12, 1960).
34. Edward J. Robinson, "How an Advertisement's Size Affects Responses to It," *Journal of Advertising Research*, 3(4), 16-25 (December, 1963).
35. R. A. Schrimper and R. J. Peeler, Jr., *Commodity Promotion: A Controlled Experiment Evaluation* (Raleigh, N. C.: North Carolina State University; April, 1965).
36. Horace S. Schwerin, "Why Television Commercials Succeed," from Robert Ferber and Hugh G. Wales (editors), *Motivation and Market Behavior* (Homewood, Ill.: Richard D. Irwin, 1958), 321-333.
37. Charles H. Sevin, "What We Know About Measuring Ad Effectiveness," *Printers' Ink*, 47-53 (July 9, 1965).
38. Aaron J. Spector, "New Test Shows Plus Value of Repeat Exposure," *Media/Scope*, 92-93 (September, 1960).
39. Irwin M. Towers, Leo A. Goodman, and Hans Zeisel, "A Method of Measuring the Effects of Television through Controlled Field Experiments," *Studies in Public Communication No. 4* (Chicago, Ill.: University of Chicago, Autumn, 1962), 87-110.

Marketing Research
40. Roger Bengston and Henry Brenner, "Product Test Results Using Three Different Methodologies," *The Journal of Marketing Research*, 1(4), 49-52 (November, 1964).
41. Roy E. Carter, Jr., Verling C. Troldahl, and R. Smith Schuneman, "Interviewer Bias in Selecting Households," *Journal of Marketing*, 27(2), 27-34 (April, 1963).
42. J. Durbin and A. Stuart, "An Experimental Comparison Between Coders," *Journal of Marketing*, 19(1), 54-66 (July, 1954).
43. Allan Greenberg, "Paired Comparisons in Consumer-Product Tests," *The Forum*, 411-414 (April, 1958).
44. Mathew Hauck, "Interviewer Compensation on Consumer Surveys," *Commentary*, 15-18 (summer 1964).
45. Andrew E. Kimball, "Increasing the Rate of Return in Mail Surveys," *Journal of Marketing*, 25(6), 63-64 (October, 1961).
46. John Neter and Joseph Waksberg, "Effects of Interviewing Designated Respondents in a Household Survey of Home Owners' Expenditures on Alterations and Repairs," *Applied Statistics*, 12(1), 46-60 (1963).

Pricing
47. Donald J. Baker and Charles H. Berry, "The Price Elasticity of Demand for Fluid Skim Milk," *Journal of Farm Economics*, 35, 124-129 (February, 1953).

48. Lawrence P. Claude, "Are the Words Price and Quality Synonymous?," a paper for a marketing class, University of Minnesota, 1966.

49. Eli Ginsberg, "Customary Prices," *American Economic Review*, 26(2), 296 (1936).

50. Edward R. Hawkins, "Methods of Estimating Demand," *Journal of Marketing*, 21(4), 428-438 (April, 1957).

51. R. A. Kelly, H. O. Werner, F. A. Krantz, Perry Hemphill, and M. E. Gravens, "Relationship of Price and Quality of Potatoes at Retail Level," *Minnesota Bulletin 406*, 3-17 (June, 1950).

52. Harold J. Leavitt, "A Note on Some Experimental Findings About the Meanings of Price," *Journal of Business*, 27, 205-210 (1954).

53. L. A. Powell, Sr., William G. O'Regan, and Marshall R. Godwin, "Experimental Pricing as an Approach to Demand Analysis: A Technical Study of the Retail Demand for Frozen Orange Concentrate," *Technical Bulletin 592* (Gainesville, Florida: Florida Agricultural Experiment Stations; March, 1958).

54. D. S. Tull, R. A. Boring, and M. H. Gonsior, "A Note on the Relationship of Price and Imputed Quality," *Journal of Business*, 37(2), 186-191 (April, 1964).

Simulation—games

55. Alderson and Sessions, "Basic Research Report on Consumer Behavior: Report on a Study of Shopping Behavior and Methods for Its Investigation," mimeographed (April, 1957).

56. Lawrence Carson, Donald Junker, Eugene Rice, Richard Teach, Douglas Tigert, and William Urban, *Experimental Research in Consumer Behavior: Four Exploratory Papers* (Lafayette, Ind.: Herman C. Krannert Graduate School of Industrial Administration, Purdue University; January, 1966).

57. "An Experimental Game," *Wood Chips*, 4(1) (November, 1959).

58. Edgar A. Pessemier, "A New Way to Determine Buying Decisions," *Journal of Marketing*, 24(2), 41-46 (October, 1959). An expanded series of experiments is reported in *Experimental Methods of Analyzing Demand for Branded Consumer Goods with Applications to Problems in Marketing Strategy* (Pullman, Wash.: Washington State University Press, 1963).

59. Vernon L. Smith, "An Experimental Study of Competitive Market Behavior," *Journal of Political Economy*, 70(2), 111-137 (April, 1962).

60. W. T. Tucker, "The Development of Brand Loyalty," *Journal of Marketing Research*, 1(3), 32-35 (August, 1964).

Taste

61. J. W. Bowles, Jr., and N. H. Pronko, "Identification of Cola Beverages: II. A Further Study," *Journal of Applied Psychology*, 32, 559-564 (1948).

62. Norman Theodore Gridgeman, "A Tasting Experiment," *Applied Statistics*, 5(2), 106-112 (June, 1956).

63. Joseph M. Kamen and Jan Eindhoven, "Instructions Affecting Food Preferences," *Journal of Advertising Research*, 3(2), 35-38 (1963).

64. James C. Makens, "Effect of Brand Preference Upon Consumers' Perceived Taste of Turkey Meat," *Journal of Applied Psychology*, 49(4), 261-263 (1964).

65. N. H. Pronko and J. W. Bowles, Jr., "Identification of Cola Beverages: I. First Study," *Journal of Applied Psychology*, 32, 304-312 (1948).

66. N. H. Pronko and J. W. Bowles, Jr., "Identification of Cola Beverages: III. A Final Study," *Journal of Applied Psychology*, 33, 605-608 (1949).

67. N. H. Pronko and D. T. Herman, "Identification of Cola Beverages: IV. Postscript," *Journal of Applied Psychology,* 34, 68-69 (1950).
68. Frederick J. Thumin, "Identification of Cola Beverages," *Journal of Applied Psychology,* 46(5), 358-360 (1962).
69. L. L. Thurstone, "Experimental Methods in Food Tasting," *Journal of Applied Psychology,* 35(3), 141-145 (June, 1951).
70. Roy Yensen, "Some Factors Affecting Taste Sensitivity in Man," *Quarterly Journal of Experimental Psychology,* 11, 221-248 (November, 1959).

Perception

71. Ralph I. Allison and Kenneth P. Uhl, "Influence of Bear Brand Identification on Taste Perception," *Journal of Marketing Research,* 1, 36-39 (August, 1964).
72. Alfred Politz, "Science and Truth in Marketing Research," *Harvard Business Review,* 35, 117-126 (January-February, 1957).
73. Samuel E. Stayton and Morton Wiener, "Value, Magnitude, and Accentuation," *Journal of Abnormal and Social Psychology,* 62(1), 145-147 (January, 1961).
74. U.S. Department of Agriculture, "Consumer Acceptance of Florida Oranges With and Without Color Added," Marketing Research Report No. 537 (Washington, D.C.: U.S. Government Printing Office, 1962).

New Products

75. B. Bliven, Jr., "Annals of Business: And Now a Word from our Sponsor," *The New Yorker,* 39, 83 (March 23, 1963).
76. David Ehlen, "A Study of Product Attributes," Master's Thesis, University of Minnesota, 1966.
77. Walter Gruen, "Preference for New Products and Its Relationship to Different Measures of Conformity," *Journal of Applied Psychology,* 44(6), 361-364 (December, 1960).
78. Keith L. Johnson, "Consumer Testing Liquid Syndets," *Soap and Chemical Specialties,* 57-60 (September, 1963).

Communications

79. Donald F. Cox, "The Measurement of Information Value: A Study in Consumer Decision-Making," in William S. Decker (editor), *Emerging Concepts in Marketing* (Chicago: American Marketing Association; December, 1962), 413-421.
80. David M. Gardner, "The Effect of Divided Attention on Attitude Change Induced by a Persuasive Marketing Communication," Ph.D. Thesis, University of Minnesota, 1966.
81. Paul E. Green, Michael H. Halbert, and J. Sayer Minal, "An Experiment in Information Buying," *Journal of Advertising Research,* 4(3), 17-23 (September, 1964).
82. Robert J. Holloway, "Experimenting with Warnings," mimeographed paper, University of Minnesota, 1965.
83. Elaine Walster and Leon Festinger, "The Effectiveness of 'Overheard' Persuasive Communications," *Journal of Abnormal and Social Psychology,* 65(6), 395-402 (December, 1962).
84. William D. Wells and Jack M. Chimsky, "Effects of Competing Messages: A Laboratory Simulation," *Journal of Marketing Research,* 2, 141-145 (May, 1965).

Merchandising

NEW EXPERIMENTAL RESEARCH IN MARKETING   429

85. William Applebaum and Richard F. Spears, "Controlled Experimentation in Marketing Research," *Journal of Marketing*, 14, 505 (January, 1950).
86. Max E. Brunk and Walter T. Federer, "How Marketing Problems of the Apple Industry Were Attacked and the Research Results Applied," *Methods of Research in Marketing Paper No. 4* (Ithaca, N.Y.: Cornell University; January, 1953).
87. Robert D. Buzzell, Walter J. Salmon, and Richard F. Vancil, *Product Profitability Measurement and Merchandising Decisions* (Boston, Mass.: Harvard Graduate School of Business, 1965).
88. Keith Cox, *The Relationship Between Shelf Space and Product Sales in Supermarkets* (Austin, Texas: University of Texas, 1964).
89. Keith Cox, "The Responsiveness of Food Sales to Supermarket Shelf Space Changes," *Journal of Marketing Research*, 1, 63-67 (May, 1964).
90. Keith Cox, "The Role of Experimentation in the Information System of a Retailer," mimeographed paper, 1965.
91. Bennett A. Dominick, Jr., "An Illustration of the Use of the Latin-Square in Measuring the Effectiveness of Retail Merchandising Practices," *Methods of Research in Marketing Paper No. 2* (Ithaca, N.Y.: Cornell University; June, 1952).
92. Kenneth R. Farrell, "Effects of Point-of-Sale Promotional Material on Sales of Cantaloupes," *Journal of Advertising*, 5(4), 8-12 (1965).
93. Max Freyd, "The Experimental Evaluation of a Merchandising Unit," *Harvard Business Review*, 4(2), 196-202 (January, 1926).
94. Peter L. Henderson, "Application of the Double Change-over Design to Measure Effects of Treatments in Controlled Experiments," *Methods of Research in Marketing Paper No. 3* (Ithaca, N.Y.: Cornell University; July, 1952).
95. Henry J. Huelskamp, William S. Hoofnagle, and Mardy Myers, "Effect of Specific Merchandising Practices on Retail Sales of Butter" (Washington, D.C.: U.S. Government Printing Office, 1956) (mimeographed paper).
96. Lennen and Newell, Inc., personal letter re packaging research, 1964.
97. Murray A. MacGregor, "Uniformity Trial Experiments in Marketing Research," *Methods of Research in Marketing Paper No. 6* (Ithaca, N.Y.: Cornell University; September, 1958).
98. "Shopping Cart Displays Soar Sales," *Tide*, 37-38 (March 3, 1950).
99. F. A. Williams, "Advertised Brands Proved to be Best Profit Makers," *Printers' Ink*, 160, 3-6 (September 29, 1932).

Social-Ethical
100. Melvin L. DeFleur and Robert M. Petranoff, "A Televised Test of Subliminal Persuasion," *Public Opinion Quarterly*, 23, 168-180 (summer 1959).
101. Robert J. Holloway and Tod White, "Ethics in Purchasing: A New Look," *North Central Purchaser*, 10(10), 48 (October, 1963).
102. James C. Naylor, "Deceptive Packaging: Are the Deceivers Being Deceived," *Journal of Applied Psychology*, 46(6), 393-398 (December, 1962).
103. Donald T. Popielarz, "A Report on an Experiment in Business Ethics," mimeographed paper, University of Minnesota, 1965.

Theoretical
104. Lee K. Anderson, James R. Taylor, and Robert J. Holloway, "The Consumer and His Alternatives," *Journal of Marketing Research*, 3, 62-67 (February, 1966).

105. Donald Auster, "Attitude Change and Cognitive Dissonance," *Journal of Marketing Research*, 2, 401-405 (November, 1965).

106. Jack W. Brehm, "Postdecision Changes in the Desirability of Alternatives," *Journal of Abnormal and Social Psychology*, 52, 384-389 (1956).

107. Richard N. Cardozo, "An Experimental Study of Customer Effort, Expectation, and Satisfaction," *Journal of Marketing Research*, 2, 244-249 (August, 1965).

108. Danuta Ehrlich, Isaiah Guttman, Peter Schönbach, and Judson Mills, "Postdecision Exposure to Relevant Information," *Journal of Abnormal and Social Psychology*, 54(1), 98-102 (1957).

109. James F. Engel, "Are Automobile Purchasers Dissonant Consumers?," *Journal of Marketing*, 27(2), 55-58 (April, 1963).

110. Leon Festinger, et al., *Conflict, Decision, and Dissonance* (Stanford, Cal.: Stanford University Press, 1964).

111. Robert J. Holloway, "Cognitive Dissonance and the Consumer—A Report of an Experiment," mimeographed paper, University of Minnesota, Center for Experimental Studies in Business, 1966.

112. Harold H. Kassarjian, "Social Character and Differential Preference for Mass Communication," *Journal of Marketing Research*, 2, 146-153 (May, 1965).

113. Judson Mills, Elliot Aronson, and Hal Robinson, "Selectivity in Exposure to Information," *Journal of Abnormal and Social Psychology*, 59(2), 250-253 (1959).

114. Donald T. Popielarz, "Category Width as a Dimension of Consumer Risk-Taking Behavior," Master's Thesis, University of Minnesota, 1966.

115. James E. Stafford, "Effects of Group Influences on Consumer Brand Preferences," *Journal of Marketing Research*, 3, 68-75 (February, 1966).

116. Venkatesan, "An Experimental Investigation in the Conditions Producing Conformity to and Independence of Group Norms in Consumer Behavior," Ph.D. Thesis, University of Minnesota (August, 1965).

Selected Negro-White Studies

117. Arnold M. Barban and Edward W. Cundiff, "Negro and White Response to Advertising Stimuli," *Journal of Marketing Research*, 1, 53-56 (November, 1964).

118. John S. Grondahl, "Experimenting with Racial Effects in Advertising," paper for a marketing class, University of Minnesota (March, 1966).

119. James W. Scheible, "Change in Consumer Preference for an Advertisement Created by the Use of a Negro in the Advertisement Picture," a paper for a marketing class, University of Minnesota (June, 1964).

120. Paul C. Patterson, a paper on the Negro in advertising for a marketing class, University of Minnesota (March, 1966).

Miscellaneous

121. G. David Hughes, "A New Tool for Sales Managers," *Journal of Marketing Research*, 1, 32-38 (May, 1964).

122. Herbert E. Krugman, "Some Applications of Pupil Measurement," *Journal of Marketing Research*, 1, 15-19 (November, 1964).

123. Herbert E. Krugman, "White and Negro Responses to Package Designs," *Journal of Marketing Research*, 3, 199-200 (May, 1966).

124. Theodore Levitt, *Industrial Purchasing Behavior* (Boston, Mass.: Harvard Graduate School of Business, 1965).

125. Irwin Weinstock and Vincent E. Cangelosi, "An Experiment with 'Goodwill' Collection Letters," *The Arkansas Economist*, 2(3), 16-21 (spring 1960).

Pupillometrics

Simply stated, pupillometrics, or perhaps more properly, *psychopupillometrics*, is an area of psychological study that is based on our finding that the pupils of the eyes dilate when we see something pleasant or positive and that they constrict when we see something unpleasant, distasteful, or negative. This occurs with illumination on the eye held constant. A more comprehensive way of dealing with the phenomenon is to state that the pupil reflects ongoing changes in the brain that mirror such psychological processes as attitude, mental effort, emotional impact, interest, and other psychological behavior. The question, therefore, really becomes that of how to adequately handle this opportunity that we have of observing the brain from the outside of the body as though we were directly observing the behavior of the brain. We must first find out the ground rules for interpretation.

While there has certainly been a suggestion in folklore and in books (for instance, Darwin's *The Expression of the Emotions in Man and Animals*) that the eye might be related to emotion, it was only through a chance remark of my wife's that I first realized that the eye might reflect an individual's subjective interests, thoughts, and attitudes.

One evening, while I was looking at a book containing some particularly good pictures of animals, my wife, who is an artist, commented that I should have more light, because my pupils were too large. Since there was more than adequate light coming over my shoulder, I was puzzled. When she repeated the remark several minutes later, I stopped to think about it. Although I had been working on perceptual problems in humans and animals for a number of years and was well aware of the relation between pupil size and emotion, I could not relate this state of dilated pupils to any physical condition. Further introspection led to the insight that it could be related to my interest in the book I was reading. My conclusion — that increased pupil size could be related to interest — was verified by some simple experiments in my laboratory the following day.

Soon, I had developed a technique for photographing pupils and measuring the changes, and in 1960 my first paper was published on the subject, in collaboration with James M. Polt.[1] In this study, we merely showed some men and women a series of pictures in which were slides of seminude males and females. On an *a priori* basis, we had the idea that both men and women would be more interested in pictures of the opposite sex, and therefore, would show greater increases in pupil size to these pictures. After testing, we also asked the subjects to rate the picture on an interest scale, so that we could compare an individual's professed interest with his pupil response. It did indeed turn out, as we reported in *Science,* that women had large responses to pictures of men, and men had large responses to pictures of women. However, an examination of the verbal ratings showed that the pictures of seminude women were rated as highly interesting by the men but, if the women were to be believed, they did not think that the pictures of males were at all interesting. We quickly realized that this disparity between the pupil response and the verbal response on the part of the women was undoubtedly a reflection of the social values of our society. Although it might be considered normal and healthy for a man to be interested in pictures of scantily clad girls (indeed, it might arouse some speculation if he were not), it is not considered quite right for "nice" girls to be interested in this type of picture of men.

This result made us aware, for perhaps the first time, of the vast potential the pupil technique might have as a research tool in numerous areas. The pupil response appeared to offer a direct measure of a person's attitudes, without depending on a verbal response that the individual could consciously or unconsciously falsify. Thus, we get to the fundamental problem; that is, to determine *a priori* which stimuli ought to be appealing and, thus, cause dilation, and which stimuli ought to be distasteful and, thus, cause constriction. Obviously, we cannot do this on the basis of asking people whether they like or dislike something because we cannot rely on their verbal statements. The very fundamental advantage of the pupil technique that we have developed is that it makes it unnecessary to ask the subject about his attitude.

But there does seem to be a way out. In some work that we have been doing at the University of Chicago under the direction of Alan Seltzer and in some work that is being carried out at the Pupil Research Center at the University of Michigan, subjects *under hypnosis* were shown slides

[1] Eckhard H. Hess and James M. Polt, "Pupil Size as Related to Interest Value of Visual Stimuli," *Science,* **132**, #3423, 349-350 (1960).

in the apparatus. Let me give you two examples of the research results obtained. Under hypnosis, a subject was shown pictures of food objects. A moderate pupil dilation was found for the food pictures. While still under hypnosis, the subject was made to feel hungry. He was then again exposed to the food pictures. At this time, the pupils grew much larger when the food pictures were shown. The subject was then led through a suggested meal and it was suggested to him that he was now fully satiated. He was again shown the food pictures and measurements were taken. At this point, his pupils constricted at the sight of the food pictures. Let me cite a second example. Hypnotized subjects were told that they were going to be shown some slides. *In fact, these slides were blank.* They were told that one of these was an extremely pleasant picture without, however, specifying what would be pleasant for that subject. The pupils dilated although the slide was blank. For another blank slide, the subjects were told that they were seeing unpleasant and distasteful pictures. Again the *actual* subject matter was unspecified. Constriction resulted. The slides that were shown without any instructions under this period of hypnosis caused no change in the pupil size. I feel that this is an extremely promising method in which we may get answers to some of the questions about what pupil changes really mean. Only in this way have we, so far, been able to get really perfect correlation between the subject's verbal attitude (which in this case, however, is given to him by the hypnotist) and pupil change. In other experiments, without hypnosis, the correlation is variable. It is often very poor when correlated with expressed verbal preferences, especially when we are dealing with items where there is strong social pressure to give the right answer. And it is often good when we are dealing with items of low social pressure and low ego involvement.

During the course of the next several years, we carried out numerous studies.[2] We also worked on many of the technical problems that had occurred to us after our first successes. One problem was the more precise control of light in the experimental situation. For example, with pictorial material, we showed a neutral control slide for ten seconds, then a stimulus slide for ten seconds. During each ten second period, our camera took twenty pictures of the eye. After the film was processed, each frame was projected on a screen and the diameter of the pupil was measured with a millimeter ruler. Then, the mean or average of the pupil size during the control period was compared with the pupil size during the stimulus period, and a plus or minus change in percentage was

[2] Eckhard H. Hess, "Attitude and Pupil Size," *Scientific American,* 212, 46-54 (1965).

arrived at. Naturally, this measure is worthless if the intensity of the light striking the eye is not equal during both periods in order to insure that the response is a reflection of what is going on inside the individual, rather than outside the individual. This problem is simplified in studies of other sensory modalities and when studying mental problem solving, which I shall discuss presently, where the subject fixates on the same visual point throughout the entire experimental run and brightness changes are not involved.

Another problem was film. Originally, our experiments were recorded on standard negative film. Because of the lack of contrast between the pupil and the iris in dark-eyed subjects, the filmed eyes of these subjects were often difficult to measure. By adapting our apparatus to infrared film, we were able to get excellent pictures of any eye.

Our original apparatus itself soon presented a problem. Much as a person might build a boat in his basement, without thought of later removal from that basement, we built this apparatus in one of our experimental rooms at the University of Chicago. When the need developed to run subjects in other places (for instance, high schools and hospitals), it soon became apparent that we should need a portable machine. The result is the Hess Pupil Response Apparatus. It is easily transported and can be set up at any location with a table, chair, and electrical outlet, in a matter of minutes.

During this same period, we were studying changes in pupil size in a variety of experimental situations. We had subjects solve problems of various sorts, from simple multiplication problems to statements requiring value judgments.

Our second publication was a report of the relationship between pupillary changes and mental activity.[3] We not only found that the pupil increases in size while the subject is solving a problem, but that this increase is a function of problem difficulty. The more difficult the problem, the greater the increase in pupil size. This is a phenomenon that many people have told me they were able to observe themselves after reading our paper, by simply looking at a person's eyes and asking him to mentally solve a problem such as 8×17.

We have also studied the effects of auditory stimuli, sounds, words, and music. In an apparatus similar to the one used for our visual experiments, we presented subjects with olfactory stimuli and taste stimuli.[4] Just as

[3] Eckhard H. Hess and James M. Polt, "Pupil Size in Relation to Mental Activity during Simple Problem Solving," *Science*, 143, #3611, 1190-1192 (1964).
[4] Eckhard H. Hess and James M. Polt, "Changes in Pupil Size as a Measure of Taste Differences," *Perceptual and Motor Skills*, in press.

with a large number of visual materials, we found that systematic changes in pupil size correlated with the presentation of these other sensory stimuli. The results of these studies led me to the conviction that the pupil reflected ongoing neurological activity in all parts of the brain.

One other study should be mentioned in a little more detail, since it neatly fits into the classical experimental paradigm, where hunger is used as a motivating force. In this study, we ran two groups of 16 people each. One group had not eaten for about five hours, while the other group had eaten shortly before being run in the apparatus. The stimuli used in this study were a series of pictures of food. The "hungry" subjects averaged increases in pupil size almost three times the magnitude of the response of the subjects who had just eaten. To me, this was an excellent example of how, without requiring a single verbal response on the part of the subject, a basic motivational state can be measured.

During the same period, our basic research was partly supported first by Interpublic and then by Marplan, a communications research organization, which has continued to show interest in our work. James M. Polt of my staff at the University of Chicago, and Paula Drillman of Marplan, New York, have worked with me since the beginning of my pupil research, and have contributed much to the development of our techniques both for basic and for applied research. During this time, I have also acted in the capacity of Consultant-Director of the Perception Laboratory of Interpublic and Marplan.

The most obvious application of our original findings was in the area of package and product design. Over the last several years, the studies that have been carried out by us and in the Marplan laboratories have included testing of different designs of watchbands, watches, and silverware patterns, where the pupil response was found to correlate well with the sale of the items. Containers and packages, as well as products themselves, at one time and another have been successfully tested. In many of these studies, the information made available through the pupil technique formed the basis for a client's decision in selecting a particular design for a new package, or in marketing a particular product. F. Van Bortel of Marplan, Chicago, has carried out research that is of practical importance to both basic and applied pupil studies, and has been instrumental in working out methods for analysis of pupil data by means of computer systems.

The pupil response technique was equally successful in the testing of advertisements. Here it was possible to test both potential ads and the client's existing ads against those of a competitor. The results provided by the pupil response often made it possible to isolate those parts of an ad that were of greatest interest to the viewer, since it is also possible with our technique to plot eye movements simultaneously with obtaining data on pupil changes. It is, of course, possible to show actual objects rather than pictures of objects to the subjects, and this has been done in several studies.

The success we had experienced with the pupil response to pictorial material led me to believe that we could also work with filmed material. This would open up an entirely new research area. After overcoming the problem of controlling for brightness, I was ready to carry out basic research along these lines. As with our previous work, this too was later incorporated into the applied research program of Marplan. Basically, this involved a Product-Moment Interest Curve, which made it possible to plot the interest value of a piece of filmed material in ½ second or one second segments. This technique has now been used successfully by Marplan, which has referred to the viewer's pupil response to a TV commercial as an "Interest Track," and which provides a pinpointing of interest changes. Since the area of attitude and attitude change has been of constant interest to the psychologist, we have begun to work more and more on these topics. We felt, early in our research, that the pupil response was a good reflection of attitude, and we reasoned that it should, therefore, be well adapted to studies of attitude change. Once again, the simplicity of this technique, and perhaps the accuracy, lies in the tapping of an involuntary response that cannot consciously be controlled by the subject.

One of the earliest studies in attitude change involved showing the subjects pictures of a popular movie actor. After obtaining an initial response to the pictures, half of the subjects were given some rather negative material to read about the actor. The other subjects read an equal amount of neutral material. The subjects were then retested on pictures of the actor. The result was that the second response of the subjects who had been given the negative material to read was significantly lower than the second response of those subjects who had read the neutral material between runs. We interpreted this as an indication that the negative material had changed the attitude of the subjects against the actor whose picture was used in the study.

A similar study was carried out last summer and reported at the 1964 American Psychological Association Meeting in Los Angeles.[5] This was more involved as a study, dealing with the two presidential candidates.

[5] Eckhard H. Hess, "Some Relationships between Pupillary Activity and Mental Activity," American Psychological Association Meeting, September, 1964.

In addition to having the subjects in the different groups read neutral material and negative statements about the candidates, we also gave other groups positive statements to read. Just as in our previous study, these results showed that the attitude of the individual was influenced in a positive or negative direction, according to the material he had read between experimental sessions.

Since the development of the technique, we have studied the effects of both filmed and pictorial material on attitude and attitude change. To me, this is a concept basic to all advertising research. So far as the good of the client is concerned, the most interesting, the cleverest, or the most beautiful advertisement is of no value, if it does not make the consumer react favorably toward the product being advertised. We have collected useful data from a number of studies showing that indeed some ads and TV commercials do change an individual's attitude toward a product in a positive way, while others have no effect, or even lead to a negative reaction.

The basic technique used in testing the effect of an ad (or series of ads) on attitude is to run each subject on a sequence: control period, product, control period, *ad*, control period, product. The analysis of a sequence of this type will give two types of information. If, for example, we are testing Ad 1 against Ad 2 (by either inserting Ad 1 in the sequence for half the subjects and Ad 2 for the other half, or running all subjects on two sequences, changing the order of the ads) we can determine the absolute interest value of the particular ad by comparing the response to the ad with the response during the previous control period, and we can also rate each ad as to what we have called the Relative Attitude Change (RAC). In the pretesting of a series of ads, those with both a high positive interest value and a high positive RAC score would be recommended most strongly for use with the public. Marplan has also adopted this procedure under the term Added Product Appeal (APA) for their applied studies.

The procedure used with TV commercials is very similar. Instead of showing slides, the sequence of: control period, product, control period, *TV commercial*, control period, product, is shown. As stated earlier, the interest value of the commercial can be analyzed in segments as small as $\frac{1}{2}$ second intervals. The RAC or APA score is derived in the same way as it is done for ads. In both cases, there is extreme flexibility as to the type of study that can be carried out for the client. For example, after it has been determined that a TV commercial has high interest value and produces a positive change of attitude, the client might be interested in the durability of the commercial. While some commercials might do their job sufficiently on the first presentation, the client might want to know the effects of repetition on both of these scores. Using the methods outlined above, it would be possible to determine whether a TV commercial still has interest value and continues to effectively change the individual's attitude toward the product after, for example, the tenth viewing. It may not be surprising that some commercials that start out high on both of the measures we have been discussing actually lead to negative responses after repeated exposure.

We have also tested subjects as to their response for an entire half-hour television drama and found tremendous pupil increases (up to 25% *average* increase in pupil diameter for a total of 50 subjects) during the climactic portions of the show. Highly significant differences in the response of men and of women to certain parts of the show were also observed. In one case, there was a continual pupil increase by men for one minute at a certain point in the drama while the pupils of women constricted continually during that same one minute period. Much useful information can obviously be obtained by studying the data from responses to a show before its final release.

Particularly during the past year, the general interest in applying our pupil technique to a number of problems has increased tremendously. Researchers at other universities, as well as at the University of Chicago, have used this technique in the study of sex roles in adolescents, in studying the development of social responses in children, in determining racial attitudes and attitude changes, in testing for creativity, and in studying the processes involved in simple and complex problem solving. Confirmation and extension of our findings have also been published by Scott[6] and by Paivio and Simpson.[7] Reports by others are currently in press. Recently, we have been concentrating our efforts on a more detailed study of the relationship of the pupil response to the nonvisual senses and to other physiological measures; for instance, E.E.G., galvanic skin changes, and heart rate.

Even though we have been working in this area for over six years, we feel that it is really still in its infancy, and that the potential as a research tool has been far from realized. We expect that, during the next several years, it will prove invaluable both to people carrying out basic research on certain problems and to those carrying out applied studies along the lines I have briefly discussed in this chapter.

[6] Thomas R. Scott, "Pupillary Response: A Fruitful Research Variable," *Newsletter for Research in Psychology*, 7, #2, 56 (1965).
[7] Allan Paivio and Herb M. Simpson, "The Effect of Word Abstractness and Pleasantness on Pupil Size during an Imagery Task," *Psychonomic Science*, 5, (2), 55-57 (1966).

SIXTEEN | *F. J. VAN BORTEL*

Commercial Applications of Pupillometrics

Eckhard Hess, Professor of Psychology at the University of Chicago, has described a new technique of pupillometric measurement.[1, 2] Hess is also a consultant to MARPLAN and professional director of the Marplan Perception Research Laboratory, which is concerned with the commercial application of the techniques and procedures developed by Hess working under a grant for basic research sponsored by MARPLAN.

It is my purpose, in this chapter, to describe a series of experiments designed to determine the ability of the pupil-response measure to predict the effectiveness of direct-response advertising.

Eckhard Hess states,[2] in part:

... the evidence suggests that at least with respect to visual material there is a continuum of responses that ranges from extreme dilation for interesting or pleasing stimuli to extreme constriction for material that is unpleasant or distasteful to the viewer. In the presence of uninteresting or boring pictures, we find only slight random variations in pupil size.

We reasoned that, if the pupil response could measure the interest and favorable response of an individual to a visual stimulus, the pupil response might also be an effective means of predicting the performance effectiveness of advertisements. Specifically, we hypothesized that advertisements that generated the greatest pupil diameter increases might also be more effective commercially than advertisements that generated only random variations in pupil response or constriction of the pupil.

The most difficult part of designing any test of the commercial utility of any research tool is in finding a situation in which the actual *behavioral* response to two or more alternatives can be accurately determined, and

---

[1] *Science*, August, 1960.
[2] *Scientific American*, April, 1965.

where it can reasonably be assumed that behavior differences are not contaminated with unmeasurable variables. For this reason, we chose to conduct our test using direct-response advertising; specifically, advertisements for Encyclopaedia Britannica.[3]

The advertisements tested were full-page magazine advertisements, largely four-color, and always run with a related postcard inserted into the binding of the magazine. The basic purpose of these advertisements is to persuade readers to send in the postcard. Consequently, the performance of any advertisement in terms of behavior response can be measured by simply counting the number of postcards returned. However, since there are seasonal fluctuations in response and differences between publications in terms of response rate, accurate measurement of response to two or more advertisements requires that they be split-run in the same issue of the same publication.

This advertiser has, for many years, used A/B split-runs to evaluate the performance effectiveness of alternative advertisements. More specifically, when the advertiser wishes to evaluate a new advertisement, half of the circulation of a magazine is exposed to a *control* advertisement known to be effective in terms of the number of postcards returned. The other half of the circulation of the magazine is exposed to the new *test* advertisement.

The fact that both the control and test advertisements run in the same issue of the same publication eliminates variations due to season or publication. Since the split-runs are made in magazines with substantial circulation, the characteristics of the populations exposed to control and test advertisements are well matched.

Thus, a simple count of the number of keyed postcards returned for the control and the test advertisement provides an accurate and objective measure of actual performance, and a good basis for test evaluation of the predictive power of the pupil-response measure. Replication studies have shown that the findings obtained in this kind of split-run testing are reliable.

Over a period of three years, we have had an opportunity to make measurements of pupil response to eleven pairs of test and control advertisements, and to compare pupil-response scores with actual performance, as measured by split-runs.[4]

In designing the pupillometric test for Encyclopaedia Britannica ad-

---

[3] I am grateful to Encyclopaedia Britannica and to McCann-Erickson for their financial support of this research project, and for their permission to discuss the findings.
[4] Findings for the first six tests were presented at the 1965 meeting of the American Marketing Association. Findings for the five remaining tests are being reported publicly for the first time here.

vertising, we began with the hypothesis that the number of postcards returned or lead-pull performance depends on two characteristics of the advertisement: initial impact and copy persuasiveness.

By *initial impact*, I mean simply the ability of the advertisement to command interested attention. Every advertisement must work in a competitive environment, and unless it commands the attention of the reader, it cannot be expected to perform effectively.

However, an advertisement may well be effective in commanding attention, but not persuasive when the copy is read, so we also wanted a measure of *copy persuasiveness*—that is, the ability of the advertisement to motivate the reader to act.

The technique used to test the hypothesis was, in part, determined by the basic pupil-measurement procedure. It is evident that when a complex stimulus such as an encyclopedia advertisement with lengthy copy is presented in the eye camera for ten seconds, we cannot expect the viewer to read the copy. We were confident that in a ten-second exposure most people would see the picture, read the headline, and get other major visual elements of the advertisement. We also felt that these major elements would be most important in determining the ability of the advertisement to command the interested attention of the magazine reader. Therefore, we reasoned that a ten-second exposure of the advertisement should measure its initial impact.

In view of the extensive copy in the test and control advertisements, we decided it would be necessary to have the viewer read the advertisements outside the eye camera. Then, after the viewer was familiar with the copy, the advertisement was shown again in the eye camera. Basic research had shown that attitudes generated through such readership tended to be reflected in eye camera response to the same stimuli after readership.

With these considerations in mind, we adopted the following research procedure:

1. Qualified subjects are shown test and control advertisements in the eye camera.

2. Subjects are removed from the eye camera, and permitted to read test and control advertisements in a normal reading situation. Readership is encouraged, but not forced.

3. Subjects are returned to the eye camera and again shown test and control advertisements.

This procedure was followed in all of the eleven tests reported in this chapter.

Fifty qualified subjects were used in each study. Subjects were qualified on demographic characteristics and stage in life cycle, based on prior knowledge of the characteristics of families that are the best prospects for purchase of an encyclopedia.

Preliminary experimentation showed that families qualified as prospects had larger pupil-response scores than families not qualified as prospects—a finding that has been consistent for other products and services. For this reason, we believe it is important to conduct all tests among qualified prospects.

Although the data in pupil measurement tends to stabilize with about 30 subjects, we set an arbitrary minimum of 50 subjects. Our first test was conducted in 1963. The control advertisement used in this first test, which we called Family Telescope, had demonstrated its ability to return leads. The test advertisement, which we called Boys in Pool, was a radical departure from the ad format previously used, and was a spread rather than a single page. The test advertisement had shown an excellent response in verbal testing techniques. Pupil-response scores for this first test are shown in Table 16.1.

TABLE 16.1   ENCYCLOPAEDIA BRITANNICA TEST NUMBER ONE

| | Pupil-Response Scores | | | |
	Initial Impact	Post-readership	Total	Lead Performance
Control				
Family telescope				
Red books	28	16	44	100%
Test				
Boys in pool	—2	—1	—3	82%

We were all surprised when the eye camera scores were conspicuously better for the old control than for the new test advertisement. In fact, Hess replicated the test in his own laboratory, and not only confirmed the findings but discovered that his own pupils behaved in the same way as those of the subjects in the study.

Pupil scores for the test advertisement differ significantly from those for the control (t test $p < 0.05$).[5]

[5] Pupil score differences in all tests were evaluated by t tests, and differences in p value 0.05 or greater were considered statistically significant.

When the split-run data were compiled, we found, as Table 16.1 indicates, that the old control advertisement had, in fact, pulled more leads than the test advertisement.

In this report of findings, the differences in lead productivity are expressed in terms of percent because we have been asked not to reveal the number of leads returned by an advertisement. Therefore, in each instance, we have simply taken the number of leads returned by the control ad as 100%. Then returns for the test advertisement are expressed as a percent of the control ad. Differences of 10% or more between the control ad and the test advertisement are considered significant.

In this first test, then, the pupil response correctly predicted lead-pull performance.

The second test used the same control ad. The test ad was a variation on the control. In the control advertisement, the color of the binding on the encyclopedias displayed in the bookcase was red. In the test advertisement, the color of the bindings was white. Otherwise, the control and test advertisements were identical.

As Table 16.2 indicates, the impact score for the test advertisement was somewhat higher on initial impact, but this difference was not statistically significant. However, the difference between test and control for the postreadership score was statistically significant.

TABLE 16.2   ENCYCLOPAEDIA BRITANNICA TEST NUMBER TWO

	Pupil-Response Scores			
	Initial Impact	Post- readership	Total	Lead Performance
Control Family telescope Red binding	28	16	44	100%
Test Family telescope White binding	34	37	71	110%

Why the postreadership score should show a greater difference than the initial-impact score is not clear, since the bookcase might well be considered one of the display elements of the advertisement.

As Table 16.2 shows, the test advertisement pulled 10% more leads than the control advertisement, and performance was again consistent with eye camera scores.

After these first two tests were conducted, there was a slight modification of our operating procedure, since Hess had developed a new and improved technique for controlling brightness. In the first two studies, there was a tendency for controls to be slightly brighter than test slides. This difference tended to make the order of magnitude of scores in these first two studies higher than those in subsequent studies. It will be necessary to bear in mind, therefore, that scores for the remaining tests cannot be compared directly with those for the first two tests.

The control advertisement in the third test was of the same vintage and in the same format as the original control advertisement. We called this one "Boy and Girl."

The new test ad was an adaptation of a technique that had proved successful in direct mail. As Table 16.3 indicates, there was a slight difference in initial-impact score in favor of the control, but this difference was not statistically significant. The postreadership scores were identical for the control and test advertisements.

TABLE 16.3   ENCYCLOPAEDIA BRITANNICA TEST NUMBER THREE

| | Pupil-Response Scores | | | Lead Performance |
	Initial Impact	Post-readership	Total	
Control				
Boy and girl				
Red binding	9	4	13	100%
Test				
Knowledge	6	4	10	99%

The lead-performance index shows that the difference in lead pull was 1%—not a significant difference in performance.

Test 4 used the same control as test 3, and was like the second test in that the test ad was identical to the control except that the color of the bindings on the books was white rather than red.

Table 16.4 shows that there was a slight difference in initial-impact score in favor of the ad with white bindings, but this difference was not statistically significant. There was a larger difference in favor of the test

TABLE 16.4 ENCYCLOPAEDIA BRITANNICA TEST NUMBER FOUR

| | Pupil-Response Score | | | |
	Initial Impact	Post-readership	Total	Lead Performance
Control				
Boy and girl				
Red binding	9	4	13	100%
Test				
Boy and girl				
White binding	11	13	24	115%

advertisement with white bindings in the postreadership score, and this difference was statistically significant.

Again, we cannot explain why the difference between the two advertisements should be greater in the postreadership score than in the initial-impact score. We can only observe that the finding was consistent in the two very similar studies.

The lead-performance index shows that the test advertisement with white bindings pulled 15% more leads.

Test 5 was initiated under somewhat different circumstances. The control advertisement used in this test had produced fewer leads than had been expected or desired, despite the fact that the format had what appeared to be an appealing picture, a good headline, and the white binding.

Since both the eye camera and split-run testing had indicated that what appeared to be relatively minor differences in format could produce significant differences in performance, it was decided that a revised version of this advertisement should be made and tested.

The revised version included a small headline under the picture, offering nine reasons for choosing the Encyclopaedia Britannica. Then each of the nine reasons was set out separately in the ad copy, as contrasted to the original in which the copy had run continuously.

On the initial-impact score, the control scored somewhat higher than the test, as shown in Table 16.5. On postreadership, the control again scored slightly higher than the test ad. Neither difference was statistically significant.

The lead-performance index shows that the difference in lead pull was 1%, and not significant.

TABLE 16.5 ENCYCLOPAEDIA BRITANNICA TEST NUMBER FIVE

	Pupil-Response Scores			
	Initial Impact	Post-readership	Total	Lead Performance
Control				
Boy on rock (Original)	6	1	7	100%
Test				
Boy on rock (Revised)	1	—2	—1	99%

In test 6, the control advertisement, "Classroom," was again an advertisement with known lead-pull performance.

The test ad was again a significant departure from the control. First, the illustration was black and white rather than in color. Also, a different layout technique was used. Black and white advertising, of course, has a considerable cost advantage, and there was a possibility that even if the black and white advertisement pulled fewer leads per thousand, it would be more cost efficient in terms of cost per lead.

Table 16.6 shows that the initial impact was substantially greater for the control ad than for the test ad. This difference was statistically significant. The control was also slightly higher than the test in the post-readership score, but the difference was not statistically significant.

The lead-performance index shows that there was a very substantial difference in lead pull in favor of the control advertisement.

TABLE 16.6 ENCYCLOPAEDIA BRITANNICA TEST NUMBER SIX

	Pupil-Response Scores			
	Initial Impact	Post-readership	Total	Lead Performance
Control				
Classroom	12	11	23	100%
Test				
Why buy?	2	8	10	70%

The difference in lead pull nearly approximated the cost difference, and the black and white advertisement did not produce more cost efficient leads.

Tests 7 through 10 were conducted simultaneously. The same control advertisement was used in all four instances, and the four different test advertisements were run in regional editions of the same publication. The demographic characteristics of the four regions were matched as closely as possible. However, the sample size delivered by regional editions of the publication is smaller than we had previously used. For that reason, the findings of the split-run test must be regarded with somewhat less confidence than previous tests.

The control advertisement used for these four tests was "Family Telescope" with white books. After the fact, the evidence suggested that this was an unfortunate choice. When this advertisement was first used as a control, it showed good eye camera scores. When tested again in 1965, it produced slightly negative eye camera scores. The data strongly suggested that this advertisement, that had had substantial exposure over a period of three years, was "worn out" at the time this group of tests was conducted.

The test advertisement in test 7 used a cartoon character, "Dennis." The test advertisement scored well in both measures, and considerably above the scores for the control. However, only the initial-impact score was significantly different.

As Table 16.7 shows, lead performance was higher for the test advertisement.

In test 8, the test advertisement used cartoon characters, the "Munsters," in the illustration. This test advertisement showed scores above the control but the differences were not statistically significant (Table

TABLE 16.7 ENCYCLOPAEDIA BRITANNICA TEST NUMBER SEVEN

	Pupil-Response Scores			
	Initial Impact	Post- readership	Total	Lead Performance
Control Family telescope White books	—9	—5	—14	100%
Test Dennis	10	10	20	114%

TABLE 16.8   ENCYCLOPAEDIA BRITANNICA TEST NUMBER EIGHT

| | Pupil-Response Scores | | | |
	Initial Impact	Post-readership	Total	Lead Performance
Control				
Family telescope				
White books	—9	—5	—14	100%
Test				
Munsters	4	1	5	108%

16.8). The lead performance of the test ad was better than that for the control, but the difference was not large enough to insure replication.

In test 9, a well-known personality, Danny Kaye, was used in the illustration.

The initial impact score was higher for the test than the control, but not significantly so.

The postreadership performance was significantly greater for the test advertisement than the control.

As Table 16.9 shows, the test ad again pulled more leads than the control, but the difference is not large enough to insure replication.

Test 10 again used an unusual illustration to emphasize the headline theme: "Hiccups."

The initial impact score for this test advertisement did not differ significantly from the control. The post readership score for the test adver-

TABLE 16.9   ENCYCLOPAEDIA BRITANNICA TEST NUMBER NINE

| | Pupil-Response Scores | | | |
	Initial Impact	Post-readership	Total	Lead Performance
Control				
Family telescope				
White books	—9	—5	—14	100%
Test				
Danny Kaye	1	11	12	107%

tisement was slightly higher than for the control advertisement, but the difference was not statistically significant.

The lead performance was greater for the test advertisement than the control. However, this particular sample was the smallest of the group and the 116% must be viewed with caution (Table 16.10).

TABLE 16.10   ENCYCLOPAEDIA BRITANNICA TEST NUMBER TEN

| | Pupil-Response Scores | | | |
	Initial Impact	Post-readership	Total	Lead Performance
Control				
Family telescope				
White binding	—9	—5	—14	100%
Test				
Hiccups	0	8	8	116%

Test 11 again employed an "old" control, "Boy and Girl," with white binding, which showed slight negative scores.

The test advertisement was "Wide Span of Books" in which the primary illustration was a set of Encyclopaedia Britannica. In initial impact, the score for "Wide Span of Books" was almost identical to the control.

The postreadership score for the test ad was slightly greater than for the control. Neither score difference was statistically significant. It was

TABLE 16.11   ENCYCLOPAEDIA BRITANNICA TEST NUMBER ELEVEN

| | Pupil-Response Scores | | | |
	Initial Impact	Post-readership	Total	Lead Performance
Control				
Boy and girl				
White binding	—6	—3	—9	100%
Test				
Wide span of				
books	—7	1	—6	111%

our judgment, prior to the split-run, that this difference was insignificant and would not result in a significant difference in lead pull.

However, as Table 16.11 indicates, there was a significant difference in lead pull, with the test advertisement outpulling the control by 11%. In this instance, the sample was large enough to provide considerable confidence in the findings.

CONCLUSIONS

Table 16.12 summarizes findings for eleven comparisons of pupil-response scores with postcard returns for test and control pairs of encyclopedia advertisements.

TABLE 16.12

Test Number	Eye Camera Score Differences between Test and Control Ads			Lead-Pull Performance Differences between Test and Control Ads (Percent)
	Initial Impact	Post-readership	Total	
1[a]	−30[b]	−17[b]	−47	−18
2[a]	+ 6	+21[b]	+27	+10
3	− 3	0	− 3	− 1
4	+ 2	+ 9[b]	+11	+15
5	− 5	− 3	− 8	− 1
6	−10[b]	− 3	−13	−30
7	+19[b]	+15	+34	+14
8	+13	+ 6	+28	+ 8
9	+10	+16[b]	+26	+ 7
10	+ 9	+13	+22	+16
11	+ 1	+ 4	+ 5	+11

[a] Procedure of testing changed after first two tests. Scores not directly comparable in order of magnitude to remaining tests.
[b] Statistically significant differences.

Our hypothesis was that, whenever there was a statistically significant difference in pupil scores between the test and control advertisement for either the initial-impact or postreadership pupil measures, we should predict a greater number of postcard returns for the advertisement achieving the significantly higher score. For those pairs of test and control advertisements showing no significant difference in either pupil response measure, we should predict no difference in postcard returns.

Of the eleven studies conducted, six showed a significant difference between the test and control advertisements on at least one of the two pupil response measures (tests 1, 2, 4, 6, 7, and 9). For these six tests, the predictions were all correct, in that the test advertisement pulled more or fewer postcard returns than the control, as the pupil score indicated. In the case of test 9, the small size of the postcard-return sample limits our confidence in the postcard-return data.

In the remaining five tests, there were no significant differences between pupil response to the test and control advertisements in either of the two pupil measures (tests 3, 5, 8, 10, and 11). Of these five cases, two (tests 3 and 5) showed no difference in postcard returns, while three cases (tests 8, 10, and 11) showed a difference in postcard returns. Again, for tests 8 and 10, we have some reservations about the adequacy of the size of the sample of postcard returns.

On the basis of our original hypothesis, then, we made eight correct predictions and three incorrect predictions in the total of eleven tests conducted.

In the three cases of incorrect prediction, we failed to predict a difference because eye camera score differences did not reach statistical significance (tests 8, 10, and 11), although in each instance each advertisement getting the higher pupil score on both measures also pulled more postcards.

Tests 8 and 10 seem understandable, in that quite substantial score differences in at least one pupil-response measure did not achieve statistical significance because of a wide range of response.

Test 11, however, is more difficult to understand. In this instance, there were no substantial score differences in either measure of pupil response, yet the difference in postcard returns is substantial and based on a very adequate sample.

It is also apparent that we have been more effective in predicting which advertisement will pull more leads than in predicting *amount* of difference.

Overall, however, the pupil response measure has proved to be a more effective predictor of lead-pull performance of advertisements than any of several other pretest techniques that have been used to evaluate encyclopedia advertisements.

As a result of these findings, the pupil-response measure is now being used to screen large numbers of potential new advertisements. Those achieving the highest pupil scores will then be split-run.

This has some very important advantages for this advertiser. While the split-run technique provides a definitive measure of the performance of advertisements, the procedure is both time consuming and costly. It takes several months to determine definitively the actual postcard return for a split-run, and there are a limited number of publications that can reasonably be used for this purpose. Therefore, the number of new advertisements that can be tested is seriously limited.

Further, use of the split-run technique predisposes the advertiser to testing minor variations. That is, a radical innovation in form may extract a severe penalty in terms of a reduced number of leads.

Consequently, the pupil-response measure has made it possible for the advertiser to experiment more boldly with new ideas, and to test far more advertisements, with good confidence that any advertisement that shows high pupil scores is a good candidate for split-run testing.

At the same time, we are continuing our study of our use of the technique, with the long-range objective of predicting more accurately the amount of difference in lead-pull performance. For example, we are currently conducting studies to determine whether there are important geographic area differences in response, comparing scores for tests conducted in New York, Los Angeles, and Chicago.

Similar tests of the predictive power of the pupil-response measure have been completed or are in progress for products, packages, basic advertising concepts, outdoor and television advertising, point of purchase material, and direct mail.

I am confident that the pupil-response measure is the best measure of involuntary response that is presently available, and will play an increasingly important role in the application of the sciences in marketing management.

SUMMARY

Eleven tests of the ability of pupil-response scores to predict which of two advertisements will pull most postcard returns in split-run tests have been conducted.

In six of the eleven tests, one of the two advertisements tested has shown a significantly higher pupil score on at least one of two pupil-response measures used and, in each instance, the advertisement with the significantly higher pupil score pulled more postcard returns.

In five of the eleven tests, there were no significant differences in pupil-response measures between the two advertisements. In two of these tests, there was no difference in postcard returns. In the remaining three instances, there was a difference in postcard returns.

In the total of eleven tests, pupil-response scores correctly predicted postcard returns in eight instances. In the remaining three tests, the advertisement getting the higher pupil score also pulled the most postcard returns, although pupil-response score differences did not meet the criterion originally set for significance.

The pupil-response technique has been more effective in predicting lead pull than alternative techniques tested previously, and is currently being used to screen large numbers of advertisements.

Index

455